Here's To It!

A Memoir by Gerald A. Jewett, Jr.

2018

FOR R'

Gerald A. Jewett Jr.

Published by BookLocker.com, Inc., St. Petersburg, Florida.

Printed on acid-free paper.

BookLocker.com, Inc.
2017

First Edition

Compiled, edited, and copyedited by Jennifer Jewett Dilley
Front cover artwork by Jake Dilley; final cover design by Todd Engel

Author's Preface

As a pre-91st birthday gift, my daughter Jennifer offered to put together a memoir about my life, with stories dictated by me. Over the years, I've had lots of interesting experiences, enough that several people have told me to write a book. But I just never wanted to tackle such a big undertaking. Now the offer has been made to do all the work for me if I just sit and tell the stories—I can do that much. My kids have oftentimes recorded me on tape and video and on their cell phone cameras when I get started reminiscing, but not really with enough material to put together any kind of an orderly book. So, I think this is a pretty smart idea, and have decided that now is as good a time as any to get some of those long-term memories onto paper for future generations. And there are scrapbooks and files full of old photos and clippings which should help add a lot more interest to the whole project.

Naturally, I was a little bit hesitant about this idea at first, because I did not necessarily want to tell my daughter, or even have in print, some of the skeletons in my closet. But Jen laughed while assuring me the book doesn't have to be a 'tell-all' deal. She also suggested inserting some historical and genealogical information about my ancestors since I always talk so much about them too—I certainly do like that whole idea. My family has kept our forefathers alive over the years with tales of their drive and determination, and those stories have helped make me who I am. Most of the ancestors, on both sides, even kept written journals (like this book will be, I'm told.) One of my great-grandfathers was also a studious researcher and genealogist in his later life, leaving us records that have assisted family members in putting things together on that side of the tree. So, this book will not only get into my own personal tales, but will also be a good reference source for my descendants who want to learn more about their heritage without having to do so much research.

It really is a good time to tackle this project since my memory is still pretty darn keen. But I just can't believe I've outlived almost everybody in my stories! Though easily recalling the names and faces of family members, friends and acquaintances when I talk about them, we have decided to eliminate most personal names for this book, unless they are already public record or we have received permission to include them here. I'm getting excited to see how this whole thing will turn out. ***Here's to it!***

Gerald A. Jewett, Jr., jerryjewett@yahoo.com, September 2016

Editor's Preface and Acknowledgments
(with Afterthoughts about this fourteen-month project!)

I'd been thinking for a long time that it would be nice to help Dad write a book about his life. Everyone has a story, of course, but many of his seem especially intriguing. The guy has always kept others fully enthralled with his compelling (and accurate) tales, not only about his own life and that of his family, but also about the rich history of our city and state. So, I had already started recording, onto paper and onto video, many recollections as Dad told them, hoping to find a way to put things into some semblance of order so that his grandchildren and his 'greats' could eventually listen to and read highlights from the life of their very colorful grandfather. Born when the Roaring 20's slammed into the Great Depression, this man was part of the 'greatest generation' that seemed to emerge as a more footloose and fancy-free bunch—and all of it somehow related to growing up between two major world wars and in an era of such tremendous industrial and technological change.

Of course, I assumed a chronicle about Dad would be a posthumous effort, as with my other genealogical endeavors, but things ramped up when he asked me to start working on his eventual obituary. I did my best to succinctly compile onto the page a lifetime of well-over-the-top activities and involvements, all the while wishing it could be enhanced with some of the back stories that accompanied those listed items. At 800 words, Dad's first reaction was that the obit was just too long, so his assigned chore was to begin crossing out whatever didn't need to be listed. The next time we sat down to look at it, he was fretting about having added even more! Consolidating one's life journey onto a single written page in small font must be daunting, and I appreciated that my father wasn't ready to eliminate any of it. Because the obituary was the origin of this project, you'll soon see that we have decided to start the book with it, giving the reader a little foretaste of the pages to come!

About a year and a half ago, it became apparent that I just needed to stop everything else that was filling up my daily schedule, in order to offer services as an editor and 'genealogist wannabe' in helping assemble pieces about this man's fascinating story while he was feeling well enough to share more about it. (Dad has been pretty healthy these past couple of years—better than he was at age 90 or even 89, when we thought we were going to lose him for one reason or another.) So, back in late August 2016, I presented him with a pre-91st birthday gift—a verbal proposal to help compile a book about his life. He took no time in accepting the offer, and we jumped headfirst into this project right after Labor Day.

Before we sat down to begin writing the first time, Dad had already been thinking a lot about it and announced that he'd like to start out with, "My name is Gerald Anson Jewett, Jr." And off we went! We have continued to meet for several hours every week in his cozy Wesley Acres apartment, and at my office in Clive. Though it's finally time to see it go to print, this really is the book with no ending—one story has unlocked the door to another and another. And when he eventually pulled out the massive scrapbook with some of the photos he wanted to include, I almost fell off the chair! Deciding how to begin the book was not a chore for Dad, but deciding how and when to end it has not been easy.

My advance apologies if any details herein have inadvertently slipped by close research scrutiny. I tried to properly vet each and every story my father gave me, making certain the dates and names and circumstances line up—sometimes it's just hard to believe he can be so accurate with that long-term memory of his. On occasion, I would stop him mid-sentence to directly question the veracity of a statement, and he'd say, "Why don't you ask the lady in your phone?!" He was always so proud when SIRI agreed with him and added even more information—what did we ever do without the amazing internet?

As a curious and avid reader of all things history, I've amassed over the years many books, boxes and file drawers of family archives, even predating the arrivals in America of our Jewett and Call forefathers—'when an old man dies, a library burns to the ground' isn't an adage that applies to this family! And my own memberships in the National Society of the Colonial Dames of America required documentation from these sides of my ancestry back to at least 1750 A.D.; for this book about Dad and the things he wanted to add about his forefathers, I have obviously gleaned much from those papers. But historical items can be especially cumbersome in footnote or endnote layout, and not every reader cares to jump to them, so I've simply woven several into the actual text of Dad's memoir... if not of interest, please just skip over the bracketed notations in smaller font to continue hearing Jerry's voice tell his story. For anyone wishing to dig deeper, a multi-page Appendix lists names of some of the books and other sources that fill my boxes and file drawers of family goodies—every possible attempt has been made to contact owners of any copyrights, and I trust due credit has been given. (Frankly, it's tough to know where some information has come from, as there is a lot of data in my head after far too many years of doing this stuff!)

Personal thanks go out to several others who have assisted in this endeavor. Though she claims not to be so interested in genealogical pursuits, I'm grateful to my sister, Stephanie Jewett, for her devotion to (and her keen recall of some details about) our father and our grandparents. Steph and her sons and grandsons live near Dad and hang out with him quite a bit, catching him retelling some stories that are included herein. Thanks go out to our paternal cousins, Chan, Kyle, Darcy, and C. J. Gibson, who grew up in the early years alongside us in Des Moines and at Lake Okoboji. Their Mom (Connie Cory, Dad's only sibling), was once a treasure trove of our family history, and I have often wished I'd picked her brain more thoroughly while she was able to clearly access the details… thankfully, she didn't keep them to herself, but freely shared great stories with her own kids and others. Though we cousins are now scattered around the country, whenever we have the chance to chat via phone or email, or even in person, the wonderful tales just start pouring out—I love that we typically end up laughing out loud like we did as kids. This book will contain some personal thoughts of recognition from each of them, and from two others (Dad's cousin, Tom Jewett; and my husband, John Dilley), all excerpted from surprise written notes that had been presented as gifts to Dad on his 91st birthday a year ago—it's certainly never too late to thank a 'second father,' or any other, for positively impacting our lives.

And gratitude goes right back to that same paternal cousin, Tom, for his ongoing Jewett family historical endeavors and book compilations; and to Dad's maternal Hutchison cousins who have assembled throughout the decades many Call family history items for all of us to enjoy. I am grateful to Jean Kramer, current President of the Kossuth County Genealogical Society, for sharing additional Algona articles and photos; to Peggy Strief and her local Delta Design team for their seemingly endless assistance with our photographs; and to Christine Karnas for offering her keen eye in the color and picture choices for the back cover (which highlights a **Here's To It!** toast from Lake Panorama a few days before Dad's 92nd birthday). My appreciation to Adam Delange of Newellco, who caught enthusiasm for this project when I requested permission to use various Dymo Label Maker references within the pages, as well as a tape likeness on the book's cover; he even offered to surprise my once-Dymo-obsessed father with the gift of a vintage machine! Thanks go out to the many other individuals and/or companies who gave permission to use a name/photo/quote here and there; and to our intellectual property attorney, Brian Laurenzo, for making sure we kept this all on the up and up! Lastly, I'm indebted to (and always amazed by) artistic son, Jake Dilley, who knocked it out of the ballpark with the delightful caricature that graces his Grandad's book; and to designer Todd Engel who seamlessly joined the front and back together to prove you *can* judge a book by its cover.

Special *posthumous* thanks get sent up to my mother (Jackie Berguin, Dad's first wife and the mother of his only two children). After their divorce, Mom became an American

History and World History teacher for the Des Moines Public Schools. I clearly recall the day I came home from my own high school and announced to her, "I just *hate* history! It's all about memorizing dates of things that don't even matter! How can you waste your time teaching such a boring subject?" My mother's simple answer changed the very course of my life… "Honey, it's all just one big story puzzle. Since you love to read and you love puzzles, put it together so the dates make sense of the story." And just that quickly, my focus changed. History suddenly came alive… so alive that it's been my own personal journey to help assemble such historical puzzle pieces for myself, and for others as well. Thanks, Mom! And thanks to all of my ancestors who have since passed, but who continue to assist with these types of genealogical pursuits—it's amazing how they seem to keep themselves quite busy, working for us and with us from the other side of the veil.

Be aware that this book has a chronological order to it, but with wanderings into topical discussions when deemed necessary for the storyline—sometimes the chronology actually develops backward but will make sense in the big picture. For every hour that Dad shared stories, I spent at least another three trying to figure out where to place the information in order to assimilate it into the whole. And every now and then, I couldn't help but add my own *{Editor's note}* with personal comments in curly brackets to help give further insight into one of his stories. Thank you for understanding the development of this project, and for just going with the unique flow—it's a hybrid book by design, a 'bio-mentary' (to coin what is likely a new term). I trust this will be an enjoyable memoir, and that the layout will contain a little something for everyone, from the casual reader to the avid history buff.

I was once admonished from the pages of a book to give my ancestors their proper due, because they gave me the ticket to my own life adventure—what a great concept! So, think of this narrative as honoring some of that debt owed to my forefathers (including Dad, who was a real trouper throughout this endeavor). There is indeed magic in looking at family history through the eyes of one who lived it, and I am thrilled to be a small part of keeping "his-story" alive. This has personally been the most fulfilling writing project of my life, and one for which I'll always be grateful—not many adult children have the opportunity to spend quality time working diligently for fourteen months on such an endeavor with a parent in his 90's (now 92, to be exact!). Which reminds me… due to being more than a year in the making, people and stories mentioned in the book have grown up right along with it, so I've adjusted any stated ages or timespans to be accurate at this time of printing.

Jennifer Jewett Dilley, jewettdilley@gmail.com, November 2017

Table of Contents

THE OBITUARY...XI

BEGINNINGS... 1

MY CALL HERITAGE... 7

THE NATIVE AMERICAN INDIANS.......................... 31

MY SHORE HERITAGE 37

SHORE FAMILY FUN.. 55

JEWETT FAMILY GATHERINGS................................ 65

THE JEWETT LUMBER COMPANY 73

HANGING OUT IN THE NEIGHBORHOOD 81

SUMMERS IN COLORADO 99

LAKE OKOBOJI COMPETES WITH COLORADO 109

OKOBOJI BECOMES PERMANENT............................. 113

MY OWN TRANSPORTATION 119

PAINTING THE TOWN RED....................................... 135

OKOBOJI GROWS UP TOO 141

MY JEWETT HERITAGE, IN PART............................... 151

GEORGE ANSON JEWETT, A MOST AMAZING MAN 155

THE JEWETT TYPEWRITER COMPANY 173

DES MOINES KEEPS GROWING 185

DRAKE UNIVERSITY GETS ITS START 201

THE SURPRISE 'JEWETT JEWETT' HERITAGE! 205

MY TERRIFIC PARENTS 209

SERVING OUR COUNTRY 227

WILD AND CRAZY UNIVERSITY DAYS 241

AND YES, THERE WERE AIRPLANES 255

MARRIAGE AND FAMILY YEARS 265

MY SINGLE-AGAIN ERA 285

SETTLING DOWN (SOME) 301

'NEAR MISSES' AND OTHER TALES 313

LIFE TRANSITIONS CONTINUE 329

LOOKING BACK 343

APPENDIX 369

Jewett

THE OBITUARY
(an interesting start to a book about one's life!)

Gerald Anson Jewett, Jr. ("Jerry"), a resident of the Wesley Acres retirement campus, was born in Des Moines, Iowa on October 21, 1925, to Gerald Anson Jewett, Sr. and Bertha Shore Jewett. A baptized member of the former Central Christian Church, he passed peacefully into the next life on _____, at the young age of ___. Other than two years spent in the United States Army Air Corps pilot training and service during WWII, Jerry was a lifelong resident of Des Moines and a nearly-lifelong summer resident of Lake Okoboji in northwest Iowa.

The kid kept his teachers on their toes at Greenwood and Callanan, before graduating as President of the Theodore Roosevelt High School class of 1943. College studies were started at Drake University and continued, following war draft obligations, at the University of Iowa, where he was President of his Sigma Nu fraternity and served on the Interfraternity Council before graduating from the College of Commerce with a degree in Business Administration. Jerry became the fourth generation to enter the family-owned Jewett Lumber Company in Des Moines, serving first as its General Manager, then Treasurer, then President. He was a perfectionist with a passion for homebuilding, and others learned much from his keen woodworking prowess. Mr. Jewett was always pleased to give of his time and talents to a variety of organizations. Though he hoped for a short newspaper obituary, it was tough to decide what to eliminate; the forthgoing list of involvements brings an appreciation to his commissioning many years ago into the Honorable Order of Kentucky Colonels…

Jerry was one of the founders of the Polk County Heart Association and served as Chairman of the American Heart Association/Iowa Affiliate. He was Chairman of the Boards of Mercy Properties and of Mercy Share Care, Ltd., and served for a number of years on the Board of the Mercy Foundation. Jerry founded and was President of the Polk County Reserve Deputy Sheriff's Association, Chairman of the Polk County Peace Officers Association, and President of the Polk County Society for Crippled Children and Adults. This gentleman was a successful fundraiser for Easter Seals' Camp Sunnyside, United Way of Central Iowa, March of Dimes, and The Salvation Army (enjoying annual turns as a skywalk bell ringer). He was a proud part of the American Legion, and a volunteer Committee member of the Employer Support of the Guard and Reserve for the State of Iowa. The man sat for many years on the Executive Board (and later, on the Advisory Council) of the Mid-Iowa Council of Boy Scouts of America, and was a Past President of the Shrimp Club and of the Pioneer Club of Des Moines. He was also a long-standing member of the Okoboji Yacht Club, a Board member of the Okoboji Protective Association, and founder and operator of the Lake Okoboji Seaplane Base. Life memberships were held in the University of Iowa Alumni Association, in Sigma Nu, and in the Jewett Family of America, Inc.

This very active individual wore a number of hats for the Greater Des Moines Chamber of Commerce (and for the Junior Chamber as a young man), chairing its annual Goodwill Tour Committee and chairing for many years its Membership Committee. Additionally, he was honored to successfully plan and carry out the big air show for Des Moines International Airport's 50th Anniversary while serving as Chairman of the Chamber's Aviation Committee. Jerry was an avid business and recreational pilot who logged more than 23,300 hours in his own 55 years of active flying and was rated as a commercial pilot for land (single and multi-engine), sea (single-engine), and instrument. He was a well-seasoned traveler with a penchant for remembering details, and was known for being a consummate storyteller (with enough material to fill the pages of his recent book, *Here's To It!,* a published memoir about one very eventful life). In addition to a passion for airplanes, classic cars, magic tricks, and Oreo cookies, Jerry's many pastimes and hobbies over the years have also included sailing, snow and water skiing, ice and roller skating, tennis, golf, hunting, fishing, horseback riding, boating, swimming, tinkering in his workshops, and wintering in Marco Island, Florida.

For well over six decades, Jerry was a member and past President of the Reciprocity Club of Des Moines and of the Quiet Birdmen pilot's organization. He was also a Paul Harris member of The Rotary Club, Honorary President of the Izaak Walton League, and on the Board of The Des Moines Club. Past memberships have included the Ad Club of Des Moines, Des Moines Golf and Country Club, Des Moines Art Center, Drake Boosters Club, Dowling Club, Planned Parenthood, Ducks Unlimited, and the YMCA. Jerry assisted with the Governor's Iowa Emergency Resource Management Plan, serving as Chief of its Supply and Requirements Division. Vocationally, he was a member of the National Association of Home Builders, President of the Iowa Lumbermens Association and of the Northwestern Lumbermens Association, President and Life Member of the Iowa Chapter of Hoo-Hoo, International, and Chairman/President of the National Lumber and Building Material Dealers Association. After the merging of two local family-owned pioneer building material businesses, he served as CEO and then as Chairman Emeritus of Gilcrest/Jewett Lumber Company until his passing.

Jerry Jewett was preceded in death by his first wife, Jackie Berguin, and second wife, Nelle Ross. Left to carry on his immediate legacy are two daughters, Jennifer (John) Dilley and Stephanie Jewett. He is also survived by sister Connie Cory, stepsons Roy (Barbara) Ross and Tom (Gay) Ross, close friend Jeanette Redman, and some very special Wesley Acres pals. Dearest to Jerry's heart were his four beloved grandsons, Joe (Carrie) and Jake Dilley, and Ryland and Kingsley Jewett; and he was simply delighted with his four little great-grandchildren, Ashton and Jack Dilley, and Anson and Jonah Jewett.

Gerald Anson Jewett, Jr. was a man who left an indelible mark on his family and on his world, and we are enriched by having known and loved him. Jerry often gratefully acknowledged the fine teamwork of physicians who kept him in such good balance over the more recent years, asking that those 'major players' be listed herein: Drs. Sean Cunningham, Josh Groben, Craig Shadur and Tom Buroker. He wished any memorial donations in his name be sent to a charity of the donor's choice or to the Wesley Life Foundation, 3520 Grand Avenue, Des Moines, Iowa, 50312.

BEGINNINGS

My name is Gerald Anson Jewett, Jr. I was born at 9:13 A.M. on Wednesday, October 21, 1925, at Methodist Hospital in Des Moines, Iowa… weighing in at 8 pounds, 4 ounces, and measuring 22 inches long. My parents were Gerald Anson Jewett, Sr. and Bertha ("Bertie") Shore Jewett. The baby book Mom kept about me states that she took me home two weeks later, on November 3—I guess they let new mothers relax for a couple of weeks back then, unless I had some newborn sickness nobody told me about.

Eventually, I did have a few unexpected childhood illnesses, the big one being double pneumonia as a fourteen-month-old. Believe it or not, I really do remember looking out of my crib during that long ordeal, especially hating those bars that caged me in. By age 3½, I also had whooping cough for six whole weeks, and then ended up with full-blown pneumonia yet again by age 4. Being confined to a bed was terribly tough on this active little kid. My parents would tell me I needed to rest, and Mother recorded that I replied, "But I'm not sleepy—see how lively and quick I am!"

I grew up at 213-38th Street Place in Des Moines, in the house my folks had built the year before I was born. The lot on which they began construction was once my mother's pony pasture, across a deep ravine that still housed her horse barn behind the 210-37th Street home of her parents, Dr. Francis Edward Victor (F. E. V.) Shore and Mrs. Bertha Call Shore. As a wedding gift to my Mom and Dad, her parents had given them the north rear portion of their large plat of land that ran from 37th Street all the way west to 38th Street Place. (My grandparents reserved the south rear portion of the plat in hopes of eventually building themselves a smaller home on it in their time of retirement.)

Two years after receiving the generous wedding gift, my parents built their first house on that back north lot. I was 4½ when my little sister, Connie, was born, and we loved growing up there. Our home was a beautiful two-story brick and stucco with a slate roof. It had four bedrooms, two baths, a fireplace, a big solarium/sunroom, a full underground basement, and a detached two-car garage.

And like in the homes of all my grandparents, we had an additional back stairway that went from the kitchen up to the second-floor bedroom of our live-in housemaid, Freda, a really nice lady who was with us a long time. I remember that Freda had an ongoing problem, however… when walking from the living room to the dining room, she regularly fell down after tripping over the edge of the oriental rug that was under our large formal dinner table! We never knew why she couldn't get that right.

There was a big metal door to a chute on the (north) driveway side of the house—that's where coal was delivered regularly and dumped down into a very dirty basement storage room. When I was old enough to help, I remember shoveling coal with Dad. We had to carry it clear over to the furnace on the southwest side of the basement, where it could be vented out of the fireplace chimney. A few houses by then were starting to be heated with oil, but ours was still heated with coal until several years later. I'll tell more soon about the workshop I built for myself in that same furnace room as a kid, and about some of the many things I constructed down there.

The northeast corner of the basement was the laundry area—we had a new-fangled electric washing machine with a wringer, but no clothes dryer. Those were the days when you just hung wet clothing items out to dry in the backyard or dangled them from a clothesline in the laundry room if the weather was bad. (And you could even send things to the cleaners when their truck came through the neighborhood every few days.) In the southeast corner of the basement, my very creative Mother had her own art room. And last, but not least, also down in our basement you'd find my Dad's little beverage still, which helped out during those Prohibition years—and no, I never got into it!

While my folks were building that first house, a little neighbor boy was playing after hours at the job site and fell down the two-story chimney the very day it had been constructed. I guess when he was found, all the bricks had to be torn out to retrieve him unharmed. Interestingly, that little boy eventually grew up to serve our country overseas in World War II and was captured—he again had to be retrieved, this time as a Prisoner of War in Germany, and again he returned home alive! (That guy is no longer living, but I finally met and had a nice time chatting with his daughter just recently at a meeting of the Des Moines Historical Society, where she was the guest speaker. Victoria Herring seemed to thoroughly enjoy hearing some neighborhood tales about her young father, and was even more intrigued to hear stories about her *grand*father—a man she never even met, who eventually became an Iowa Governor and U.S. Senator. Victoria has since written a kind note granting permission to use any names of her family members in this book, so the reader will have the treat of learning a little more about some of them in upcoming pages.)

There was no such thing as a television set back then, but we did have a radio (a Philco console with push buttons) that we kept in the living room. One of the buttons on it said, "TV SOUND," and we all wondered what that meant. Now we know the company was way ahead of its time in preparing its products for such a thing as television. My Dad was always up on the latest models of electronics, which is likely why we had that fancy Philco. We all listened to the radio as a family, but I really only liked hearing the Sunday funny papers read aloud on it. Other than that, my family would go over to my grandparents' house across the ravine on Sunday nights where we all listened to Jack Benny on *their* radio, an old thing that had a box battery about a foot square, which was full of acid to run it—it was real, real primitive, but my grandfather just loved it. Usually, my folks' very close friends, Peg and Woody, would come over for that Sunday night affair too—it was my job to pop popcorn and make fudge for everyone, which of course helped the Jack Benny Show sound even better!

There was also a telephone in our new house, and it was kept on a little drop leaf desk at the top of the stairs. My folks later added another phone, moving this one into their bedroom and putting a second one in the downstairs solarium. Our phone was originally on a party line… you just picked up the hand-held receiver and the call went through an operator. By junior high and high school, I was able to call my friends whenever I wanted, with the exception of one guy who lived clear out in Valley Junction (now known as West Des Moines)—I wasn't supposed to ring him because it cost a nickel to call that far.

Our first phone number was simply '505.' As Des Moines grew in size, preface names were added to the phone numbers—the first two letters of the new preface names corresponded to the first two numbers on the phone dial. Our '505' became 'BL-505' (the 'BL' stood for 'Blackburn;' other preface names were 'AM' for 'Amherst,' 'CH' for 'Cherry,' 'CR' for 'Crestwood,' and so on—longtime Des Moines residents will remember those.) Years later, two numbers were then added to the *end* of phone numbers, and ours became BL-505-25. Eventually, 'BL-505-25' became '25-505-25' or as written today, '255-0525.' (Area codes came along much later, of course.) This may seem boring, but

I wanted to bring up the phone number story for a good reason… When my parents eventually moved from that first home in their later retirement years, they kept the same 255-0525 phone number. And after my parents had both passed away, my daughter Stephanie was able to secure that very same phone number for herself. Believe it or not, our original 'BL-505-25' is still Steph's landline number all these decades later!

Our house on 38th Street Place wasn't really all that fancy, though it was in a fairly fancy neighborhood. But across our backyard and ravine, the homes along 37th Street where my grandparents lived were, in fact, *really* fancy. I guess there was only one house that wasn't… it was the 'bookshop house' north of Greenwood School. The lady who lived there was a widow, a friend of my mother's, and had sold her large house a few blocks east after her husband passed away. She moved into the small home next door to my school and kept it so nice and neat and well-arranged. Her front room was covered in books, and that's where I took reading lessons. I was far-sighted and had to wear glasses to read as a kid. Jennifer just asked if they were wire-rimmed glasses and, yes, they were—I don't think there were plastic rims back then. As a matter of fact, I don't recall anything made of plastic that early. The first car we ever had with a plastic steering wheel that replaced the wooden wheel was about a 1938 Ford, I think. *{Editor's note: Readers will learn that Dad determines history by the cars of the era!}* Anyway, the tutoring must have helped because I didn't seem to need special lessons after that. I still don't consider myself a fast reader though, and am almost dreading reading the final draft of this book about my life for fear it

will take me until I'm 94 years old to get through it. Whenever I think about that reading tutor who lived next to Greenwood School, for some reason I think about the pair of hand-me-down pants 'inherited' from her son, Tom. I just hated those pants because they had a little spot on the front of one leg that Mom could never get out, so I finally just refused to wear them.

As a little kid, I sure loved Winnie-the-Pooh, the character introduced by author A. A. Milne the year after I was born. I had my own Pooh bear, sleeping with it every single night and carrying it around wherever I went during the day. Long before I could read by myself, Mother would sit and read to me about the adventures of this new little Pooh guy bumping down the stairs behind Christopher Robin. Naturally, it was fun to pretend I was Christopher Robin with my head full of light-colored hair like his (but you can see that mine had lots of curls peeking out of some very stylish hats!).

Mom also read to me about other A. A. Milne characters, like the three little foxes who didn't wear shoes and didn't wear soxes and kept their handkerchiefs in cardboard boxes. Those particular foxes must have made quite an impression on me, and I always kept plenty of handkerchiefs myself. I grew up sneezing a lot, with allergies to things like goose feathers, household dust, powder, white potatoes, cocoa, insecticides, corn, and ragweed. And because of hay fever, there was a special air filter in my bedroom. I remember having a 'Schick test' back then to see what things I was allergic to—my doctor scratched a place on my back and then gave my folks a huge list of far too many things I was supposed to stay away from! (All these decades later, I no longer keep my handkerchiefs in cardboard boxes, but do continue to regularly use a fresh cotton one carried daily in my pocket! I've dealt with other sensitivities to a few things over the years, and an annoying itch sometimes brings them to my attention. But a recent blood test shows no food or environmental allergies at this time, and it's a great relief to know that chocolate isn't a current problem—you're reading about a self-confessed chocoholic who has been addicted to Hydrox and then Oreo cookies since childhood!)

I just loved my little crank-up record player with its small vinyl disc full of Pooh songs, and would sing them all day long. First, I had to crank and crank and crank, then the player would play and I would sing along with it until the words started slowing down, then I'd crank and crank and crank again to be able to finish songs. My parents and sister talked for years about how I used to sing the songs as a little kid just exactly as I heard them, with all the warps and skips and varying speeds! One of my favorites was about the changing of guards at Buckingham Palace, and how Christopher Robin went down there with Alice. There are several verses to that song, and I memorized them all—they were to come in so handy in the future when singing those childhood songs to my own daughters (and singing to myself to stay awake while flying airplanes solo). Another favorite poem by the same author was about the King and Queen having breakfast—it also had several verses, and I memorized them too, of course. That particular recording on my vinyl disc sounded just like live theater, and I loved to repeat the breakfast poem with the same distinguished voice for the Queen and the same high-pitched little voice for the Dairymaid. *{Editor's note: For me, the all-time best day Dad and I spent in writing this book was the day he tapped into his memories of the Pooh songs and poems. We both began to sing, smiling at each other in wide-eyed surprise that either of us recalled them… gotta love that long-term memory!}*

When putting me down to bed at night, my folks and I always prayed a popular prayer that starts, "Now I lay me down to sleep, I pray the Lord my soul to keep...," but I often asked Mother to read to me the one from my Pooh book where Christopher Robin asks for blessings on everybody in his family, but almost forgets to add, "God bless *me*!" I really did want God to bless us all.

Evidently, I was a very observant little guy and must have had a lot of questions. Mom said that I asked her when I was two years old if the trees were electric since their leaves moved in the breeze—it's so great she wrote down that statement in my baby book, or I might have forgotten it. I do recall thinking that electricity was magic and that if anything moved it must be electric. By the time I was about four, a friend of Dad's had given me a little electric motor that you plugged into the wall, and I used it to make the engine-like hum when playing with my toy cars—that was the best sound!

Even though it was fun playing indoors with my cars and singing songs along with my record player, I was also a busy little kid who loved to be outdoors, not only in my own backyard but all over our neighborhood and beyond. And I especially enjoyed spending a lot of time at my grandparents' home across the ravine. One day I was playing with my toy cars in Grandma Shore's living room while she was having Bridge Club. I remember one of the women saying to my grandmother, "Bertha, where were you from originally?" and Grandma answered, "I was a Call girl from Algona." All the ladies laughed, but I didn't know what they were laughing at...

MY CALL HERITAGE

"Call" was Grandma Shore's maiden name. Her father, Ambrose Adolphus Call (along with his older brother Asa Cyrus Call), founded the Iowa town of Algona in 1854. The two boys had been born in Ohio, and both soon became young patriots with an inner urge for adventure. Their grandfather was a Minute Man in the Revolutionary War of 1776 [Asa Call, Sr., 1763-1825, whose "immediate cause of death was the wound in his head which he received in battle and which troubled him for years"], and their father had served in the War of 1812. Their father had been a widower with no children, before marrying his second wife (their mother, Mary "Polly" Metcalf), with whom he fathered eight. Ambrose, born on June 9, 1833, was the youngest of those eight children—he would one day become my great-grandfather. [And only a few generations before that, ancestor Ralph Sprague (1599-1650) had originally arrived in Salem, Massachusetts from Upway, Dorsetshire, England on the ship 'Abigail.' He is attributed with being one of the founders of Charlestown (Boston) and of Malden, Massachusetts; additionally, he became a Deputy to the General Court, as well as a Lieutenant of the Charlestown Company.]

The story of Ambrose and Asa, the two Call brothers, is terribly fascinating to me, so I wanted to make certain we put some things about them here. The boys' father [Asa Call, Jr., 2/4/1792 - 3/13/1833] had died at the early age of 41, just a couple of months before my great-grandfather Ambrose was born. Their father's lengthy medical problems had drained all financial resources of the family, and their young widowed mother was forced to move away from Ohio with her kids. Though born in Vermont, she had relatives and supportive friends in western New York, so she moved back there with her children. After five years, she and the kids all headed west again and relocated in South Bend, Indiana for a lengthy period of time. [In 1848, after fifteen years as a widow, Ambrose and Asa's mother married James Finch in Fulton, Illinois, just across the Mississippi River from Clinton, Iowa. The couple resided in the Clinton area (in a town then known as Lyons, Iowa) until Mr. Finch's death there in 1862. Mary Metcalf Call Finch eventually moved to Algona, Iowa, to live near her sons, Ambrose and Asa, in the town they had founded in 1854. She passed away in Algona on September 19, 1868, at the age of 69 (having been born on May 24, 1799, in Corinth, Vermont). Mary "Polly" Finch is buried with her sons and families in the Riverview Cemetery in Algona, Iowa.]

So, my great-grandfather, Ambrose, and his Call siblings received their later public education in South Bend. By the time their mother remarried, Ambrose was striking out on his own as a 15-year-old teenager. He headed back to Ohio (the state of his birth) to attend commercial college while also establishing a news depot in Dayton, "delivering to subscribers the Cincinnati dailies ahead of the mails." My great-grandfather's pioneering spirit was strong and by the age of 20, he headed westward, exploring new lands by starting at the headwaters of the St. Croix River in Wisconsin and then traveling downstream. In the meantime, Ambrose's older brother, Asa, caught a bad case of 'Gold Rush Fever' and had struck out for California in 1849, walking with a herd of cattle all the way from St. Louis to San Francisco. He was a survivor of the famous sinking of the Winfield Scott steamer off the Channel Islands near Santa Barbara on December 1, 1853, but that's another story! [The wreck site is part of the Channel Islands National Park and Marine Sanctuary, and has been listed on the National Register of Historic Places since 1988.] Not long after surviving the shipwreck, just four years after heading west, Asa returned to Iowa from the California gold fields (where he had amassed a small fortune of $6000 in gold, secretly sewn into the lining of his buckskin coat for the trip back east).

[Before heading west in 1849, Asa had done some school teaching while he also attended, and graduated with honors from, Oberlin College Institute in Ohio (following his public schooling in South Bend). Having had experience with Native Americans while making his western trek, Asa was then appointed by the Army in California as 'Indian Commissioner,' with the rank of Captain. His duties, along with the 100 men under his command, were many, including recovery of stolen cattle from the Snake Indians (Native American tribes near the Snake River, which eventually included the Northern Paiute, Bannock, and Shoshone) and the pursuit of ongoing negotiations with the tribes. While in California, Asa was also a correspondent for the *National Era*, an abolitionist newspaper published for several years in Washington, D.C. Asa's great-great-grandson, John R. Call (and wife Vanessa) did two years of extensive editing work on the journals of Asa Call, kindly gifting us with a copy of their final 1998 edition of *The Diaries of Asa Cyrus Call: March 28, 1850-December 26, 1853.*]

After then getting married, Asa and his new wife settled in Iowa City, the capital of our state at that time. He regarded their Iowa City home as temporary, however, having decided to select some "eligible site" for a new town of his *own* making. As quoted by Asa in his personal journal, "I had for several years intended to found a new town. I was determined to find a place where I could get fine lands and as many other advantages as possible." Asa had apparently explored the upper Mississippi, where every available site was already occupied; he also explored the western shores of Lake Superior, where he found good harbors but no land. Eventually Asa decided to look inland.

[It was likely while on his explorations further east that Asa had met and soon married Sarah Heckert, daughter of John and Elizabeth (Fisher) Heckert of Elkhart County, Indiana. After they wed on June 13, 1854, Asa and Sarah then traveled 300 miles west, ending up in Iowa City. Historically, the first capital of the Iowa Territory had been in Burlington (at one time called 'Flint Hills'). Iowa was still uncharted territory when Burlington became the capital, and squatters crossed the Mississippi River to begin clearing the land and building cabins and fences. But they were driven back east across the river by American soldiers who burned those cabins and fences, because the government had promised the Indians that no white settlers would come into the Iowa land before June 1833. After that date, there was a population explosion and by 1838, the 'Territory of Iowa' was formed. It wasn't long before the early settlers realized that a more central location for a capital would soon have to be chosen. By 1839, a spot nearer the center of the growing population movement westward was found on the Iowa River in Johnson County—then called

'City of Iowa' and now 'Iowa City'—one log cabin served as the Capitol Building for the Iowa Territory until a larger structure was finally completed in 1842. Iowa officially became a state in late December of 1846. By the time newlyweds Asa and Sarah Call moved to Iowa City in 1854, the legislature was already deciding to move the capital from Iowa City to Fort Des Moines, to be near the fork of the Raccoon and Des Moines Rivers. (For confusion purposes, 'capital' is not spelled 'capitol' unless referring to an actual building, and is not 'capitalized' unless referring to the state or U.S. 'Capitol Building' by name!) Iowa's capital move finally happened by 1857— the same year the word 'Fort' was dropped from 'Des Moines.' The State University of Iowa, called the 'University of Iowa' since 1964, had been founded in Iowa City in 1847, just two months after Iowa became a state. Once the seat of government moved out of Iowa City, the entire State University of Iowa was housed in the old Capitol Building ("Old Cap") for another six years until a second structure was built on that land owned by the University.]

In the meantime, Asa's youngest brother (my eventual great-grandfather Ambrose) was temporarily living in Stillwater, Minnesota, a logging center on the west banks of the St. Croix River. The boys must have kept in touch somewhat, because Ambrose received a letter from Asa, persuading him to head south in order to discuss a joint exploration venture of founding a town in unsettled northern Iowa. So, Ambrose took a boat down the river to Muscatine, apparently meeting up with Asa and taking a stage together over to Iowa City. The two of them laid out their plan and finally headed west to Fort Des Moines (as our city was first called), then turned north to follow the Des Moines River into the 'Upper Des Moines country' and beyond. The pioneering brothers were fully aware that they would be entering uncharted and hostile Indian territories, but both had valuable experience dealing with that. So, they chose to proceed with the adventure into northern Iowa—Asa was almost 29-years-old, and my great-grandfather Ambrose had just turned 21.

[At that time, "there was across eastern Iowa a definite path one hundred miles long to guide the movers going west. No furrow had been plowed in northern Iowa, but there remained a faint trail as far as the abandoned military post at Fort Dodge. Three tribes of Indians who for centuries had roamed Iowa—the Sioux, the Winnebagos, and the Sacs and Foxes—had been shrewdly bargained with by their white brothers, and for a few paltry dollars and the hope of much firewater had parted with their ancestral hunting grounds and fishing streams and lakes, and were moving westward. They were not happy in their bargain and were loath to go. Tribe hating tribe, and all suspicious of the white man, they lingered and begged and thieved and robbed in small bands, keeping the settlers and each other in a constant state of alarm and suspense."]

My grandmother told me that when her father (Ambrose) and her uncle (Asa) went north from Fort Des Moines and moved up the Des Moines River, they were armed with one rifle and were walking, carrying their only belongings in knapsacks. Along the trail, they came upon a man riding an old pack horse, and were able to purchase the animal and take turns riding with their goods on its back. They were relieved when finally making it to the very small settlement of Fort Dodge, 90 or more miles later. It's kind of interesting that there were government surveyors who had been assigned to the area north of Fort Dodge the week before the brothers arrived, but they had been robbed by Indians and had retreated forty miles back down to that Fort as well. The surveyors talked of the great and beautiful land to the north, however, which further motivated Ambrose and Asa to forge ahead in order to find the spot they would claim as their own. The excited brothers then purchased a second rifle and another horse, along with a wagon to carry their new homesteading provisions, and kept proceeding northward. [The surveyors also had encountered extreme amounts of mosquitoes, writing, "the air would be literally thick with them… if we talked they would get in our mouth, they would fly into our eyes and ears, would cover our faces and hands, and not an inch of our bodies unprotected by clothing would escape them. In going to and from camp we would carry our tools so as to have one hand free to fight these little torments." Later accounts by early settlers tell of tacking cloth mosquito netting to cover the windows of the log houses in the spring.]

Grandma said that when her father and uncle finally came upon the big bluff located where Algona is today, they both thought it would make a beautiful place for a town. The date was July 9, 1854. Asa wrote in his journal, "At the site of Algona I found a tract of good land, with a fair supply of timber, some water power, and near the center of the county… at that time there was no settlement north of Fort Dodge." Ambrose recorded that they used a spade and "investigated the nature of the soil," then "drew up our team on the high ground… noted the beauty of the location overlooking the river and the bluffs beyond, with a fine grove of timber to the north and south… My brother said, Ambrose, I believe this is the place for our city—we will build the court house right here on this high ground." My great-grandfather Ambrose later wrote more emotionally about how he felt upon that first sighting of their new home: "It was a beautiful inverted mirage that appeared in the clouds after sunset, outlining to us the groves of timber along the Des Moines River west and north of our camp clear to the Minnesota line. The mirage is common in all prairie and desert countries both in summer and winter when atmospheric conditions are favorable, but I have never since seen a double mirage, and never before or since did I see so beautiful a picture in the heavens."

Because Algona land was still unsurveyed, they could 'take up government claims.' So, the Calls wasted no time… my great-grandfather Ambrose made this important entry about staking the first claim in Kossuth County the very next day: "We made our camp at noon… and while dinner was preparing and the team eating I made my way through the jungles to the river at the Indian ford, just above the bridge, where I found plenty of moccasin tracks. On my return to camp with my hatchet I blazed a walnut tree and wrote: Ambrose A. Call claims all that part of section 11, Tp. 95, Rg. 29, lying south of the river. Dated July 10, 1854." The Call boys were then the only white settlers north of Fort Dodge and west of the

Cedar River in the state of Iowa. [Staking a claim back in those days was just as it sounds—literally hammering down a stake on a portion of land that had not yet been declared as owned by anyone else. Since the territory had yet to be fully surveyed, settlers held their land by 'right of possession.' One book on the history of Iowa and of Kossuth County details, "When Iowa had been a state for four years, the code of 1850 had declared that any person occupying any part of the public lands not yet in the market and having his claim plainly marked out should have constructive possession of the same to the amount of 320 acres... sometimes it was difficult to measure the land exactly when it followed the winding course of the river, but if there was any uncertainty, the settler usually claimed enough to cover all contingencies... In order to avoid trouble, the few settlers decided to follow the example of older groups on the frontier and organized a 'Claim Club.' This was the first formal meeting ever held in Kossuth County and undertook to protect each member in the peaceable possession of his claim."]

After staking their claims, Asa and Ambrose returned to Fort Dodge and then to Boonesboro to collect the necessities for a pioneer existence. From there, Asa continued heading south and east, back to Iowa City to reunite with his new wife [where they were temporarily living as boarders in the local hotel] and to begin preparations for their return to Algona together in the late fall. Ambrose realized he would need help in completing some of the huge tasks ahead of him over the next few weeks, so he invited another man, William T. Smith, to join him in first finding the best route back to Algona. Call and Smith flattened a good trail along the way by hitching a log under the rear axle of the wagon to drag down the grass, allowing others to eventually follow their trail north. My great-grandfather and Mr. Smith then began building a 14' x 16' log cabin on Ambrose's chosen site. He later told my grandmother and her siblings that the cabin was "built exactly as Great-grandfather built in Vermont and similar to the one in which Abraham Lincoln learned to read his Bible." The logs were "as large as two men could raise, with a door made of puncheons hewn from basswood logs, a one-sash window 10 x 12 inches, a chimney made of sticks

with mortar made of yellow clay, a fireplace of boulders, and a hearth of dirt." It was the first cabin built by white men in Kossuth County and was tucked high in the rugged hills which were surrounded by old growth forest, forty miles from the nearest cabin.

The hand-drawn sketch here is dated December 17, 1856, and comes from the many written journals of my great-grandfather, Ambrose. This must have been what his original cabin looked like, and it appears he had added an outbuilding by the time he drew the peaceful setting two years after he started to reside there. I'm guessing the stumps in the drawing are from trees he felled to build the structures or to fill his fireplace. It's hard to imagine these few original settlers braving the harsh northern Iowa winters, and without much interpersonal contact once they had laid up sufficient wood to burn and game to eat throughout the severe months when only tallow candles furnished light as needed. It had to have been lonely living in such a vast, silent wilderness; and yet my great-grandfather Ambrose thrived.

[The settlement was originally named 'Call's Grove,' after which 'Callville' was presented as a potential replacement name. Asa wrote, "It was quite a study to get a name that was suitable. We came to the conclusion that we would not tack a city to our name. We thought if it ever came to be a city, people would find it out and it would only be ridiculous to make it a part of the name. It was finally left for my wife to name the place and she decided to call it 'Algona.' This was not a pure Indian name…" When Asa's wife, Sarah, and her husband joined back up with Ambrose at their new settlement several months after the brothers founded it, she may have suggested the name to signify nearby waters belonging to the Algonquin tribe. But there also seem to be other accounts of how 'Algona' got its name. It is likely some sort of combination of 'Algonquin' and 'Algoma' (a name often found in regions of the eastern U.S. and Canada). The name's history does signify water, which would make sense for this new community, surrounded on three sides by the winding of the Des Moines River.]

That site is now part of the 138 acres known as the Ambrose A. Call State Park—the land was gifted to the state and was dedicated as a park in July of 1929 at the three-day 75th Diamond Jubilee Anniversary celebration of the founding of Algona. Development for such a park had taken place on that original tract of great-grandfather Ambrose's land, and it opened with new "splendid roads, beautiful picnic spots, deep well water supply, and a large and comfortable shelter house." Most importantly, in honor of Ambrose and his love of the wild, the park's commitment was to keep the native timber and shrubbery and wildflowers in their natural state.

My grandparents likely attended that big Call Park event in 1929. Mom and Dad and I may have been there too, but I really have no recollection of it. [In attendance and speaking at that gala affair were Governor John Hammill, as well as Senator George Patterson and Congressman L. J. Dickinson. Others addressing the group included the Secretary of State, members of the Board of Conservation, and representatives of the Call family. (Ambrose's eldest daughter, Florence Call Cowles, was slated to speak but became ill during the trip to Algona from Des Moines and had to return home—her son Gardner Cowles, Jr. spoke in her stead.)] I do remember, however, all the picnics we have had in the Ambrose A. Call State Park over the years since then—more than I can even count. We always stopped there on our travels to and from Lake Okoboji during the summers. The cabin that currently sits in the heavily wooded park is not the original one that my great-grandfather built and lived in, but is a close replica and near the spot where his sat.

Back in July of 2004, I participated in the 150th Sesquicentennial Anniversary celebration of the founding of the town of Algona. In attendance for that weekend were several surviving great-grandchildren of the founders, including my sister and myself and a few of our relatives from around the country. The local Des Moines cousins also in attendance included David Kruidenier, Ted and Tom Hutchison, and L. Call Dickinson, Jr. [Gerald Jewett, Jr. and Constance Jewett Cory are the grandchildren of Bertha Call Shore, David Kruidenier was the grandson of Florence Call Cowles, Ted and Tom Hutchison are/were the grandsons of Edith Call Hutchison, and L. Call Dickinson was the grandson of Myrtle Call Dickinson.] Each of us rode as Grand Marshalls in one of five open convertibles, while our own children and grandchildren (more than 100 descendants of Ambrose and Asa) rode on or walked behind a trolley bus that carried members of the Call family along the eighteen-block parade route. It was quite an event, with Algona residents cheering and yelling thanks to us as we paraded through their town.

On the final day of that 2004 celebration event, the Mayor and others topped off the weekend by providing us with a lovely Sunday luncheon in the park that carries my great-grandfather's name. Sis Connie and I were still in attendance for this final day picture, as were my wife (Nelle), niece (Kyle), daughter (Jennifer), and son-in-law (John). A local newspaper article prior to the big weekend celebration had quoted their Mayor (Mr. Lynn Kueck, who still serves in that capacity) as saying, "These descendants are like celebrities—I want them to go home and say, 'Wow! We were treated like royalty.'" Sure enough, I went home and said, "Wow! We *were* treated like royalty!"

Just recently, in July of 2017, son-in-law John drove me (and Jen) up to Algona for several hours of enjoyment at their Founders' Day Weekend. After first cruising by the County Historical Museum at the Fairgrounds in order to look at a fine outdoor display of vintage cars, tractors, motorcycles, and race cars, we then met up with members of the Kossuth County Genealogical Society for a nice personal chat. Our next stop was at the public library to view an art exhibit (generously sponsored by the Stinson Prairie Arts Council) of original paintings by Mary Call, daughter of Asa and Sarah Call. Mary's art looked so much like the paintings done by my own mother—it was hard to believe it wasn't Mom's work, but that of her cousin [once removed] instead. We were then able to squeeze in a quick tour of Algona's WWII P.O.W. Museum and to take in its historical audio-visual presentation. Stopping there was especially meaningful since I had personally seen that P.O.W. camp in Algona during the war days—the tall barbed wire fences that contained 10,000 or so prisoners left quite an impression on me back then.

We ended our afternoon trek to that recent Founders' Day Weekend by taking an educational walking tour led by Mayor Kueck, observing the river country with its tall grasses and woods and ponds on some of the original ground once owned by my great-grandfather. (Fortunately, I didn't have to actually walk it, as the Mayor had kindly arranged for me to ride in a Polaris Ranger driven by the man who owns the 240 acres of land on which part of the tour took place). It was such an interesting historical excursion—all of the

participants enjoyed learning even more about the rich history of the Algona territory founded by the Call brothers. After the other tour-takers left, the generous landowner then took the three of us on our own private tour of his 'Wildhaven Campus' (I was still a passenger on his Ranger, and John and Jen drove a John Deere Gator), venturing even further into the rough native lands once owned by Ambrose. It was exciting to find ourselves deep within the thick overgrowth, encountering several more acres of silent territory inhabited by all sorts of wildlife. A pair of bald eagles faced each other from their perches on two tall posts overlooking what was likely a favorite pond full of fish; their *huge* nest was in a nearby tree. All agreed this four-wheel adventure was our trip highlight.

But we had also stumbled upon another fun affair earlier in the afternoon when stopping in at the 'Train Wreck Winery,' owned by area native NFL Super Bowl Champion, Dallas Clark. Their actual vineyard is located on the Clark family's Century Farm south of nearby Livermore (next to the site of a 1920 famous train wreck, thus the name); the retail

operation we wanted to see occupies the refurbished old 'Chicago and North Western' railroad station that had been built in 1917 and sits next to a north-south track on the east end of Algona.

Unbeknownst to us, we happened in on the very day the local managers and personnel were celebrating the Depot's 100th Anniversary, and I was just in time to be served the first piece from the sheet cake prepared for that birthday party. Along with the complimentary cheese and crackers and a glass of "Kate," their best-selling sweet red table wine (this one named in honor of railroad heroine Kate Shelley), we learned there really *is* such a thing as a free lunch!

Before leaving the winery, each of the patrons in the establishment had entered our names into a drawing for a free T-shirt; believe it or not, my name was drawn as the winner of that! And after the managers learned of this book being compiled about my life, they offered for us to come to Algona to hold a signing party in their Depot, which we may indeed do. (The Kossuth County Genealogical Society had already offered to sponsor such a book signing event up there, and now it looks like we'll have a place to hold it.) All in all, the railroad station celebration was a terrific unplanned stop for us.

This is probably an appropriate time to tell of another type of transportation network—The *Underground* Railroad—which was taking place behind the scenes back when my great-grandfather and his brother were founding and settling Algona. [Wikipedia most succinctly describes the Underground Railroad as "a network of secret routes and safe houses" used by tens of thousands of African American slaves "to escape into free states and Canada with the aid of abolitionists and allies who were sympathetic to their cause."] I'd heard stories about this slave freedom network running east and west through Central Iowa, but had really not heard about any connections through the undeveloped land further north. Of course, there had to be some who escaped in that direction too, in order to reach Canada, and I was proud to learn that my great-grandfather and the new Algona settlers were able to assist a black slave in his bold escape to freedom in the summer of 1855, exactly a year after the Call brothers had founded the town.

[A short recap of the Underground Railroad story, as recorded (portion in quotes) by Ambrose himself: "…A young black man, haggard and hungry, tattered and torn, hatless and barefooted… showed up at (my brother) Asa's cabin door… Our guest was a colored boy about 25 years old who had escaped from slavery in southern Missouri. Fleeing for his liberty, he had followed the north star by night until he came to the end of the road. He then followed the trail across the prairie until he found our settlement. After a week's rest our wayfarer was supplied with shoes, hat and clothing sufficient to keep the sun from blistering his naked body, and a supply of bread and meat sufficient to last until he reached the Mankato settlement. He was then started on his way rejoicing. One of our number accompanied him for half a day to the end of Union Slough and charged him to keep on the east bank and on the east bank of the stream flowing north from it until he reached the settlement. We heard later that he reached it safely… A week or two later, there was loud talking outside the first meeting of the Claim Club. On going to the door we discovered the contention was caused by two long-haired men loaded down with revolvers, on lank, jaded horses. The question had been asked by one of our party what they expected to do with so much artillery." As it turned out, the two guys were looking for the slave that Ambrose and Asa and friends had housed and helped. Thinking the slave was still in the vicinity, the two men planned to capture him, but "when they saw some ten or fifteen men emerging from the cabin, each with a long rifle in his hands… (they) turned their horses' heads to the south and rode away." The two frightened slave hunters later reported back to others that "in Call's settlement, the settlers had gathered with their guns to protect him." The two guys also said they "considered themselves fortunate to escape with their lives."]

In 1856, a new family arrived at the Algona settlement—the Hendersons, whose ancestors had already come to prominence as well-known settlers of the state of Kentucky. Most important to this story of *my* life is the "red-cheeked twelve-year-old," Nancy Eliza Henderson, who eventually became my great-grandmother. The Hendersons had heard about the new opportunities for growth in northern Iowa and had come west in a covered 'prairie schooner' wagon—Nancy's father, stepmother, and all her siblings, step-siblings, and half-siblings. Through subsequent years, Nan was known for fondly recounting some great stories about incidents that happened during that harrowing and yet exciting trip west. [Nan's mother (Nancy Hill Henderson) had died in Indiana shortly after Nan's birth, and the little girl had resided for several years in Charleston, Illinois with her maternal grandparents (her Grandfather Hill was a Presbyterian minister). Nan's father, (Hezekiah "Ki" Ashmore Henderson) married a second time, to a widow with several of her own children, and together they added even more children to their brood.]

Though Nan's restless pioneering father, Hezekiah ("Ki") Henderson, and family didn't stay in Algona more than a couple of years, Ki was highly involved in its early physical growth. Hezekiah Henderson was an energetic construction maverick, and right away had built the largest log cabin in the settlement—not only did it house his family, but it also had an upper sleeping loft that held 12-15 men who had come to work the land. Ki holds the distinction of being the area's first 'landlord,' and his wife baked the very first bread out of flour made from wheat raised locally.

By that time, Asa Call and his wife Sarah had built their own log cabin (after spending their first winter in Ambrose's) and had begun harvesting sod corn—the first crops raised in the county. Sarah wrote, "Our little cabin was made of poles, a stick chimney and a little clap board door about four feet high... but we soon fixed it comfortable... The room was so small that when strangers came in the country and stopped with us, as they usually did, we were obliged to set our table and chairs out of doors and make beds on the floor..." She also journaled, "We opened a sugar camp which is now in Ambrose Call's grove... We invited all our neighbors, three families, to help us sugar off. Someone got up on a stump and made a speech. I remember only one remark: he predicted a bright future for Algona."

And a bright future it was. The little community really blossomed during the summer of 1856, after having been platted that spring. "Improvements of importance were made, and quite a few settlers, among them a number of intelligent and ambitious men, found homes in Algona and its vicinity," my great-grandfather wrote. The time was "particularly prosperous and hopeful... the crops were fine, the seed-corn and potatoes yielded abundantly... everybody seemed pleased they had come to Algona."

Then the winter of 1856-57 hit with a vengeance. There was so much snow, with never-ending blizzards, and the cold was terribly intense. The Henderson 'log hotel' sent men many miles away on foot, with hand sleds, to get flour. Several residents were caught in storms, causing amputation of hands and feet due to them being so badly frozen. Family animals died of exposure. Snow drifted over the cabins so that only a chimney pouring smoke was visible. Neighbors didn't see one another for weeks at a time. Provisions were scarce, and "there was alarm about it," according to accounts.

Finally, spring arrived, but with it slowly came word that the terrible Spirit Lake Massacre had occurred. Asa journaled, "After the Spirit Lake Massacre it was necessary to take some measure of safety. We sent out scouts in every direction... who explored the whole country and reported that there were Indians on our rivers and that we were at the frontier, all the settlers beyond us having fled." Stockades were built at Algona and nearby Irvington to help keep the Indians out of the settlement. One account describes, "They had a sawmill at Irvington and plank(s) were sawed at the mill. They were stuck up endways in the ground. The fort was built with bastions on the corners which commanded a view of anyone approaching from two directions..." Asa himself reported of the stockade that he "considered it entirely safe against any Indians that had no artillery."

And my great-grandfather Ambrose journaled some additional thoughts to help describe the spring that had everyone on edge: "The snow was mostly gone, the streams and sloughs all bankfull of water with no bridges or boats, which made travel almost impossible and added to the fear and panic of the settlers... the air was filled with rumors, every stranger was viewed with suspicion... many settlers fled, and some never returned..." By summer, things had settled down somewhat in Algona, and a number of speculating young men arrived from the New England states, grabbing up land that had been abandoned by those who had fled, hoping to sell it for a profit the next year.

But the next year brought its own troubles! My great-grandfather wrote, "We had a repetition of Noah's flood. The Des Moines River was a sea from its source up in Minnesota to its mouth; every ravine was a mill stream and every slough a pond. No newcomers came, but the reverse. Added to our local troubles a general financial depression existed throughout the country causing universal stagnation in all business enterprises. Emigration ceased and speculation in lands and town lots was a thing of the past. The speculators and land owners refused to pay their taxes and it was impossible for the newly organized counties to collect sufficient money on the tax list with which to transact the ordinary course of business."

Most of the hearty settlers (the Call brothers in particular) stuck it out and made the best of it, however. They were strong and ambitious, always looking for and finding ways to improve their plight and to strengthen the settlement. One of the first obvious needs had been for a grindstone to sharpen tools. My great-grandfather wrote that he had searched the area until he located a stone quarry several miles away and used his ax to "attack" a ledge of rocks, hauling back to Algona a two-foot square slab to be used by settlers far and wide. Word spread that Ambrose Call, "the man who had a grindstone," lived in the area; my great-grandfather wrote, "I can say without fear of contradiction that while this grindstone lasted I was the most popular man in northern Iowa."

His brother, Asa, had soon realized the need for a sawmill so that crude log cabins could be replaced by wooden structures, and sent the younger Ambrose east to Dubuque and then even further east across the Mississippi River into Illinois to obtain and then haul machinery (by a team of oxen) back to Algona. The new combined 'grist and sawmill' was obviously a huge overnight success in the community. (I sure do love these stories about the resourcefulness of my ancestors and other Iowa pioneers, and was especially interested in learning about this first area milling operation. And believe it or not, that first 'lumber company' was later lost to a fire, like my own a century later!).

Nan's father, Ki Henderson, had erected (with newly milled lumber) a building in town—it was a 'storefront' structure, which over the decades served as the post office, a storeroom, and even the Courthouse. Ki and his family left Algona after a couple of years, and Nan returned to her grandparents' home in Illinois for just one more year of school. After that, at age 15, she and her elder brother [Milton Henderson] boarded another prairie schooner and headed back to Algona to live permanently.

{Editor's note: This female pioneer ancestor of ours seems to have walked off the pages of a Laura Ingalls Wilder book. One later newspaper article states that she was "possessed of high spirits and a charming personality, and was the belle of the frontier settlement." I just can't help but wonder if an adolescent Nan (at ages 12-14) had met and fallen in love with the handsome and adventurous young twenty-something Ambrose Call while living in Algona with her Henderson family during those two years, before heading back to her grandparents' home for only one year of school. Unless we uncover other reasons for her return so soon, I like to think of it as the lure of love that boldly brought Nan back to Algona as a 15-year-old girl, accompanied by one brother as her only family member.}

It was so fortunate for Algona that Ambrose and Asa Call both had keen business minds. Because of the depressed tax situation at the time, "the 8th General Assembly enacted a stringent revenue law authorizing county treasurers to advertise and sell lands upon which the taxes had become delinquent and allowing a liberal price for publishing the same, which was to be done by the paper in the county having the largest circulation." Kossuth County didn't have a newspaper, so the resourceful Call brothers got creative once again… "My brother Asa and I thought we saw in this law an opportunity to get a newspaper for Algona, an ambition we had long cherished, and we at once set to work with this end in view." He describes searching various places around Iowa until "we finally heard of a printing outfit at Fort Des Moines which he offered to sell to us for $600 in county warrants at their face. We accepted his offer and had the press and fixtures hauled up by ox teams. The machine was a used Washington press which… seemed quite old and the type was badly worn. We managed to get the press up in time to get the tax list out," and "after the tax list was finished the paper went to sleep until the next spring!" By agreement of the brothers to then split their joint assets, Ambrose took possession of the printing operation and commenced publication of the *Algona Pioneer Press*, putting himself in the editorial chair to get it up and running over the next three years.

It was only a year or so after young Nancy Eliza Henderson had returned to Algona that she and Ambrose Call were married. The bride was 16 and the groom 27 when they drove in a wagon down to Oskaloosa, Iowa for their wedding [on October 30, 1860] at the town in which Nan's father and family had since settled. Upon returning to Algona, a five-day wagon trip using horse or oxen, the young couple continued helping to establish their new town while also establishing their new home—baby daughter Florence was born ten months later.

Pioneering women were obviously made of hearty stock, and it could safely be assumed that Ambrose's wife, Nancy, and Asa's wife, Sarah, surely must have been two of the heartiest. There are many stories of the things these two women did to advance the early settlement of Algona, while living without the 'creature comforts' now taken for granted. One prime example is a story about great-grandmother Nan, a young woman still in her twenties when she had a toothache that took her to the local veterinarian (since there were no dentists in the area) … "The horse doctor proceeded to pull out all of her teeth in one sitting, after which false teeth were eventually ordered from the Montgomery Ward or the Sears Roebuck catalog." Decades later, Nan replied to one of her granddaughters [Bertha Cowles Quarton] who had just paid her a compliment about her lovely looks, "I wish you could have seen me with my own teeth!"

Apparently, Ambrose had moved out of his bachelor log cabin before his marriage, residing for awhile with his sister and her husband. [John Ellison Blackford was married to Asa and Ambrose's sister, Mary Minerva Call. Mary was six years older than Ambrose, and was the only Call sibling who came to Algona—she and Mr. Blackford had moved there from northern Indiana the year after it was founded by her brothers, and became very prominent settlers of the community. Their daughter, Ella Algona Blackford (Clarke), was the first white child born in Algona.] This was likely during the time that Ambrose was building a new home for himself and his soon-to-be bride on a lot with several acres of land he had secured a couple miles north and closer to other settlers. Ambrose and Nan put down their roots in the new dwelling, adding onto their home as more children came along.

RESIDENCE of **AMBROSE A. CALL**,
ALGONA, KOSSUTH CO.

The family experienced a big house fire during the winter of 1868, but rebuilt and lived comfortably there for another seventeen years. At the time of this fire, Nan would have been very pregnant with their fourth child, my grandmother. The eldest two children (six-year-old Florence and four-year-old Edith) had been rolled up in quilts and whisked off to the home of the nearest neighbors. They survived, as did two-year-old Etta, "thanks to the quick work of their hired hand and all the neighbors" who came to their rescue. In spite of the icy cold weather and living through something as terrible as a winter house fire in those early days, the children of Algona seemed to really love the Iowa winters. As an adult, Ambrose and Nancy's daughter Florence reflected, "Instead of dreading the cold, we loved the fierce storms that built drifts so one could walk for weeks over gates and fences on the hard crust, and nothing was so musical to our ears as the sharp crunch of the snow under our feet when the thermometer was 10 or 20 degrees below zero… On the long winter evenings we cracked nuts around the fire and listened to the stories our fathers and mothers told of earlier days of danger and hardship, making them seem as heroes in our eyes."

Growth in the community of Algona continued, and its people seemed almost enchanted with the place. Rivers were full of fish; large and small game were found everywhere; cattle and rabbits and prairie chickens were plentiful. All the children were kept as busy as the adults in the wild country of northern Iowa, bringing in wood and picking up kindling and digging potatoes and hunting eggs and carrying milk pails and churning butter and cleaning dishes—it wasn't an easy existence by today's standards, but the pioneer communities that thrived were made up of such people.

[Eldest daughter, Florence, also wrote extensively as an adult about those early days in the once-primitive Algona… "There was hardship, to be sure. There was crudity of living conditions, deprivation, much loneliness, even peril. But also there was opportunity—and it was this which had brought them. Besides ability to break the sod, to combat the physical hazards and obstacles, to build and organize communities—to do all the things that energy and courage could do—there had to be vision. And many of the pioneers possessed it—the capacity to think, the talent for dreaming realizable dreams, the passion for education, the appreciation of culture, the persistent reaching toward the spiritual." And Ambrose himself wrote of his early co-settlers, "A little spice of danger seemed to be an incentive to them." By 1871, the *Algona Times* proclaimed, "This town has acquired an importance within the past two years that few towns can boast of. It is located in the center of one of the finest agricultural districts of Iowa and possesses natural facilities and advantages which in a few years will make it one of the best towns in the state." Already platted as a town back in 1856, Algona was finally incorporated in 1872 and a brand-new Courthouse was built—the population was then approximately 400 people.]

It wasn't long before Algona was truly a thriving community in northwest Iowa. Thanks to Asa's foresight regarding future transportation needs of their town, and to Ambrose's railway scouting expeditions that had begun many years before, a railroad line was finally built across the state of Iowa from east to west (and through the town of Algona) almost *fifteen years* after their initial efforts! [The full story of the Call brothers' ongoing work to bring a railroad through undeveloped northern Iowa is such an inspiring one, and could be a chapter in and of itself. It would include the details of these two enterprising young men first building their strong wagon, then procuring a telescope, a surveyor's compass, a tent, etc. There was the winter Asa spent in Washington, D.C. working to get a bill passed to grant Iowa sections of railroad, followed by his work with our state legislature to make Algona a stopping point on the railroad. Then there was the task of plotting out the eventual route of the network, etc., etc.]

My great-aunt, Florence, described her rail recollections this way, "…When the railroad was actually being built, the town was full of rough, whiskey-drinking men who were grading the road… At last there was the fascinating smell of the coal smoke from a puffing engine… we arose long before daybreak amidst much excitement and rode in a lumbering vehicle miles from our homes to 'the depot.' There we bought a ticket from Mr. Lantry and went on an excursion away off to Clear Lake [45 miles] … It would be difficult at this time for a young person to realize the intensity of delight we children of the early pioneers experienced when we took our first journey by rail."

By the fall of 1885, and likely in celebration of their own 25th wedding anniversary, my great-grandparents began excavation for a basement and foundation on which they would build a spacious Victorian mansion on their acreage. The home itself was finally erected on what is now the southwest corner of Hall and College Streets, and featured the 'Call Coat-of-Arms' on each of the facing sides of the large cupola that highlighted the third-floor ballroom with its balconies. When they undertook the building of their mansion, Ambrose was serving as President of the First National Bank

(which he had founded as the 'Bank of Algona' five years before). A reporter at the time wrote of the soon-to-be home, "It is expected that Mr. Call will erect a residence which will be second in beauty and desirableness to no residence so far built among us. It will overlook the river and bluffs south of town, which form a magnificent view." And it really was quite fancy, with seven fireplaces (five of them finished in various hand-carved woods—mahogany, cherry, and oak—and two finished in marble believed to have been imported from Italy). The stairway to the second floor was of solid walnut with a hand-carved corner post. The floors were soundproof, built with three layers of flooring and a layer of filling. The 2" x 6" walls were back-plastered for insulating purposes (and I understand each wall had a diagonal 2 x 6 board placed every two feet).

The Call home remained intact throughout the lives of my great-grandparents and beyond [Nancy lived on the family homestead site 62 years, until her passing in 1922]. Their huge house eventually

became the Kossuth Hospital from 1929 until 1949, after which it was used as a series of nursing homes until 1966. In the summer of 1973, plans were underway to demolish my great-grandparents' eighty-eight-year-old home. I flew some of my Des Moines cousins to Algona to join up with other family members in order to investigate the possibility of restoring the old structure, and also to see if there were any items we wanted to salvage from the house. There wasn't anything much worth rescuing—even the beautiful handrails and ornate fireplace mantels had already been stolen or in some way removed from the place. We returned home empty-handed in that regard and had to finally make the difficult decision not to undertake such a long-distance and terribly expensive project (which would have required much more than just restoration, due to all the rotting wood, etc.). I know the town hoped that we great-grandchildren or some other group would rise to the challenge, but that was not to be... the stately and once-beautiful mansion was demolished in 1974.

Although that portion of Ambrose Call's land covered what is now several city blocks, a short brick condominium building (with a current address of 408 South Hall Street) sits on the old home site. There really is no longer a "magnificent view overlooking the river and bluffs south of town," as development has sprouted up all around the original land. It was meaningful for me to take another drive past the homesite this summer, and to again be reminded of that "magnificent view" it must have once had. I recall reading that the large (15' diameter x 22' high) cupola from the third story of the home was to be saved and placed in the Ambrose A. Call State Park, but I'm not sure that structure ever made it to the park—it certainly has not been there more in recent years.

Eight children were born to Ambrose and Nancy Call, and the kids were "inculcated with her high principles and sterling qualities," according to my great-grandmother's September 1922 obituary. Their eight children included the first four daughters (my grandmother, Bertha Angelina Call, was number four), followed by a rather lengthy gap before the last three children were born. A long-awaited first son, Ambrose Glen, had come along prior to those final three children, but he died unexpectedly at age 2½.

[The first children were Florence Maud (called "Flora"), Mary Edith (called "Edie" or "Eda"), Etta L., and Bertha Angelina. A newspaper obituary from 2/12/1873 gives no reason for the death of fifth child, son Ambrose Glen (called "Glen"), but apparently it was due to a sudden illness, describing "a robust, healthy child until within two days of his death," and the "bitter affliction" of his parents due to his passing. A few years after the death of little Glen, Ambrose and Nancy's final three children were born: Chester C., followed by twins Roscoe and Myrtle.]

Ambrose and Nan went to great lengths to educate their children at home from an early age, long prior to their attending school. And by the time they got a little older, Ambrose was willing to make financial sacrifices to ensure that they all continue to be well-educated, during and beyond the high school level. [The idea of upper education had been unusual for women until this time, but colleges began to be founded in order to educate women on how to become teachers—a noble profession that nicely complemented a woman's "true calling to be a good wife and mother."]

At that time, it was common and proper for women to be interested in painting and drawing, as were the Call daughters, but not to be studying art at a higher level. So, when eldest daughter, Florence, left home to study at the Chicago Art Institute, it must have been quite a big step for an Iowa pioneer family. [Women were often not even allowed in such institutions until the late 1800's; one hundred years later, 75% of all American art students were women.]

Florence first studied at the Art Institute and later graduated in 1884 from Northwestern University in Evanston, Illinois with a Bachelor's degree in Literature. Second daughter, Edith, who excelled greatly in the French language, was also educated at Northwestern and had become a teacher in Irvington, Iowa in 1883. Third daughter, Etta, attended St. Mary's Academy, a private Catholic school in Notre Dame, Indiana, from which she graduated with honors in 1885. And fourth daughter, Bertha (my grandmother) also graduated from Northwestern University in Evanston, where she was a member of the Alpha Phi sorority. By the time the three younger children eventually came of age, upper education in the Call family was quite routine!

Ambrose and Nan's daughters were well-educated young women, but they also eventually married well-educated (and well-to-do) men. And the Call sons put their own college degrees to good use too, as they climbed the corporate ladder to top rungs of a national life insurance company. [Florence married Gardner Cowles, the Algona school Superintendent and banker who eventually owned the *Des Moines Register and Tribune*; Edith married Archibald Hutchison, a graduate of Cornell College who became a real estate attorney and Justice of the Peace; Etta married William K. Ferguson, who became President (after Ambrose) of First National Bank in Algona; Bertha married the town doctor, F. E. V. Shore, moving to Des Moines to open a specialized practice after studying overseas; Myrtle married attorney Lester J. Dickinson, who later became a United States Representative and then a United States Senator; Chester graduated from Northwestern University like three of his sisters, and moved to Kirkwood, Missouri as the Chief Executive Officer of Kansas City Life Insurance Company; and Roscoe graduated from the law department of the University of Michigan at Ann Arbor, after which he first became a dealer in investments and securities in Algona, then moved to Des Moines to run the offices of Kansas City Life Insurance Company there.]

On our automobile trips to and from Lake Okoboji over the decades, not only did we picnic in the Ambrose A. Call State Park, but also typically stopped to see our various relatives still living in Algona. I remember spending the night in my great-aunt Edie Hutchison's huge home there and playing in their big sandbox as a kid. The Call sisters all remained close, though third daughter Etta had passed away several years before I was born. [Etta Call Ferguson tragically died in Rochester, Minnesota on December 26, 1907, following surgery at the Mayo Clinic Hospital. She would have been 42-years-old the following month. Their only child, son Arthur, was 17-years-old when his mother passed. Etta's husband, William K. Ferguson, eventually remarried.]

I sure do love this Call family picture, taken in front of their five-year-old mansion in the late summer/early fall of 1890. The picture includes my great-grandparents and all of their children, sons-in-law, and grandchildren—already an extended family of fifteen.

Standing, from left to right: **Dr. F. E. V. Shore** *(my grandfather)*, Chester Call, **Bertha Call Shore** *(my grandmother)*, young Myrtle Call (Dickinson), Edith Call (Hutchison), Florence Call (Cowles), Gardner Cowles, and William K. Ferguson. Seated from left to right: Roscoe Call (twin brother of Myrtle), **Nancy Henderson Call** *(my great-grandmother)*, little Russell Cowles, **Ambrose A. Call** *(my great-grandfather)*, Helen Cowles (LeCron), Etta Call (Ferguson), and baby Arthur Ferguson.

Though I never met my great-grandparents or stayed in their family mansion in Algona, my mother talked of how her grandma and grandpa's neat and clean house always smelled so good—she remembered breakfasts of pork chops with fried apples and fried potatoes, a fire in the living room, and a maid named Lollie. And I know that my great-grandfather paid close attention to dressing smartly… It is recorded that one time he came home after being with the local tailor for a fitting, and reported to Nancy that the tailor told him one of his shoulders was higher than the other. My spunky great-grandmother responded with something like, "Well, did you hit him?" That particular story is not only cute, but is especially interesting to me because my own tailor told me the same thing recently after I took him my ill-fitting vests and sport coats needing to be adjusted (only to learn it was for the same darn reason!)

Ambrose Call stayed personally involved in so many things that helped grow his community, including erecting the Call Opera House in town by 1893. 'The Call' was intended to be a hall of culture and entertainment, and became the site of all the crowd events in Algona for the next forty-four years, including stage plays and high school class plays, and movies (the first 'talking pictures'). Though Ambrose certainly wanted to bring culture and entertainment to his new town, the overriding incentive for such opera houses springing up around the country was economic—a worthy lure for new residents. [Promoters of opera houses had to contend with the more rigid settlers, however, who felt that new cultural centers might lower moral standards in the community.] Completed at a cost of $25,000, the theater had 600 seats, with one balcony and two boxes. People came from all towns within a 35-mile radius to see its first play, "Gloriana" by the Chas. Frohman Company, on February 16, 1893—gross receipts totaled $1,000 for opening night. One newspaper article stated that The Call was quite a progressive step for the town… "The good people of Algona are to be congratulated upon the possession of such a perfect playhouse." Sadly, on April 18, 1937, The Call burned to the ground, with flames fed in part by the barrels of oil stored in the stage area to supply the popular lobby popcorn machine. Nevertheless, the fine facility had a wonderful run for nearly four-and-a-half decades.

As already detailed earlier, Ambrose had worked with his brother to establish the first newspaper in the county, editing it before selling it three years later due to his many other involvements. He was elected the first County Supervisor when that office came into existence and was appointed Assistant Assessor of Internal Revenue for several years. Not only did he have the banking interests reported earlier, but he also spent four decades as a government mail contractor with one of the most extensive routes in the west, continuing in that capacity until the 'Star Route' business in the mail service was abandoned. I understand that his work actually took him to every state [45 at the time] in the Union. Ambrose explained his decision to finally lease and then sell the paper, journaling, "In the spring of 1863 I found myself with more work on my hands than I could attend to:

the government had awarded me several long mail routes beyond the frontier, which I had to stock up; I had accepted the appointment of internal revenue assessor with eight counties in my division…" My great-grandfather remained such a busy man throughout his entire life. He was a prominent Mason and, though declining repeated requests to run for various political offices, represented his town and his county as a staunch Republican at several meetings and conventions. I understand that he always claimed to be a farmer and was often dealing in real estate, owning property in other states too (like a large rice plantation in Louisiana!) as well as a considerable portion of the best farming land in the county. Ambrose was known as a generous man, "never turning a deaf ear to a worthy subject soliciting charity." Oh, and in his spare time, my great-grandfather additionally founded the nearby town of Bancroft, 15 miles north of Algona.

[Ambrose's older brother, Asa, was elected a Judge in 1855, which certainly helped him accomplish so very much for their community and the county as well. Asa lived in Algona for 33 years and died at the early age of 62 while visiting in San Francisco, California, on a trip that was hoped to help strengthen his ailing body. He had been born on September 2, 1825, and left this earthly journey on January 6, 1888. His capable wife, Sarah Heckert Call, had passed away during childbirth at only 40 years of age, leaving Asa a widower for his final twelve years of life. They were parents of seven children. John R. Call's edition of his great-great-grandfather Asa's diaries, as bracketed earlier, pays proper tribute to the monumental contributions made in such a short lifetime by this utterly amazing man—details on that publication can be found in the Appendix to this book.]

Ambrose Adolphus Call lived out his life in the first town he founded, and still owned over 2,000 acres of Iowa land at the time of his death in 1908—he had come a long way since proudly digging the first crop of potatoes next to his little log cabin. People said of him that his word was his bond—and that's the best compliment a guy can receive, in my opinion. My great-grandfather was only 75 when he died of "old age," according to one newspaper account. I guess 75 might be considered old when compared with his brother's death at age 62. In reality, Ambrose had heart disease and had been ill for about a year before passing. [Ambrose had been born on June 9, 1833, in Huron County, Ohio, and died on October 22, 1908, in Algona, Iowa.]

As was customary for the time, his funeral service was held in their mansion. After Ambrose's death, their youngest son Roscoe (and his wife) moved into the Call mansion to care for his mother, Nancy. A few years after that, Nan fell and broke her hip, necessitating the use of a crutch to get around. Two years later her crutch slipped and she again broke the same hip, causing her to live the rest of her life more or less as an invalid; the ongoing presence and assistance of Roscoe was of great consolation to her, of course. My great-grandmother, Nancy Henderson Call, died in her own bed after suffering a "stroke of paralysis" in September of 1922, three months before her 79th birthday.

At the time of her passing, Nan was still survived by most of her children, as well as by nineteen grandchildren and eight great-grandchildren. [Nancy had been born in Clark County, Illinois on December 14, 1843, and died on September 11, 1922, in Algona. Cerebral hemorrhage was listed as the official cause of death.] My great-grandparents are both buried in the Ambrose Call family plot, located in the Riverview Cemetery at the north end of Algona.

As an interesting side story, the first settler to have been buried at Riverview Cemetery was the maternal uncle of Asa's wife, Sarah [Michael Fisher, who had come to Algona with the rest of Sarah's Heckert family in May of 1856]. By 1891, Asa and Sarah's son, George Casper Call, built

a family vault into the cemetery hill—inside were twelve crypts, created for the purpose of transferring and housing the remains of his parents and other members of Asa and Sarah's immediate family (including Asa and Ambrose's mother, Mary "Polly" Metcalf Call Finch). In 1972, vandals broke into the Asa Call family hillside vault, using crowbars and drills to bust through the massive metal door on the outside, then prying loose and damaging the very heavy marble faces of the crypts.

I wish I'd personally met my great-grandparents [Nancy Eliza Henderson Call, left, and Ambrose Adolphus Call, right], as well as my great-great-grandparents too—people with such vision and stamina. But it really does feel as if I've gotten to know them because of their terrific journals and photos and tales passed down through the years. (Now I'm thankful to keep their stories alive in this book about me!)

THE NATIVE AMERICAN INDIANS

I often asked Grandma to tell me stories about when she was a little girl growing up in early Algona. She had lots of tales about their pioneer family helping to settle a very primitive Iowa, and thought correctly I'd like hearing ones that involved native Indians. Since my grandmother was the youngest of the first four daughters, she was in charge of babysitting a lot for her three little siblings who had been born all those years later. [When the baby twins were born, Bertha was 11-years-old. Eldest sister, Florence, was turning 18 and preparing to leave for The Art Institute in Chicago; sisters Edith and Etta were 15 and 13, and preparing to leave for private schooling in South Bend, Indiana; and little Chester was just 2½. It seems that their mother Nan was suffering from some post-partum depression after the birth of the twins, according to a letter sent that next spring from Ambrose to his daughter Florence—in that communication Ambrose requested that Florence leave Chicago and her school, and return right away to Algona to assist in childcare and other responsibilities in order to give an "ailing" Nan (who hadn't even been out of the house for several weeks) "a vacation."]

Grandma told me about one time when her father came home and asked her, "Bertha, where is Myrtie?" My twelve-year-old grandma, who had been caring for her baby sister and little brothers, replied, "She was crying so much that I gave her away." And he said, "Who did you give her to?" She answered, "To the Indian chief." My grandmother said her father went to the nearby Indian reservation and was able to retrieve his daughter unharmed, and then again instructed his children to not associate with the Indians without him present because they *could* be very dangerous.

My great-grandfather Ambrose was not an Indian hater by any means, quite the opposite actually, but there were various massacres that had occurred in northern Iowa since he had arrived there, including the famous attack on the settlements near Lake Okoboji and Spirit Lake by 1857. He had come to Algona three years before that massacre, and had encountered his first Indian a month after that arrival. In describing that chance meeting, Ambrose recorded that he had been exploring the woods up the river when he heard a gunshot, which startled him since he thought he "owned the only gun within fifty miles." He wrote that he hid in the trees and crept to the bank of the river where he saw the Indian, who had just discovered Ambrose's footprints… "I knew that if the presence of a white man was suspected before I had interviewed them, the chances were that I would not see them at all, unless greatly to my disadvantage." When Ambrose felt certain they were the only two people around, he stood up and said to the Indian, "How." The Indian started to go for his gun, "which was lying right under my feet on the bank of the river." Ambrose again quickly said, "How, How." The startled Indian just stood there until Ambrose calmly walked up to him and held out his hand and said, "How," yet again. The native then seemed reassured enough to grasp Ambrose's hand. After learning of the turtles that the Indian was killing, "I picked up and handed him his gun and bow, which he slung over his back. We then walked up the river to the bend, where I left him, motioning him on and telling him puckachee." After that instruction for the Indian and his tribe to leave the area, Ambrose "hastened to the cabin" and made sure his oxen and pony were secure. When he later scouted the area for more Indians, he found where their tepee had been and the trail they left behind as they 'puck-a-cheed' northwesterly out of the Algona area.

Ambrose wrote that his first knowledge of Native American presence in their actual settlement had been when "a burly Indian tagged by his squaw" suddenly appeared at his bachelor cabin in the woods saying, "How, How," and wanting to trade moccasins for bullets. My great-grandfather asked where they were camped and how many tepees they had, learning there were forty tepees. Ambrose and some other men visited the native village and requested that the Indians leave the area. The next day the Indians scattered through the settlement and visited every cabin, sometimes merely begging for food and other times plundering. This went on for days and is clearly documented in many accounts. The Indians made all their raids during daylight hours, and were "most annoying and very alarming." The settlers learned to be prepared for such visits, and that the natives could sometimes be lured away with food. Though often able to bargain for their lives, raids by the Indians became increasingly hostile, and the white men (and women) were many times threatened, bound, gagged, and held against their will.

In one attempt to settle the Native Americans after a very harrowing raid on the cabin of one of the new settlers, my great-grandfather and a few others attempted to end the pillaging and terrorizing death threats once and for all. He wrote, "…We found their village. It fell to my lot to be spokesman. The chief's tepee stood near the center and was a very large one. We walked rapidly to it and went in without ceremony. The chief was a large man, past middle age who seemed to be lame, having one foot bandaged with rags. I accosted him roughly and seizing his tent gave it a hard jerk to give emphasis to my words and show him what I wanted, telling him to 'puckachee.' He seemed very much frightened but after a moment's hesitation explained that a part of his young men had gone after elk, pointing in a southeasterly direction, and would not be back until after dark; that the next morning at sunrise they would pull down the teepees and 'puckachee Dakota.' He made a circular motion with his arm showing that he would go around (our) settlement, thence north, thence west. He watched with considerable interest while we discussed his proposition and seemed relieved when I nodded my head in assent and took his hand." Ambrose continued to record about the incident, "…Few eyes were closed in sleep during the night before their departure and their every motion was watched… I have said the people of our settlement did not fully realize the terrible danger they had passed through. They did not know what bloodthirsty, villainous murderers these (particular) Indians were. Ink-pa-du-tah [sic] had not established his reputation as the fiend incarnate he proved himself to be a year later at Spirit Lake. This was the first time and the only time he and his band were ever successfully resisted." In a book about the history of Kossuth County, there is an interesting quote from one settler's journal concerning the scary event: "Had it not been for Ambrose Call I believe the whole settlement would have been murdered." [In another later editorial about that same event, Ambrose described the intricacies of Inkpaduta's teepee: "It was very conspicuous. I never before nor since have seen one on which so much painting, for decorative purposes, had been done, or where so much pains had been taken to beautify it. The material was elk skins neatly sewed together and around the whole teepee, beginning about four feet from the ground, were three broad bands painted in red, which were each about a foot in width and painted in the form of looped-up drapery. The teepee was very large and the artist evinced considerable skill in the painting. The Indians themselves when they visited us had their faces more or less painted with the same material… I was struck with the beauty of the big teepee and of course knew it was occupied by the chief, so I unceremoniously pulled the door to one side and walked in, I having learned that this was not a violation of Indian etiquette if one did not stand in the doorway."]

It's almost unbelievable to me that my own great-grandfather personally encountered and turned away Inkpaduta, the famous Indian Chief who was determined to seek justice for the killing of his brother and his brother's family by a white man [Henry Lott] not long before. The Sioux Indian band had headquartered in a grove in the Call's Woods area and had harassed settlers there. But then they headed north and west, eventually showing up in the area of Lake Okoboji. In the famous 1857 'Spirit Lake Massacre,' Inkpaduta led the Sioux Indians in the killing of 40 or so Lakes region settlers, taking captive four young women. It was an especially famous massacre since the youngest one captured, 14-year-old Abigail Gardner, was kept a few months before being ransomed. She lived to tell the story and, almost thirty years later, published a book detailing the incident and her captivity. [Abbie Gardner-Sharp's *History of the Spirit Lake Massacre and Captivity of Miss Abbie Gardner: The Raid of the Santee Sioux Against the Iowa Frontier Settlements, 1857*, is one of the last narratives written about European Americans being held by Native Americans. Thankfully, the Spirit Lake Massacre was the last attack by Indians on settlers in Iowa, but the terror that was spread by the incident caused the Algona settlers to build stockades in order to insulate themselves. Additionally, the 'Northern Iowa Brigade' helped patrol and protect from further attacks.]

As a kid and as an adult, I have always been interested in the Spirit Lake massacre story, and have visited so many times the original Gardner cabin that still stands in the Arnolds Park area of Okoboji. I was quite interested in the cabin itself and how it was built, so I enjoyed studying that log construction up close. But it was also pretty unsettling to think that the Indians had stood right there on the spot where I was now standing and had killed all those people except the young girl they spared because her light-colored hair was so unique to them. *{Editor's note: Whenever over at the Park for a weekend nutty bar, we typically stopped to look at the cabin and to again hear about the horrible massacre. I was always personally ill at ease when visiting the site as a child. It was such a stark reminder of our family's Call heritage, and how close we likely came to the same grim ending in our own early Iowa pioneering efforts. Family members were told 'the other side of the story,' of course, but I'm not sure we ever really understood or fully appreciated the cruel injustices and unfairnesses to the Native Americans by many of the first white settlers and by the early laws of our country. With or without full blame, Inkpaduta felt he had good reason to avenge the murder of his brother and his brother's family by the white men.}*

Ten years after founding Algona, my great-grandfather was awarded credentials for his Civil War service as "Major, Northern Iowa Brigade, Army of the Ohio, 8th Division." The Civil War was a time of intense patriotism across the country, and many brave boys from Kossuth County headed south, never to return. Adding to the trying times, terrible Indian attacks were taking place just over the border up in Minnesota, causing alarmed Iowa settlers to flee the territory. As protection from further attacks and to furnish a feeling of security, a small force of mounted men was formed (The Northern Border Brigade) to act with the United States troops already stationed to the north. The Brigade was comprised of frontiersmen familiar with the habits of the Indians, and they constantly scouted the border while also building stockades and taking other security measures.

[One account tells of wartime Indian exploits of Ambrose and his very close friend, William Ingham, who had come to Algona the year after the Call brothers arrived… "Cpts. William Ingham and Ambrose Call, of the Northern Iowa Brigade, rose west from the settlement now known as Estherville. This country was then profuse with high reeds and underbrush so that without a clear point of vision nothing could be discerned within a distance of approximately two hundred yards. About twelve miles out from the settlement, in the late afternoon, they heard a noise which Cpt. Call identified as an Indian signal and later, witnessing smoke, they realized they had entered a territory which was swarming with the Sioux who had so recently massacred the settlers at Spirit Lake. In the early evening, just as they were about to make camp, Ingham suddenly reached for his gun when a huge Indian, dressed in war paint and riding a 'painted pony' silently rode up to their camp-fire. Call, who was familiar with their language, engaged him in conversation and soon learned that he represented a band of some sixty braves, only a half mile away from the camp-site… As Ingham was dressed in the cavalry uniform and Call was not, Call advised the 'chief' that they represented a brigade from Ft. Dodge, which was encamped only five miles distant. He suggested to the chief that he and his braves had better 'puck-a-chee South Dakota'—in other words get out of Iowa as soon as possible. The big Indian asked for tobacco and liquor. Ingham and Call provided him with a box of tobacco and a flask of brandy. He wheeled his pony, saluted and rode westward…"]

Forty years after his service in the Northern Iowa Brigade, the elderly Ambrose gave a speech at Algona's 50th birthday party, held on the 4th of July in 1904, and included his history with the Native Americans: "They have said that I was an 'Indian fighter,' but that is not true. When I was a boy I spent a lot of time with the Winnebagos, Chippewas and Ojibways up in Wisconsin and Michigan… there I learned the rudiments of the Indian language and contrary to popular opinion, if you can speak or communicate with one Indian tribe in this country, you can communicate with them all."

[Ambrose's speech continued with details about the above-bracketed incident that had taken place with his friend, Captain Ingham. Ambrose recalled, "Whether the Indian whom Captain Ingham and I met and thwarted up on the plains west of Estherville was in fact Inkpaduta, I could not positively assert. I do think however, that Inkpaduta, like Jesse James, received credit for a great many crimes which he, himself, was not capable of committing, no matter how wicked he may have been. When the Northern Iowa Brigade went south in the spring of 1863 to join General Sherman at Memphis, I had not the slightest fear of any Indian trouble in Kossuth County and, in fact, except for the roving bands of Indian gypsies who appeared from time to time along the Des Moines River, there was never a fright nor a fear of an Indian uprising in northern Iowa after that time…" Ambrose then concluded his speech for Algona's 50th birthday party with an interesting follow up to that very story: "Many years later, when I was on a business trip in Sioux Falls, a man halloo'ed at me from across the main street. He was dressed in a brightly checkered suit. Upon greeting him I realized that he was an Indian. "Mr. Call," he said, "I am running 400 cattle. You remember when you told me 'puck-a-chee South Dakota'?" "Yes!" I said, "I remember!" "Well," he said, "You better puck-a-chee Iowa— 'cause I got all the money there is here!"]

Not long after Ambrose had retrieved his daughter, baby Myrtle, from the reservation back when my grandmother had been babysitting for her siblings, there was a knock on the door of the Call home. Grandma told me she looked through the side window and saw that it was the same Indian chief to whom she had given little Myrtie. After running to get her father, she said that she and her siblings all hid and listened while Ambrose went to the door. She told me that the Indian spoke to her father saying, "You have birch tree… I want. You give me, and I make boat for you and boat for me," and that my great-grandfather said, "OK." Sure enough, the chief made two beautiful birchbark boats out of that big front yard tree, and Grandma said that she and the other Call children had a lot of fun playing for many years in their new boat in the river at Algona.

We descendants are so very fortunate that Ambrose kept a written journal—his family called it "Pa's Diary"—a large leather-bound book of about 800 pages, in which he recorded a brief daily record of events of interest to him for the decade from 1862-1872. [Several years ago, Hutchison relatives gifted family members with the journals scanned onto CDs. The free-flowing handwritten font is not an easy read, however, with some pages very light and difficult to decipher; and the style is much different than that to which we are now accustomed, both in sentence structure and in punctuation.]

Additionally, a paper called *"The Bee"* had been written by early Algona pioneers in 1857-1858, before the day of newspapers north of Ft. Dodge—we have several of Ambrose's ongoing *Bee* articles entitled, "Politics in the Fifties." And of course, there are copies of *The Algona Pioneer Press*, first edited and published by Ambrose himself (with the used, and rather impaired, printing machinery mentioned in the last chapter) beginning back in 1861, when he was just 28-years-old.

Throughout my life, I've been told so many bits and pieces about the early efforts of my ancestors in settling and growing their town, but it has really come to life for me now that we have been putting it into a bigger picture for this book. It's no wonder that this little town in northern Iowa was on the map! And bringing the railroad line through there might have been my ancestors' most instrumental accomplishment since early travelers were then able to discover Algona, personally experiencing its richness and perhaps even deciding to stay. And 'staying' is especially important to this story, because the year after my great-grandparents started building their lovely mansion on the bluff, a newcomer arrived in town on that train—the dashing young Dr. Francis Edward Victor Shore, from Canada.

Meet my grandfather…

MY SHORE HERITAGE

Francis Edward Victor Shore was born [on December 7, 1864] in Toronto, Ontario. His father, Richard Boyle Shore, was a native of Canada [with Irish lineage back to Carrick-on-Shannon]; his mother, Elizabeth, was also from an old Canadian family. I don't remember ever meeting my Shore great-grandparents and don't know quite as much about the history of that side of our family, but my daughters always thought it was pretty funny that Great-grandmother Shore's maiden name was 'Elizabeth Taylor.' And our whole family thought it was somewhat strange that my grandfather had two middle names, especially when my mother (his only daughter) didn't have a given middle name at all!

F. E. V. Shore apparently had a brother named Montague [a teacher in Goodlands, Manitoba], who I don't remember ever meeting or even hearing about. He also had a sister named Grace—I do remember her somewhat, and that she was married to a doctor up in Canada. [Grace taught school in Canada at Winnipeg Collegiate. A note in the 1905 medical journal, *Canada Lancet*, reads, "An interesting ceremony was performed at the residence of Mrs. Elizabeth Shore, 102 Charlotte Street, Winnipeg, January 11, when her only daughter, E. Grace, was united in marriage to Dr. I. Herbert Davidson of Manitoba."] My great-aunt Grace came to Des Moines every now and then to visit, and for some reason I recall that one time she had brought several silver spoons for my grandmother, sewn into the inside of her garment in order to cross the border without declaring them—that seemed pretty adventurous to a kid like me.

My grandfather, Francis ("Frank") Shore, had pursued his early education in the Toronto public schools and at the Collegiate Institute in Winnipeg. He then graduated from Medical School at the University of Michigan in Ann Arbor in June of 1886, at the early age of 21, after which he wanted to live in the states rather than return to Canada. We don't really know why he traveled by train to Algona, Iowa, getting off there and deciding to stay, but perhaps the town was advertising for a physician. In any event, that's where the new Dr. Shore moved in the summer of 1886, devoting the next four-and-a-half years there to a general practice of medicine, while becoming increasingly interested and educated in the treatment of diseases of the eye, ear, nose and throat (and also increasingly interested in a very special young lady) …

On March 19, 1889, after almost three years in Algona, the beloved town doctor, Francis Edward Victor Shore, married Bertha Angelina Call, fourth daughter of the town's respected founder. Following in the footsteps of her older sisters, Bertha was well-schooled, both at home and outside of it and, as mentioned before, had earned her degree from Northwestern University in Evanston. The couple had met when Bertha was home from college for the summer, perhaps the first year that Dr. Shore arrived in Algona. Their wedding took place in the Call mansion, after which the local newspaper announced that "the newlyweds made hasty preparations to take the evening Milwaukee train for Chicago… from Chicago they go by Cincinnati and Nashville… and will spend a couple of weeks in New Orleans and along the coast, taking a short gulf trip to Florida." (I hadn't realized until recently reading the newspaper article that my grandparents honeymooned in New Orleans and along the coast, then took a short gulf trip to Florida—that was also *my own* honeymoon path 61 years later!)

The Shore newlyweds returned to Algona and settled into a home they remodeled, also doing some traveling abroad during the next two years while Frank was practicing medicine locally. Realizing he needed a "broader field of labor" than was offered a physician in their small town, my grandparents moved in April of 1891 from Algona to Des Moines, where Dr. Shore firmly established his specialized EENT practice. An article from the *Upper Des Moines* newspaper one month later proclaimed the success of his new endeavor, stating, "Dr. Shore is doing much better than he had any reason to expect" down in the big city. I understand that my grandfather continued to excel greatly, especially after additional studies "with eminent oculists and aurists" in New York, London and Paris. [Those studies must have occurred just prior to their move from Algona to Des Moines. There are documented snippets of a trip to England, with the young couple sailing for Liverpool on 1/7/1891, and record of a return from Europe on 3/25/1891. Unless we learn otherwise, they likely stayed overseas for that entire twelve-week period of time, while Frank pursued his "additional EENT studies" already mentioned, and Bertha availed herself of specialized art training. They would have also celebrated their second anniversary on 3/19/1891, just before returning to the states and opening the medical practice in Des Moines.]

The young couple probably continued more traveling while my grandfather established his new private practice, and I understand that he also attended national conventions as a part of his growing involvement with the Masons. An August 1892 article from the *Algona Republican* puts him at a Knight Templar's Conclave in Denver, while his wife stayed in Iowa visiting her family in Algona. My grandparents didn't start a family until almost nine years after they married, but apparently tried to conceive several times before that. Grandma Bertha Shore is reported to have had several "failed pregnancies." *{Editor's note: We are unable to find a record of the dates of the miscarriages. One genealogical chart, however, shows that Frank and Bertha's first-born child was actually a son named Joseph (and called "Joe"), who did not survive. Perhaps he died at or shortly after birth—the fact that he was given a name likely means he survived the birth process.}*

Grandfather Shore (known to me as "Pop") was an Eye, Ear, Nose and Throat physician, and I used to watch him do surgery on a number of patients in his office on the 2nd floor of the Empire Building that sat on the northeast corner of 6th and Walnut Streets in downtown Des Moines. His office faced 6th Street near the alley and, when (one of) my uncles picked him up after work in the afternoons, they would just toot the horn down on the street and Pop would wave his hand out the window and then come on down. He told me that he was never concerned about being around blood—that he could be "in it up to his elbows" and it still wouldn't bother him.

Pop made a special little stool for me to stand on so I could watch him operate, and I clearly remember him doing things like removing tonsils, stitching eyeballs, and so forth. He would tell me, "Jerry, go over and get another can of ether," which I would bring from the shelf and give to his nurse so she could administer the ether on a piece of cotton under the patient's nose. When I was barely four-years-old, he assisted in removing my own infected mastoid; though he was affiliated with Mercy Hospital, I can clearly remember him reassuring me before the operation, which took place at Methodist. (Just for the record, Pop had also removed my tonsils when I was still three but, for some reason, I don't remember anything about that particular operation.). I learned something new and very interesting while working on this book…. Apparently, my Pop Shore also had to do mastoid surgery, a *double* mastoid surgery in fact, on his own daughter—my mother—when she was a little girl too. As the EENT specialist in the area back then, I guess he did what he had to do. My grandmother wrote that her husband was very strong before performing the operation on their daughter, but that after it was over he was emotionally exhausted and could not work for several days.

When they first arrived in Des Moines in 1891, I'm not sure where my Shore grandparents lived. It's likely that they started out in what came to be known as the 'Sherman Hills' neighborhood, because that's the area where Pop and Grandma Shore ended up building their first home six years later at 696-19th Street, on the southwest corner of 19th and Pleasant Streets. [The 'Sherman Hills' neighborhood is named after Mr. Hoyt Sherman who arrived in Des Moines from Ohio in 1848, at the age of 20, and quickly become involved in the city's early origins (including various pursuits in law, banking, railroad, education, and insurance). After being named Postmaster the year after he arrived, Sherman used his own money to construct the first dedicated post office building in town. Additionally, he was appointed by President Lincoln as Union Paymaster in 1860, giving him the title of Major during the Civil War. Ten years before that, Mr. Sherman had purchased five acres of land (paying a total $105 at an auction) just northwest of downtown Des Moines. By 1877, the 50-year-old community activist completed construction of a hillside mansion on his land, described as "a society showplace of the grandest scale," and it wasn't long before other homes were being built on the surrounding hills ("Sherman Hills"). The Shermans reared five children during their decades in Des Moines. Mrs. Sherman passed away in 1887, ten years after the mansion was constructed.]

Grandma Shore's handwriting on the back of this 1898 picture describes it as "The first house Frank and I built and owned, built in 1897." My grandmother and her visiting sister-in-law, Grace Shore, are enjoying the view from the first floor's wraparound front porch. Documents tell of a large barn toward the back, with a big side lot for their first four children to play.

The second photo [used by permission] was just taken in the summer of 2017. The home's exterior doesn't appear to have changed much over the 120 years since it was constructed, perhaps because the entire 80-acre Sherman Hills District of 120 historic structures is listed on the National Register of Historic Places. (The current owners of 696-19th Street have kindly invited us to come take an inside tour of their lovely place, which we intend to do very soon… I've never been in it!)

Back then, it was considered a big bonus that the streetcar went down 19th, running right in front of the Shore house. Written records show that my grandmother loved to step onto it to go shopping downtown, especially every Wednesday, and that she was finely dressed in "lacy shoes and real jewelry." Any packages from shopping trips were delivered later, directly to the back of the home, as were semiweekly deliveries by the one-horse wagon from Tingley's Meat Market. There was also an ice cart that came by regularly, with customers putting 12" high cards into their windows requesting the number of pounds of ice they needed that day—25, 50, or 100.

Every month, a seamstress came to their home, according to family documents; and when my great-grandmother Elizabeth visited from Canada, I understand she was always fitted for a new dress with lots of ribbons and lace. My mother said that her family took the streetcar almost everywhere, but that they also had a buggy with fringe, and a parasol that "had little black silk ruffles and the handle was split so that you could hold it from either side." The gardener did not live in their house but he was the one who took the children to and from their parties, carrying them inside and out if there was inclement weather.

Mother once drew a picture as she told about the inside layout of the 19th Street house, where she had been born and lived until she was eight-years-old. By then, she also had three (of her four) brothers. Mom described the center hall entrance with a fancy stairway. The south side of the home had a parlor, and behind it a sitting room. In the sitting room was a fireplace, and Mom told of how the Shore children loved to lie on the floor in front of the fireplace to read the funnies, especially "The Katzenjammer Kids." The sitting room opened into a large formal dining room, where the family always ate dinner at the big table and children of all ages wore bibs. Though they had a cook, I understand that Grandma Shore often burned sugar in a pan on the stove to fill the house with a sweet toasty smell and to cover up other cooking odors. Children were not allowed in the kitchen, though there was a day for baking bread and cookies and they were probably allowed to have some part in that. There must have been five bedrooms, all upstairs, with the master bedroom opening onto a second-floor wrap-around deck to duplicate the same wrap-around porch below it. Mom said the nursemaid's room was near the back stairs, and that the maid shared a room with the cook. Sounds like a pretty fancy place to me!

This is the home where my mother, as a young girl, was asked to bring a washcloth to the dining room table to wipe the face of one of her little brothers. Bertie went up to the bathroom to retrieve the washcloth, and thought it would be funny if she threw the cloth from the upstairs at such an angle that it would come sliding onto the table. She then leaned over the banister to do just that and fell to the first floor, breaking her back! My grandfather took my mother all over the country to see various orthopedists and specialists about her back. They eventually traveled to Portland, Maine, during one Christmas holiday when my mother was in about fourth grade, to see a specialist who had connections to a physician in Des Moines. According to Mom, that doctor "forced (my) bones the opposite direction, but it didn't work... it was deeper than that."

To make the most of that particular trip out east, Pop took my mother on a boat down the Hudson River into New York City, and on a horse-driven streetcar uptown. They went to Coney Island, and he had Mom's hair done at the hotel, among other perks. Pop also took his only daughter, who was a very picky eater until then, to different foreign restaurants and said that my mother actually enjoyed trying unique Austrian, Greek, and Italian foods. He also admitted that he was exhausted by the trip, but that little Bertie, in spite of her back pain, "never seemed to tire at all!" I would say that the treatments on Mom must have worked well somewhere along the line, as her issues with posture were not terribly noticeable. She did have some exaggerated forward rounding of her back and shoulders, however, and later osteoporosis added to that.

My grandparents and these good friends and neighbors in their early Sherman Hills area had what was called a culture club, or conversational club—get-togethers during which they would "gather at one house or the other, have a glass of brandy or sherry, and discuss higher things." We have a picture of the 1914 gathering of the Des Moines (Women's) Conversational Club, of which my grandmother and her eldest sister, Florence, were members. Florence and her husband, Gardner Cowles, Sr., had moved from Algona to a home on 17th Street in the Sherman Hills area of Des Moines just a few years after my grandparents built their place at 19th and Pleasant Streets. My mother remembered how excited they all were to have "Aunt Flora" and "Uncle Gardie" move down here. Notes also show that Henry C. and May Wallace, and Charles and Nell Cumming were also a part of the "erudite" conversational club of people. The Wallaces and my grandparents became best of friends and eventually purchased land in Colorado, where our family made such lasting memories every summer when I was a kid.

Great-aunt Flora was almost seven years older than Grandma, but the sisters were very close. Not only had they grown up as a tightly-knit pioneer family, but both girls had also graduated from Northwestern, with a keen interest in art and culture. After college, Flora had returned to Algona to teach school, later falling in love with and marrying the Principal/Superintendent, Mr. Cowles—the couple moved to Des Moines in 1903 when Gardie purchased a major interest in the *Register and Leader* (which became *The Des Moines Register*). [Gardner Cowles had studied at Penn and Grinnell Colleges in Iowa, after which he graduated from Iowa Wesleyan before taking the job at Algona. "Gardie" then left the educational field to join his father-in-law, Ambrose Call, servicing rural mail routes for awhile, then pursued interests in banking and real estate/loans; he later became one of the owners and editors of *The Algona Republican* newspaper, before moving his career to Des Moines. Five years after purchasing the *Des Moines Register*, he purchased the *Des Moines Tribune*.]

My grandmother also stayed very close to her second-born sister, Edith, who was four years older than Grandma. Edie's husband, Archie Hutchison, was from Algona and the couple continued to reside up there. So, my grandmother would often go back to her hometown to see the rest of her family, and especially to spend time with Edie. The two sisters just seemed to have a special bond, according to everything written about them. "… Bertha and Edie would share a room and get giggling over something so hard and loud that the rest of the family would come running to see if they were hurt." [One time, Edie came to Des Moines to help Bertha with a difficult pregnancy, and the two of them decided the pillows on the bed needing fluffing. Edie shook a pillow out the window so hard that it broke, and both sisters erupted into laughter that wouldn't stop. Bertha later lost the baby, and Edie was so worried that she had caused the miscarriage. Their physician father continued to assure his distraught daughters that such was not the case.]

After living in the Sherman Hills area several years, my Shore grandparents bought a large piece of land covering the area from 37th Street on the east to 38th Street Place on the west, at about the halfway point south of Grand Avenue and north of John Lynde Road. [The lot was part of a huge plat that had been purchased by Gardner and Florence Cowles not long after they moved to Des Moines. The land, legally known as "Cowles Place," ran from Grand Avenue all the way south to John Lynde Road, and from 37th Street all the way west to 38th Street Place, also including some land southwest of that over to Tonawanda Drive.] My grandparents had the choice of purchasing this particular plat of land on the unpaved 37th Street (next to a lot that Flora and Gardie Cowles were to build on) or of purchasing a piece of ground about a mile-and-a-half northwest on Harwood Drive— then called "Country Club Drive" because it was near the original Des Moines Golf and Country Club on Polk Boulevard [40-acres of field leased for 20 years to the Club by attorney Jefferson S. Polk]. Though it must have been a less swanky location at the time, I'd imagine they opted for the 37th Street location so that sisters Bertha and Florence could live next to each other.

Another likely drawing card for choosing the 37th Street plat was the new elementary school—Greenwood—that had been built toward the north end of that street in 1901. The school was the only structure north of the Shore property at that time, and there were just two other homes planned for construction to the south. [The Gardner Cowles home at 100-37th Street was the first to be completed in 1909. The Shore home at 210-37th Street, immediately north of Cowles' and south of Greenwood School, was completed by 1910. The last home slated to be built on the street was down at the far south end and belonged to the Henry C. Wallace family (50-37th Street, completed in 1912). The Wallaces filled their home with six children—three girls and three boys, as did the Cowles.' The Shores filled theirs with five children—one girl and four boys. It's likely that having a school nearby was a big plus for those three families.]

In 1908, my grandparents had started construction of their new residence on 37th Street, but due to some workmanship imperfections during the building process, Pop Shore required that the existing plasterwork be torn out and that the entire house be re-plastered (with further build-out taken up from there) before his family would take possession of the home. So, my grandparents and their four young children had to first make a transitional move out of their 19th Street Sherman Hills home, where the kids had all been born and had later been baptized together in the front parlor. The Shores temporarily moved into a great big house on the southwest corner of 31st Street and Cottage Grove Avenue for over a year. That's where their youngest child, Francis Edward Victor Shore II, was born in 1908. (The house is still on that corner today, and I believe it was made into several apartments many years ago for nearby Drake University students.)

The new Shore house on 37th Street south of Grand was considered quite elegant, inside and out. Since my grandparents were concerned about new-fangled electric lights perhaps not working out as touted, they also installed gas lights in their new home—so all the light fixtures were double ones! Additionally, they were all burnished brass and from Tiffany's in New York (as were their furnishings, fabrics, and fine trim). I understand that my mother, their only daughter, was doll crazy and kept her lovely collection in a big case behind glass doors that slid up. One of the silly things I remember about their house is that the bathrooms had toilets with the water tanks clear up by the ceiling. Back then, toilets flushed by gravity rather than by water pressure, so it made sense, but those always looked

so strange to me. My grandmother was just a wonderful gardener, quite proud of her zinnias and delphiniums; and Pop himself raised roses, which his children regularly sprayed and dusted for him. Their entire outdoor setting was (and still is, even today) just beautiful, and I love looking again and again at this shot of Mom and her four brothers enjoying a horse and buggy ride in their lush front yard.

All the bedrooms in the Shore home were upstairs, with another door to a back stairway that led up to a huge full-sized attic where the children could play. (A generation later, Connie and I loved spending time up there too.) In the rear of the basement of my grandparents' new home was a large workshop that Pop and his sons built across the entire back wall. You walked through the workroom to get to the new two-car tandem garage that they later added under the lengthy enclosed porch that stretched front-to-back along the entire south side of the home (on left side in picture). They had hesitated about adding the garage due to concerns about toxic exhaust fumes getting into the house, but putting it under the porch area must have seemed safe. Pop and his boys used to make all sorts of stuff down in that workshop—that's where he built the little stool for me to stand on in his office. I loved watching Pop build things and enjoyed just looking at that workshop design, figuring out how I could make one much like it for myself in my folks' basement.

Those three original homes, as well as the stately Greenwood School, still line the west side of 37th Street today. And so many more lovely residences have been added in-between them over the years. Though these three families lived "next door" to one another back then, the lots were so huge that there was a good distance from one house to the next. The Cowles and Shore sisters and their families had always spent Thanksgiving and Christmas at one another's homes, and wrote of frustration one winter when there was enough snow that the Cowles' could not get up their portion of 37th Street to the Shore home "until about 5 PM!" *{Editor's note: Dad and I laughed reading this account, agreeing that these dear Call women, once little pioneer girls living through severe snow blizzards and ice storms and house fires and prairie wildfires and a devastating grasshopper invasion (not to mention travel by cart along rutted dirt paths), might have become a bit soft by now!}*

Long before I was born, The Cowles house in our neighborhood saw lots of famous people come and go as guests. And there were several more by the time I was a kid—the list just goes on and on. I especially remember Wendell Wilkie staying there when running for President in 1940 against Franklin Roosevelt, and what a big deal that was. My parents and sister and I periodically would have lunch at my great-uncle and great-aunt Cowles' house. It seemed so huge, and I loved playing on their elevator just inside the gracious front door entrance. Luncheons at their home were quite formal, and my sister said she didn't like going over there because she never knew which fork or spoon to use. On one occasion, my father said, "Connie, just watch me, and do what I do." So, Connie watched him, as instructed. But when the Hollandaise sauce was served, Dad put it on his potatoes rather than on his asparagus where it must have belonged. Connie said she was glad that she watched everybody else, following their lead instead!

In Henry Wallace's front yard at 50-37th Street, just to the south of the Cowles' house, there was a photo taken May 27, 1918, of a local Boy Scout troop posing with former President Teddy Roosevelt. My uncle, Dick Shore, is in the picture (standing, third from left) as a young Scout. And they kindly let his little brother (Victor Shore, sitting on ground on the front bottom right and likely wearing glasses), be a part of the photo even though he wasn't a Scout. Several other boys who grew up to become prominent citizens of Des Moines were part of that same troop. I was so proud when becoming a Boy Scout myself many years later, because two of my uncles had been in a picture with a former President of the United States who was visiting in our very neighborhood! [Theodore Roosevelt was in town for a speaking engagement at the old Coliseum downtown. The event was sponsored by the National Security League, and Roosevelt spoke on "English as the Sole Language for the Schools."] I remember this picture so well because it hung proudly in my grandparents' home. We are grateful to Uncle Dick's son-in-law, Gerald Jacobs, who kindly had a plate made of the original photo and sent it to us for use in this book.

It would be nice if I could report enjoying being a Boy Scout, like a couple of my neighborhood friends. Going to Scout camp for a few summers was fun, but the regular local meetings were boring and our Scoutmaster wasn't all that great—it seems that all he had us do was play basketball in the gym of the Plymouth Congregational Church. One time we did get to take a trip a few miles across town to hike in the woods on the north side of Hickman Road, east of where Broadlawns Hospital is today, but that's about my only positive memory of a group activity. (I put all that behind me as an adult, however, becoming an active Committee member of the Executive Board, and later of the Advisory Council, for the Mid-Iowa Council of Boy Scouts.)

Pop Shore had graduated from Medical School at the University of Michigan, as had Dr. William Mayo. The Mayo Clinic founding brothers, William and Charlie (and their families) continued an ongoing close friendship with my grandparents over the years. My mother used to tell me about going up to Minnesota fairly often with her parents to visit the Drs. Mayo, and staying in their lovely homes. I wonder now if the trips to see the two brothers also had anything to do with consultations or treatments for my mother's broken back. Mom said she especially loved Dr. Charlie's huge mansion (Mayowood is nowadays open for tours, though I've never taken one), and how much she adored the man. Though known as "Dr. Charlie" to others, Dr. Mayo reminded my mother on several occasions, "Bertie, my name is *Uncle* Charlie to you."

I have often thought about that story when going up to the Mayo Clinic in Rochester for annual comprehensive physicals myself over the years, and then as a surgical patient two separate times at the Mayo Methodist Hospital campus following cancer diagnoses at the Clinic. I was operated on for colon cancer up there in 1982, during which they removed eighteen inches of my large intestine, joining the new ends and sewing it back together—they said I supposedly wouldn't be as susceptible to polyps with that section removed, but I certainly have had lots of them taken out over the decades since! Then ten years later, in 1992, I underwent surgery to remove part of my liver after 'seeds' from the 1982 colon cancer operation had apparently dropped into that area and started to grow. I was told that the guy who operated on me was the only liver surgeon in Rochester at the time, and I was extremely grateful that he wanted to get that cancer out of me quickly—my appointment with him was on a Friday and I was being operated on by Monday. Learning that the liver is the one organ able to regenerate itself gave me some consolation when undergoing that surgery, and I'm so thankful to have very quickly grown another healthy one in just ninety days! I did take chemotherapy in Des Moines following the 1992 surgery, and afterward had to use a cane for awhile—when I told my doctor about how bad my legs hurt when walking very far, he answered, "So do mine!" In other words, he wasn't going to give me anything for it, so I just learned to live with the pain until it eventually went away. For the record, an oncology nurse later told me that leg pain, along with so many other things of course, can be a side effect of chemo treatments. (And I guess leg pain is also a part of aging, at least for me—some days they just hurt, and I don't know if it's due to exercise or the lack of it!)

It's almost hard to believe I've had regular clean reports ever since those two major cancer events twenty-five and thirty-five years ago. I'm truly grateful for such fine care, by the

Mayo doctors and by my Des Moines team as well. Recently I've made it a point to personally look into the eyes and thank the four main physicians who have kept me alive these past several years, and I've included their names in my obituary already composed for publication in the *Des Moines Register* (and included as the first chapter of this book). If it weren't for the keen brains of my main docs consistently thinking up ways to keep my cancer, heart, kidneys, and overall physical health in balance, I'd surely be a goner by now—medicine has certainly come a long way.

Now back to the 37th Street home of my Shore grandparents... It was quite fancy, as I've said, but the home that was eventually built on land immediately south of their place (between my grandparents and the Cowles') was far fancier yet! It was a huge brick mansion constructed and owned by a man named Clyde Herring, who had a Ford automobile dealership and auto parts business. The gentleman had originally lived and worked as a jeweler in Detroit, Michigan, where he personally repaired watches for *the* Henry Ford. After relocating to Iowa, and eventually to Des Moines, Mr. Herring had a personal contract with Mr. Ford—it was impressive to me that he drove a free car and got a commission for every Model T ever sold in our state! By the time I was born and got to know him, Mr. Herring must have become a pretty wealthy guy, because his local company factory built over thirty Fords every day and delivered more vehicles than any other automobile agency in the United States.

I spent a lot of time as a little kid playing at the Herring mansion next door to Pop and Grandma Shore's place. It had been built five years after my grandparents' house, still ten years before I was born, and was one of the largest homes on 37th Street. It didn't have an attached garage, but the big detached one had servant's quarters above, like a carriage house—I'm not sure who, if anyone, lived up there. And if memory serves me, their family also owned another smaller 'cottage house' on 38th Street Place (my street) directly behind their 37th Street house, and I believe one of their sons stayed in it.

My grandma told me that Mr. Ford used to come to Des Moines on occasion to see Mr. Herring. On one of those visits, my Uncle Victor (who was just a little kid at the time—maybe about the same age as in the previous photo with Teddy Roosevelt) hid in the bushes of the next-door mansion to peek at Henry Ford when he arrived. When Mr. Herring came out of his house to greet Henry Ford, he saw little Victor in the bushes and called him to come out and meet Mr. Ford. Mr. Herring introduced Victor by saying, "Victor's folks live right next door and once purchased a Model T from me." Then my young uncle blurted out, "Yes, but the blame thing never ran!" I was told Henry Ford got such a kick out of that! And it still makes *me* smile too.

By the time I was a little kid, the Herring neighbors had become close friends of the Shores, of course, and they always welcomed me coming over next door for a visit. The Herring's had a caretaker named "Mackie," who was a heck of a nice guy. Mackie's daughter and I were the same age, and we often played together in that huge yard with the fish pond and the fancy greenhouse that sat between the Herrings and the Shores. It was fun to ride my trike over there almost every day to see what was going on at the big mansion. (Yes, it's really me!)

Mackie also was the caretaker for the huge Hoyt Sherman Place at 15th and Woodland, home of the Des Moines Women's Club. Grandma Shore and her sister, Florence Cowles, had been Presidents of (and Grandma remained very involved in) the Women's Club, so they regularly saw Mackie working over there too. [The opening page of desmoineswomensclub.com shows a black and white photo of early Club 'movers and shakers'... Bertha Call Shore is pictured on the upper right of that group of 13 ladies. The Club had been founded in 1885 and moved into Hoyt Sherman Place in 1907, three years after the mansion sat empty following the death of Mr. Sherman. Des Moines Women's Club constructed the new auditorium in 1923.] I got to know Mackie well enough that when I went over to the Women's Club with Grandma, he would take me all around the big place. I recall many times he let me turn on and off the different lights and play on the stage in the newer 1400-seat auditorium. Mackie's own home was behind the Woodland Cemetery and I remember that he had no doors to enclose his double garage; my father gave him the set of doors off our two-car garage when we replaced them with overhead ones.

Some of my favorite memories include sitting on Mr. Herring's lap many times at his huge dining room table while he and his wife were being served dinner by Mackie. I must have been only three, or maybe four-years-old at the most. After the meal, Mr. Herring would smoke his cigar, then he always gave me two cigars to take home to my Pop Shore next door. So, I would get on my tricycle and pull into a special place in the bushes between their houses, where I lit up one of the cigars with a match from my pocket and puffed away at it, before soon delivering the other fresh one to Pop! Remember that those were the days when men smoked regularly and openly, and even threw their cigar and cigarette butts on the ground. As a little guy, when downtown shopping with my mother, people would look at me funny because I'd be walking along with a cigarette or cigar butt in my mouth after picking one up off the sidewalk.

Eventually, the house and grounds of the Herring home became terribly run down. I remember that the fish pond ended up covered with scum, the greenhouse windows looked perpetually dirty, and the grounds were unkempt. I didn't understand it at the time, but the family had lost everything due to the Great Depression. I have since learned that their big home had gone back to the bank, but that they were able to pay rent to the bank and continue to live there while rebuilding their lives. And rebuild they did… Mr. Herring one day became the Governor of Iowa, and later one of our United States Senators! After the Herring family moved out, their big house eventually was the home of our local Catholic Bishop, and has since been used as a private residence.

Much of what I knew over the years about Governor Clyde L. Herring was already a matter of public record, but my own personal childhood memories about him and his family were not. Because of that, we were at first careful not to use his name or those of any of his family members in this book about me. But, as luck would have it, I finally had the chance to meet his granddaughter this spring, as mentioned earlier. It was fun to be at that local meeting of our local Historical Society and to relate some of these Herring tales to her. Though she hadn't ever met her grandfather, she fondly remembered Mackie, which was nice to hear. Most of my stories were about her grandfather, but she was delighted to hear a few about her own father too… as I mentioned earlier, she sure laughed when learning that her Dad was the little kid who had to be removed from our chimney during construction of my folks' first home on 38th Street Place back in 1924!

My own grandparents just loved their 37th Street neighborhood, and I sure enjoyed crossing the ravine to spend time with them over there. In the evening, Pop would sit in his overstuffed chair in the living room, facing the fireplace with his back toward the front windows while smoking a cigar and sipping on something. I was too busy playing with my cars to recall much of what he was doing other than laughing at my little antics, but think he was also oftentimes reading some book or magazine while in that cozy chair. I understood that he and my grandmother regularly read aloud to one another too. I never saw Pop with playing cards, but learned that he was terrific at Bridge, and told others that you could tell all about a person by the way he played a hand of it. Being around Pop in his living room is a warm memory for me, and I'm grateful for the time spent with him there.

Not only did he have his thriving private medical practice but, in 1922, Pop also became the fourth Chief of Staff at Mercy Hospital in Des Moines. Though not a Catholic, he was instrumental in bringing the facility to our city—his name was listed on an original scroll to that effect. Pop's photo is still displayed today on a wall in the hospital with the other Chiefs of Staff, and I really enjoy stopping to look at it whenever I am over at Mercy for some reason. [The Sisters of Mercy was an order that had been founded in Ireland, and had brought hospitals to the United States in the mid-to-late 1800's. By 1893, one of their extension hospitals was brought to Des Moines, occupying rented space in the Hoyt Sherman mansion on Woodland during construction of the hospital's own building, just north of downtown on 4th Street. By 1895, Mercy Hospital moved into their new building at 4th and Ascension Streets, becoming the first permanent hospital in Des Moines. (For the record, Methodist Hospital had its Des Moines beginnings in 1901.) During that same time frame, the Mayo brothers (close friends of Dr. Shore) had also started working with a different order of nuns, the Sisters of St. Francis, and soon opened St. Mary's Hospital in Rochester with that affiliation.]

Dr. F. E. V. Shore was a member of the College of Surgeons, a former President of the Polk County Medical Society, and a member of the Iowa State Medical Society and the American Medical Association. While originally working in Algona, Pop had been appointed local surgeon for the Milwaukee Railroad, then became the eye and ear surgeon for the Rock Island Railroad Company after moving to Des Moines. The 1911 *Iowa Medical Journal* contained an interesting entry about him that read, "Dr. F. E. V. Shore of Des Moines was the victim of an auto accident last month. While cranking his machine it kicked, breaking the bones of his right forearm." And *I* got a kick out of reading about that just recently—it happened many years before I was born, but I do remember someone telling me about that incident, a cute story for a car lover like me.

In addition to his occupational pursuits, my grandfather had been an active member of the Wakonda Club and of St. Paul's Episcopal Church downtown. The priest from St. Paul's was the one who had come to their original 19th Street home to baptize each of the first four Shore children (at one time) in the front parlor. Records indicate that their baptismal clothes "were all from Best's," and that "there were presents and food" at the home celebration. [F. E. V. Shore's family roots include several Episcopalian ministers, both in England and in Ireland. One written account states that when Frank and Bertha Shore were in London on an overseas adventure, they retreated into a church to get out of a cold fog and were surprised to find themselves standing on a grave of a 'Shore' under their feet, while looking at the markings of another 'Shore' on the wall above them!]

Pop was a leading Mason, belonging to Capital Lodge, A.F. & A. M., the Knight Templar Commandery, and to the Mystic Shrine; he was likewise a member of Knights of Pythias Lodge and had filled all the chairs. Sadly, Pop died in 1931, at the early age of 66, from complications of an 'undetected brain tumor,' I was told. [Francis Edward Victor Shore had been born on December 7, 1864, and died on February 9, 1931. His certificate lists cerebral arteriosclerosis as cause of death.] He had been ill for a month and was hospitalized the last week of his life—at Mercy, of course. I understand that he became rather confused in the final days of his illness, telling my grandmother that *she* was the sick one who needed to be in the hospital; so, Grandma, being a loving and dutiful wife, moved into a hospital room next to his and stayed there until he passed! She was only 62-years-old when preparing for the loss of her dear husband.

Grandma's sister, Edie Call Hutchison, came to Des Moines to help keep up the Shore house during Pop's illness. After his death, I clearly recall that Pop's body was kept in a casket in their library on 37th Street, and that someone sat up with it all night until the day of his funeral. I was only 5½-years-old when he died, but really do have such terrific and very vivid memories of my early life with Pop Shore. He often told me he hoped I'd grow up to become a physician too, so I soon appointed myself the neighborhood doctor to help keep everyone healthy (and to examine all the girls).

It's hard to believe nowadays, but my Shore grandparents had traveled regularly with another couple who had a motor home—one of the first of its kind. They all went south together during the cold Iowa winter months. The large Shore house on 37th Street was too big to 'close down' for the season, so my family would drain the pipes in our smaller home on 38th Place and move across the ravine into theirs for the winter! Looking back, I realize that the winter moves to our grandparents' home were clever ways to save energy costs, especially during those Depression years. After Pop died, two of my Shore uncles—Mom's eldest and youngest brothers, Philip and Victor—continued to live with Grandma to help oversee and keep up the place, but my own family still moved over there every winter while my grandmother traveled south. She never remarried, continuing to devote herself to our family and to her many outside interests.

Here's a cute picture of Grandma Shore and some other ladies on a tour of the Panama Canal in April of 1935. They are apparently being lifted onto or off of a ship. Scrapbooks show that Grandma had traveled down there at the time to meet up with the Cowles' (her sister Florence and husband Gardner). Grandma Shore is the one furthest away on left—she's wearing the white hat with the black band.

I remember one winter while we were living in Grandma's house, Connie got the measles and I got the mumps. After we were both over those diseases, then *I* got the measles and *she* got the mumps! Just like in my early childhood days, I hated being quarantined for such a long period of time. Our doctor, who lived only a few blocks away, stopped by every night on his way home just to check on us until the long ordeal was finally over. That was back in the days when house calls by physicians were more commonplace, of course, but this guy had also been a close friend of Pop Shore's.

After five years as a widow, Grandma Shore finally sold the big house on 37th Street, and built a nice two-story four-bedroom home [at 211-38th Street Place] for herself and her sons, Philip and Victor, on the south lot next to our house—it was still a part of my grandparents' original plat and was kept available for this very reason. (It was also the piece of land which had once held my clubhouse and my pony as a little kid.) Grandma then lived in that house, next door south of ours, the rest of her life.

In the summer of 1948, while I was home on college break and working at the family lumber company, Grandma Bertha Call Shore became quite ill. I asked if I could sit up with her every night, in the chair by her bed, and was so glad to be right there next to her when she passed on June 30, 1948, at 3:00 A.M. She had been bedridden her last three weeks, and was 80-years-old [Bertha's date of birth was May 2, 1868] when arteriosclerosis caused my grandmother's heart to finally fail. And right there next to Grandma's bed was also a walnut-stained side table I'd so lovingly made for her in my 'Manual Training' woodworking class at Callanan Junior High School nine years earlier. I was proud that she even found the little drawer in it to be handy—I'd designed it to hold a phone book, and that was exactly how it was used!

{Editor's note: The little handwrought table has an ongoing family history of its own. After 14-year-old Jerry made and gifted it to his Grandma Shore, she kept it next to her bed for those final nine years. Once his grandmother passed, Dad's mother (my Nana) held onto it for another 23 years, until gifting it to me in 1971 when I got married. For the next 40+ years, the sweet table had a place of honor in the guest room of our home, looking so handsome next to the ornate antique walnut-stained four-poster bed I'd slept in as a girl. Knowing that Dad had forgotten all about my inheriting that little piece from his mother, I wanted to surprise him with it almost five years ago to use in his future new apartment at Wesley Acres. Imagine his delighted face when the table he had once so carefully crafted for his Grandma peeked at him from under my Christmas tree, wrapped in a great big bow! Today it sits in his living room next to the large navy-blue leather recliner that Santa had also given him a few years before that. A phone book is in the table drawer, of course. And to sweeten the story just a little bit more, my own nearly-seven-year-old granddaughter out in California now sleeps on the antique four-poster bed I had as a girl (which will one day again be accompanied by a little table that was handcrafted in a junior high shop class by her great-grandfather, Gerald Anson Jewett, Jr., as a gift for her own great-great-great-grandmother, Bertha Angelina Call Shore, all those decades ago!}

SHORE FAMILY FUN

As a little kid, I really had a lot of fun, especially with tricycles and then bicycles and cars and airplanes—anything to get me from one place to another. Each Christmas Eve I asked my parents to take me to the airport so I could see Jesus fly in for his birthday party. To top off those exciting Christmas Eves, Connie and I would sneak out of bed late at night and try to peek down the stairs into the living room to see what might be tucked under the tree for us to discover the next morning. I felt so sick to my stomach with excitement every year. On one especially memorable occasion, Connie and I tiptoed out to the landing, and she suddenly turned to me wide-eyed, whispering, "Jerry, you got it, you got it… there's a bike!" And I threw up right then and there. The next morning, when Mom and Dad called us down for gift time, I was still so sick that all I could do was crawl down the steps and across the living room floor on my hands and knees to pet the tires of my brand-new and very first bicycle, a Western Flyer in my favorite color—blue!

Christmas Day was always a great celebration, often with all the Shore and Jewett relatives in one place at one time. I just loved it when everyone was together (and being the center of attention as the oldest grandchild and great-grandchild!). We first had our own time of celebrating as a family foursome early Christmas morning. After that, my relatives would gather, either at our house on 38th Street Place or at the home of one of my grandparents, or over at my great-aunt and great-uncle's big place on Grand. Let me first introduce you to my mother's terrific side of the family. Her four brothers—Philip, Ambrose, Dick, and Victor Shore—made every gathering such a memorable occasion. None of my uncles were married when I was a little kid, and they were all so much fun to be around…

Uncle Phil ('Philip Call Shore') was the only one older than my Mom, and he remained single all of his life. Phil had lost most of his hearing at an early age after he and a neighborhood girl ate poisonous berries off a house plant at her home while Phil and my grandmother were over there for a visit—both children got 'brain fever,' and the little girl died. After his lengthy illness as a child, Uncle Phil required more one-on-one attention over the years. I knew Phil the best, as he was the only Shore son who lived his entire life in Des Moines. He had attended the neighborhood Greenwood Elementary School and old West High School, and also attended Western Military Academy in Racine, Wisconsin. As a young boy who loved music, Phil sang in the choir of St. Paul's Episcopal Church, but I'm not sure if that was before or after he was so sick and lost his hearing. Though handicapped by deafness and some loss of brain function, Uncle Phil was still pretty darn sharp of mind, asking endless questions and kidding around a lot. He also loved animals, and had many pets throughout his lifetime. He never complained about the loneliness of total deafness, and even pretended that he heard and understood what others said to him. Phil usually smoked a pipe, and it smelled so good. For my fifth birthday, he gave me a corn cob pipe of my own, and I smoked everything that would burn in it—pine needles, coffee grounds, and so forth. (You'll recall that I always kept matches close at hand too!)

I understand that, as little kids, Phil and my mother often found ways to get into trouble. He was only 1½ years older than Mom, and they must have played together a lot. I guess one time the two of them hid under the dining room table with scissors, and proceeded to cut the fringe off Grandma's fancy tablecloth. There were all sorts of stories about their shenanigans, but a favorite one Mom told us is about the day she and Phil decided to slide down the coal chute at their home on 19th Street after the door to it had accidentally been left open. Apparently, the cook leaned out the back door and told them to stop, but Phil egged his little sister on and told her to pretend she couldn't hear the cook. When their mother, my grandmother Shore, returned home to find her two coal-smeared kids, she gave naughty big brother Phil a choice of punishment or of going without dinner (I understand he chose the punishment, though I don't know what that was!). Then my mother was put into the bath, where the coal just smeared when she tried to wash it off. She was very young, but said she always remembered how her own mother laughed and laughed while watching little Bertie try to scrub herself clean!

Due to his disabilities, Uncle Phil was never able to earn an income for himself, so my mother and father continued to financially provide for him after my grandmother passed. In his later adult years, Mom and Dad purchased for Phil a little one-bedroom house on Hickman Road, immediately east of 48th Street. For the rest of his life, our family members would regularly stop by the house, where the back door was never locked. People just came on in through the kitchen and walked right into the living room, typically finding Phil sitting in his big overstuffed rocking recliner reading the newspaper. He'd always loved participating in and watching sports of all kinds, so the television would usually be blaring with some game, though he couldn't hear a word being said on it. When he saw that he had visitors, my uncle would excitedly yell his greetings (not knowing how loud he was yelling) and invite us in, dropping his very mussed-up newspaper sections to the floor and immediately starting in with questions. Phil read each and every article in the papers and somehow seemed to absorb them—people were always astounded at his near-total recall memory, and he really was quite sharp on every redundant detail he communicated.

After buying Phil a home, my father then asked his local Cadillac dealer friend for recommendations on a good car from their used lot for Phil. Dad ended up buying him a dependable Buick, the one and only car that my uncle then drove the rest of his life. Unfortunately, Uncle Phil—we fondly called him "Uncle Phoo-Phoo"—was somewhat of a terror behind the wheel. At the end of our family gatherings over the years (to which he typically arrived about an hour early) someone would announce that Uncle Phoo-Phoo was leaving, and everyone would hurry outside to watch him pull away in his car. It was always quite the scene and nobody wanted to miss out on it. Being deaf, Phil couldn't hear the revving of the engine as he accelerated, so he would regularly back too quickly out of the driveway before then throwing the car into gear and laying rubber for several feet. He sometimes backed into the bushes across the street from the driveway of my house—after one Christmas gathering, the back end of the Buick had to be 'lifted' out of the snowy bushes with the help of family members!

I'll never forget the weekend I got a call from a contractor who was building a new duplex on 48th Street, just west of Phil's home. The guy had thought it was safe to park his Volkswagen Karmann Ghia in Phil's gravel driveway for a few minutes while checking on the construction progress next door. Unfortunately, Phil didn't realize there was a car parked in his driveway, and never thought to look behind him after climbing into the big Buick for a trip to the grocery store. Uncle Phil revved his engine and quickly threw the car into 'Reverse,' unable to get but a few feet. Thinking his rutty gravel driveway was the problem, he threw the car into 'Forward' and then into 'Reverse' again, thinking he'd get a good run for it through the ruts. This time he smacked that Karmann Ghia clear across the four-lane street and onto the parking on the south side of Hickman Road! The contractor heard the commotion and came running over, waving and yelling to get Phil's attention, telling my uncle to look at what he had done to the poor guy's car. A surprised Phil simply said, "Oh! I didn't do any damage to it, did I?" In fact, he'd demolished the car.

On October 19 of 1983, at the age of 84, Uncle Phoo-Phoo passed away, not long after being taken to the hospital from that little house on Hickman. Though he was quite ill and in pain the night before he died, he continued to be concerned with the welfare of others. He asked me if his sister (my Mom) was still planning to return to Des Moines the next day from Okoboji, and also asked whether Jennifer had given birth yet to her second child.

{Editor's note: John and I lived just a mile from Great-uncle Phil for our first several years of marriage, and I stopped over to see him regularly (with our little boy, Joe). Phil was quite worried about me when our second child hadn't been born on his 'due date' in early October. Jake finally arrived not long after Uncle Phoo-Phoo passed.}

So, Uncle Phil was the eldest of the Shore kids, and my mother was their second child. Then two years later Ambrose ("Ams") Call Shore was born and was named after his grandfather who had founded Algona. I remember when Ams was terribly, terribly sick as a young man still living at home on 37th Street, bedridden for a long time with gallstones which were eventually removed during a very painful procedure. Ams had been encouraged to be a printer by his Uncle Gardie (Cowles), who owned the *Register and Tribune*. After going away for school to study the skills of a pressman, he did work for a brief time at the *R&T* until learning that they didn't condone the hiring of relatives! So, Uncle Ams started his own print shop, located in one of the garages of the Shore Apartments in Sherman Hills, on the north side of Woodland at 14th—my grandparents owned the property and had a manager who lived in the basement of that building.

Ambrose also opened a little diner called "Waffle Gables" in a cute free-standing cottage at 41st Street and University Avenue (in what was, and still is, known as the Uptown area of Des Moines), and we were over there for breakfast quite often as a family. I had no idea at the time, but the sign says the place was open from 7 am to 1 am—that's a lot of waffle-making! (It also shows that the noon special was a plate lunch and the evening special was a steak dinner, but I'm only remembering the wonderful weekend breakfasts of waffles and maple syrup.) My mother, the family artist, painted the big sign that hung outside of Ambrose's café, a perfect spot for little Connie and her big brother to stop for a winter pose.

Ams eventually married girlfriend Lulu, with the wedding taking place in the Shore home on 37th Street. The young newlyweds moved around quite a lot, due to Ams always looking for better newspaper jobs. They were living in Washington, D.C. and working for a government printing operation when their son, Ronald, was born in January of 1942. Due to a blackout during the war days "not being very conducive to trying to warm up bottles for a baby," they decided to leave D.C. Cousin Ron remembers living in about five different states by age 15, after which his father started work with *The Kansas City Star* for a brief time. A move to the Los Angeles area the next year to take a job with the *Herald Examiner* was successful until Ams was forced into early retirement due to an ugly and prolonged strike by his union (and the eventual closing down of the paper)—it seemed he just couldn't ever find the right job at the right time. Uncle Ams was such a kind and gentle man who remained very close to my mother all through the years, and we would make it a point to see him whenever traveling west. Ams' only child, my cousin Ron, has one son and two stepdaughters; he and his wife still live in southern California, where Ron recently retired after a long career with IBM.

The third Shore son was my Uncle Dick, formally named 'Richard Boyle Shore' after his Canadian grandfather (F. E. V.'s father). Uncle Dick was very bright and was always clowning around. When the young Shore family had first moved into their new house on 37th Street in 1910, I understand that my Mom had a brace she was supposed to get into and hang from a door header to help straighten her back. That brace was kept on the stairway up to the attic. Uncle Dick liked to play hide-and-seek with a young buddy who had lived in their Sherman Hills neighborhood, and who now lived across the street on the

Young Shore Carves Spanish Galleon, Accurate in All the Minutest Details

Ship Is As Correct Historically As Possible.

east side of 37th (on the north T-corner at St. John's Road). I guess that one time, Dick hung in Mom's brace to scare his buddy when the door to the attic was opened, bragging for the next year or so that the scare even made his friend "wet his pants!"

Uncle Dick was a very, very fine craftsman, and learned his building skills in that basement workshop of his parents' home on 37th Street. While away at college, he carved (by whittling) an ornate model ship as a Christmas present for his sister, my mother. It had electric lights and a place to hold incense so that the guns on the ship would smoke! (I made the newspaper as a two-year-old, being ever so gentle with Uncle Dick's newest creation.) While still living at home as a high school kid, he had even built my mother and father's bedroom set for their wedding present, with beautiful inlaid woods. I'm remembering that the set included a headboard, footboard, and a dressing table with its matching bench—I'm so glad Dick's family now has those wonderful pieces.

My uncle eventually became a mechanical engineer after studying at Iowa State and at Michigan State Universities. He married Dorothy and began working for a big farm implement manufacturer, moving first to Waterloo, Iowa, then to Bettendorf, Iowa (before finally moving to Moorhead, Minnesota after retirement to be closer to their only child, daughter Nancy, and her husband and their sons.) We visited Uncle Dick's family in all of their homes. I especially remember the ranch house he built (completely by himself) on one of the hills in a very nice section of Bettendorf [at 30 Riverview Park Place], supported in the middle by a big steel beam that he insisted on personally moving and placing all alone. That Bettendorf house actually had special secret compartments so a person could go unseen from one room to another in the basement. There was a big recreation room where he had a lot of things he'd crafted by hand, including that pictured model Spanish Galleon with the guns that really put out smoke. He also displayed in that wonderful rec room an antique ax that his grandfather, Ambrose Call, was carrying when he founded Algona. *{Editor's note: When Dad mentioned the ax, I excitedly wondered about it perhaps being the one that Ambrose journaled about—the 'hatchet' he used to carve his name and date into the walnut tree to stake the first Algona claim back in 1854. But Dad recalled it to be a rather large tool, less hatchet-like and more of a size used to hew logs into lumber. Dick's son-in-law, who now has the ax, confirmed that recollection.}*

As an adult, Uncle Dick was most often seen with a big cigar in his mouth and making silly faces—I tried to mimic him by doing the same goofy looks, especially during family photos or films. He was just full of jokes, and everybody loved being around the guy. I remember when Dick had an old stripped-down Ford Model T with a box behind the front seat. He told me how he was on a date one time when he got out of his Model T, picked up a horseshoe from the back box and threw it as far as he could, then told his date that his 'luck had just run out.' I still laugh at that, even when telling it for this book!

Dick became quite the inventor over the years. While still working for one of the farm implement companies, I remember that he invented front-wheel shock absorbers, so that when the two tractor wheels that are close together came to a rock, one wheel could go up independent of the other wheel. Mother once told me that her brother got $1000 from his company for that invention, but no further royalties. Dick's son-in-law recently told

Jennifer about a few more of my uncle's inventions that I didn't recall: One was the 'inner buffer' tire which allowed a tire not to go completely flat clear down to the rim before being changed (evidently, a manufacturing firm waited seventeen years for the original patent on that inner buffer to run out before finally making it themselves!). Another invention was the corn picker, co-developed with a partner, but which never worked out due to the lack of connections with purchasers the partner had supposedly lined up. And last, but not least, was the first dishwasher... My uncle apparently couldn't come up with a way to rid the machine of the food waste, however; when his boss asked about how the invention was coming long, Dick replied, "It stinks!"

Before retiring, Uncle Dick had worked as the head of development for the Army Weapons Command in Rock Island, Illinois, across the Mississippi River from his Bettendorf, Iowa home. While working there, his son-in-law reports that Dick invented a new mortar for the Army's use—it was called the "Mantis" and allowed mortar shells to be fired accurately on the first shot. Apparently, the Mantis was never used at that point in time because it wouldn't hold up under actual battlefield conditions. Uncle Dick was compensated in part for his inventions but apparently didn't have ownership of his patents, which always seemed sad to me. He was such a creative guy and just loved tinkering around and coming up with new things—maybe that's more important to an inventor than being compensated. Though always hard of hearing, I'm told that Dick continued to be sharp of mind to the very end, sitting in his big chair and reading every night before bed. I'm also told he continued to smoke his beloved cigars, chewing them down to nothing. Dick eventually died of colon cancer in 1978 (as did his daughter, my cousin Nancy, more than five years ago now). Nancy and her widower, Jerry, have been blessed with three sons, eight grandchildren, and three great-grandchildren.

The last child born to my grandparents, Frank and Bertha Shore, was yet another son. Uncle Victor was several years younger than his sister and brothers (born in 1908, almost nine years after eldest sibling, Philip). Victor's full name was Francis Edward Victor Shore II, so named after Pop. He was a wonderful man who worked hard to overcome some handicaps from a very early age. As mentioned earlier, Victor had been born in the temporary residence on Cottage Grove Avenue, the house (near Drake) that the family had moved into while in the final construction process of their 37th Street home. My mother wrote down some notes about her little brother, Victor: "The Cottage Grove house had a porte-cochere, a big playroom and a parlor. Victor was born there. He had been a healthy baby, but he caught from the neighbor boy whooping cough, measles, and chicken pox.

The doctors would come. They would hold him up. They said he would die. My father said, 'No, this baby is not going to die.' When Victor did recover, he wouldn't eat except white food—mashed potatoes, milk, etc. He always had a nurse. (In the next house) at 210-37th Street, I would take him wheeling. He couldn't sit up. He would smile and his skin was so white and his hair had no color."

While growing up, Victor just loved railroads, and for years kept a written timetable of the incoming and departing trains even as an adult. He went downtown to the Rock Island Depot regularly just to watch the locomotives. After he fell in love with and married his girlfriend, Helen "Louise" (who I understand he perhaps met at a local drug store), they moved to Tucson, Arizona, and I recall visiting their first little house with a dirt floor. Victor worked security at a local high-rise retirement village run by the City of Tucson, and passed away in 1979 at the age of 70. He always continued to love trains, and was excited to be one of those who celebrated our country's Bicentennial in 1976 by watching the 'American Freedom (Steam) Train' come through Arizona on its tour from California to the Atlantic coast.

Victor and Louise's daughter, named Helen Bertha and called "Nellie," also had some handicaps and illnesses, and passed away from throat cancer ten or so years ago at the early age of 61. Their son, my cousin Frank (actually "Francis Edward Victor Shore III"), recently retired after many years with the Tucson Electric Power Company. Frank is a peach of a guy with the stamina and know-how to restore old cars from scratch, literally building the automobiles from parts in a bucket! When Frank finishes a car, it always looks brand-new. He still keeps a beautifully restored 1914 Model T under cover, and is currently dealing with the headaches (at least to me!) of restoring a 1927 Ford Model T coupe. Frank and his wife have one son who is a recently married detective with the Tucson Police Department. My cousin Frank says he and his wife broke tradition by not naming their son "Francis Edward Victor Shore *IV*," and that their son rather wishes they had done so—they did give him the middle name of "Francis," however. *{Editor's note: We are grateful to Frank for mailing us boxes of historical family pictures and publications for use in this book and for safe-keeping with other family archives.}*

I'll end this section about my Shore heritage with a nice photo of a family gathering in the front yard of the 213-38th Street home where Connie and I grew up. Nobody dated the picture, as usual, but by looking at the car in the driveway and the fact that new cousin Ronnie Shore is on Grandma's lap, I figure it was the summer of 1942.

Left to right, standing, are: **Uncle Ams**, Me, Dad, Mom, Aunt Dorothy (Dick's wife), Aunt Lulu (Ams' wife), and **Uncle Dick**. Seated in front of me and my father is **Uncle Victor,** and standing off to the right is Dick and Dorothy's daughter, my cousin Nancy. In front, my sister Connie is leaning on the chair in which **Grandma Bertha Call Shore** is holding baby Ron (son of Ams and Lulu). To the right, **Uncle Phil** is petting the dog.

I just couldn't be more grateful for the Call and Shore family traditions inherited from Mom's side of the family. And now it's time to tell about Dad's people too…

JEWETT FAMILY GATHERINGS

Here's a Christmas 1931 four-generation shot of the Jewett clan—I had recently turned six-years-old, and my little sister, Connie [born April 2, 1930] would be two in the spring. Family members in the photo include: front row—*me*; second row, seated left to right—Bonnie Jewett Welpton (my great-aunt), George Anson Jewett and Annie Henry Jewett (my great-grandparents); third row, standing—Dr. Hugh Welpton (husband of my great-aunt Bonnie), David "Warren" Jewett (my uncle), Margaret Jewett Jewett (my short little grandmother), Gerald Anson Jewett, Sr. (my father), Bertha Shore Jewett (my mother), Dorothy Izene Shaw (fiancé of my uncle Warren), David Lewis Jewett (my grandfather) holding Constance "Connie" Jewett (my sister), and Homer Henry Jewett (my uncle).

Dad and his two brothers loved electronics and were always experimenting with gadgets. I remember that Uncle Homer had brought along this new-fangled timer gizmo that he could rig up to a camera and take our family photo that year. We were all excited and curious to see what happened when he set the timer, and watched as he ran to get into the picture before the shutter snapped. We waited and waited, not certain if it would ever take the shot… and obviously, most of us were not at all ready when it did!

That family picture was taken in front of the west windows in the living room of my great-aunt Bonnie and great-uncle Hugh Welpton's house. For some reason, several of our eyes were looking over toward the front door. I don't recall anyone else being there, but something seems to have distracted a few of us while waiting for the camera to snap the shot. A local photographer recently told us these non-professional settings make for the best kind of pictures, and that we are fortunate to have one like it. (And it's especially meaningful to have this particular Christmas photo—by the next year my great-grandmother, Annie, was quite ill, passing away on New Year's Day of 1933.)

Bonnie and Hugh's home at 2413 Grand Avenue was a great big place, which was perfect for so many family gatherings. Bonnie had drawn the plans for the house, which was built for just the two of them. In this photo of the three Jewett sons, Dad is  on the left, Warren in the middle, and youngest brother Homer on the right. The house was located across the street from the Terrace Hill mansion at 2300 Grand (now our Governor's residence). The Welpton place was so large that it eventually became the J. M. O'Meara (and later Conley-O'Meara) Funeral Home when Hugh and Bonnie were ready to sell.

Another fun gathering spot for all of us was at the High Street home of my Jewett grandparents, just a few blocks north and east of Bonnie and Hugh's place. To be honest, I really didn't care *where* we got together, but only *that* we got together! I'd have to say that my favorite times as a kid were the many big Jewett (and/or Shore) family dinners, which not only occurred on holidays but also took place every Sunday. We might end up at the home of either set of my grandparents, or at the home of one of my uncles, or even at our own house—but wherever we were, the whole family was always there. And the best part of those weekly and holiday dinners, for me at least, was eating the leg of lamb with mint sauce because I was the one who got to go out and pick the mint leaves (everybody had a patch of that growing outside their kitchen door)!

My paternal grandparents, David Lewis (called "D. L." by most) and Margaret Jewett, built

a large home for their growing family at 2105 High Street [just three blocks west and one long block north of their original residence at 1814 Ingersoll Avenue]. The High Street area was a popular and newer neighborhood up on a knoll that overlooked the Ingersoll Avenue hub of action to its south. [The back double-car garage and wrap-around driveway for 2105 High Street were accessed by an alley that came in off 21st Street (now called Martin Luther King Parkway). The same alley serviced the back entrances to houses like theirs that faced south with a High Street address, as well as to houses that faced north with a Woodland Avenue address. Just north of the home that was built behind the David Jewett place was (and still is) the entrance to the Woodland Cemetery. On the southeast (catty) corner of 21st Street and Woodland Ave. sat Bird Elementary School, and on the southeast (catty) corner from the Jewett house at 21st and High Streets sat the Iowa Children's Home.]

The house itself sat on a rather narrow east-west lot but extended quite deep to the north. They also owned the lot next door west, where they had a huge garden, regularly tended to so lovingly by my grandfather David (known to me as *"Pops"* with an '*s*', so as not to be confused with my *Pop* Shore). Connie remembers even better than I do taking walks with Pops Jewett, carrying fresh flowers—a large bouquet and a small one—to place on the grave of his first wife and baby who were buried in the nearby Woodland Cemetery. [David graduated from Drake University in 1887 and married Lillian Maud Howell, daughter of Adam and Mary (Sanderson) Howell, on New Year's Day, January 1, 1890. Lillian and their baby son, George Adam, both died during childbirth on April 16, 1892. Lillian had been born September 26, 1866, and was only 25-years-old when she passed.] It seemed a tender thing to do, but we really didn't understand much back then about his taking flowers to decorate that headstone at the cemetery. (In later years, Connie said she wondered how Grandmother Margaret felt about Pops' regular flower walks to the grave of his first wife. I'll talk a lot more about my Pops and my grandmother, Margaret, soon… their own surprise love story is one for any book, and especially for this one!)

On the land between Ingersoll to the south and my grandparents' High Street house was a great big ballpark that their three sons just loved. Not only did my father and his two brothers have that wonderful park to play in, but they had another favorite spot too… under the ground between their house and the ballpark ran a great big storm sewer that also apparently served as a play area for them when not full of water! I'm under the impression that the sewer started at about Polk Boulevard three miles to the west—that's where Greenwood Park used to be. Then it ran all the way east several miles, passing in front of my grandparents' house before eventually emptying into the Des Moines River downtown. I hadn't appreciated how big that storm sewer was until Dahl's was remodeling their grocery store at 35th and Ingersoll several years ago and I got to see it when they were digging—it was a big old cement thing that looked at least six-foot square. Dad had told stories about playing in that storm sewer, so seeing it helped me picture the fun he and his brothers must have had doing that.

My grandparents' house had a living room all across the front end of it, and Margaret's grand piano sat just inside the entry by a big window. The rest of the main floor seemed pretty dark to me, especially the interior den with its fireplace and half-bath. Connie and I had our toy closet under the stairway in that den, so that's the room where Pops used to play a lot with the two of us. We had a toy truck that hauled sand, and we would make the truck go up a ramp and dump the sand into a certain area of the play station. Pops also had a little table-top pinball machine—he and I used to have contests against each other with that. Jen has asked me to further describe my grandparents' house since she didn't remember much about that second or third story. So, I drew a more detailed diagram of the upstairs layout for her, where there were five bedrooms at the top of the first set of stairs. I suppose my grandparents slept in the same bedroom while their sons were growing up, but they each had their own separate bedrooms by the time Connie and I were kids. [The front three bedrooms at the top of the stairs changed hands many times over the years. The first room to the right was Margaret's; the first little room to the left with the single bed was the maid's (which eventually became Bonnie's room for awhile after she was widowed). Straight ahead in the southeast corner was the guest bedroom where Connie and Jerry slept whenever spending the night—that bedroom later became David's until he died, after which it was taken over by Bonnie until she passed. The two back bedrooms are detailed in the below text.]

You had to turn left to get to Pops' bedroom at the northeast end of the upstairs hall—his was on the other side of the only bathroom and he had a neat little walkout porch that was over the main kitchen entry below, though I never once saw him go out on it. (There was also a doorway on that second floor that led to yet another staircase taking you up to a top level—a full attic where their sons could play and do projects. My Dad had the first wireless radio station in Iowa as a kid, and it was located up in that third story.) The fifth bedroom on the second floor, located back in the northwest corner, was where my *great-*grandfather, George A. Jewett, had an office! That bedroom office could also be accessed by a back stairway that came in off a second (and more private) northwest driveway entrance, with a landing that led into the kitchen and to the basement below it. George's daughter (my grandmother, Margaret) was his secretary, taking dictation in the bedroom-turned-office and typing everything on a JEWETT typewriter. The JEWETT was quite a machine in its day, sold all over the world (and deserving of its own upcoming chapter).

{Editor's note: That very same typewriter unit was once on display in our Iowa State Historical Museum, after having been donated by Dad's uncle, Homer Jewett, who was in charge of transferring such estate items many years ago. Homer also donated one typewriter to the Polk County Historical Society, for display in the Postal Exhibit at Polk County Heritage Gallery. The Des Moines Historical Society currently possesses (but doesn't display) my great-grandmother Margaret's original typing machine; our family has requested to one day have it donated back to us, if and when the Historical Society chooses to "dispose of, at their own discretion" such a donation, per their written policy. It would be wonderful if the very JEWETT that Margaret used in that bedroom office could be safely stored and displayed with other family archives.}

The only other portion of my grandparents' High Street home that still needs mentioning is the dark and damp underground basement where a partial dirt floor went across the entire front of the house. My sister recalls the "wonderful earthy smell" of that basement, but I don't remember it being wonderful at all—I thought it smelled musty! I'm guessing that Pops left part of the floor dirt so that he could do any repairs that might be necessary, since he was such a handy do-it-yourselfer. And sure enough, when their sewer pipe got a hole in it and started leaking, I recall him digging it up and repairing it himself, then putting the dirt back in place. One would think that Pops Jewett, a business landlord who was always fixing things, would have had a nicely organized workshop down in that basement… but in reality, there was absolutely no rhyme or reason to where he kept his tools or equipment! It never made any sense to me, but just piling stuff onto a table or into a corner seemed to work well enough for him.

Most of that basement dirt floor was just stacked and stacked with JEWETT typewriters—they were all over the place, clear up to the ceiling! And on the cement portion of the floor, which covered the north three-fourths of the basement, there was typewriter machinery.

I remember belts and lathes and all sorts of parts from that company, some even hanging from a long axle strung across the ceiling, and that Uncle Homer used to like messing around with all that typewriter equipment. He was nine years younger than Dad and eight years younger than Warren, and likely had to create ways to keep busy once Dad left home for WWI training and then for the University of Pennsylvania, and Warren was finishing high school and starting college. Homer also had a lathe down in that basement, where he turned wood, making bowls and other beautiful inlaid items—he was just busy doing stuff like that all the time, and ended up with several patented inventions.

[Homer wrote of the Jewett typewriter parts kept in that basement… "The factory (was) located in the middle of the block on the north side of Court Ave., between Second and Third. I can remember my father Dave taking me down there to help clean out the building when I was just a little boy." In putting together this book, there has been no record found that the typewriter 'factory' was ever located on Court Avenue—the only address in family files, and also listed on advertisements for the machine, show it to be in the 900 block of Grand Avenue. The Court Avenue location recalled by a young Homer may have been just a place to store typewriter parts when the company was sold by 1912 (Homer was born in December of 1908). Or the Court Avenue spot may indeed have been the south entrance to yet another location about which we recently learned… There is written reference to a 212-3rd Street location for the Jewett Typewriter Company, further described as a site "built by the Des Moines Commercial Club" who "raised $200,000 to build the building as an incentive to keep the Jewett Typewriter Company in Des Moines." Surviving family members keen on Jewett history have never even heard of that location. In attempting to put the puzzle pieces together on this matter, it is jointly concluded that George Jewett was looking to close down the Grand Avenue typewriter business location after encountering a potential takeover that was in the works, and perhaps moved it to the 212-3rd Street location to save the operation or to save money (or perhaps to save 'face') after the $200,000 was raised to build and help keep his company in Des Moines. Homer seemed to clearly recall cleaning out a downtown storage location and correctly mentions "setting up a complete parts department in the basement" of his parents' home at 2105 High Street, where he "was still getting requests for parts until 1956."]

Also, down in the basement of the High Street house was this metal 'shoeshine thing'—all the men went down there and shined our shoes on it! The apparatus had a removable arm that went into a holster on the wall and held one shoe at a time while you hand-polished it. For some reason, it was always a meaningful thing to me when four generations of Jewetts (and sometimes even three generations of Shores) would head down there to shine our shoes whenever over at David and Margaret's home.

Long after my grandparents had passed away, their High Street residence stood empty with no real plan for its use. Eventually, the house was slated to be torn down to make way for a local business that had bought the land. The business owner got in touch with me to see if there might be anything I'd like to salvage from the place before it was demolished. So, I went over to my grandparents' old High Street house and walked right down into the basement, unscrewing that shoeshine apparatus and carrying it out with me! That's the only real meaningful item that I wanted to take (other than the once ornate front door, which was in such bad shape that someone threw it out after I temporarily stored it in the materials yard at the lumber company). After getting the 'shoeshine thing' home, I cleaned it all up and gave it a new coat of paint, then hung it in the basement workshop of my Des Moines house, where it got plenty of use for years. It's still in terrific shape, and I'm thrilled that my son-in-law now uses it regularly in his own garage shop.

THE JEWETT LUMBER COMPANY

My great-grandfather, George Anson Jewett, was quite the pioneer entrepreneur in our city, starting several businesses and outreaches in the Des Moines area over the years, not the least of which was the Jewett Lumber Company. In August of 1865, as a 17-year-old young man, George had walked forty miles to Des Moines from Pella in search of work. He first took a job earning $20 per month as a bookkeeper for the Brown, Beattie & Spofford agricultural implement dealer located on the corner of First Street and Court Avenue; by the time he left them eight years later, George was managing the operation and earning $125 per month. For the next six years, he worked for (and soon became manager of) the H. F. Getchell & Sons lumber dealers, "these years revealing the choice of a future business career." [George had also organized and become general manager in 1871 of the Des Moines Scale Company, one of the first manufacturing enterprises in the city—associates in that 'hay and stock scales' endeavor were S. F. Spofford, Wesley Redhead, H. F. Getchell & Sons, J. D. Seeberger, F. R. West, and others. George Jewett also helped organize the Iowa Loan and Trust Company in 1872, with a limited capital of one million dollars to make loans on real estate—others in this venture included Coryden Fuller, John Elliott, James Callanan, Samuel Merrill, John Ulm, James Heartwell, John Coggeshall, John Owens, M. T. Russell, C. C. Carpenter, Brown & Dudley, I. N. Thomas, and J. G. Weeks.]

By 1879, George Jewett was ready to go into business for himself, choosing two good friends as partners [David R. Ewing and Ed S. Chandler] and organizing the firm of 'Ewing, Jewett and Chandler, Lumber Merchants.' A brief time later, Mr. Chandler moved to California and sold his shares to the other two—the new company was then known as 'Ewing and Jewett, Lumber Dealers.' Their business was originally located on the southwest corner of 5th & Cherry Streets, just south of the Polk County Courthouse, next to the railroad tracks. When the Wabash Railroad took over that property by condemnation two years later in order to turn it into a new passenger depot, the lumber firm of 'Ewing and Jewett' was forced to move. They relocated a few blocks west-northwest of that spot after my great-grandfather paid $28,000 to the City of Des Moines to purchase the full city block from Grand Avenue to Locust Street and between 9th and 10th Streets. (Interestingly, I was told that the City of Des Moines had paid only $10,000 for that entire block two years earlier, turning it into a city park.)

In 1902, partner David Ewing passed away. George Jewett bought out his deceased

partner's interest by giving to the Ewing family the south half of the block where the main offices had been located, which meant physically moving their general office building over to the southwest

corner of 9th and Grand. The Ewing family then built an apartment building on that half-block of land that stretched from 9th to 10th Streets facing Locust, as shown on the left side of this above 1912 pic. [The Voya Financial building now sits there.]

The right photo shows that a second story was then added to the main office (and with more signage to better describe the full nature of the business—early 'corporate branding!').

While Mr. Ewing was still alive, the 'Ewing and Jewett' firm had also purchased a *second* piece of property which included the east half of the block between E. 6th and E. 7th Streets, from Walnut to Court; in addition, they leased the one-quarter-block across the street, immediately north (the leased building is shown below in the early 1900's). That entire location then operated as

the east-side branch yard, while the main office and yard continued to do business out of the 9th and Grand site shown above. (By the way, these are not customers parked and waiting to enter the east-side location—they are independent vendors lined up to haul goods for customers before the days when the company delivered. Just like the taxicab lineup at an airport today, the first vendor in line was waved over into the main yard across the street and loaded up for delivery. I actually remember this system as a little kid!)

About 1905, the old lumber company structures at the east-side location had been torn down to make way for more modern offices and a warehouse. For the main building, they used a brand-new method of concrete construction, called 'tilt-up.' Just as it sounds, forms for the walls were laid on the ground and reinforced concrete was poured in place, then the walls were tilted-up with the use of horses. Our new corporate logo was engraved over the large entry. Jewett Lumber Company was the first tilt-up concrete building in the entire United States and was written up in many cement industry publications before the process later became quite common across the country.

When the firm had become known as the 'Jewett Lumber Company' after 1902, my great-grandfather George held titles of President and General Manager, and my grandfather D. L. became the firm's Secretary (D. L. had originally started his own career with the 'Ewing and Jewett Lumber Company' after graduating from Drake in 1887 and quickly becoming Manager of their east yard location.) Because George Jewett was such an entrepreneur, he had also started a separate entity known as the 'Jewett Realty Company' to handle real estate that had been accumulated when people were unable to pay their lumber bills and wanted to settle up with property instead of cash—George installed himself as President and General Manager of the real estate business, naming D. L. as *its* Secretary as well. And believe it or not, the two of them also held the same titles in *yet another* business developed by George—the Jewett Typewriter Company (as already stated, that whole endeavor deserves, and will be given, its own upcoming chapter).

The lumber business provided a wide variety of building materials, true to its company motto, "Everything From the Foundation to the Chimney Top." Though my great-grandfather started the Jewett Lumber Company (and the Jewett Realty Company and the Jewett Typewriter Company), as well as many other enterprises prior to those, George A. didn't keep a private office at his various businesses, preferring to be in the middle of the action in order to better interact with the employees and customers. He and

his on-site secretary are off to the far right in this lumber company photo taken about 1910 in the beautifully-appointed main offices at 9th and Grand.

George A. Jewett firmly believed in advertising and was a charter member of the Ad Club of Des Moines. On April 25, 1918, the *Des Moines Register* ran an article entitled, "Jewett's Ads Are Famous." The article states that a Harvard professor in their Graduate School of Business Administration wrote to George, "I have frequently heard your advertising methods favorably mentioned... If you have any printed matter which shows what you are doing, and you have no objection... I would appreciate copies or at least hearing more about your work." The professor might have been referring to George's large personalized lumber company ads like the one on the next page... he had a nice homey style that attracted buyers, with his ongoing soap-opera type of saga known as "A Serial for Home Builders."

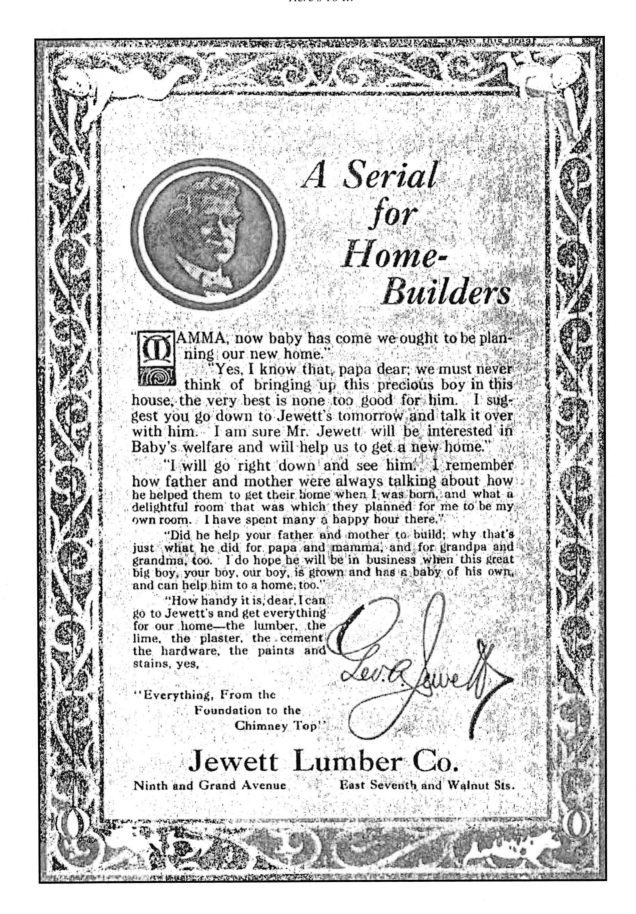

By 1920 Des Moines was growing rapidly and the half-block location on Grand Avenue between 9th and 10th Streets was considered far too valuable for a lumberyard. So, that piece of property was leased by my great-grandfather to a group of real estate investors for 99 years at a net rent of $25,000—the investors then erected 'The Jewett Building' on the site in 1921, creating enough interior space to house a wide variety of retail businesses and offices. All storage and deliveries for George's lumber operation were then handled through their east-side location at 615 E. Walnut, while they kept the main offices and a hardware and paint store in the new Jewett Building [at 412-414 9th Street]. George ran an article (with a coupon, no less) in the May 11, 1921 *Des Moines Register*, telling of the lumber company's grand re-opening in the new building, complete with decorating demonstrations by paint experts and an invitation to the public to "come and give us a boost on the *next* forty years."

The large commercial Jewett Building also housed the Jewett Realty Company, along with tens of other businesses, including the Northwestern Bell Telephone Company. One first floor tenant was The Jewett Market—a retail and wholesale grocery that I recall knowing absolutely nothing about! [The grocery store was run by a gentleman named Sandahl and was likely named 'Jewett Market' due to its location. The Sandahls later had a large grocery store across the street to the east of their original Jewett Building location, on the southeast corner of 9th and Locust, and became close friends of the Jewett family through future generations.]

A *Des Moines Register* article about the property stated that "The Jewett Building is a two-story brick structure. It has a frontage of 281 feet on Grand Avenue, and a depth of 126 feet on both Ninth and Tenth streets… It is considered one of the most attractive pieces of income property in the downtown district. The first floor is occupied by more than thirty retail stores and other tenants, while the second floor is devoted largely to offices." It was such a wise investment by my great-grandfather, at least for a few years.

But by 1927, our country was starting into a period of economic recession, and the lumber company found itself hard-pressed to keep operating at the pace it was going. So, my great-grandfather moved all the main offices into a small room in a corner of the other yard in east Des Moines. The old pot belly stove was converted into a furnace, which sat along the west wall of the hardware section. Uncle Homer even rigged up a special in-office fan system to help better move warm air throughout the entire building. George then "sold" the big Jewett Building on Grand Avenue to tax-exempt Drake University for $1, giving himself tax relief and helping to make Drake stronger financially.

George passed away in 1934, and that's when D. L. Jewett—my 'Pops'—moved up to the position of President of the Jewett Lumber Company, but just for a short while… Pops soon decided he was best suited to further develop George's real estate endeavor mentioned earlier, so D. L. handed off the reins of the lumber company to his eldest son (my father, Gerald). Pops then took over as President of the Jewett Realty Company, while also establishing and becoming a partner with his three boys in yet *another* business endeavor—D. L. Jewett & Sons—an insurance and investment agency! These ancestors of mine were sure determined entrepreneurs. Pops leased some additional downtown space and hired a secretary for the 'D. L. Jewett and Sons' business, and I remember that office well. It sat in the northwest corner on the 2nd floor of the Royal Union Building (which was in the 700 block of Grand Avenue, where part of the current Marriott sits). The building had old cast-iron open-cage elevators, and I just loved to ride on those. At that time, the building was owned by a real estate huckster, a landlord who regularly gave my grandfather fits. One time a window in Pops' office got a hole in it and, rather than repairing it, the cheap landlord just stuck a rag in it!

When not working downtown in that insurance and investment office, you could find Pops driving around town for his real estate business. He owned a lot of property by then, and it took a keen eye (and a nice selection of cars!) to oversee all of it. Sometimes in the evenings and on weekends, I recall people coming to the door of my grandparents' home to settle an outstanding rent bill, or what have you. Pops would use my grandmother's grand piano as a desk to write the receipts. He had to steady his writing hand with his other one because it shook so badly—he called it 'the palsy.' (I seem to have developed some of that similar shakiness especially in one hand over these past years, as did my father and both of his brothers—one of my uncles even had to take medication to keep it in check. It can't help but make me wonder if some of the same shakiness of my sister, Connie, has been incorrectly attributed to her Parkinson's disease.)

HANGING OUT IN THE NEIGHBORHOOD

Though I loved the Thanksgiving and Christmas holiday-time, it was always great when spring came and I could be playing outside even more. Trikes and bikes and cars and airplanes were my real passions, as already mentioned, but playing ball in our big backyard and in the rear driveway area was also a great way just to pass the time. Spring also brought Easter, which was fun because we got to try our hand at raising baby rabbits and chickens—one of our family videos from back then shows Connie and me cuddling with our little Easter chicks right after they had hatched. (I enjoyed watching that again recently!)

And we had dogs most of the years I was growing up, but they all seemed to live such short lives. One of our dogs (I think he was owned by my folks before I was born) was named, "Flash," a beautiful collie that just up and died. We named another early dog, "Christopher Clumsy," and he was just a little thing—I have no idea what breed, and think we just got him at the pound. My bedroom windows overlooked the front yard, and one day I was upstairs and supposed to be taking a nap. I looked out my window after hearing a 'yap,' just in time to see our neighbor's St. Bernard take a bite out of our little dog's neck… and then Christopher's head just fell off! (The owner of that St. Bernard was none other than Ford dealer and eventual Governor, Clyde Herring.) "Jumbo Trapeze" was our female dog that I watched give birth to a bunch of pups in just one litter—I guess she was my favorite, and we had her the longest. One day I was going with a neighborhood friend to spend the day at Riverview Park—we boarded the streetcar at 39th and Ingersoll, and Jumbo had made the trek with us. My friend and I walked to the back of the tram and heard a 'yap,' looking out just in time to see that my dog had been cut in half by the streetcar! My family then replaced Jumbo with a little white dog, naming him "Snowball," and during a snowstorm he went outside and simply disappeared!

I don't recall having any more dogs as a kid, and that was OK—I really didn't want to get close to animals after all those losses, to tell you the truth. Also, I was allergic to dog hair, along with the many other things listed earlier in this book, and preferred not having a dog around. (Until years later, however, when my own daughters were young—a guy I knew from Izaak Walton told me about a litter of English Setters he had, and I went over to his house to choose a nice one from that bunch. I presented the cute little male pup to my girls in a gift box that Christmas morning. We all took the doggy outdoors to the snowy side yard of our home, where the little guy just tumbled all the way down the hill. Youngest daughter, Stephanie, immediately named him "Tumbly." I had hoped to eventually use Tumbly for hunting and to keep him and his hair outside in the nice doghouse I built, but neither of those personal plans worked out. The girls really bonded with Tumbly— especially Stephanie, who insisted on letting him live inside, sharing her food with him, and taking him with her wherever she went.)

I grew up just three doors away from Greenwood, the same grade school my mother and her brothers had attended. The school property ran the full distance from 37th Street (on the east) to 38th Street Place (on the west), just like the Shore property did. I've already mentioned that when my grandmother and her Shore siblings were growing up, Greenwood was the only building north of their home on 37th Street. By the time I started to attend Greenwood, however, there were a couple of houses that had been built on 37th Street between *their* house and the school, and a couple of houses that had also been built on 38th Street Place between *our* house and the school—the neighborhood had sure grown in those twenty years. From the very first day at Greenwood, I just hated kindergarten and couldn't wait to get out of that place. One day I ran away from class, and the teacher chased me and fell down, tearing her hose and dress; I remember that my mother bought her a new outfit!

During that same time, I fell in love with a neighbor girl who lived a few doors away. She's probably the real reason I stayed in kindergarten. While attending Greenwood together, the other kids would give us each a marble to see us kiss, and we ended up with everybody's marbles. I finally decided to elope with that kindergarten girlfriend, so I packed my wagon with toys and my little razor and moved into her house. Her mother and father were so wonderful to me; she and I were bathed together every night in the bathtub by her mother, then were put into the big double bed. During that time, her brother got a sore throat and I, being the self-appointed neighborhood doctor, looked down his throat— everything looked OK to *me*! But then the local pediatrician, the same one our own family had (the friend of my Pop Shore's), came over to the house and diagnosed her brother with "infantile paralysis"—more commonly known as polio! That very quickly was the end of my honeymoon; my mother and father met me at my girlfriend's door where I was packing my wagon with the toys and razor to move back home. (By the way, that older brother of hers recovered quite well, with only a slightly noticeable handicap through life. We remained close, and I was asked to fly his company's airplane full of family and friends out to his wedding in California years later.)

My home and the home of my Shore grandparents were separated by the big deep valley or ravine that I'd have to run through to get from one house to the other. Sometimes there were bums who had wandered up from the railroad tracks that ran not too far south of our neighborhood, and the bums would sleep in my mother's old pony barn down in the ravine to get warm. So, it was pretty scary to cross the valley, especially in the dark… I was glad that my other grandmother, Margaret Jewett, was a very religious lady who taught me about the Bible and had introduced me to the 23rd Psalm. It was the first thing I ever memorized, and I found myself reciting it almost every day as I ran through that valley of the shadow of death to get from the Shore home to my own home. Then when I was old enough to ride a bike, I'd ride like the wind down the hill and back up the other side, all the while reciting the 23rd Psalm. (A few years ago, when completing my 'final arrangements' packet with Dunn's Funeral Home, I asked to have Psalm 23 put onto my visitation handout, just the way Grandmother Margaret taught it to me—it's important enough that I'm adding it to this book too.)

"The Lord is my Shepherd; I shall not want. He maketh me to lie down in green pastures: he leadeth me beside the still waters. He restoreth my soul: he leadeth me in the paths of righteousness for his name's sake. Yea, though I walk through the valley of the shadow of death, I will fear no evil: for thou art with me; thy rod and thy staff they comfort me. Thou preparest a table before me in the presence of my enemies: thou anointest my head with oil; my cup runneth over. Surely goodness and mercy shall follow me all the days of my life: and I will dwell in the house of the Lord forever." (KJV)

Eventually I had my very own pony to ride across that valley, given to me by one of Dad's business friends. "Pete the Pony" was kept in the vacant lot just to the south of our home, right near where I later had a little hand-built clubhouse. The lot was that piece of the Shore family ground I already mentioned, land that was being saved for my grandparents to eventually downsize and build a house on in their retirement years. I found out that keeping a pony was a lot of work… feeding, watering, washing, brushing, and all that. And every time I'd put the saddle on Pete, that son of a gun would turn his head around and bite me in the seat of the pants! On a few occasions, we would get a phone call at 4 or 5 o'clock in the morning telling us that Pete had gotten loose and was down in somebody's yard eating their flowers. Back in those days, our neighborhood seemed so safe, and we just left our cars in the driveway with the keys in the ignition and the house all unlocked. I don't recall us ever having a problem with theft, but one day my neighborhood friends entered our home, just long enough to put Pete into our living room while we were away! I finally grew weary of having a horse of my own to care for, frankly, and I think we ended up just giving him back to my father's friend.

While growing up, I was obviously very close to all four of my grandparents. And it was terrific that both of my grandfathers and some of my uncles, on both sides, were so handy in making wooden products. I remember the time one of my friends got a brand-new fancy wooden wheelbarrow when I was in kindergarten and he was in first grade… I sure wanted one like it, so Pop Shore made an identical one for me in his own basement workshop. And since the other side of my family was in the building materials business, everybody always had all the scrap lumber and other stuff that we needed to create things—I was one lucky little kid!

By this time, my father and his youngest brother, Homer, were both actively managing the Jewett Lumber Company, which had been started by their grandfather. Since Uncle Homer was nine years younger than Dad, I especially liked being around him—people used to think we were brothers. He had a keen mind and was always busy tinkering around and inventing things (like my uncle Dick Shore had done), first in that basement of his parents' house at 2105 High Street and later at the new home he built for his own family at 2101-39th Street, just south of Hickman on the east side of the street. We used to go over to Homer and Marie's house every now and then for the Sunday family dinner, and I just loved seeing what my uncle was up to. One of Homer's inventions during that time was a smoke bomb of some sort—I remember it was supposed to be for "government use." My other Jewett uncle, Warren, was in on this particular invention and when they finally tested it in the basement of Homer's 39th Street house, smoke was pouring out of the windows and it got so bad that they had to call the Fire Department. Another of Homer's inventions had to do with hydraulic brakes for automobiles, and he built a miniature prototype car about two feet long—I recall how all the brake line tubes went to the wheels.

Homer and his wife adopted two sons, my cousins David and Tom, and moved into a larger house on Harwood Drive, just north of Ingersoll. It was a lovely and very tall two-story brick and stucco home with a big attic for storing inventions and Jewett family memorabilia. We have a list, hand-typed by Uncle Homer, of his inventions from 1933 through 1971. There were several, but I think his most famous one was the snow thrower (labeled by the United States Patent Office in 1959 as 'Snow Removal Implement'). He also invented with another Des Moines gentleman a generator, patented in 1968 as 'Electrostatic Power Generator Driven by Pneumatic Power Means.' *{Editor's note:*

I cherish the original patent documents that Homer's son, Tom, recently passed on to me for safe-keeping with other family heirlooms. Homer's U.S. patents are complete, with official red seals affixed to the blue silk ribbon strands that join the document pages.}

Like my Uncle Homer, I loved to work on stuff too, but my inventions were mostly made of wood. One of my first big projects, at age six, was to build myself a workshop in our basement on 38th Street Place, much like the one I admired in the basement of Pop Shore's home on 37th. I had lots of power tools, even as a little kid… a lathe, a skill saw, a grindstone, a drill press, a table saw, and so forth. One day I sawed into my pointer finger, enough that you could see light through the slice—that's when I learned to keep hands out of the way of power tools! For a few years, I built a lot of push cars, as already discussed, and my little girlfriend (the one I'd eloped with in kindergarten) would push me around the street in front of my house—we even have a videotape of her doing that!

I eventually built myself a clubhouse, which looked like an outhouse, and put it on the land just south of our home, the lot where Pete used to be kept—I could continue practicing my doctor skills out there. I remember also building a clubhouse in the rafters of a neighborhood kid's garage. His mother was so excited about the project that she drove us both down to the lumberyard so I could get the extra supplies I needed to complete the job. The clubhouse was eventually nailed into the rafters, and we had such fun playing up there. You had to crawl through a dog tunnel door to get into the thing from the outside, and we even put a window in it. When we got tired of being inside the clubhouse, we'd go play in the wooded ravine that ran up and down Tonawanda Drive right by his house. He and I would swing naked on the vines just like Tarzan. One time my friend ended up infected with poison ivy all over his body, so the two Tarzans always wore clothing after that.

One of the very first things I built down in my workshop was a 'pop stand' on wheels, and kept it in Grandma Shore's garage on 37th Street. I was still only six-years-old, and my Pop Shore had just recently passed away. I would wheel that stand up to 37th and Grand, just north of Greenwood School, and park it on the southwest corner in front of the old Polk mansion (today it is the location of the P.E.O. International headquarters), where there was more traffic. A number of the big beverage trucks, like Coca-Cola, would stop there and unload whatever I needed; the big ice trucks would also stop, and I'd get a 100-pound cake of ice to chop up in a barrel and keep my pop cold. I sure wish there was a photo somewhere of my pop stand, which was a pretty big deal in the neighborhood. My business was so successful that I built another stand on wheels to use a few blocks west, at the southeast corner of 42ⁿᵈ Street and Grand Avenue. That location was run every day by a good friend who lived close by on Greenwood Drive, and then we'd wheel it down to her house at night—we charged a nickel a bottle, and drank most of our profits.

During the same time that I was running the pop stand at 37ᵗʰ and Grand, the big Christian Science Church was in the final stages of construction of their new building just east of 38ᵗʰ Street Place, and the contractors had building materials stuck all up and down the parking on Grand. The big long steeple, or spire, for the church was laid along the parking, starting right by the pop stand. My friend who lived in the Bolton Apartments near that intersection would join me in trying to walk along the spire and keep our balance. (Now that I'm 92-years-young, there are a lot of interesting overlaps due to being in this same neighborhood most of my life. Today I'm living on a Wesley Life Foundation retirement campus located just east of my old pop stand location at 37ᵗʰ and Grand. The campus also now includes the Bolton Apartments where my friend grew up long before Wesley Life purchased that building. The Foundation also recently acquired the old Christian Science Church that was being built during those pop stand days. And as for trying to walk along a spire and keep from falling these days… well, most of my friends and I are taking balance classes here at Wesley just to walk *anywhere* without falling!)

It was wonderful to grow up (and to enjoy the rest of my life) in this same centralized area of Des Moines since most conveniences have always been quite close to home. Back in my early years, it seemed like there were an awful lot of grocery stores around. Those were the days when a house had only an icebox to keep food fresh, so quick daily trips to a market for items were oftentimes necessary. The truck from Des Moines Ice and Fuel Company came by every other day or so, and the delivery guy would look for the card in our window to know how many pounds of ice to leave us. Eventually, we had one of the first electric ice boxes in the neighborhood—it had a big coil on top, but I don't recall much else about it. And then, of course, refrigerators cooled by Freon came into being by the time I got a little older. The closest grocery to us was the Red Ball Store at 37ᵗʰ and Ingersoll (where the Greenwood Tavern is now located), and I remember it best for one reason… in 1929, when I was not yet four-years-old, I started up my Mother's Cadillac Touring Sedan convertible when she had gone inside to pick up an item at the Red Ball. I don't remember actually starting up the car, but do remember my mother's reaction to it—I wouldn't say she was mad, really, but she kind of had a fit about it! I'm certain she was scared to death thinking about what might have happened had the car been put in gear.

Besides the Red Ball store, we also had several other groceries nearby. 'Matulef's' and 'Barnard's' were both in the Roosevelt Shopping Center, 'Bassman' and 'Grand' were on different corners at 15th and Grand Avenue, 'Jack Love' was at 35th and Ingersoll, 'Swanson' was at 38th & Ingersoll, 'Hood's' (later Dahl's) was at 48th & Grand, 'Vatruba's' was at 56th and Grand (and later at 59th and Grand). There was also an open-air Central Market downtown at 2nd and Locust, which was quite popular due to all the fresh fruits and vegetables—it was like our current day farmer's market. The 'Pewless' grocery, owned by parents of a classmate, was north of Ingersoll on 35th Street at Rollins—their old brick building has been home to several small businesses since then and is still there, sitting immediately south of what is now I-235. And there was another little grocery store next door to my great-aunt Bonnie and great-uncle Hugh Welpton's big home on Grand, but I can't seem to recall the name of that one—little markets like those were just all over the place. One day I stopped with my grandfather, Pops Jewett, into the Grand grocery store on the northwest corner of 15th and Grand (where the Gas Lamp bar is now located) so that he could pick up a loaf of bread, and I remember that it cost him a whole nickel.

There were a lot of drug stores in the neighborhood too, and a few were frequented quite regularly during the Prohibition era when the purchase of alcohol for consumption was illegal. During those days, businessmen 'in the know' could stop in at a drug store for a shot of whiskey on their way to and from work. Here are some of the more prominent drug stores that I remember in our neighborhood (not all of them were known for that backroom activity, of course): Curtis Drug, owned by Jack Curtis, was across from Greenwood Park on Grand Avenue. Bauder Pharmacy was at 38th and Ingersoll, and Reppert Pharmacy was just three blocks down from there on the northwest corner of 35th & Ingersoll (one of my teachers dated the guy who owned that, and I'd see her in there having green rivers and chocolate cokes with him!). Bright Pharmacy was on the southeast corner of 28th and Ingersoll, and Brady Pharmacy (owned by the Dad of a classmate of mine) was at 31st and Ingersoll. A little further out was Crews across from the airport on SW 21st, Greenwalt further down on Grand, and Cardamon's City Drug on the southwest corner of 5th & Grand. The old Brown Drug owned by Joe Clay and Johnny Carr was downtown too, in the 1500 block of Grand.

There also seemed to be an abundance of dairies in Des Moines, including Maple Leaf, Iowa Noah, Weiser, Northland, Flynn, Jones, and Anderson-Erickson. We bought most of our milk from Weiser and from Flynn as a kid. The horse-drawn Flynn milk wagon stopped in front of our house right at the end of our driveway, where the milkman would step off carrying his wire crate full of bottles that he hoped we would take off his hands that morning. In the meantime, the horse and cart would go on down the hill and just stop and wait for him at the end of Woods Drive at Tonawanda, until the delivery guy had called at the other houses on the block. (If my 'Pete the Pony' would have just behaved like that Flynn Dairy horse, I might have kept him!) Another truck that came around the neighborhood on a regular basis was the one from the Cascade Laundry Company. Their main plant was located on the northwest corner of 13th and Grand, but you didn't have to bother driving there since they would pick up and deliver right to your house. We kids just loved it whenever the truck came around because we could yell at the driver to honk his horn—and when he did, it played that little jingle, 'This Is The Way We Wash Our Clothes, Wash Our Clothes, Wash Our Clothes...'

There were several ice cream places around town too, but not with home delivery. Reed's seemed to be the most famous because of all the outlying stands—their main headquarters was at 21st and Forest, but our closest Reed's shacks were at 38th and Ingersoll (run by "Old Bess"), and in the Roosevelt Shopping Center (run by "Andy"). Lambert's was clear over on E. 14th and Aurora Avenue, and later there was Skondra's downtown on 6th Avenue across from the Equitable Building. Bauder's, which was near our house, always had (and still does) some of the greatest flavors around. And the *fanciest* ice cream parlor in Des Moines was called 'Fox,' and was clear down on Keo Way—if I was a good boy, my folks would take me to Fox (I didn't get to go there very often!).

In the summer of 1933, when I was still seven-years-old, a couple of major events took place in Des Moines. First was the opening of the brand-new Des Moines Municipal Airport on S.W. 21st Street (now Fleur Drive). The southern city limit line was Watrous Avenue back then, and the airport was still another mile or more beyond that. My folks knew how much I loved airplanes, so Mom drove me out to the big grand opening. I remember there was a fellow selling tickets for rides over Des Moines in his Ford Trimotor plane, also known as 'The Tin Goose.' Mom and I climbed into those wicker seats and up we went—what a thrill! From then on, I was hooked. One day I found myself jumping on my bike to ride out to the airport by myself... after all, I was a pretty savvy navigator with my blue Western Flyer (and it was only an eleven-mile round-trip). So, I hopped on the bike and headed east down Grand Avenue. Immediately south of the Ford Motor Company Model T assembly plant at 18th and Grand was a terribly rickety old iron bridge heading over railroad tracks and the Raccoon River, connecting Grand Avenue with S.W. 21st Street. It was a *very single* two-lane bridge... if there was a truck going over it, an approaching car had to wait. Every time you crossed over, a horrendous noise made you think it would surely collapse. Once I got over that bridge, S.W. 21st was paved with brick all the way out to my destination, and I got there safely. (Just for the record, if streets were 'paved' back then, it was with wood or with clay tile paving brick—Merle Hay Road, Grand Avenue, and Ashworth Road were done in brick, the same way S.W. 21st Street was. I guess that's why we had some large clay brick plants around the city, like Goodwin's Brick out on Thomas Beck Road.)

On my return trip from the airport, I rode like the wind back over that rickety old bridge and was tempted to stop in and visit a couple of buddies on my way home. The first stop would have been at the house of a kid who lived about halfway between the Ford Motor plant and my place. He'd just gotten a new BB gun and had wanted to make sure it sighted up properly with a target; somehow a BB found its way through a storm window and a paned window and into the bedroom of the house across the street! He was still in big trouble for that, so I decided that stopping there was probably not such a good idea. I kept on riding until passing in front of the home of another friend who was in some trouble after putting a potato into each of the twin tailpipes of his mean stepdad's Cadillac and then having to pay for the garage wall repair after the potatoes blew two holes in it. Deciding it was best not to stop there either, I ended up heading on home. That might have been the first day I discovered how fun it was to play on the garage roof—I got out the ladder and leaned it against the south side of the garage and climbed on up, just to see if I could. Another kid from the neighborhood went up there with me too. My mother knew about it, I guess, but for some reason she let us do it anyway. (Thinking about that all these years later, and especially for this book, I'll bet Mom was worried sick about me possibly falling from that garage roof, especially in light of her own fall into the stairwell of her childhood home and the resulting broken back.)

The other major happening in the summer of 1933 was when a well-known group of gangsters known as the Barrow Gang were on a big cross-country bank robbery spree and were ambushed while sleeping in an abandoned park just west of Des Moines. It really put Central Iowa on the map, and everyone was talking about it for a long time. All members of the gang were shot in the ambush out near Dexter, but a wounded Bonnie Parker and Clyde Barrow escaped on foot, stealing a car and carrying out their robberies and killings around the country for another year or so. Bonnie and Clyde were eventually shot to death the following May as they attempted to escape from Louisiana in a stolen 1934 Ford V-8. Not long after that, the bullet-ridden car went on display around the country…

Every year the Ford Motor Company held a car show on their factory lawns at 18th and Grand to display the newest models of Fords on the market. The summer after Bonnie and Clyde were killed was a big deal around here because the shot-up automobile in which they died was going to be in Des Moines, and on display at the annual auto show. I badly wanted to see that 1934 Ford Deluxe 4-door with the doors that opened from the front, so my father took me to the big event. Dad had lots of friends in various branches of law enforcement, and they were there at the show in plain clothes, but well-prepared in case any of the gang members returned to see the car and stir up trouble. Dad asked one of his undercover friends to "show Jerry what you have," and boy, was I surprised to see a real submachine gun hidden under the guy's overcoat! Thankfully, it was never necessary for anybody to engage a weapon since none of the Barrow gang members showed up that day. [Ford Motor Co. later sold that Grand Avenue factory property to the Solar Aircraft Co. for producing parts during WWII. In 1950, it was purchased by the Des Moines Public Schools for their 'Technical High School,' and now is the location of their 'Central Campus.']

With the Herring Ford Company owners living in our neighborhood, and the Ford Model T assembly plant only a couple miles east on Grand Avenue, that particular make of auto was quite popular in Des Moines. But so were others, and a guy would see some pretty nice cars while driving around our area of town. Along with a love of airplanes, I've always been car crazy, so none of the cars on any given street slipped by me without a second look. I may not have known a cow from a horse (my mother and sister always kidded me about that), but seemed to know most every model of car and year of make! Except Buick—I just wasn't up on those for some reason, even though I liked their look and eventually even had one. I sure loved sitting in the various automobiles of my folks and all my relatives; one of our cleaning women had a brand-new Model T, and she'd let me go outside and sit in that too. So, bicycles eventually took a back seat to automobiles. And by the time I started building push cars, my friends and I spent most of our free time getting around the neighborhood in those. It was a big deal for us to run alongside our cars, pushing them as fast as we could, then to jump in and drive until they finally stopped.

I remember my 8th birthday in 1933 especially well, because Dad borrowed a little gasoline-driven car for a day from the guy he knew who owned Globe Machinery and Hoist Company. The little car had been manufactured there and looked almost like one that my friend's dad had recently bought him. The car that my father got to borrow was big enough to carry me and my 3½-year-old sister, Connie. The two of us rode in that thing all over my grandparents' front yard and driveway, then up and down 37th Street (since 37th had a sidewalk and our street didn't). Connie and I even rode clear up to the Grand Avenue corner where I had run my pop stand the past couple of summers. That birthday 'loaner' car had a corner of the front bumper broken off, which of course bothered me, but it was still so much more elegant than my friend's older model. My friend drove his car so much that it was pretty beat up; he would regularly throw a casing off the tire, then he'd have to stop and pick it up and put on a fresh casing before he could get going again. (Jen asked me to explain what a 'casing' was and how it worked… it was just an old tire with the inside cut out so that it could be easily slipped over a new tire to keep the new tire fresh. Bear in mind that new tires for a little gasoline-driven car were pretty expensive, with the economy the way it was. So, you'd want to cover the nice new tire with an old casing. You just had to let a little air out of the good tire, slip the casing onto it, then you'd blow it back up and be on your way!)

The winter before that 8th birthday, Dad had purchased an 8mm Kodak movie camera that got good use right out of the box. It was one of the first 8mm cameras around and enabled him to take moving pictures of our entire family, including my great-grandparents. We are so thankful that my father purchased it in time to take film video of our 1932 Christmas gatherings, and of our 1933 Easter with baby chicks, and of so many other celebrations. My 8th birthday that following October, with me driving the little gasoline-driven car, is really something to watch nowadays. It's especially meaningful to me, because seventy-plus years later Connie and I made another video much like it, showing us driving off together in one of my antique convertibles and waving at the camera like we had done back on that 8th birthday. *{**Editor's note:** A few years ago, Dad had all the 8mm film from those very early years made into VHS tapes, and more recently transferred onto CD's, a most meaningful gift for his daughters and grandsons, and for Jewett generations to come.}*

About 1936 my folks had a beautiful two-room playhouse built in our backyard for my little sister—it had knotty pine paneling, electric wall plugs, and so on. I especially enjoyed it because, after sneaking out of the house and sleeping outside in a pup tent a lot in the summertime, Connie let me bunk down in her fine playhouse. Different friends of mine would spend the night with me in that playhouse too and, by staying out there, we had an opportunity to roam the neighborhood at night, peeking into the windows of the houses down the hill just west of our place. And everybody played outside in the wintertime too, always finding plenty of stuff to do (like having contests after each newly fallen snow, watching to see which one of us could unzip and most legibly 'write' our names in the white stuff). I have had such wonderful buddies my entire life, and so many of those relationships started when we were just boys being boys.

Proof they began racing in 1936 —

Every single day I drove with one of my closest friends (the kid who lived in the Bolton Apartments) up and down 37th Street, and soon ventured further south toward the railroad tracks, into the grounds belonging to the Des Moines City Water Works. We also drove around the ravine on Tonawanda Drive just west of my house, doing that in our spare time for years.

This picture was dated 1936, but we were racing our push cars long before that. The year after this shot was taken, the kid from the Bolton got an engine-driven 'speed model' of our original cars, a nice custom-made miniature automobile. We have a 1937 newspaper clipping showing him and another buddy of ours standing next to that new rig, with a caption reading, "The boys have to fuel with a pint or so of gas now and then and it takes a lot of tinkering too, to keep it running like a bird." The thing was still way underpowered though, with a 1/2 or 3/4 hp engine that wouldn't even take you up hills.

The buddy who was helping my friend with that new rig became a very, very close pal to me until his death just a few years ago. He was a year older, and we spent lots of time together as kids, with me staying at his house or him staying at mine. Some Sundays I got to go with him and his family to the Temple at 51st Street and Grand Avenue; other Sundays he would attend my church (Central Christian), where I regularly went with my great-grandfather, George A. Jewett. One year that buddy was given a little gasoline engine by a friend of his Dad's, so I built a car for it in my workshop and attached a 'Ford' front emblem. Then my grandfather, Pops Jewett, helped rig up a clutch mechanism

for stopping and starting the car—it turned out to be a pretty nice unit for us to share, but it was way underpowered as well! We guys did the best with what we had, though, and it sure was terrific to get around without actually having to push our cars everywhere.

To go places outside our neighborhood, we could ride on the streetcar, but we had to save up for it. Streetcars were trolley buses or trams that ran up and down the unpaved middle of wide Ingersoll, and it was a quick way to get downtown. The cost to see a movie alone was 16 cents (15 cents plus tax), so it was cheapest to just head on our bikes to the 'Uptown' at 41st and University or to the 'Roosevelt' in the Roosevelt Shopping Center since we could get to both of those without also paying to ride the streetcars. But going downtown to the 'Orpheum' or the 'Paramount' or the 'Des Moines' theaters was a real treat, so it was sometimes worth the extra nickel to get down there (and another nickel to get back). When I was around 8, or maybe 9 years of age, my parents took me downtown to see Houdini and Blackstone putting on a show together at the Orpheum Theater on 8th Street between Grand and Locust. I was already a fan of magic tricks, but this really whetted my appetite for more. It was a great show, and the theater itself was considered quite impressive. It was said that the temperature could be 30 degrees outside, but the Orpheum required no heat—a full house kept it at 70 degrees inside. (After that performance, magic shows became more of a routine for me. In my adult years, I liked to hire magicians to do acts for various club gatherings and for lumber company parties and picnics. And one year I hired a guy to entertain at a private party in my home basement— the same guy who had been performing his stuff at our latest company Christmas event. Magicians were always a huge hit for me, and I continue to this day to let myself be fascinated by how they do their tricks. For my 90th birthday, my family sent me downtown—though not on a streetcar—to the Des Moines Civic Center for a Broadway production called 'The Illusionists,' which showcased several of the greatest magicians performing nowadays… that was such a treat.)

One of our favorite trolley trips as kids was to Riverview Park, where we could ram into each other in the bumper cars. But to get out to the amusement park, you had to have a transfer pass. We boarded the streetcar at 39th and Ingersoll, then got off downtown and used the special pass to get onto the 6th Avenue tram, which took us north on 6th and clear up to Riverview. Not only were the bumper cars a big draw, but I liked the thrill of riding the roller coaster, followed by the quietness of the canal ride through its dark tunnels. We usually ate an ice cream cone while we stopped to watch the older people in the dancehall too. The father of a friend of mine owned Riverview Park and, unless they were having one of their '2 cent special' days, I remember it cost us kids just a nickel to get in. With the nickel ride on the streetcar to get there, and the nickel ride to get home, as well as a nickel for ice cream or pop, most of us did odd jobs during the week to save up the twenty cents or more for outings like these.

Fortunately, I was a resourceful kid and really liked making and selling things to get some spending money. My family was full of people who 'worked harder in order to play harder,' so that's just what I did from an early age too. Having done well with the pop stands, I kept coming up with ideas like that. And working at the family lumber company since age 8 gave me some creative opportunities. One money-making brainstorm came to me when working with 100-pound kegs that nails came in—I just cut out the top half of the kegs, leaving enough for a handle that held the bottom half. The little baskets that resulted were awfully handy to carry garden tools and to use as a wastebasket or a magazine holder, or as a container for just about anything. I think my mother mostly sold them to her friends! Around age 10, I sold sawdust logs. They were made by The Weyerhauser Company out of sawdust that was compressed so hard that the product was held together without any glue—they came six to a bundle. The logs arrived on a rail car, and I would buy them from the lumber company and resell them for a little profit. People used the product in fireplaces, where they would burn all night. Weyerhauser also came out with the same size *colored* sawdust fire-starters that burned various colors all at once—a box of 4 colored logs cost $1.50/box and sold like hotcakes.

During the winter season, another kid and I sold Christmas wreaths, which we purchased for a buck or so at Wilson Florist on the southeast corner of 35th Street and Woodland. Mom would drive us over and we'd fill up her car with a bunch of wreaths, then go around the neighborhood reselling them for $1.50 and up, depending on how fancy they were. When I got older, I resold Christmas trees that I also purchased at Wilson Florist. Another job I had was helping a kid a couple of years older than I was with his *Des Moines Tribune* paper route. I must have been about 12. We folded the papers into little 7" or 8" squares, then we'd sail them up to the houses. Sometimes the thing would land on the roof or in the bushes, so we'd have to sail another. The paper was considered rather expensive at 25 cents per week, and even some of the wealthier people didn't take it. (And if they did, they sure didn't want to pay when I came around to collect, even turning off their house lights when they saw me coming!) My friend gave me some easy routes too, such as inside the Commodore Hotel, so cold or rainy weather was a snap. I really did enjoy helping that kid deliver his papers, and didn't even mind not getting paid—at least it was something to do!

I got to meet one buddy (who became another of my closest friends for life) simply because of a big new house being built a few blocks away from my own. After getting out of school each day, I always headed over to that construction site to check out the day's progress and to play around there for awhile after the workmen left. One day there was a pile of fresh cement just lying there, so I started making some balls from the dumped-out wet cement to throw at other kids from the upstairs windows of the framed house. To my surprise, there was a much older kid there who was doing the same thing that day, so we did it together and that was the start of a lifetime of friendship. This new buddy was exactly seven years older, with an October birthday the week before mine. He had attended a special school somewhere in the east due to a severe hearing handicap—for all practical purposes, the kid was deaf. But he was highly intelligent and could read lips darn well. I learned that his family had property at Lake Okoboji, where ours had also started to go for summer vacations, so this quickly became a year-round friendship. (And the two of us eventually ran around with one another when I wasn't away at college or in the service, even living together in his house when we were both divorcees in the early 1960's. He became one of my very closest friends, so you'll be hearing a lot about him in this book—I'll just call him my cement ball buddy.)

That deaf cement ball buddy soon introduced me to one of his own friends who was his same age and who lived in a *humongous* home just a few blocks away from my house— a place that took five years and $3 million to build, with its 28,000 square feet and 42 rooms! The residence sat on a few wooded acres and was a genuine replica of an English mansion. Since the sons who lived in that new mansion were all several years older, I didn't really know any of them… that is, until my cement ball buddy introduced me to the youngest one and we three started spending a lot of time together. My mother and the mother of my new 'mansion friend' were both artists who were also busy in civic affairs, so they already knew each other. One morning the lady who lived in the mansion told Mom over the telephone that she had finished her daily exercises by walking into all the rooms of her house, and that she was simply worn out after doing so! My mother was still laughing about that comment, even decades later. *{Editor's note: The mansion was known for its lovely gardens as well. Back in 1971, my husband and I were the first couple to be married outdoors in the main garden and on the cobblestone walkways and steps that spill from its south entrance. Over the 46+ years since, it has been an extremely popular spot for weddings and other gatherings, with its natural floral and woodland beauty against the majestic backdrop of the massive brick and stone structure.}*

One evening I got a telephone call from my new friend who lived in the mansion, inviting me to come over for a party in his basement. The home was so huge that I had to ask him which of the many doors to go in, and he told me to use a certain one off the back courtyard. When I got inside the house, ready to go down the stairway to the basement, I heard a voice say, "Hello." I didn't see anybody, but answered back, "Hello." Again, the voice said, "Hello," but I still didn't see anybody. It turned out that the voice was coming from a talking parrot! Even though my own home was several blocks away from that mansion, I could clearly hear it when this kid's older brother tuned the air horns on his Cadillac out in the courtyard behind their place—you could feel them vibrate our house! I really loved that noise and hurried over to watch him whenever he was tuning them up. (I was only about 7 or 8, and that older brother of my new friend was about 20 or 21.) The horn-tuning sure made an impression on me, as did the life of that same older brother, who ended up graduating from the Wharton School of Finance at the University of Pennsylvania (like my Dad had), and who continued to love cars and planes and boats throughout his life (like I did!). The older brother was the only one of the four sons of the mansion family to end up staying in the Des Moines area, and I was honored to become his close friend and to follow his adult career as an antique plane collector and an experienced boat racer. And he married a lovely lady whose father was a *world-famous* boat racer!

(Here's an interesting side note to the story of that older boating brother who lived in the mansion: Years later, when I was a student at the University of Iowa, one of my Sigma Nu brothers loved to race speedboats, which was difficult because he had contracted polio during WWII, leaving him very crippled. In order to race a boat, my fraternity brother had to literally be placed into the thing; then the watercraft, with him in it, was hoisted up and carefully set down into the water. One day that frat brother asked me if I knew this famous racer from Des Moines because he wanted to try to buy an award-winning speedboat from him. I replied that I knew the older mansion brother well, and agreed to get in touch with him for my fraternity brother—I ended up handling the deal for them, and that brother raced the beloved boat purchased from my Des Moines friend for many years, winning several awards himself.)

That older brother from the mansion eventually built himself an all-steel Lustron house on a 2½-acre portion of the family land next door west of the mansion. His new place was actually two pre-fab metal houses put together. I sure enjoyed swimming in the big pool that was at the south end of the house in an atrium that connected the two. Since my father was in the building materials business, people would ask him what he thought of the

Lustron house. Dad said he really didn't know anything about the construction, but that he wouldn't want to be in there during one of our Midwest thunder and lightning storms! (I thought that was such a clever thing for a lumber dealer to use as an answer.) In the end, those homes were only manufactured for a short time.

A few years after meeting the sons who lived in that mansion, my Dad bought a brand-new 1939 Ford coupe and I was given permission to take it for a little neighborhood joy ride. I was still just 13 and showing off while driving it, especially when I got down in the area of my friends' mansion. While going around a sharp corner much too fast, I hit a telephone pole on Tonawanda Drive behind their big place, tearing off the left front fender of Dad's new car. When I got back home, I wanted to break the news of the accident to my father slowly, so I told him I had bumped the left front fender. When he came out to look at the car, the whole fender was missing! He did not say a word, and I never knew what was going to happen to me as punishment. Nothing ever did, and that was the worst treatment he could have given me. Dad was pretty savvy about disciplining me when I needed it, and he always found ways of doing it with words rather than actions. He was such a wise man, and I respected him a lot. One time a neighborhood kid and I got into a fight over something—the kid threw a hammer and cut my head. I went home to get my head patched, and Dad said, "Jerry, you can get in all the fights you want, and lose an arm or a leg or even your life. But just remember one thing… a fight never settles an argument." I never forgot that, and tried to steer clear of fights that can sometimes break out, especially during a guy's teenage years.

SUMMERS IN COLORADO

Even though I had such fun playing with my friends in and around the neighborhood, our summer vacations were exciting too. My family began their close connection to Colorado after Pop Shore had discovered the beauty of the Colorado Springs area while his own children were still young, long before I was born. This must have been about the time that Spencer Penrose was making his fortune in Cripple Creek and pouring money into various Colorado Springs developments. My parents told me that Mr. Penrose originally got his money from owning a gold mine in Cripple Creek, a big busy town of over 50,000 people after gold was discovered there. Mr. Penrose was quite a philanthropist who then built the Broadmoor Hotel and the Cheyenne Zoo and all sorts of things in that area of the state—his name was always being mentioned for something.

I guess Pop and Grandma Shore used to go out to Colorado and stay regularly in a little rustic Green Mountain Falls hotel. They loved it so much that they ended up purchasing the top half of a mountain that was for sale there! So, my mother and her brothers grew up spending their family summers in Colorado. Mom remembered that her father put his family on the narrow-gauge railroad to gather wildflowers on the mountaintop—they were supposed to identify and make a book about the flowers they found. My mother said she won a whole dollar from her father for her wonderful book. By 1912, the road up to Pikes Peak was opened (also by Mr. Penrose), and flocks of tourists started coming to the area. But Pop could never get a permit to build a house on his mountaintop land. In the meantime, his close Des Moines friend, Henry C. (called "Harry") Wallace, purchased some Green Mountain Falls property that was below the rather useless upper portion of the mountain already owned by our Shore family. The Wallaces then built two homes there—a large bark-covered pine log cottage on higher ground (called "May's-Mount" after Mrs. Wallace's middle name), and a smaller cabin on lower ground (called "Estherview" for its glimpse of Mount Esther). Pop Shore and Harry Wallace had a personal agreement that Pop would 'give' the Wallaces our top part of the mountain, in exchange for them letting our family spend a month or so each summer in one of the two homes built below it.

On the next page is a photo of some of my clan on a Colorado trip back in what I'm guessing to be 1922. I'm thinking my parents were probably engaged, and to be married that September—Mom might even be showing off a ring on her left hand. Uncle Victor (Mom's youngest brother) is seated on the front of the car, and would be about 14.

My grandma, Bertha Call Shore, is leaning on the car while looking at my (eventual) parents, Bertie and Gerald; Pop (Dr. F. E. V.) Shore is standing on the other side of my Dad. I wish my family would have been better at labeling photos so I didn't have to determine dates according to the cars in the picture—this was an especially tough one since I can't get a good look at the entire body of that Cadillac convertible!

Even though Harry Wallace died in 1924 and Pop Shore in 1931, the Wallace family kept their housing agreement with our Shore family for many years—I can remember going out there until about the start of WWII. The son of Henry C. Wallace was Henry A. Wallace, who became the U.S. Secretary of Agriculture (like his father), then became a U.S. Vice President. Sometimes the Wallace family would also be staying in one of their cabins while we stayed in the other… I so enjoyed playing tennis with Henry A.'s daughter, Jean, who was a few years older and who really beat the socks off of me! It didn't matter whether our family stayed in the large 'May's-Mount' or in the smaller 'Estherview'—neither had running water or electricity. For an ice box, we put our food outside into a big cement container about three feet long, then let the stream of water coming down the mountain run over and around it to cool the food. We put things like butter up on rocks so those wouldn't be sitting directly in the water. Without electricity, we used kerosene lanterns for our lights, which worked out just fine. Every morning we would watch the empty gold ore trains go through Green Mountain Falls on their way up to Cripple Creek, with three or four engines pulling the empty cars all the way up there. Then in the evening, we watched the loaded gold ore cars coming back down from Cripple Creek—the engines had to keep the brakes on to slow up the heavy train cars on their descent. The trains were then heading on over to Manitou Springs, where gold was extracted from the gold ore.

Talking about the Wallaces reminds me that I heard about some excitement that went on in Des Moines one summer regarding President Calvin Coolidge, who had been one of then-deceased Mr. Wallace's former personal friends. I guess Coolidge (who was President when I was born), considered living for one summer in a Des Moines mansion—it was a big residence in the 3800 block of Greenwood Drive, down the hill from our house, and belonged to one of my Dad's University of Pennsylvania fraternity brothers. My family said they thought it would be terrific to have the 'Western White House' in our neighborhood for several weeks, and I guess everybody was disappointed that President Coolidge did not end up accepting the offer. If I remember correctly, they said he took a place instead in the Black Hills region of South Dakota that summer, near the area where the Mount Rushmore carvings had been started.

I recall several transportation arrangements for our weeks in Colorado. We typically first sent our luggage out there by train. Then Mother, Dad, Connie and I would drive Mom's car out together for a few days, and Dad would take the train back to Des Moines for most of the work week. Sometimes he would drive back out to Colorado in his own car, but I think the train was his regular method of commuting because I remember being at the station a few times. I especially recall our summer trek to Colorado in 1932, a year after Pop Shore passed away. Mom's older brother, my Uncle Phil, came with us. We sent our luggage, then all drove out there in Mother's older, but very dependable Cadillac Touring Sedan convertible. There were so many fun experiences during the month or so we spent in Colorado each summer. Every summer our family members rode horses together up the mountain with a whole group of people to a skeleton ghost ranch where there were regular big barbeques with square dancing. We rented very tame horses from the Brockhurst Stables out of Green Mountain Falls. The first year that my sister was able to ride alone, she was too small to fit into the equipment they had available, so the stable owners bought a new saddle just for her! *{Editor's note: We have an adorable film clip of Connie in her beautiful new leather saddle, with everyone loading up to start out on one excursion.}* The trail ride cost a certain amount per person, which included the horse and the dinner and the dancing—Connie and I didn't square dance, but our folks and their friends sure enjoyed taking part in that. And I'll never forget the one time that Mother rode up beside me on her rented horse to say hi, and then her horse just laid down and died right on the trail! After that, they all jokingly started calling my rather petite mother, "Big Bertha!"

My parents also rode burros up the mountain one year, and enjoyed the adventure of that all-night ride with a bunch of their friends just to see the sunrise from the top of Pikes Peak—we have lots of video of that particular adventure too. Connie and I were too young to go along, and I actually wasn't at all interested anyway—an overnight ride on a burro to see a sunrise couldn't be as good as spending it back at the cabin or messing around with the car. Most people I know have liked riding the Cog Railway up to the Peak too, and find it hard to believe when I tell them I've never even done that. The Railway has an interesting history and seems to be a great and safe way to get to the summit, but I've always just preferred to drive it.

Each year we all went to watch the annual Pikes Peak Auto Hill Climb (the 'Race to the Clouds'). People lined up and down the 19½-mile dirt road to watch the cars compete for the shortest time it took to climb up to the 14,115-foot-high finish line while speeding around all the tight hairpin turns in pursuit of the coveted Penrose Trophy. The first summer out there, we didn't know where to go to best watch the races; so, we all rode horses out to Woodland Park, where the event

started. But that didn't put us high enough to really get a good look, so we rode back through Green Mountain Falls and eventually found a better spot that we returned to each year after that. Our new viewing location was situated much higher on the actual Pikes Peak mountain, and we got up there by car instead of by horse after that first summer. (On my 92nd birthday, I got to ride up to the top of the Peak again—what a cold and windy spot just to have one's picture taken! And that sharply curving road without any guardrails still gets my attention. At the admission gate to enter the park, I'd been given a Park Service 'Junior Ranger' badge, which I'm now proudly showing off around Des Moines.)

By 1933, my father had purchased a new 1933 Ford V-8 with a radio, and we made the annual summer family trip to Colorado in that. Dad was so excited when he was able to receive Des Moines' local WHO-Radio station from the driveway of the big cottage! Before then, there were no radios or even clocks in cars. I remember how the first automobile clocks ran slowly in winter and fast in summer—if your wristwatch was within ten minutes of the car clock, that was pretty good. Toward the end of that August in 1933, my Jewett grandparents drove another car out with Dad one weekend to spend the last week or so with us in Colorado. We were all staying in the big cottage and discovered bees living in a basement room. Pops Jewett showed me how to get those bees out of there—we put nets over our heads and caps on top of the nets, then went into the room to spray bug killer. That took care of it. For some reason, neither one of us got stung, even though bees were all over our netting!

Even as a 7½-year-old kid, I was already driving my parents' and grandparents' vehicles a good deal of the time. My folks' cars both had front bucket seats that tilted up to access the back seat, so I made two blocks of wood for the driver's side, which kept the seat tilted forward when I was driving. Making that little adjustment, along with adding a cushion, I could see out better and could also reach the pedals! At the end of that August of 1933, my folks and Connie stayed to vacation a few more days in Colorado, but I had to be back in Des Moines for the start of the school year. So, I got to drive Grandmother Margaret and Pops Jewett from Colorado back to Des Moines in that brand-new 1933 Ford with a radio. On the way home, we had eight flat tires; I was the one who repaired the tires and pumped each one back up by hand. A lot of the roads through Colorado were not paved back then, and this bumpy trip took us three full days; it was fun to stay in the motels along the route.

After returning to Des Moines from that vacation, I lived for a few days at my grandparent Jewett's home at 21st and High Street, and they dropped me off in the mornings at Greenwood Grade School. Once they were well out of sight, I would then run three doors to my own home and crawl into Dad's '33 Ford, which had been parked in our driveway after the trip home from Colorado. Then I drove that car clear around the block to the main entrance of Greenwood on 37th Street, parking it right in front to show off to my friends. One day, the Des Moines Chief of Police was putting on a safety program at our school and, when I saw his car parked outside, I thought he had really shown up to arrest me! I quickly drove Dad's Ford back to my house and high-tailed it on foot to school. I was more careful after that, but it was not unusual for me to borrow my folks' cars and take my neighborhood friends for a late ride many nights whenever my parents were away.

I was fairly certain that our live-in housemaid, Freda, never knew about all that, but maybe I was wrong… we came across a little letter from me that Mom kept, after dating it April 24, 1933. It had been written in the spring, just before that family summer in Colorado—my folks must have been on a business trip somewhere. I wrote, "Dear Mother, Freda lets

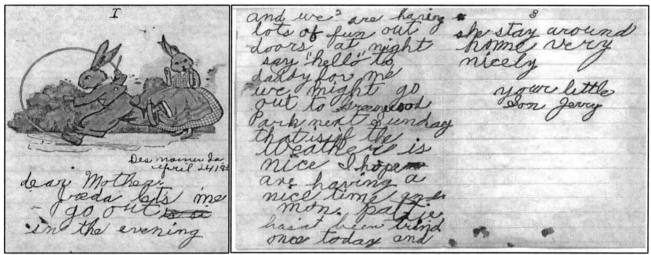

me go out in the evening and we are having lots of fun outdoors at night…" So maybe Freda knew after all! (I also made mention of another dog named 'Pattie.' To be honest, I truly had forgotten about Pattie until recently coming across this little letter in my baby scrapbook. Pattie probably died in some freak accident too.)

Summertime in Iowa also meant heading to YMCA Camp, from about 1932-1935. In those days, the Interurban electric train went from Des Moines to the 'Y' Camp north of Boone and first ran right past our east-side lumber facility. I remember boarding the train at the northeast corner of 2nd and Grand, then going south on 2nd to Walnut Street, then straight over to East 7th before turning south again to cross Court Avenue in order to get to the other railroad tracks. I loved riding the train to camp, waving to everybody in the lumber company as I passed by it on my way out of town. Once out of the city, the other guys and I quickly started filling paper cups with water to drop out of the window like little bombs when we crossed over one of the highest railroad bridges in the country (just north of Boone). I really don't seem to remember as much about camp as I do about those terrific train rides to and from the place. *{Editor's note: We were unable to secure permission to use a publication photograph of the Interurban from one of the books in our family library, but have listed its full reference data in the Appendix (see* Pure Nostalgia, *by Carl Hamilton, ed.) for readers interested in seeing what the little train running through Des Moines looked like. When first discovering the photo, Dad exclaimed, "That's IT!"}*

Our east lumberyard location was also right on the route for many city parades, including the one that signaled the official start of the annual Iowa State Fair. [The Iowa State Fair had been held in the town of Fairfield until moving to Des Moines in 1879. That was also the year several new businesses, including the Jewett Lumber Company, got their starts in Des Moines.] The parades used to wind all through town from east to west, starting at Capitol Hill and heading down Walnut Street right past the lumber company, finally ending at up the entrance to the Woodland Cemetery at the northwest corner of 21st Street and Woodland Avenue. Since my Jewett grandparents' home was just half a block south of the cemetery entrance, their drive was another fine place for me to set up one of my pop stands and sell to the people watching the end of the various parades. And I remember there was always a 21-gun salute as the Memorial Day ones ended, which was quite meaningful.

An especially positive fair memory happened to me years later, in August of 1956. That was when cowboy Roy Rogers and his wife Dale Evans, along with Roy's horse, Trigger, came to the Iowa State Fair. For some reason, Mr. Rogers had made advance arrangements with my father to leave the horse in our lumberyard until the parade started, and I got to sit on the famous animal. Even as a thirty-year-old adult, I sure felt like a kid that day! My Dad was such a big supporter of the Iowa State Fair and, all through the decades of his lumber company management, gave our employees a paid half-day off to attend it. While on the subject of the Iowa State Fair, this is a good place to mention that I've never missed it. These past few years, however, haven't been as enjoyable walking around the grounds in the hot weather and with legs that don't move as fast. So, nowadays I just show up on the Wednesday night before it starts, pulling up in my car to the southwest gate and telling them I'm going to the Administration Building. For some reason, they seem to let me in, and I park right in front of the Varied Industries Building and get myself a corn dog before slowly walking through to see all the exhibits (most of which are manned). Then I head down to Diamond Jack's across from the big horse arena and get a cocktail while watching people dance to the sounds of whatever band is playing. Most of the food stands are already up and running because I think the pre-opening Wednesday might be employee night. I just love continuing to show my support of the annual event in this way, and still remember fondly the Iowa State Fair Parade coming down Walnut Street as such a positive memory of the family business days of my youth (and even as an adult, clear up until that east yard location on the parade route burned to the ground in October of 1968).

When I was eight-years-old, I had started working at the lumber company. As already mentioned, George founded it back in 1879, and two of his grandsons (Dad and Uncle

Homer) were by then involved in the management of it. My grandfather (Pops) also remained active, but only as an Officer due to those other businesses he ran. Even at age eight, I was pretty well running the hardware department and putting up orders of paint, door locks, nails, and so forth. Unable to lift a 100-lb. keg of nails in those days, I'd roll into the hardware store the wooden barrels of whatever size nails were needed, break the wooden top, then tip the top of the barrel toward the bin until the nails fell out. One day I mixed '8-penny finish' with '8-penny case,' and had to sort out two barrels of nails—after that, I really knew the difference! To recycle glass containers and fill orders for customers who needed bottles of linseed oil, turpentine, and other liquids, I'd crank the smaller amounts out of 55-gallon drums.

The hardware set-up I worked in at our big east-side store didn't look nearly as fancy as this first one that George had at 9th and Grand in the Jewett Building, where the back of the hardware store also had a single-car garage with a Model T Ford pickup truck, parked for fast deliveries by way of the rear alley.

And repairing broken toys during the holiday season was another of George's novel ideas. Santa's sign promises that the restored items would then get a coat

of Jap-a-Lac, a terrific and very popular stain and varnish made by the Glidden Company.

Not only did I start in the indoor hardware department at eight years of age, but I also got to begin working outside that summer, in the actual lumberyard part of the business. One of my jobs had to do with dirty old cloth cement bags that people returned for a nickel. I'd place the bags into a machine (that my grandfather had invented) which first shook out any cement left in them. Then I had to bundle the filthy old sacks, 50 to a bundle, using a split table with a pole lying on top. I'd step on the lever to fold the table up which, in turn, folded the bags and then wrapped two wires around each bundle before removing the pole so we could take the bag back out of the machine. That was definitely the dirtiest job I ever had.

And one of the *hottest* jobs I ever had while working in the yard was unloading boxcars by hand in the heat of summer—we'd have to remove boards, unloading the bigger pieces one at a time. And we'd also unload paper bags full of plaster powder. On hot days, those sacks seemed to heat up inside so much that you wondered why the paper bags didn't burn. We wore gloves, of course, but it was still rough and grimy work. Lots of jobs in the yard made a guy dirty though. Back then we sold a product called asbestos board, in 4 x 8 sheets. We would cut the asbestos board into smaller pieces for customers, and I remember being covered by asbestos dust from the saw throwing it all over me. Of course, we had no idea at that time of the cancer-causing danger of asbestos, and it now makes me wonder if that's where my cancer had started before it finally appeared fifty years later.

In those days, guys never stopped for a coffee break while on the job out in the yard, but if it was really hot, we had a coke machine so that the boys could buy a bottle of that for a nickel. Most of the yardmen smoked, and they rolled their cigarettes by hand and lit them by striking a wooden match off the side of their pants. We had a number of Italian guys working in our yard, and I was especially close to one of them—I used to go regularly to his south-side house in 'Little Italy' for a lunch of his mom's homemade spaghetti. Then when I finally invited him over to our house for lunch, my Mom opened up a plain old can of Chef Boyardee to serve us! A prominent gossip columnist for *The Des Moines Register* caught wind of that story and thought it was funny enough to put in the paper.

LAKE OKOBOJI COMPETES WITH COLORADO

Along with our Colorado months, we also began (in the summer of 1931) a love affair with a large group of natural lakes in northwest Iowa. It was quite an adjustment for everyone after Pop Shore had passed away in February of that year. So, Dad rented us a getaway vacation cottage, with no running water, on the north end of Manhattan Beach on beautiful West Lake Okoboji. We brushed our teeth at a pump in the side yard and bathed in the lake, which was down a few steps. The old Manhattan Beach Hotel was still located there, and our cottage was about eight or ten doors north of it—they had very popular weekend dances at the Hotel, like the ones that were also held at The Inn across the lake. After the Hotel was demolished a couple of years later, they built several more of the individual cottages, each with direct lake access, which seemed to be renting like hotcakes by then.

I'll always remember that very first Okoboji summer. We had taken two vehicles up to the Lakes, and Dad had driven back to Des Moines in his car for the work week. My Uncle Ambrose (Mom's brother) was staying with us in the lake cabin too. Mother was very ill and spent most of her time in bed… *{Editor's note: I immediately had to stop Dad right here in his story. This was certainly the first time I'd heard of my grandmother being ill and spending most of her time in bed (ever!). Nana was such a vibrant woman who loved to be out and about, a real 'party gal' who took part in most every event, even in her middle age and elder years while I knew and loved her. When asking Dad what her illness was, he said he couldn't remember, adding, "she was just sick!" My heart began to break for my Nana as I started to put the probable puzzle pieces together… This dear woman was only 30-years-old and had just lost her 66-year-old father four months earlier to a sudden unexpected brain tumor. Now she was holed up in a rustic lake cabin with no running water, several hours away from her husband during the work week, and all the while coping with an overly active 5½-year-old son and a ten-month-old daughter! I'm thinking that life's twists and turns may have seemed overwhelming to her during this time.}*

… It was late June, and word came up the beach that there was a terrible fire in the town of Spencer, just a few miles south of us, and that the whole town was going to burn to the ground! I quickly ran down to the lake and picked up our swimming tubes that had come off Mom's Cadillac Touring Sedan. After helping Uncle Ams deflate the tubes, we reinstalled the tubes into the tires of the car and pumped them back up. (In those days, you didn't ever need to drive around during the daytime, with a grocery market right across the road where we were able to buy our staples, so removing the inner tubes from the car tires in order to use them for lake play was a regular routine.) We reinstalled the wheels onto Mom's car, then I crawled under it to throw out the logs that the car was resting on, and we all (Mother too) drove down to Spencer to watch the disaster. I understand that the million dollar fire that day was the catalyst for making Iowa the first state to ban fireworks a few years later, because it had been a kid with a lit stick of punk walking into a drug store firework display that was blamed for starting the 1931 spectacular horror. (Just this year, 2017, fireworks are no longer banned in our state… you can now buy them for use, but only on certain days of the year and supposedly with a special permit to actually light them. It's a confusing new law that I'm hoping gets rescinded or repealed, frankly.)

By 1936, five years after our first encounter with the Iowa Great Lakes, we had regularly been spending summer months out in Colorado *and* up at Lake Okoboji. I especially remember that particular spring because Mom had gotten a brand-new powder blue '36 Ford that had been all dolled up to look like an Easter egg on the showroom floor of the Jensen-Dunn dealership on Keosauqua Way. That summer my father rented one of the little cottages on Okoboji's Crescent Beach, which also had a Lodge, and we spent a few weeks there. Some of my folks' good friends and their two daughters, one my age and one Connie's age, traveled often with us and had rented the beach cottage next door to ours. Their father had lost his leg in WWI and, every Saturday morning, I was impressed when he took his leg apart and oiled it. One day he said to me, "Jerry, I'll leave my leg off and hop on one leg, racing you while you go backward." And he beat me all to pieces! Sometime later, this same family was at our Des Moines house, and the adults were having a cocktail on the patio before dinner. I was showing off for the eldest daughter, and threw a firecracker out of the upstairs bedroom window; that poor man, a WWI vet, jumped a mile high. I really felt terrible, not thinking at all about it before I did it. (That story alone is reason enough for me to hope our state gets rid of the new firecracker law.)

Okoboji vacations started to become more of a regular event than did Colorado vacations as we got older, but we still spent time doing both. A couple of memorable Colorado events took place in the summer of 1938 when we had Dad's white 1938 Ford two-door coach. The same family with the two daughters came out to vacation with us there, and I wanted to again impress the girl my age, this time by taking her for a ride clear up to Pikes Peak in our new Ford. I took the sides off the engine hood to allow more cool air to circulate through it during the long climb. The two of us started out on the surfaced road at a little village called Cascade, a few miles south of Green Mountain Falls. When we got to the restaurant at the top of the peak, which is right at 14,115-feet in elevation, we didn't even get out of the car, but just enjoyed the view and then drove back down. She and I loved traveling all over that area and into some other mountains. What made it all especially memorable was that the high-altitude travel brought on that gal's first menstrual period, and I was asked by my mother to drive the girl to the drugstore in Green Mountain Falls the next day to get some feminine supplies! After all these years, I still consider that woman one of my girlfriends—she is widowed like I am, but is alive and well (I called her from Pikes Peak on my 92nd birthday, just for old times' sake). We keep in touch regularly and have laughed so many times about that 1938 incident and how embarrassing it was... for both of us! The other important Colorado event that happened the same summer, when I was still 12, was when my mother and father took us over to the famous Broadmoor Hotel in Colorado Springs. I remember there was a big crowd of people gathered in the front driveway, and Spencer Penrose (who owned the Broadmoor, as mentioned earlier) was sitting in a chair elevated way up, with ten-year-old movie star Shirley Temple sitting on his lap! Miss Temple was just a couple years younger than I was, and all the guys my age had a crush on her, so seeing her in person absolutely made my summer.

Spending time in Colorado has always been special for me, not only as a kid but even as an adult. Though we didn't go there as regularly after the WWII days, I found excuses to make stops out that way whenever I could, just to take in the beauty of the place and to visit my Jewett relatives (Uncle Warren's family all eventually lived in the Colorado Springs area, and many still do).

In one of the special memory notes written to me for my 91st birthday, niece Kyle recalled a time in the spring of 1962 when I flew out to Colorado Springs to bring my her and her siblings back to Des Moines after they had taken the train out there with my sister for a little Broadmoor vacation... "Before we flew home, you got a car and drove us into the mountains, wanting us to see the family cabin visited every summer. It was a wonderful old cabin, tucked under the pines. You pointed to a picnic table and wondered aloud if it could possibly be the same one into which you'd carved your initials as a little boy. You walked over to it, lifted it to get the sunlight on the spot... and there they were: 'GAJ Jr.' carved with precision! And at that moment I felt there was a bit of magic about Uncle Jerry." Was I ever proud when I got that new Boy Scout knife as a kid, and just wanted to carve my initials into a lot of things. I will never forget the very day I bought it at Frankel

Clothing in downtown Des Moines, between 5th and 6th on the north side of Walnut—they carried a lot of the Boy Scouts of America line of clothes and accessories back then.

My own fond memories of summers in Colorado took me back out there yet again ten years ago, in October of 2007, when I heard that the Wallace land in Green Mountain Falls was for sale (and for a reasonable price). I had a silly notion to perhaps buy the place so that my kids and grandkids could go out there and enjoy it like I did, and hoped that maybe Jen and John would want to take on such a building project. So, they rode out there with me, as did my girlfriend. That 2007 trip out to see the Wallace property for sale was a fun step back in time, but the area was more run down than I recalled—the big cottage was long gone and the little one was pretty rustic, ramshackle was more like it. We realized it would take a heck of a lot of work (and special permits) to build something on the land that would be anything close to what might be enjoyed by my family in this day and age. Maybe I should listen better to the old saying that 'you should never go back,' but it's just hard to stay away from wanting to revisit some of those memorable places from my Colorado youth. I can't believe I'm saying this, but driving a car that far myself doesn't interest me anymore, so the kids drove me back out to Colorado for my birthday last month too. I'd hoped to wait another week to be out there over the Halloween weekend, in order to again take in the annual Emma Crawford Coffin Race, but thought it might be too cold.

{Editor's note: Emma Crawford was a young woman afflicted with tuberculosis back in the late 1800's. Her parents took her to Manitou Springs, Colorado in hopes the healing miracle waters there would restore her health; unfortunately, Emma died in 1890 and was buried, per her request, at the top of Red Mountain. After years of harsh weather and severe snowmelt and rains on the mountain, her casket was dislodged and slid down into Ruxton Canyon. More than a century later, some creative residents came up with the idea to hold a town race with that theme—costumed participants would push downhill the homemade wheeled 'coffins' that look somewhat like Dad's early push cars, with one team member (an 'Emma') riding in the casket. Thousands of spectators now line the several blocks of Manitou's main street to watch the annual wild and zany event, wisely sponsored by the local Chamber of Commerce. Prizes are awarded for the fastest teams, the best coffin, and the best Emma. We just happened to be in the nearby Green Mountain Falls area to look at the Wallace cabin in late October of 2007, when learning of the Emma Crawford celebration the very next day; we twisted Dad's arm to stay an extra night so we could all cross off our 'bucket lists' an item we didn't even know existed. And he loved it!}

OKOBOJI BECOMES PERMANENT

In the summer of 1939, my paternal grandfather, Pops Jewett, ended up purchasing a home on West Lake Okoboji, at about the midway point of Dixon Beach. He knew how much his kids and grandkids loved going up there, and wanted us all to have a place of our own. I remember the realtor telling my grandfather out in the front yard of the cottage, "Mr. Jewett, the lot alone is really worth the $3,500—they just threw the house in." As a 13-year-old, I thought it was pretty great that Pops got a free house!

My Dad had recently purchased the new 1939 Ford coupe (the one I'd driven around our neighborhood that time the fender ended up missing) and had planned to take it up to the Lakes for the weekend, before heading back to Des Moines in it for the work week. But I badly wanted to drive it up there for him that Friday night, suggesting that he and Mom ride up together in her car. Luckily, that became the plan… my folks drove her car, and I got to drive the '39 Ford, but with the additional understanding that I would be *very, very* careful. Of course, I drove it up there *very* carefully and went out partying *very* carefully around Okoboji that night, then returned it *very* carefully to the new cottage driveway before finally going to bed.

The next morning, my father yelled upstairs and wanted to know what I had done with his new car because it wasn't in the drive that morning. I got up, quickly got dressed, and ran downstairs. When looking out the window, the car was not where I had parked it the night before! After running out the back door, I discovered that the planks under the gravel driveway had rotted out, and Dad's brand-new Ford had dropped into the septic tank below… after two wreckers removed the car basically unharmed, I spent the rest of the weekend cleaning the vehicle. I didn't seem to have a lot of good fortune whenever borrowing that car, although I kept a mattress in the trunk, so it couldn't have been all bad! I'm not sure if my father ever even knew of that mattress, now that I think about it. *{Editor's note: Seriously?!}*

Also in that same summer of 1939, when I was still 13, I got to drive my 75-year-old Pops, and my Uncle Homer and Aunt Marie Jewett, to the World's Fair in San Francisco! The only other time I'd been to a World's Fair was when it was in Chicago a few years earlier, back in 1933, and my folks took me there on the train (that was also the year I drove my grandparents from Colorado to Des Moines, and I thought Mom and Dad should have let me get us to Chicago too, of course; but the family train ride was great fun.) I just loved being able to drive, not only because I really liked it, but because I easily became car sick when not in the driver's seat. On this particular 1939 road trip to and from California for the World's Fair, I drove the four of us all the way out west and up the coast and then back to Iowa in Pops' brand-new '39 Plymouth Deluxe. My uncle was filming the trip with his new movie camera, which was doggone nice to have. We took the southern route out and stopped along the way at Carlsbad Caverns in New Mexico, the Grand Canyon and the Petrified Forest in Arizona, and the Boulder Dam (now called the Hoover Dam) in Nevada. When returning home a week or so later, we took the northern route. While coming through the Hollywood, California, area early in the trip, we visited the studio where Shirley Temple worked—I'm thinking it was RKO. They had built a little house to a smaller scale that was just for her. We got to tour that house, and I remember having to duck to get through the door. It was especially fun for me to be there since I had just seen her in person at the Broadmoor in Colorado Springs the summer before, and still had a crush on her! Uncle Homer and Aunt Marie decided to take a side boat trip from Hollywood out to Catalina Island before meeting back up with Pops and me near San Francisco—they must have taken the train back north for that portion of the trip.

Pops was one of the ten California children of George "Enoch" Jewett (and was named after Enoch's father, another 'David Lewis Jewett'). In addition to the World's Fair, our trip west was a chance for Pops to reconnect with his siblings and their kids and grandkids. Pops' story puts an exciting twist in our family tree, and I'll talk more about that soon, so get ready for one big surprise. Pops had been born in Petaluma and had grown up in that area north of San Francisco. By the time we made this trip in 1939, four of his nine other siblings were deceased, but I'm thinking the rest of his brothers and sisters were living fairly close to the area. I had never met any of them, so this trip west was also a time for me to meet and get acquainted with some of my California family.

Our first stay was in the home of Pops' brother, Frank, who had recently passed away at the young age of 68. His widow, Eva, was so welcoming. We were given a very nice bedroom to sleep in, but I remember the beacon on Alcatraz Island went around and around and kept flashing into the room—enough to keep me awake. Alcatraz had started to be used as a Federal Penitentiary just five years before this, and it was scary to me thinking about those guys locked up out there. (I later toured Alcatraz as a 50-year-old adult and found it terribly interesting.) Frank Jewett had a son, George Daryl, who had been killed in an airplane accident in France during WWI. Frank also had a daughter and two granddaughters, and one of them was sure cute! (Just for the record, since our grandfathers were brothers, that cute one and I kept in touch somewhat over the next twenty-plus years. Then about 1960, she came to Des Moines for an extended visit during the time I was divorced—she stayed with my Mom and Dad, and we had a lot of fun together for weeks.)

The next relative we met up with while on that 1939 road trip to California was one of Pops' sisters, Ida Jewett Silk, who lived in little Forestville, where I had fun swimming with some of my 'new' cousins in the nearby Russian River. If I remember correctly, Ida's husband, Tom Silk, was from England. I think he was the Mayor and Postmaster, and that he also had the bank there in town. They had a huge home and two grown children, but I'm not recalling meeting either of them. I believe their son moved to the east coast and became a professor or something. We had a big family reunion picnic in Tom and Ida's yard, which was lots of fun for everybody.

I guess my most memorable stay on that California adventure was at the ranch of another of Pops' brothers, Bert Jewett. Great-uncle Bert and his wife, Eva (not to be confused with *Frank's* widow, Eva, back in Berkeley) had a dairy ranch near Sebastopol where they also grew hops. And I remember meeting their daughter, my 'new' Aunt June, who was a very nice lady too—I later kept in touch with June and her husband for many years. Sonoma County was known for being in the heart of wine country, and I had such fun driving Pops and Bert around while they sampled various types of local wines. Pops was the eldest brother, and Great-uncle Bert was the youngest (by ten years). Bert was an inventor, of sorts, and showed us all kinds of things he had rigged up around his place. One was a gizmo where he could go to the back door and reach up and pull a wire which opened a gate about a block away for the cows to come in. He also could open his mailbox out by the road and bring the mail in with the same type of rigged rope and pulley system. He had an arrangement of mirrors that allowed him to cut his own hair, which impressed me so much that I used the same arrangement to begin cutting my own hair when I got back home (which saved the 50 cents you had to pay to have it cut down at Pope's Barber Shop on Ingersoll!) But the best invention was Bert's "Do-Nothing Machine," which had won first prize after he entered it in the local fair. It had bells that clanged, and wheels that turned, and whistles that whistled, and colored lights that blinked on and off... and it did absolutely nothing! The thing really made us laugh, but the heartiest laughter came from Bert himself while showing it off—he just loved it. Bert and Eva eventually sold their farm and moved closer into town, retiring in a beautiful home that he built by himself at age 80.

Great-uncle Bert was full of stories. I'm not sure whether to believe this or not, but he swore it was true… He was the music director for the local high school and told us that the President of the United States (it would have had to have been William McKinley) came to visit one year and that the school band was supposed to play for him. The only tune they knew well enough to play on such short notice was 'The Death March.' Uncle Bert said, "Well, the President of the United States ain't going to know the difference… we'll just play it." Not long after, the President was assassinated, according to Bert! *{Editor's note: While that story has been popular family lore all these decades, we really can't seem to vet the tale. Dad was pretty insistent that it be included here anyway, and still laughs when remembering his Great-uncle Bert telling it—that guy must have been quite a character!}*

Pops Jewett and his four brothers were pretty musical guys, and my family always enjoyed this photo taken at their Forestville family farm, long before my grandfather became my grandfather. (I'm so glad that Connie has the framed original of this cute picture.) Pops was the eldest of the five sons— I think he's the guy in the middle.

At some point in time, well before I was born, Great-uncle Bert had also moved to Des Moines for awhile to work for my great-grandfather, George A. Jewett, at the lumber company. Bert told how George was a stickler about recording all sales and making certain the cash drawer balanced to the penny at the end of each day. Of course, that was back before cash registers kept track of such transactions, and Uncle Bert told me that practically every night after work they had to put money into their own pockets in order for the drawer to balance! (I'm pretty certain he wasn't making up that story.)

[George A. Jewett wrote in his 1930 *Memoirs*, "While I was in Old Central College, one of our much loved teachers said to me, 'George you ought to take a motto like the Knights of Old, who had their motto emblazoned on their banners. Here is a good one for you—Whatever is worth doing at all is worth doing my very best.'… She said 'write that 100 times and bring it with you next week.' And do you know that Motto has stuck by me all these years. As a bookkeeper perhaps my Final Balance would be out of balance a small amount and I would be tempted to let it go, then that Motto would stare me in the face and I would say if its worth doing at all its worth doing my very best. Then in Business College the Professor said when you make an entry make it with the thought that were you to die the next minute, make it so complete that your successor will know what you meant."]

One thing I recall about the California clan is that they all had such a wry sense of humor. Now that I think of it, the Des Moines Jewett boys (Dad and his brothers, Warren and Homer) had that same type of humor, and it must have been due to the influence of their father, my Pops, who had grown up with those nine siblings out west. I remember one time we went out for breakfast on that 1939 Fair trip and Pops asked the waiter if the diner's pancakes were any good. The waiter replied that they were "the best in the world," so Pops ordered us two helpings. The waiter went to the window that opened into the kitchen and yelled, "TWO ORDERS OF PANCAKES." Then he went back into the kitchen himself and made the pancakes—turns out, the waiter was the only employee in the joint! Afterwards, he asked my grandfather, "So, was the double order of pancakes the best in the world?" Pops, who was an excellent cook said, "Well, you were about *half* right." That kind of quick humor kept this grandson in stitches most of the time. Though the trip to California was supposedly to see the World's Fair, I really don't remember much about it! There was just so much other stuff to take in. I guess I do recall that it was held between San Francisco and Berkeley on land called Treasure Island, which had been dredged out of the ocean just for the Fair, and I thought that whole construction story was pretty interesting. But the other memories from that 5,000-mile trip overshadowed going to any Fair, at least for me.

The year after the 1939 California trip, I got to drive my same aunt and uncle and Pops to another World's Fair, this time in New York. Can you believe my good luck? It was the summer of 1940 and I was 14-years-old. I just loved being behind the wheel of Pops' brand-new 1940 Plymouth. Best of all, I got to drive around the 'Indy 500' racetrack for twenty-five cents when we went through Indianapolis. I really wanted to race cars someday, and remember rounding the curves and seeing the big holes that had been cemented up where racing drivers had collided with the walls—that really made an impression on me.

After 1940, I don't recall any other summer road trips to other World Fairs, but that was alright with me—just spending time in Colorado and up at Okoboji took up most of my time and created enough great memories. Additionally, I was beginning to get quite busy with my own adolescent life and…

MY OWN TRANSPORTATION

I always wanted a car of my own and my father told me when I was old enough to get a license to drive, I could buy one if I had enough money saved—that meant $100. In October of 1939, between those two World's Fair trips, I had finally reached age 14 and could get a school permit. So, I went downtown looking at cars, and found a 1930 Model A Ford Cabriolet convertible with a rumble seat and roll-up windows (instead of plastic side curtains), and fell in love with it. I came home and told my father, "I found the car I want." The price tag on it was $95 and Dad said, "How much have you got for insurance?" I answered, "Not enough." He said, "You can't get into the driver's seat without insurance on your car." My father accompanied me downtown to look at the car and he was able to purchase it for $55, which left me with enough to buy insurance. My artistic mother then painted my initials on the outside upper armrest areas of my driver and passenger doors. It was such a pretty convertible, with just one front bench seat (and a rumble seat).

Dad had a keen business mind, having graduated with a B.S. in Economics from the Wharton School of Finance at the University of Pennsylvania in Philadelphia (alma mater of President Donald J. Trump, businessman Warren Buffett, and Tesla inventor Elon Musk, among so many others). In addition to being appointed as General Manager of the family lumber business right out of college, Dad also assumed the position of Vice President and General Manager of another local implement company that manufactured threshing and harvesting machines. As if that wasn't enough, my father also had been appointed by President Hoover in 1931 to be Collector of Internal Revenue for the State of Iowa! He really was a busy guy, working out of three different offices around town.

I remember back when the finishing touches were being completed at the big Federal building between E. 1st and 2nd Streets on the south side of Walnut, there was one great big slab of granite left over, and the contractor didn't know what to do with it. For some reason, my father told the workers they could haul that piece of granite to our back yard and dump it, which they did—right in our back driveway! I'm not at all certain what Dad had in mind for the eventual use of that big old rock at our house, but whatever it was never came about. I was a kid who loved being out in the back yard and rear driveway, and that thing just laid around there for a number of years, always in the way, until we finally had a big hole dug and the slab was (thankfully) shoved into it!

With a school permit, I started driving my 'new' 1930 Cabriolet to Callanan Junior High School in 1939. As the only kid in school who had a car, the director of the athletic department let me use it to drag the dirt track behind the school, pulling a smoothing device behind my car to flatten track ruts. I parked my convertible every day in the same place on the west side of Callanan, right on 31st Street. Many days I'd come out to find my car gone… kids would 'borrow' it and coast down the hill to Brady Drug Store on the northeast corner of 31st and Ingersoll for lunch. Without a key to my ignition, they just left the car down there and had to walk back up the hill to school. (And I had to walk down it to get my car at the end of the school day!) Speaking of hills, at the end of our own street, 38th Place became steep Marsh Drive, which I always tried to climb after first speeding around the corner from Tonawanda in high gear… that Model A could never get more than halfway up before having to throw it into second gear, but it sure was fun to keep trying.

When still only 14, the Bolton Apartments neighborhood friend and I took many trips in my old Cabriolet. I had only a school permit but figured if the car was driving us to a school somewhere, that permit should work just fine. So, our first road trip was down to the Military Academy in Mexico, Missouri to see a friend of ours—he was the kid who had put the potatoes into the tailpipes of his stepdad's car, which may have had something to do with his going away to military school. My traveling friend and I lifted out the back of the front seat and laid it on the floor of the rumble seat and slept in the car while down there. On that trip, the cover fell off the manifold heater and it was hot as the dickens inside the car, so we stuck a rag in the manifold heater pipe and it caught fire. Another time on that same jaunt, we had to stop and hammer some nails into the convertible top which was starting to blow off. Needing an excuse for another road trip with my school permit, he and I then drove up to Minneapolis to see a good friend who was attending St. John's Prep School; on the way home, we stopped in Faribault, Minnesota to visit a number of buddies who were attending Shattuck Academy. We didn't want our Des Moines boys to feel all alone when away from home, so always did our level best to keep them company.

I usually parked my Model A Cabriolet in a vacant lot across the street from our house on 38th Place, and in cold weather would sometimes have to build a fire under the engine to heat the oil. During that time, while 14- and 15-years-old, I voluntarily worked without pay at the Standard Oil filling station on the northwest corner of 37th and Ingersoll, and got to grease my car up on the hoist for nothing. The father of my 'mansion friend' drove in regularly with his Cadillac for an oil change and grease job—instead of throwing his old oil away, I would save it and put it into my Model A, which just worked out great. I sure spent a lot of time at that filling station. Mom sent me down there to use their bathroom fairly often anyway because she didn't want me clogging our toilet at home after a few days of irregularity, so I got to know the place pretty well. The man who owned it was a peach of a guy—I never heard him swear, and he always just seemed so 'up.' His filling station was close enough to the fire station that those guys liked to go down there too, as did a man who worked for the City, regularly fixing natural gas problems in nearby homes. And, come to think of it, the paperboy hung around there too—we'd all oftentimes have lunch together, cooking ourselves something on the station owner's hotplate.

But there was another filling station, just a block away, where I also sometimes hung out—it was a Skelly station on the southeast corner of 36th and Ingersoll and was managed by a tough young guy who loved to get into fights (just the opposite of the Standard Oil man). I'd go on over there to check in on occasion, and especially to hear stories about guys doing naughty things. One kid who hung out there regularly was a real terror—he was four years older, and did stuff like taking grease guns from the filling station and loading them with water, then heading down to Greenwood Park and pulling up next to another car to squirt the riders with water when they rolled down their windows. One time he took a .22 rifle he got for Christmas and shot out the beacon at the new Des Moines Municipal Airport—boy, did he get in trouble with the FAA for that stunt! I couldn't believe the stories he would come up with… he was just one of those kids who was always thinking up ways to misbehave. And, come to think of it, so was his sister—she was my age and was a lot of fun, a real addition to any party. I remember one day when she got into the habit closet at St. Joseph's Academy and dressed up like a nun. Pulling stunts like that was a regular routine for her, and she continued to be that same way even into her adult years. She was a very creative woman, and eventually got a lot of money for coming up with a famous slogan used for a long time by a national toy company.

Anyway, I loved being out and about in that Model A Cabriolet, and spent a good deal of my time tinkering with it, either in the empty lot across the street from our house or in the north half of our garage where I hung the engine off the rafters to overhaul it (and also cut off the running boards to give the car a sleeker look). I spent so much time working on my Model A Ford, but it sure was a cold hobby in the winter months. So, you can imagine my excitement when Mr. Dunn of Jensen-Dunn Ford offered to let me work on my car in their shop for free whenever I wanted—we were very good customers of theirs, buying my Model A (as well as most of our personal cars and company trucks) from them. There was also a welding shop across the street from Jensen-Dunn—I was in there a good deal of the time getting something welded, so hanging around at the dealership was really quite handy. Mr. Dunn eventually even ordered me a mechanic outfit so I'd look like his other employees. The lettering on my uniform had my name on the front pocket like the other guys; on the back, however, instead of saying, "JENSEN-DUNN FORD," like everyone else's, my back lettering said, "JEWETT'S FLASHY SERVICE—OPEN ALL NIGHT." Anyway, I felt like I fit in pretty well with the employees and did have a lot of fun working on my car down there. *{Editor's note: When cleaning out our family home in order for Dad to move to the Wesley campus almost five years ago, I inadvertently left that mechanic outfit hanging behind the door of his basement workroom. Not knowing the origin or sentimental value of the overalls, they were apparently hauled away with other seemingly non-essential items. It surely came as a surprise when someone later forwarded Dad a picture of those very overalls for sale on eBay. Now that he is fondly recollecting the story about the mechanic uniform for this book, I wish we had it back to hang in his apartment!}*

I was born and bred a Ford guy, at least during my early car years. Dad liked doing business with Jensen-Dunn and continued that relationship for a long time. But eventually, they sold out to a big national franchise, which caused their demise. The new owners were two slick car salesmen who had developed a get-rich-quick scheme back in the '40's, starting their operation in Memphis, Tennessee and expanding from there. Their reputation was not stellar, and most people in Des Moines weren't falling for their tactics. We knew of a guy who bought a brand-new car from them and took it on a road trip, stopping somewhere south of town to have his oil checked. While under the hood, the filling station attendant asked this Des Moines man how the new V-6 engine was performing. The car owner said, "V-6? But I bought a V-8!" Sure enough, they'd sold him a V-6 for the price of a V-8, and he was furious! Another guy we knew took his car in to potentially trade for a new vehicle, leaving his to be appraised while taking a test drive… when he returned to the dealership, his car had been sold! Those kinds of stories were all over town back then. Not long after the new franchise opened up in our city, I went into their store to charge something on our family's longstanding (Jensen-Dunn) account, only to be told they wouldn't charge to me. I said, "What do you mean? We've always had a family charge account here." They still refused me credit. My father said they'd be lucky to last six months here in Des Moines, and that was about it if I remember correctly. (For some reason, those Hull-Dobbs people also got into the restaurant business, starting it up out of Memphis as well. They opened a diner-style operation that was supposed to compete with the Toddle House chain. In Des Moines, the Dobbs House diner was located in the 1400 block of Grand Avenue. Several years later, sometime in the 60's, Dobbs bought out the Toddle House franchise of 200 or so restaurants around the country. And I remember eventually seeing the 'Dobbs House' name on airline catering vehicles for quite some time, so it must have been a better enterprise for them than the automobile business.)

I really liked working on cars, and by now have had several to tinker with throughout my life. While owning the Model A, I also picked up an old four-door Model T Touring Sedan, but it was so much work to maintain that I quickly got rid of it. In that north half of our home garage where I worked on my cars, I had also built a framework rack to hold a 55-gallon drum full of gasoline—it had a cap on the top, and I poured five-gallon cans of gas into it, one at a time. It was a darn expensive fill for me since gas cost 10-cents-a-gallon, but it sure was worth it to have my own supply. Back then, you never had to look very far to find a filling station. I'm not exaggerating when I say there were almost too many to choose from. And they were all full-service, meaning you drove in and stayed in the vehicle while the attendant filled you up, checked your oil, tested the air pressure in your tires, and washed your window. Filling station attendants would be happy to change oil and replace burned-out light bulbs; but when your vehicle needed additional attention, you'd take it to the Auto Testing Station, located just east of the Police Station on the south side of Court Avenue—they had all the equipment to test all the systems. That's also where auto owners were required to take vehicles to have the lights, wipers, brakes, hand brake, front and tail lights, horn, and everything else tested annually. I remember they always got a kick out of me bringing in my Model A since it was a pretty fancy car for a kid to be driving around town. I'm not recalling exactly when the Auto Testing Station closed down, but it must have been 1965 because the last car I remember taking in there was Mom's Okoboji car... a '56 Ford Parklane station wagon which is still in the family and still has the required sticker on the window showing it passed inspection in 1965.

Back to our neighborhood filling stations... I already said that Standard Oil was on the northwest corner of 37th and Ingersoll, and that there was a Skelly station that sat on the southeast corner of 36th and Ingersoll. On the southwest corner of that same intersection was yet another (where Frenchway Cleaners is now); and just across the street, on the northeast corner, there was a Phillips 66 station. Shell was located on the southwest corner of 35th and Ingersoll, and still another station sat catty-corner to it (then W.T. Dahl bought that whole northeast corner to build his grocery store, tearing out everything that was there, including the Wilson Greenhouse at 35th and Woodland). The intersection of 28th and Grand had a filling station on each corner except the northwest one. The Trax station was one block east of that intersection, with another Shell station a block east of Trax and a Standard station at 18th and Grand that was open 24 hours. There were still others along Ingersoll Avenue, like on the northwest corner of 21st (Harding Road) and the like.

Gas stations are no longer on every corner, and the gas prices are no longer so stable. Several years ago, in my travels here and there around town, I began noting the cheapest places to fill up—it wasn't so long ago, but it was before we had regular internet help like GasBuddy to give us local prices. I regularly reported back to my friends as to where they could find the cheapest place to fill up that week. After months and months of giving these regular reports, one of my friends asked me, "Jerry, how much money do you think you save a year running around town to find the cheapest gas?" I thought a minute and said, "Well, at least $100." His reply to me was, "How about I give you $100 to not tell us about it anymore?!" I got the picture. (For the record, a few weeks ago, the cheapest gas around Des Moines was $2.039/gallon; then after the hurricane hit southeast Texas, our gas prices jumped overnight to $2.599/gallon.)

I was never without available fuel, even back in the days of my first cars, and took advantage of filling my tank with 'regular' grade whenever I could. (There was also 'white' gas, which was the cheapest because of the lowest octane amount, but usually caused a knock in the engine. And then there was the more expensive 'ethyl' grade with higher octane.) I drove my Model A so many miles—a lot of times over 100 miles—around town on any given night. Once when I was still 15, my 16-year-old Jewish neighborhood friend and I were heading east on Grand Avenue and waving at some girls working at the A & W Root Beer place next door west of the Dunn's Funeral Home at 21st and Grand. We ran smack into a parked car in front of the little Toddle House restaurant across the street from Dunn's. When the police arrived on the scene of the accident, my friend was sitting on the curb holding his broken jaw after going through the windshield of my Cabriolet. Since I had only a school permit and my friend had a license, he claimed to be the driver—now that's a friend for life! (And he really was... I sure do miss the decades of fun we had.) My wrecked Model A was towed to the Yellow Cab Company garage, owned by the uncle of another kid I ran around with. The car wasn't in real bad shape, being made of iron back then, and it was soon repaired.

While mentioning The Toddle House, I should add that it was a very popular diner, known for cheeseburgers and chocolate pie. It was real tiny, with just one row of stools at the counter, and you watched them cook your meal with great flair, flipping burgers in the air and that sort of thing. It was an especially crowded place after midnight, and it might have even been open all night. After being handed your check, the waiter watched while you paid the bill based on the honor system, putting your money into a glass-enclosed collection box at the door. The waiter could see for the most part how much money you put into the top of the box, then he stepped on a pedal behind the counter to open a hatch door that dropped the money into the bottom (opaque) half of the box. They were pretty well protected from being robbed because of that system.

There were so many other restaurants in Des Moines at that time, as there are now. Some readers of this book may enjoy recalling the more well-known eating places like the Younkers Tea Room inside the downtown department store, and Grace Ransom's 2nd floor Tea Room on the south side of Locust across the street from the Register & Tribune Building. The White Palace hamburger place was on the north side of 16th & Grand—my folks gave me 16 cents to go down there, so I could get one of their 10-cent burgers and a 5-cent milk (plus have the extra penny to pay the one-cent tax). The Butterfly, a Greek place owned by the father of a Greenwood classmate, was south of Grand on 7th Street. Another friend of mine and his new wife later had a trendy restaurant off the sidewalk behind the Liberty Building in the 600 block of Grand, where she ran the register. Then they later bought Boyce's, where she also cashiered. Of course, the infamous Babe's was on 6th Avenue, the Chickadee (which became Gino's in the 1960's) was further north on 6th, and the Hi-Ho Grill was on the north side of Euclid, just east of 6th Avenue, in Highland Park. I think Chuck's also opened on 6th in that same neighborhood about the time Gino's did. Vic's Tally Ho, at 5601 Douglas, would grill steaks, custom-ordered, right in the middle of the dining room; and Scarpino's was just a shack of a place that sat on the west side of the street, south of the intersection of 73rd and University. Wally's Drive-In was at Harding Road and Ingersoll, and I already told about A & W Root Beer being just west of Dunn's at 21st and Grand. Bolton & Hay was (and still is) known as a supplier of restaurant equipment, but they also once had eight fast-food diners downtown at one time—their waiters wore white shirts and black slacks, as well as black leather bow ties!

Piccolo Pete's at 27th & Ingersoll was a crowded hangout for Drake kids. Lane's Beer Garden was on the north side of Ingersoll east of 36th Street, and Bucknam's Imperial House, also on Ingersoll (on the northwest corner of 19th Street) was a great place for steaks. Jesse's Embers at 33rd Street quickly became a popular place in the 60's, and is still a busy Ingersoll Avenue hangout even today—that's where my 90th birthday party was held. Canfield's on the southwest corner of Fleur Drive and Valley Drive (now George Flagg Parkway) was noted for its fried chicken—it later became known as Michael's, and still had terrific food. The famous Wimpy's Steak House was on South Union, and Rocky's White Shutter Inn was on Fleur Drive. Across from the airport on Fleur were The Mainliner, The Runway Grille, Connie's Skyliner, Johnny & Kay's, Warren's Steakhouse (just north of Johnny and Kay's), and Caesar's Orchard Inn (just north of Warren's). If you ventured further from the central Des Moines hub of activity, you could find the Latin King restaurant which was (and still is) on Hubbell Avenue over on the east side of town. And Ricelli's was another marvelous Italian steakhouse way out on Indianola Road, southeast of East 14th Street.

Johnny's was supposedly a 'private' Veteran's Club at 63rd and Railroad in Valley Junction, but it was also open to the public and was very, very popular. There was a window in the door that they'd open to see who was knocking, like a Chicago speakeasy, then they could make a decision whether or not to let you in. But I'll bet the owner never turned anyone away (I always just went in through the kitchen though, so I'm not really certain of that!) The restaurant was located in this little old house where the owner had grown up, and it sat on low ground near the Raccoon River—low enough to have been flooded several times over the years. I remember that their water supply was provided by that river through an old-fashioned 'sand point' well, and I don't think they ever did connect to city water. *{Editor's note: So, I wondered aloud if it was safe to order a glass of water with dinner at Johnny's. Dad quickly replied, without skipping a beat, "Well, I sure had plenty of safe scotch and waters out there over the years!"}*

If you didn't mind driving a little west of Des Moines, the Lighthouse Inn was clear out at the northeast corner of 60th & Ashworth in West Des Moines. Even further west and north, outside of the little burg of Waukee, was Alice's Spaghetti Land in the Shuler mining community just north of Hickman on R-30 (now also called 'Alice's Road'). Another notable restaurant in its day was the Horse & Buggy at the west end of the town of Adel on old Highway 6, but it was another fifteen-minute drive west of Alice's.

Since talking about a few of the old popular restaurants we used to visit, it might also be fun to mention the best-known hotels back in the day. There was The Commodore, a very stylish hotel *and* residence at 3440 Grand Avenue—I think that was the furthest west hotel that I remember in town. And there were a few others out south by the airport, of course, like Johnny & Kay's Motel, which had been added to their already-existing restaurant. Most of the other hotels were downtown… the Brown was in the 400 block of Keo Way, on the north side of the street in front of where the old Broadlawns Hospital was located. The Northwestern was next to what used to be the railroad tracks on the southwest corner of E. 4th & Walnut, and the Victoria was out on 6th Avenue. The Franklin, that sat on the northwest corner of 5th & Locust, was where I learned to drink beer. (Years later, I bought into the Franklin with a bunch of other investors. We planned to tear it down and two of the guys wanted to really clean up that corner. We built a gravel parking lot, but not much happened after that. I finally just got out and got my money back—the investment seemed to be going nowhere, and they ended up selling it to Keck to become a parking ramp.)

The Chamberlain Hotel was on the northeast corner of 7th & Locust, where the Ruan Center is now—it had been built in 1911 by the same D. S. Chamberlain who built the mansion just outside my apartment window on the current Wesley Acres property. The downtown Chamberlain Hotel with its Dutch Room restaurant was once labeled "The Finest Hotel in the Middle West," but much later became even more famous for an unsolved murder that took place there in 1967. The Savery Hotel and the Hotel Fort Des Moines were both fashionable, even back then. [The Savery (built in 1887) had been the first in Iowa to have a lavatory in every hotel room by 1919, which was the year the Hotel Fort Des Moines was built.] And nobody can forget The Cargill, which was the local whorehouse! There were other little hotels, like The Milner (I'm remembering the name of the place, but for some reason not recalling right now where it was located), and The Elliott on the east side of 4th Street between Walnut and Court. The Randolph, owned by Boss Hotels, was on the northwest corner of 4th and Court, and there was the Tangney Hotel which was later the Kirkwood (and has now been made into condos).

{Editor's note: It's obvious to the reader by now that Dad is persnickety about his directions. He would often stop me when reading back his dictated stories for this book, wanting to add even more precision to a location description. When Steph and I were very young, our dinner table conversation regularly revolved around learning directions. He felt it was important that we understood how to find our way around town and to talk in north/south/east/west terms, so Dad would quiz his daughters to sharpen us on the skill… "If you were at Barbie's house and walked straight out the front door, which direction would you be heading? Then if you wanted to go from there to Dahl's, which direction would you have to turn?" Dad's girls don't need to rely on popular GPS programs these days—we still just use the early compasses firmly embedded in our psyches!}

There were plenty of places for kids to hang out too, and I made certain to be at all of them! A lot of times we went to each other's houses and listened to records, usually in somebody's basement. One of my friends lived clear out on the southwest corner of S.W. 21st and Watrous Avenue (where the popular Skip's restaurant has been for years). Her dad told my father back then that he wanted to buy just outside the edge of the city limits to save on property taxes; so that's what he did, giving his daughter the old garage that sat just west of the house. A bunch of us painted the walls of the garage and threw a rug over the dirt floor—it was probably more fun than anywhere else to go since it really wasn't a part of anybody's house at all. Every now and then while listening to songs out in that garage, we'd hear an explosion and the ground would shake because they were dynamiting in the coal mines that were all around the south side. Des Moines once sat on an abundance of coal, and the mining industry was big in our city clear up until about WWII. The South Des Moines Coal Company was one of the largest producers since so many acres of mines were located in that area of town. Even to this day, we occasionally have news stories about a sinkhole or even a big cave-in occurring in and around Des Moines, including areas other than the south part (I remember a fairly recent one around E. 16th & Capitol).

I had another friend who lived out on S.W. 21st, but not as far as the Watrous Avenue city limits. His house was just north of Park Avenue and backed up to the old shaft of a coal mine that started at S.W. 23rd and Park. One day three of us guys decided to break into the old shaft and see what was there. We took a bunch of rope, and each had our own flashlights. We didn't want to die without oxygen though, so we also took a canary with us to test it out! Uncle Phil had given my mother this canary, and Mom just hated having to feed and water it all the time. So, it seemed logical to take the canary with us into the shaft—if the canary died, we'd all get out quickly, and Mom wouldn't be upset since she didn't like it anyway. So, the three of us broke in and began to explore the entrance to the mine. But before the canary even had a chance to start gasping for air, we all ran out so darn fast—it was *really spooky* down there! My mother never did find out about that whole thing, which was probably best.

In the wintertime, we kids spent our weekends ice skating or sledding on the lagoon in Greenwood Park. And in the summer, we were at the Ashworth pool in the Park most days. The pool had two cupolas you could swim into, one in the southeast corner of the pool and one in the northeast—they were just big enough that you could hide in them and hug the girls so the lifeguards didn't see you. Those were the days when there weren't many private pools, to speak of. The only one I even remember in our area was the one that my great-uncle Gardie and great-aunt Florence Cowles had behind their house on 37th Street. They also had a tennis court and a bathhouse with separate dressing rooms for men and women. I went swimming at the Cowles house a lot, which was always fun. And it got even more fun as I grew older, when their granddaughter (my second cousin) invited other girls to go swimming over there. Doors weren't locked back then, of course, so my friends and I would sneak into the Cowles' basement to watch through the pool window that was in their recreation room, hoping to sneak a peek at girls swimming in the nude. One time that window broke and the pool water poured down the hill west, flooding all the houses clear over on Tonawanda Drive.

There were lots of places outside of the neighborhood to find fun too. Back then, Des Moines had a Coliseum located on the river at 1st Street between Locust and Grand (before it burned down and the YMCA later built on that property). The Coliseum was the main auditorium in town and it was where lots of gatherings were held, including all the speeches by Presidents and political candidates who stumped here. And there was an old guy named Charlie Cain who walked around downtown, wearing a tattered hat and some raggedy old clothes and talking nonstop, while also carrying a big sandwich board sign that advertised Coliseum events. The Circus occupied the Coliseum whenever it came to town, as did large exhibits (an annual auto show, an annual home show, etc.) that are held these days in the Events Center and in the Varied Industries Building and other spots on the State Fairgrounds. The Coliseum was the place to go for lots of sporting events, like Drake University basketball games, and golden gloves boxing and wrestling matches every Friday night in the winter time—Al ("Babe") Bisignano and Earl ("Rabbit Punch") Wampler sure did draw big crowds. In the summertime, the wrestling and boxing matches were held out at Riverview Park and at the KRNT Theater in the 900 block of Pleasant.

Best of all, the Coliseum even had a roller skating rink upstairs that was quite the crowd-pleaser, especially with teenagers. There was also a roller skating rink on the 2nd floor of a building on the northwest corner of 7th and Grand, and still another rink on the southwest corner of 11th & Walnut, before WHO studios moved in there. There were places to go bowling in town too, with the best alley out on 5th Avenue north of Keo Way. And the only ballpark at that time was on the west side of 6th Avenue at Holcomb, just north of the Des Moines River (across the street west from where North High School is today). Back then, it was called Western League Park, and it had permanent lights so you could watch the Des Moines Demons play at night. I believe it's still a city-owned field.

Lambert's at E. 14th and Aurora was actually a dairy, but also had a dance floor where they held teenage events outside—we used to go there during high school for ice cream and dancing. There was also a terrific dancehall in downtown Des Moines—it was called Tom Archer's 'Tromar,' and was located on the northwest corner of 5th and Park Streets, not too far south of the bowling alley just mentioned. The Tromar pre-dated the Val Air out on Ashworth Road in West Des Moines, a building which had originally been built as a tire factory—the guys who built the tire place were out of Chicago and had put up a factory at E. 18th and Court by the Fairgrounds as well. Automobiles were becoming quite popular, so these guys thought they'd make some quick money by getting people to invest in a tire company… they collected money and put up the structures, but it was just a fraud, and they skipped town when it all came to light. That's when Tom Archer, who owned the Tromar, bought the West Des Moines tire place and turned it into another dancehall—he put a wooden framed shack enclosure on top of the cement structure, with shutters that opened so you could dance out in the moonlight. Tom named it the 'Val Air,' likely due to open air dancing in the Valley Junction area of town. It's been a dancehall since the late 1930's and was once a really nice place to go for an evening.

Driving out to Valley Junction, and even much further west, was a heck of a lot of fun back then. I sure tore around town, starting with that first Model A, and have gotten to know this city pretty darn well all these years since. I remember oftentimes parking in the Cabriolet in a cornfield at 22nd Street on the south side of Ashworth Road in West Des Moines—one time, my girlfriend accidentally kicked the shut-off valve from the gas tank to the engine, and my car wouldn't start. After frantically looking everything over, I finally discovered what had happened, and turned the valve open again. In those days, many of the streets around town were wood or paving brick, like I mentioned before, but some were still just dirt. It was quite an adventure to drive on Ashworth clear out west of 60th Street in West

Des Moines, which was then their western city limit. But you didn't want to get caught west of there if it was raining because you'd likely end up stuck in the mud.

In thinking of old West Des Moines, I also recall the night I was getting ready to race my car with another childhood friend. He was hurrying to meet up with me after having dinner with his folks at the old Des Moines Golf and Country Club on Ashworth Road. The Club had two long driveways, one for incoming cars and one for those departing; the drives were separated by about thirty feet, and that center area was lined all the way with big bushes hiding a masonry fence. After finishing his dinner, my friend got into his father's new Chevy convertible and headed down the hill from the parking area up by the Club entrance. He suddenly decided to take a shortcut to Ashworth Road by going between the two driveways. My friend was already speeding when he hit that hidden masonry fence, losing all his teeth and ending up in really bad shape. Three or four cars full of his pals all waited in the ER inside the east hill entrance down at Methodist Hospital until we knew he was going to be alright. It was a pretty scary deal and we were all very worried about him. Thankfully he recovered and went on to be one of my first two roommates in the Sigma Nu house in college, so the crazy stories about him didn't stop back with that Des Moines Golf and Country Club driveway.

Many in the crowd of kids I ran around with had great cars, and we were probably some of the first to 'scoop the loop' in our city. One day I was in my Model A, heading down Ingersoll, racing a friend of mine in his old Essex (which also had a rumble seat)—he was the guy who had gotten the new BB gun and shot out the window across the street from his house a few years before. For this auto chase, each of us had a passenger in our cars as well. In those days, Ingersoll Avenue ended on the east at 17th Street, where a big building stood. The Cummings School of Art had moved from the old library building downtown into that structure at the east end of Ingersoll. On the southwest corner, there used to be a filling station that had been taken down, but the road was still there and it ran right behind Gold Medal Ice Cream on Grand Avenue. (Incidentally, heading west from 17th and Ingersoll, there were streetcar tracks that ran down the center of Ingersoll way out to West Des Moines, beyond 63rd Street. Ingersoll wasn't paved where the tracks were until years later when one of our city Street Commissioners decided it would be wise to just pave over the top of the tracks, making Ingersoll a nice wide street. That's when the electric curbliner buses came in all over town—they were much more nimble and could pull around cars, and what have you.)

But back to that car chase… The friend who was racing me suddenly cut through the old filling station that had been at 17th, and went on down to Grand, where he turned west and sped up the Grand Avenue hill in front of the old Ford Motor Company assembly plant at 18th Street (which, as mentioned, is now the Des Moines Public Schools' Central Campus). I was behind him, keeping right on his heels, when a police car with two officers stopped me in front of the Ford plant. One of the policemen got out to stay with me, while the other chased down my friend, catching up with him in front of the Hubbell mansion on Terrace Hill (now the Governor's Mansion) at 23rd and Grand. The policeman who had been dropped off with me asked for my drivers' license, looked at it and said, "Oh, a school permit, huh?" I said, "Yes sir, I'm coming from school." He said, "Uh-huh." Then he said to the other kid in my front seat, "What's your name?" The passenger with me happened to be the son of our State Governor (not to be confused with the former Governor's kid that I had also gone to grade school with). The policeman immediately recognized his name, quickly changing his tune and saying very nicely, "Now boys, I don't want you to get in trouble… you go on now, and just proceed carefully." It turns out that my racing friend up the hill in his Essex wasn't quite so lucky—the officer who stopped him ended up impounding his car and taking him and his passenger to jail! And that's how I learned it's not *what* you know, it's *who* you know.

I continued to spend some weekends and part of the summers as a kid working in the family lumberyard, which became more fun as I got old enough to drive their various pieces of machinery around. We had an old 1923 Republic truck that I loved operating… it had hard rubber tires, a chain drive, and a crank starter. Its air compression horn running off one cylinder made such a funny squawk when you pulled on the wire to release the exhaust through the horn—it was called an 'exhaust whistle.' By age 16, I wasn't really old enough to be driving an actual lumber truck on the street—you couldn't get a chauffeur's license in Iowa until age 18—but I knew a kid who got one at age 16 in order to haul burlap bags for his own family's business. Burlap could be used for lots of things back then; in particular, when you couldn't buy roofing membrane during the war, it came in handy for flat roof maintenance to keep tar from running, so it quickly became a pretty big business. That kid I knew got to drive over to Omaha and bring loads of burlap bags back for his mother to wash and sew together for his father to sell. My Dad placed an order for acres of the stitched bags, and when the kid delivered the order, I thought he was a pretty lucky guy getting to drive a truck on the road like that. So, I asked my father if he could try to get me a chauffeur's license too, since it would come in handy for driving various trucks at the lumber company. Dad picked up the phone to call an Iowa Highway Patrol friend of his who was in charge of the motor vehicle license department down at the State Capitol Building. The guy told him to have me come on over and see him, which I did. The license department was located in a hallway in the basement, so I went down and met up with him there. He said, "What have you got to drive right now, Jerry?" and I said, "I've got a Model A." He said, "Well if you can drive a Model A, I guess you can drive a lumber truck!" I proudly received my chauffeur's license in 1941, and with a silver badge that I wore on my cap to confirm it—another reminder of "it's *who* you know."

I learned one of my best lessons about driving while working as a teenager at that east-side lumber company location. A man owned the Shell service station directly across the street on the southeast corner of E. 7th and Walnut Streets, and his son worked on cars there. One day I happened to be over there getting my own car serviced when his son backed another car out of the service garage real fast and ran over a hydraulic automobile jack. The station owner turned to me and said, "There's rule number one, Jerry—never go fast when you back up because you can't always see what's there." That very word of caution has helped me avoid trouble over my long lifetime of active driving. Backing up slowly was also one of the first things taught to my own daughters and grandsons when they started to drive. I had encouraged all of them to learn to drive long before they had permits to do so—we would go to an untraveled area where they could try out their skills, just like I had learned it back in the day (but they weren't so young that they needed a cushion and blocks of wood tilting the driver's seat enough to reach the pedals!). I also let my eldest grandson drive my cabin cruiser up at Okoboji when he was not even five-years-old, and remember how cute he looked standing up in front of the seat so he could see out the windshield.

Now that I think about it there is another driving habit, picked up at an early age, that nobody in my family has ever really cared for… *{Editor's note: Not to be confused with another annoying habit of topping off the gas tank, which Dad won't be mentioning here since unable to admit that it's a bad practice, and one that has spun well out of control.}* … Back then, there were no hydraulic brakes on cars or trucks and, since lumber trucks were terribly heavy, we learned that the best way to decelerate was to downshift and let the engine help you come to a stop. It was also a must, in order to slow down while driving in the Colorado mountains. Over the years since, I've continued to use that trick, much to the dismay of those passengers riding with me. I'm the one with the last laugh though, typically going 40,000-50,000 miles before needing new brakes (and, after all, car parts like brakes need replacing, but transmissions are under warranty!).

PAINTING THE TOWN RED

In the late 30's and early 40's, whenever I had spare time, my deaf cement ball buddy and I had started to party together a lot. Since he was seven years older, he was able to get us into places I really shouldn't have been going because I was just a kid (and always reminding him that he was nothing but a bad influence on me!). We spent many nights at some of Des Moines' finer establishments like the Keo Nightclub at 18th & Keo and the old Tally-Rand, two places where you could catch Speck Redd on the piano. Then there was the Garden of Italy at 12th and High Streets, and the old Standard Club in the 600 block of High, just next-door west of St. Ambrose Cathedral. The Blue Moon, a notorious place to buy bootleg bottles of whiskey for a dollar, was on 6th Avenue south of where North High School is today; also on 6th Avenue were the Twin Oaks, the Wooden Shoe, and the Casa Loma. Mommie's was on the west side of 4th Street between Walnut and Court, just north of the Randolph Hotel. Critelli's Stage Show Bar was immediately north of Grand on 6th Avenue on the west side of the street and had great steaks, onion rings, and dance music. (And just next door to Critelli's there was a big advertisement for the Ted McGrevey taxicab company, with one of their real taxicabs enclosed in glass at the height of a second story, and with bright spotlights shining down onto the cab! They had another McGrevey billboard at 9th and Keo with a real cab coming out of it too. Those were sure something.)

Babe had the upstairs 'Jungle Club' above his restaurant at 6th and Grand, with Frenchie Graffaleer on the piano—it was a great WACs hangout where you could get cocktails and gamble on the machines. The Sepia Supper Club had terrific jazz and was in the heart of the black community at 11th and Crocker. The basement bar at The Commodore Hotel at 3440 Grand was popular with politicians when they were in town during the legislative months. The ever-crowded Moonlight (where Dutch Reagan used to hang out) was clear out on the southwest corner of 73rd and University. And I'd better mention the Pastime and the Green Circle since they were both so trendy too.

Thinking about the Green Circle reminds me of the Saturday night that two of my high school friends had a chase in their vehicles after we'd all had malts at Reed's Ice Cream in the Roosevelt Shopping Center. The action started at Reed's on 42nd, then went west to the Green Circle, which sat on the north side of Hickman Road just west of the T-intersection at 63rd. Several others of us were following their chase in our automobiles. As soon as the first of the two cars whipped left onto Hickman from 63rd, it rolled over on its right side.

Our friend driving the second vehicle swerved in time to miss doing the same thing. The rest of us immediately stopped our cars and ran to the scene. My friend from the Bolton Apartments and a girl I was crazy about were backseat passengers in that first car. Thankfully, nobody was hurt. When I asked my friend to tell me how bad the accident was, he said, "Well, I didn't lose my *ice cream*!"

The owner (and driver) of the car that rolled had to take his widowed mother to church the next morning. He didn't want her to know about the accident and that his passenger door wouldn't open. So, he pulled up tight to the house to make getting in impossible from that side of the car, then had his mother scoot across into the passenger seat through the driver's side! And as for the girl I was crazy about… not long after that, she ended up getting acute infectious mono and was terribly sick, off and on, for several months. Then she went away to boarding school with another girlfriend whose father was well-to-do and paid her expenses to go there. When she returned to Des Moines, that gal just looked so great! I was excited to have her back, and we even continued our relationship while I was in the service—she wrote me every single day while I was away, and ended up coming to see me with my folks one weekend during my College Training Detachment time in Cincinnati. (She never really got well after that bout with mono, though, and I just knew she was going to die an early death. After we broke up, she married another high school friend. Her final wish, even as a young woman, was to die up at Lake Okoboji, so her husband rented a home on Des Moines Beach and they moved up there until she passed away shortly after finally being transferred to the hospital.)

Anyway, my deaf buddy and I hit all those hot spots just listed (and more) around town. Since he was so hard of hearing, these evenings usually started out very quiet. We just winked at the girls in other booths and he would read their lips and inform me first-hand how we stood with each of the "chicks." As the nights drug on, my friend's eyesight would grow blurry, and about midnight his old-fashioned eight-hour hearing aid batteries would go dead (which presented additional obstacles for a successful evening!). One time we stopped back over at his house for a few minutes, and when I came out of the bathroom he seemed to have disappeared. Then I heard his voice coming from the basement. I went down and discovered him checking a big box of old hearing aid batteries, trying to find any with enough life to carry him through the evening. I'll never forget him sitting on this table down there, inserting batteries one by one and then yelling into his hearing aid, "HELLO? HELLO? HELLO?" Then I'd hear, "NO GOOD!" followed by a crash as each battery hit the trash barrel. One night a bunch of us were down at the Rendezvous Room at the

Randolph Hotel. Somebody asked my buddy if he'd ever been into the brothel across the street (which was an apartment with a long stairway up). He said "No," so we all hauled him over to the place. We climbed the tall stairs and knocked on the door of the apartment and, when the woman in the negligee opened the door, she immediately recognized my buddy and called him by name, asking, "How the heck *are* you, honey?"

When I began at Theodore Roosevelt High School (TRHS) with my Model A in 1940, every day I picked up my childhood friend who still lived at the Bolton Apartments on 37th Street, and another guy who lived on the north side of Grand at that same intersection, driving the three of us to school. But the next year, 1941, I finally traded my 1930 Model A

for a newer car—a 1936 Ford convertible Club Coupe with a *real* back seat—which I loved, naturally, since it hauled more kids around and everybody could talk and hear one another from the front to the back of the car. I got a trunk release off a 1938 Ford, which was a winged two-sided handle, and put that onto my '36 Ford to open the trunk. My model was a Deluxe, with two extended taillights, chrome dual horns, and a little more chrome trim. (For the record, by 1937 Ford's Club Coupes had a fixed metal top, and by 1959 they came out with a retractable steel-top convertible.) The 1936 was originally kind of a big ugly maroon 'flivver' that needed some special TLC. But it was all worth it once I got it into tip-top shape and eventually had the thing painted fire engine red. The gentleman I hired to do the paint job was a real craftsman, but was also an alcoholic… while painting my car he was apparently leaning on the left front fender. The car looked perfect when he got through, except where he had painted over the top of his hand on that fender! It was the only blemish on the entire vehicle, and he later repainted it for me, of course—it just turned out great.

By that school year of 1941-42, most of my other friends also had wheels, and we really got around. I started taking pictures of our cars to put into a big scrapbook—each car and owner are individually identified on the pages entitled "Cars in My Crowd—1942". There is a shot of the big old Chevy station wagon that was jointly owned by three guys, as well as a gorgeous blue Dodge convertible (owned by a gorgeous gal who lived out in the country where her mother raised turkeys—they also had a big pool and we'd go out there to swim). There is a 1941 blue Plymouth white-top convertible, as well as a shiny black Chrysler that lost its shininess for awhile after rolling over in that car chase out in front of the Green Circle. The scrapbook pages also show a Ford Coach, a blue 1940 Ford convertible, a '41 Plymouth, a 1938 Ford station wagon, one very sharp Buick, a Lincoln convertible, and a sweet 1941 Cadillac. Looking at those pictures sure stirs up memories.

Here's a photo of seven of us showing off, all at one time. This shot was taken on Foster Drive and was just one of our regular auto line-ups. My '36 Ford is on the far left. The annual yearbooks for TRHS always had a section called, "A Day With Our Students," where they listed hourly happenings during a  typical school day. In the spring 1942 edition of the *Roosevelt Roundup* (at the end of my junior year) a reader will find this entry: "8:17 A.M.: Jerry Jewett's car screams to a stop— Wooden, Hunter, Bolton, Lane, and monkey wrench fall out." That was pretty accurate!

By the time our final high school year was coming up, quite a few of my friends were heading away—girls to finishing and boarding schools like Madeira outside of Washington, D.C., and more guys to various military academies or prep schools. So, after two years at Roosevelt, in the fall of 1942, my parents decided to send me away too— to the Lake Forest Academy (in Lake Forest, Illinois, a suburb of Chicago). I guess naughty boys went there. So, I packed my '36 Ford convertible and headed east, taking along a good friend of mine, who rode as far as Chicago on his way to attend Harvard University. While entering the City we had a flat tire. His steamer trunk was on the back seat and the tire tools were under the back seat, so we had to unload all that out onto the parking. My spare tire was in the trunk, with all my clothes on top of it. So, we unloaded all that onto the parking too, and finally got the dang tire changed.

Upon arriving at my new school in Lake Forest, I was told by other kids that students were not allowed to have cars! I immediately found a vacant lot to park my Ford and, for weeks, my new friends and I drove all over Chicago in it. One day, the head of the school called me into his office and told me he understood I had a car there against school policy. He also told me that Lake Forest had not yet accepted all my high school credits from Roosevelt and that it would be two years before I could graduate… *two years instead of one*! The part I remember most about our conversation is him telling me I'd have to send my car home. That's when I agreed it would be a good time to send my car home, and with *me* driving it! So, that's what I did. When I got back to Des Moines, my folks were thrilled to death to see me and to have me back home. I really don't think they ever wanted me to go away to school anyway, to be honest. Leaving Lake Forest Academy turned out to be a very good decision because the war was well underway and I was going to be drafted. I was able to re-enroll at Roosevelt with no problem and enjoyed knowing I would be graduating in just *one* year.

It was so great being back in the old neighborhood, getting around my own hometown again in the bright red '36 Ford. And just to sweeten the ride even more, a friend in the Polk County Sheriff's garage gave me a police radio receiver to put in it. (The guy also worked part-time at that Skelly filling station on the southeast corner of 36th and Ingersoll, and I got to know him while hanging around there.) My father and two other gentlemen had just recently founded the Des Moines Junior Chamber of Commerce ("Jaycees"), and their first project was to get radio receivers into all the Des Moines police cars, so I thought having my own was really something. But it just seemed as if that piece of equipment would make even more sense if I also had a siren, like the older brother of a friend of mine had on his Model T—he got to install a big chrome siren and a red light on the front of his car because he represented American LaFrance, the manufacturer of fire trucks. That kid first had a contract to sell company products, then eventually ended up going to work for our local Fire Department (selling them even more products!). I used to hang out and pass the time with him and the other firemen down at the local station on 40th Street, between Grand and Ingersoll. It was fun to be over there talking with those guys, but they usually seemed a little bored… they would joke around, telling me and my friends to go on down to the Tonawanda ravine or somewhere else to start a fire so they'd have something to do!

Anyway, I sure thought that kid's American LaFrance siren was pretty nifty, and eventually obtained one myself and installed it down inside the second front grill of my '36 Club Coupe where it could not be seen. And from time to time, I'd use it, of course. One evening, a bunch of us were all out at the Hyperion Country Club for some event. As we got back into my car to leave, a police call came over the receiver about something we decided we'd better go see. So, after turning on the siren we roared out of the Hyperion entrance gates, heading south on Merle Hay Road. There was a tavern on the southwest corner of Merle Hay and the east-west road that ran along the south side of the Club, and two friends of mine were illegally in that bar having a beer. We went past the tavern with the siren blaring—they thought it was a raid, and one of them jumped out the tavern window! He later found out it was my car and was awfully mad at me for awhile.

One day not long after that, my childhood push car friend and I were in my driveway polishing the '36 Ford (with Mom's 'sanitary napkins'—those worked great!). The police radio was on and we heard about a hold-up downtown at the bank south of the Equitable Building, just across the alley on the north end of the Utica Clothing Store. He and I decided we'd better go check out that robbery scene, so we sped down Grand Avenue, then on down Locust with the siren blaring. We got to 6th Street, where the policeman directing traffic waved us through the other cars and right over to the bank—so, we parked out front and raced inside! It was a pretty exciting event for us. But a few days later, I was stopped by a local State Bureau of Investigation (SBI) agent who had been told to check out my car for a siren. The siren was hidden so far down in that second grill that he could not see it, so he let me go. A short time later, however, there was a bad accident with a truck full of WAACs going out to the Fort Des Moines Army Post—their military truck had been sideswiped by another truck and a lot of the WAACs had been badly hurt. [The Women's Army Auxiliary Corps (WAAC) was later known as the Women's Army Corps (WAC), and thousands ended up training at Fort Des Moines during the war years.] I heard the call come over my police radio and went out to see the accident, again with that push car friend. The same special agent of the SBI was on the scene of the accident and said to me, "Jerry, I know you have a siren, so turn it on and follow my car… we need to get these ambulances up to Broadlawns as fast as we can." So, I turned on my siren and followed him, proud to be helping out! (For the record, Broadlawns Hospital looked like an old schoolhouse back then, and was located between 4th and 5th Streets on Keo, behind the Brown Hotel.)

That sweet car and so many wonderful friends helped make the last year of high school really fly by, and I graduated as President of the TRHS class of 1943 (and having finally achieved my stated ambition!).

AMBITION
"To get out of school"

June 1943

GERALD JEWETT

OKOBOJI GROWS UP TOO

After living in our first Okoboji cottage during those summers back in 1939 and 1940, Pops Jewett had decided the home he purchased was in a 'low spot' and would always have a musty smell. Also, it was a pretty rustic place. I remember that you could look right through the walls to the outside—it was just the studs with outdoor siding on them; there was no insulation or any inside walls, so light came through each crack. There were plenty of cracks in the ceiling too—if someone was upstairs sweeping the bedroom floors, they'd have to say, "Look out below, I'm sweeping up here."

The residence just two doors south sat on higher ground and came up for sale. Not only was it quite a bit larger, but it also had a furnace on the first floor and a radiator at the top of the stairs as you walked up. So, my grandfather purchased it for $5000 and we moved there after selling the first place. For some reason, I don't really remember my Jewett grandparents coming up to the cottage much at all after purchasing it, but their three sons (Gerald, Warren, and Homer) and our respective families spent a number of summers at that location, sharing in the use of the house. Even though the new place had a furnace, it was the type of coal furnace used in filling stations, with only two or three radiators. It was not toasty warm at all, and you could still see outside between the slats of the vertical board siding in many places. But we all simply loved it.

Uncle Homer and his wife, Marie, bought a little X-class sailboat after we moved to the big cottage. Theirs was the boat that Connie and I got to use when learning to sail, and they were our excellent teachers. We learned the hard way… by just going out and sailing! My sister recalled one especially funny story about Aunt Marie taking Connie and Mother out to teach them how to lower the jib sail upon docking. When the three of them came toward the dock after the lesson, they were a little short. Aunt Marie made a valiant leap for the dock, getting both feet around a dock post while her hands still held onto the jib. As they'd been trained (but in this case, the wrong maneuver), Connie and Mother dropped the jib, horrified to then see Aunt Marie still clutching the post with her feet and the jib in her hands, while she slowly sunk into the water!

In those days, we always carried a cup in the sailboat—whenever we wanted a drink of water, we'd just dip the cup in the lake and get one. Okoboji has always been considered a very clean natural lake, supposedly one of three 'blue water' ones in the world, but I'm not sure that was ever a proven fact. It is a beautiful body of water and quite deep in some places (up to almost 140 feet), having been formed by glacier movements thousands of years ago. I can't believe that drinking water straight out of Okoboji hurt me all that much; but to be honest, I wouldn't be doing it today.

Connie and I learned most other water sports by just going out and doing them too. Not only were we always swimming, but we also spent a lot of time waterskiing and skiboarding. I built my own skiboard out of plywood one year and had others pull me around on it. We had acquired our first motorboat—a wooden Chris Craft—when we moved into the big cottage, and had rented a hoist for it. Then Uncle Homer designed and drew diagrams of a better hoist system with a big wheel to get the boat out of the water. From Uncle Homer's sketches, I then built the new boat hoist in my folks' backyard on 38th Street Place in Des Moines, painting and labeling where each board went, before taking it all apart. I loaded the pieces onto a lumber truck and hauled it all downtown to the railroad freight house to have it shipped by train to Arnolds Park. When we got up to Okoboji that next weekend, I borrowed a truck and drove to the Arnolds Park railroad depot and freight house to pick up the hoist pieces and haul them back to the cottage for reassembly. Since the planks were numbered and labeled, it was fairly easy, and I reassembled it all in the front yard overlooking the lake.

The next task was to get the hoist down the high bank and into the water. We installed wagon wheels on each side of the structure, and I built a track system out of wood on

which we could lower it and later take it back up at the end of the season, all with a block and tackle pulley system. Homer and Marie then purchased their sailboat and Homer drew up plans for a customized hoist for it too, with a cut-out section to accept the mast. I built that second lift in my folks' Des Moines backyard as well, labeling all the pieces before taking it apart and loading it onto a truck to be dropped at the depot freight house before again being shipped up to Arnolds Park. And that's how we ended up with two very fine hoists that lasted

many years. I remember every spring, it was quite the big event to watch me and my uncle lowering those lifts down the bank, then every fall watching us pull them up out of the water for winter storage in our front yard. Even the neighbors gathered to be a part of the installation and removal 'ceremonies,' signaling the beginning and end of the Okoboji season. Those boat hoists were so satisfactory that a prominent manufacturing plant owner came over to Okoboji one day and went down on our dock, making sketches of the units. He later began manufacturing hoists, a very popular brand yet today, at his own plant outside a small Iowa town. Several years later, I went to that small Iowa town on a Chamber of Commerce Goodwill Tour and had lunch with the very gentleman who owned the hoist manufacturing plant. Our group dined out on an island where the man had built a clubhouse and a miniature large boat just for show—it was out near the airport, where he also kept his twin-engine airplane in its own hangar with a fancy inlaid floor of colored tile! I talked with the gentleman that day, and he confirmed he had been on our Okoboji dock all those years ago. (His company manufactured lots of other things at their huge plant too, including small radio-controlled airplanes. I remember that they later sold that part of the business to an outfit near Des Moines which held an annual air show of these small planes 'dog fighting,' like this man had done back in the small town. They had a beautiful B-25 twin-engine bomber replica on top of a fencepost to promote their air show, with bomber props that turned in the wind, but that whole endeavor didn't last very long.)

Shortly after we moved into the big cottage, probably by the summer of 1941 or '42, I built a skin diving helmet out of some sheet metal and got a guy to weld a window in it. I put a one-way valve at the top for air to get in and connected it to a garden hose and a pump, then hung weights on it to get the thing to go down under the water. I put the helmet into the lake off the end of our dock, then jumped in and came up inside of it. Dad was stationed on the dock to pump air through the hose while I attempted that first dive with my new invention. I immediately got claustrophobia and quickly pushed myself out of the helmet, realizing a guy could drown down there. It was just so spooky being under the water like that, so I quickly surfaced. And there on the dock stood my dear father just pumping his heart out, thinking I was still down there needing air. My invention really wasn't very satisfactory, at least for me—it was fun to build, but it was just a Rube Goldberg that didn't work out.

Connie and I both loved sailing enough that we ended up crewing regularly for others who had larger boats. By the late '40s, I had an airplane and was flying us to summer regattas at Lake Lotawana down by Kansas City, or to Lake Minnetonka and White Bear in Minnesota, and the like. That went on during the '50s too, flying a single-engine Beech Bonanza when my wife, Jackie, crewed regularly for a seasoned Okoboji sailor and I crewed for another. My sister remembered that the sailors would polish and polish their hulls back then, before coating them with Teflon; I'd almost forgotten that at one regatta, the boat of Jackie's sailor slid right off his trailer! Our family owned other sailing boats ourselves over the years—wooden 'X' and 'Y' class ones, and then we even had a big wooden 'E' class boat (which took five sailors to handle on a windy day, but sure was fun). The 'E' leaked a bit, so Uncle Homer and I finished the bottom of it one summer in our backyard while we were drinking rum and cokes… we both got plowed and when we got through with the boat, it seemed to leak worse than before we even started! One time that 'E' turned turtle just off Fort Dodge point; the mast was so long that it busted when hitting the lake bottom. The guy who owned one of the local boat works came out and got us towed into shore at his place—I don't remember much else about it, other than the fact that he was pretty put out with us for trying to handle the 'E' without more sailors on board.

We also had a few very trustworthy wooden motor boats over the years. In 1965, I broke tradition and purchased something other than a Chris Craft. Jennifer remembers going with me down to Clear Lake to test drive a clean used Century runabout, privately listed for sale by a guy who owned a nearby recreational vehicle manufacturing plant. That blue-upholstered beauty was a honey of a boat, and we kept it in the family for many years.

Then after buying my own cottage a decade or so later, I ended up purchasing a brand-new fiberglass Bayliner cabin cruiser from Okoboji Boats, dubbing it "Little Nelle." It was certainly a lot of fun, even on colder days, and we loved having an ice box and a sink to take friends on cocktail cruises at night. The only real drawback after a late outing on the water was that our cottage sat up on a very high bank, which meant climbing 72 steps to get from the dock back up to the house—it's no wonder my legs are so sore today!

The Jewett cottage had originally been purchased in the name of Pops' insurance and investment company, D. L. Jewett & Sons. When Pops passed away in 1951, his business and the lake place were inherited by my father, Gerald, and his two brothers, Warren and Homer. Dad and Uncle Homer were still actively involved in management of the Jewett Lumber Company, while Uncle Warren was the one who typically ran D. L. Jewett & Sons. Warren decided he'd like to learn to fly, supposedly in order to do a better job selling aviation insurance… the truth was that he loved flying! When WWII started, Uncle Warren enlisted in the Army Air Corps as a service pilot… but really just so he could fly government planes! [The current United States (U.S.) Air Force was originally known as 'The Aeronautical Division of the U.S. Army' prior to WWI, and then as 'The Aviation Section of the U.S. Army' during that actual war. By 1918, it was called the 'U.S. Army Air Service' until 1926, after which it was known as the 'U.S. Army Air Corps' until 1941, and then as the 'U.S. Army Air Forces,' during WWII. It wasn't until 1947 that the air division became a separate military service known as the 'U.S. Air Force.']

As a side note, the man who originally lived next door to us at Okoboji in the 40's owned several filling stations, and he very kindly offered us gasoline coupons when fuel was being rationed during and even after WWII. We obviously weren't flying an airplane during that time of rationing, but continued driving cars to the Lakes regularly. Since we owned a lumber company with delivery trucks and vehicles needing fuel, we were usually able to get plenty of coupons, but we did take our neighbor up on his offer to fill our tanks in Spirit Lake a couple of times. We had understood that government inspectors went around to the various oil stations during those years, checking the dipsticks in the tanks to make sure the owners were properly complying with the rationing and were keeping accurate records of amounts dispersed. It was interesting to learn that many station owners had ways of getting around the compliance tests by mismarking the dipsticks, knowing the inspectors would never actually dig up the tanks to double-check the levels.

My father eventually bought out the Okoboji cottage interest of his two brothers, and began to use that lake home for business as well as pleasure. He regularly entertained many lumber industry associates and customers up at the lake and kept a detailed log of who was staying there and when. He even let some customers take over the whole place for a week or so. Every year, the Master Builders of Iowa held a convention at Lake Okoboji, and we always threw a gala cocktail party for them—about 100 people showed up at our cottage for those. I always flew up food from the Des Moines Club, along with a waiter in full uniform who then set up all the food and served as the bartender (Dad and I helped too).

We also held another annual event up at my folks' cottage, where our competing male lumber dealer owners (15 or 16 of us) would gather for a fun getaway weekend, purely for pleasure and camaraderie. Each year we had a different theme for the party—this shot is from the time we were all firemen and had the City's fire truck pick us up at our cottage and take us to dinner and

back. (Jen says I'm the guy with 'one leg up' on the competition.) One year we were fishermen, another year sailors, etc. We once rented the big Queen excursion boat and spent the day riding around on it before having dinner in the Park. The guys always enjoyed sticking with the theme throughout the entire two days, and it was a lot of fun. We never had meetings during those outings, so as not to be accused of any price-setting.

One year, Dad and I decided on a Western motif for the lumbermen's outing, with slot machines and so forth. For that particular party, I stopped in to see a guy in Des Moines who loaned out vending machines, including slots. The machines were illegal in Iowa, but the police just didn't seem to enforce the law against using them—this guy had put slots in places all around the Lakes, like The Okoboji Club and the Higgins Mansion in Millers Bay. So, I told the owner of the Des Moines operation that I wanted three slot machines in nickel, dime, and quarter denominations and that I'd like them delivered around 4:30 in the afternoon on the Friday of the outing, to be picked back up on Sunday afternoon around 4:30. He immediately dialed his secretary to put him through to 'so-and-so' in Arnolds Park. The Friday of the party, I was up at the cottage getting things ready and, at exactly 4:30 sharp that afternoon, a pickup truck backed up to the cottage, driving across the yard. Two guys got out, threw a tarp over the slot machines, walked directly into the cottage without knocking, placed the machines on the big long dining room table, and walked out.

Then on Sunday afternoon at precisely 4:30, the same pickup truck again backed across the yard and up to the door. Two men walked into our cottage without knocking, found their slot machines, threw a tarp over them, carried them back out to the truck, and drove off! The years we didn't go to the Okoboji Jewett cottage for our annual lumbermen's retreat, we guys still went on an outing together to places like Woodland Park, Colorado; Marcell, Minnesota; International Falls, Minnesota; Saratoga, Wyoming; Santa Fe, New Mexico; Portland, Oregon; Divide, Colorado; Grant, Colorado; Libby, Montana; East Glacier, Montana; Hot Springs, Arkansas; San Francisco and Northern California (Redwood Forest); and Vancouver, British Columbia. Dad and Homer and I made great memories during those trips, and a good time was had by each and every guy.

Prior to Dad purchasing the Okoboji property from his brothers in the late '60s, Uncle Warren and his wife Dorothy had already moved with their two daughters [Margaret Ann and Mary Frances] from Des Moines. They lived in San Antonio, Texas during WWII service days and after, then I believe they next moved directly to Pueblo, Colorado, where their third child [son David Warren Jewett, Jr.] was born. They eventually retired in San Antonio, but later ended up out west, living the rest of their lives near their children in Colorado Springs. Other than myself, Uncle Warren outlived all the Jewetts, passing away less than eight weeks before his 92nd birthday (suffering periods of dementia in his final months). [David Warren Jewett, Sr. had been born on February 14, 1901, in Des Moines, Iowa and died on December 23, 1992, in Colorado Springs, Colorado. Dorothy Izene Shaw Jewett was born February 25, 1907, in Garden Grove, Iowa, and died on November 13, 1991, in Colorado Springs, Colorado. They had been married on June 10, 1933.]

Uncle Homer and Aunt Marie and their sons [David Homer and Thomas Edward] had remained in Des Moines, where Homer was active in the family lumber business for all those years. Then in 1967, my aunt and uncle moved full-time into a new home they had built on the northeast part of West Lake Okoboji, just south of the Methodist Camp. Their son, Tom, recently mentioned that the new house had been his parents' joint dream and retirement project, though they evidently had first looked at lovely potential residences on Lake Geneva in Wisconsin. I hadn't realized they were looking elsewhere at the time, and am so glad they didn't move away—it was terrific seeing and being with my uncle and aunt up at Okoboji. When finally residing at the lake year-round, Uncle Homer enjoyed some product sales work in the general offices of Berkley and Company in nearby Spirit Lake. [The Berkley firm got its start in 1937 as a local manufacturer of fishing tackle and was, by the time Homer started working there, gaining international recognition]. After Aunt Marie passed away at the young age of 62, Homer eventually remarried, retired from Berkley, and moved to Austin, Texas, where he and his second wife lived out the rest of their lives. [Homer Henry Jewett was born on December 7, 1908, in Des Moines, Iowa and died on April 14, 1996, in Austin, Texas. His first wife, Marie Lampman Jewett, was born on April 10, 1911, in New York City, New York and died May 28, 1973, in Spirit Lake, Iowa. They had been married on August 11, 1934.]

My cousin Tom wrote a 'fond memory' note to me for my 91ˢᵗ birthday, recalling his gratitude after Connie and I drove down to Austin for our Uncle Homer's funeral. He thanked me in the note, adding, "It was an amazing courtesy that touched all of us." And Connie and I were so glad to have been able to be there too. On the trip to and from Austin, she and I stayed in motels along the way, getting *two* rooms upon checking in—Connie thought it was funny that I found it necessary to explain at each motel that the lovely woman with me was my sister! (Just for the record, Connie and I had made that round-trip in a brand-new 1996 Cadillac, one of my 'retirement' gifts received from Gilcrest/Jewett. I really disliked that car because the back fenders came down over the wheels too far— it just was *not* a good look, and the fenders were a son of a gun to clean!)

Once the Jewett cottage belonged solely to my folks, I spent many of my winters remodeling it by insulating walls and ceilings, paneling various rooms, changing out some of the windows, and the like. When it came time to replace the outside siding and install new roofing, we got a contractor from Des Moines and let him live in the house with his  family while he finished up the rest of the work. Every single day of that month-long outdoor project, the guy and his son started working at 8 AM, and every single afternoon they stopped at 4 PM to go fishing and boating—it was a win-win for both of us. They also rebuilt the big boathouse entirely and replaced the wonderful large deck on top of it.

At a later date, we had a foundation dug under part of the house, with a cement floor and an outside stairway to get to it. We put the original furnace down in the basement after converting it to oil, then a friend helped me run a heat duct to the first floor and another one up to the second floor—we didn't run heat to any of the seven bedrooms or to the bathrooms, but it was a big improvement over what we had. After running the ducts, my friend and his wife spent the night in a lower level bedroom through which the new plenum ran to the upstairs. They laughed when recently reminding me how the two of them were shocked to wake up that morning and see black faces when looking at each other—the dang furnace had backfired in the night! I guess we were all lucky that we lived to tell the story of taking on a project like that without really knowing what we were doing. That same couple were part of a group who flew up to the cottage with me on another winter weekend, only to learn upon our arrival that the house water pipes were frozen. My friend who had helped me install the new furnace system took it upon himself to try to thaw out the pipes with a blowtorch. While he spent the next hour down in the cold basement, the rest of us toasted him with an extra long cocktail hour before leaving for dinner—the guy still won't let me forget that weekend either!

MY JEWETT HERITAGE, IN PART

Halfway through my sophomore year at Roosevelt High School, back on January 2, 1941, a local physician had removed a cyst from the side of my neck—the operation was in the same area as the mastoidectomy I'd had twelve years before. I remember that day well because there had been a big snowstorm starting on New Year's Eve (December 31, 1940), making it difficult and dangerous for people to drive anyplace in Des Moines for a few days. Early on that New Year's Eve, I was driving Mom's brand-new 1940 yellow Mercury four-door just to show it off to my friends. It was already snowing, so I was being extra careful. After first stopping at Reed's in the Roosevelt Shopping Center, the plan was to drive on over to an annual party at the big south-side home of one of my friends. Unfortunately, the snowstorm started to get really bad while I was at Reed's, and my mother's new Mercury got stuck in the alley behind the shopping center. I had to leave it there while I found another ride to the party that evening. The snow kept accumulating overnight and when I was able to return to retrieve her car the next day, the snow had drifted over the top of it because of being up next to the building. It was still rather dangerous to be out on the streets, but somehow my friends and I braved it and got over to Reed's—we finally dug out Mom's car that New Year's Day, then had to also shovel the alley enough so that I could drive it out and get her vehicle safely home.

The day after that, on January 2 of 1941, I was already pre-scheduled to have the cyst removed from the side of my neck. It was still dangerous for people to drive around Des Moines due to the snowstorm's aftermath, and my folks didn't want to take any chances getting me to the hospital for that procedure. They were going to call the surgeon and cancel the whole thing, but I wasn't at all worried about driving—it was just another automobile adventure to me. I still had my Model A Cabriolet at that time and had installed snow chains on the front and rear tires, so it was easy getting around. They finally agreed that I could drive myself downtown, even though I was fifteen with only a school permit. So, I hopped in the car and headed down to the hospital.

While driving there that day, I can still remember thinking about my grandmother Margaret (Jewett) telling me of her early days as a little girl walking to school. Her former school building was once located in the southern section of Methodist Hospital, right where I was headed…

My grandmother's parents, George Anson Jewett and Annie Henry Jewett, were married in 1868; by 1869, they'd built a fine two-story house "out west in the country" in the 1200 block of Locust. Readers who know Des Moines will appreciate that the now-bustling Locust was not yet a street back then—it was more of a wide dirt path. Annie talked of her husband George climbing a fence to pick out the lot he wanted to purchase on the undeveloped block, and that sounded like such a fun adventure to me.

Most houses back then were big and deep and sat close to the roadway—and theirs was no exception. The Jewett's horse and buggy barn (carriage house) was behind their 1219 Locust Street home, with its back driveway that came in off Grand Avenue. A young 22-year-old George Jewett had invested a total of $5,000 to purchase the land and build the stately place, where he and his family then lived for the next 37 years, selling it in 1906 for

$27,000. He was a big advocate of home ownership and considered it a great investment.

George and Annie Jewett lost their first child during or shortly after her birth [their daughter had died on April 15, 1870—the little gravestone marked 'Our Baby' sits among the others in the Jewett plot at Des Moines' Woodland Cemetery], but were later blessed with two more healthy daughters, Bonnie Ella [born July 22, 1872], and her little sister Margaret [born December 6, 1877]. Margaret, who became my grandmother, told me that she and Bonnie walked to school every day by going down Locust and climbing over a stile at 12th Street, and then heading north on 12th Street to 'Callanan College' (which was not at all like what we know as a 'college' today—it was actually a grade school, junior high, and high school). The Jewetts were friends of the Callanans, a pioneer family who had started the 'college' and who lived on the northwest corner of 28th and High Streets, which is now the Scottish Rite Park retirement campus. My grandmother told me she used to "just love" going to tea parties at the big Callanan home (and I could picture her doing that, especially as a young girl, but sure couldn't understand how anybody would "just love" going to one of those!).

[James Callanan was a prominent Des Moines banker and land speculator who owned all the property from High Street on the south to Center Street on the north, and from 28ᵗʰ Street on the east to 31ˢᵗ Street on the west. After the death of Mr. Callanan in 1904, the original homestead at 28ᵗʰ and High Street became a facility for the mentally ill, first known as Hill's Retreat and later as Hillcrest Hospital by 1948. The hospital closed in 1964, and was eventually torn down to make way in 1973 for the ten-acre Scottish Rite Park. Much of the remainder of the family land was eventually sold to the city, and still houses three schools—Ruby Van Meter, Smouse, and Callanan.]

I understood that the original Callanan College had been started by James Callanan in about 1879, the same year my great-grandfather established his lumber business in town. Due to the eventual growth of public and private schools, the Callanan College that my grandmother attended was closed by the end of the century. In 1900, the Methodist Hospital Association was formed in Des Moines, and Mr. Callanan was approached as a potential benefactor—he sold to the Association (and apparently for a very low price) the two buildings that had once been Callanan College, and Iowa Methodist Hospital officially opened its doors there in 1901.

So, as a fifteen-year-old kid with only a school permit, I was headed downtown on snowy streets in my 1930 Cabriolet to have the cyst removed, and to have it done in the very same building where my grandmother attended school as a little girl all those decades earlier! Incidentally, when a new public middle school was built at 31ˢᵗ and Center in 1927, on the northwest end of the property owned by the Callanan's, it was named 'Callanan Junior High.' And of course, that's the school to which I had daily driven the same Cabriolet while attending there! Everything in Des Moines really does somehow seem connected when you have lived this long.

When I was growing up, Grandmother Margaret's folks were still very much alive, and I especially spent a good deal of time with my great-grandfather, George. He didn't die until I was almost nine, and he let me ride all over the place with him in his chauffeured 1923 Jewett, a big four-door sedan. As the reader already knows, George Anson Jewett was an active Des Moines businessman, but I haven't spent much time talking about his humble beginnings and his enormous efforts as a church leader, philanthropist, world traveler and, in later years, genealogist. A decade or so ago, my cousin, Tom Jewett, compiled George Anson's personal *Memoirs* and other historical records to produce a book about his unbelievable life; my daughter, Jennifer, more recently copyedited and helped revise it for an updated 2015 re-publication of *George Anson Jewett, Pioneering Iowa Entrepreneur: In His Own Words*.

I've decided to spend some time telling more about my great-grandfather in this book about me, because I was in so many ways shaped by him—you'll soon learn why he was considered such an amazing individual! Also, his story gives a good peek into the early formation days of Central Iowa and the city of Des Moines…

GEORGE ANSON JEWETT, A MOST AMAZING MAN

My great-grandfather, George A. Jewett, was a 'Dapper Dan' type of gentleman who always wore a suit and necktie—every single day he looked like a successful businessman, which he was. Even when having this picture taken with his first grandchild (my Dad) George looks ready to head to an important function. I never, ever saw my great-grandfather dressed any other way, even on a relaxing weekend (but I'm not sure he ever really relaxed!) He had been known for many years by his full head of white hair and bushy white mustache, much like the famous Mark Twain (Samuel Clemens). I'll tell later about the personal meetings with Clemens, considered his look-alike in those days.

By the time I came along, though, the elder George (now holding his little *great*-grandson, Jerry) was clean-shaven, resembling Luther Burbank and Thomas Edison—believe it or not, you'll be reading about his personal meetings with both of those look-alikes too! In this second photo, the little boy who lovingly embraced his grandfather in the above shot has grown up and become my father, standing behind me here.

George Anson Jewett was born in a Red Rock, Iowa log cabin on September 9, 1847 [he liked to say, "on the ninth day of the ninth month, at nine minutes after nine," but *time* of birth is not confirmed] to George "Enoch" Jewett and Patty Maria (Matthews) Jewett. He was the middle child of three, having an older brother and a younger sister. Little George was born into a long line of pioneering and adventurous people, on his father's Jewett side *and* on his mother's Matthews and Bell sides. These early pioneers were a restless bunch, always ready to move west from territory to territory, conquering new land. George's grandparents and parents were no exception, and had made their own moves westward—settling in Red Rock was due to it being as far west in Iowa as the white man was allowed to go at the time.

[Much like the 'Call' and 'Sprague' family lines discussed earlier in this book, the 'Jewett' and 'Matthews' lines also include men who were willing to abandon their homes to sail from England and Wales in the mid-1600's seeking liberty and peace as Puritans in America. They proactively helped to settle new towns (i.e., the Spragues in Charlestown and Malden, Massachusetts; the Jewetts in Rowley, Massachusetts; the Matthews' in New Haven, Connecticut). They were also the leaders of new colonies (i.e., ancestor Governor Thomas Dudley of Massachusetts, and his daughter, Anne Dudley Bradstreet, considered the first American poetess). These forefathers quickly moved inland after arriving on the Massachusetts shores, far less fearful about being attacked by Indians than about being attacked by sea—disgruntled English were increasingly enraged about the departure of so many thousands from that country. The lifestyle of those first newcomers to America is worth noting. One of George's cousins wrote about her own father's description of his early life here in America: "The first settlers had to be entirely self-sufficient. The farmsteads had to supply almost all human needs. The virgin forest had to be laid low and rocks removed to open up fields for cultivation. Iron nails were rarely used and their place was taken by wooden pegs of all sizes which met every conceivable need. Horses were at first almost unknown; only oxen were used. The women manufactured all the clothing used and the food eaten by their families. They crushed wheat and corn in hand-turned stone mills, producing flour for bread and porridge. Pigs, sheep, scrawny cattle, and wild game provided meats and fats. Sweets were wild honey and maple syrup. Tea was scarce, coffee unknown. Sheep furnished pelts and wool for clothing. The women clipped the wool, washed, corded, spun and wove it into cloth, and then they tailored it into the satisfactory linsey-woolsey garments of colonial times. Luxuries were few or unknown. The farmsteads yielded two rich returns, abundant crops and numerous children. The land was virgin soil untouched for numberless centuries. Life was simple, wants were few."]

Little George Anson Jewett must have felt the brunt of that generational restlessness when his father, George "Enoch" Jewett, soon left his wife and children in Iowa to embark on a journey to California in April of 1849… young Homer was not quite 7, George was just 1½, and baby Cora was either a newborn or soon-to-be-born. [Cora's full date of birth has never been determined, other than the year of 1849. There had also been another daughter born to Enoch and Patty—first child, Mary, born in 1840, died in infancy.] Gold fever had swept America, and 29-year-old "Enoch" Jewett hoped to strike it rich for his family. And he was not alone, as over 55,000 Americans were lured to California that April. One of Enoch's cousins later wrote of such a westward trek, "If we could have foreseen the trials that were before us, the experiences we would pass through, I think we would have paused and retreated. Our better judgment would have told us to remain and be content. But it was a hopeful, ambitious company that started from that little town that morning, lured by the imaginative glitter of the far famed golden fields."

Enoch and a group of relatives and friends from the Red Rock, Iowa area had planned their trip for some time, then finally started out on their journey with 18 wagons, some horses and cattle, and all their wares. The group safely reached the planned California destination in seven months, with Enoch journaling his travels along the way. My cousin, Tom Jewett, compiled another book several years ago about George Enoch's journey too (*It is One*

Grand Rush For Gold: George E. Jewett's 1849-1850 California Gold Rush Journal), and Jennifer recently copyedited and did additional research on it to help Enoch's journey really come alive for modern readers. It's such a compelling story.

Anyway, Enoch Jewett never returned to Iowa and was eventually divorced by Patty for desertion in 1852 (the same year Homer and George Anson's little sister, Cora, died!). So, Patty was legally left to rear her two sons alone. It's interesting that great-grandfathers on both sides of my family (George Anson Jewett and Ambrose Adolphus Call) were 'orphaned' in their early lives… George at age 1½ due to the *desertion* of his father, and Ambrose just prior to his birth due to the *death* of his father. It's tough for me to imagine making it in the world without my own wonderful Dad by my side every step of the way, and certainly makes me further appreciate these two great-grandfathers of mine—men who were on their own from an early age, and yet developed the drive and determination to become such fine husbands, fathers, and leaders in their communities.

I remember my great-grandfather George telling me about having fun playing as a little kid with the Indians. He referred to them as the boys of the forest… "I could really beat the socks off the boys of the forest at marbles, but they always outshot me with bows and arrows!" He also told me that the boys of the forest could come across a line to play, but that the white boys couldn't go across it in the other direction. In his eventual personal *Memoirs*, George A. wrote, "The Treaty of 1843 [sic] had said that the white man must not go west of a line drawn north and south which crossed the Des Moines River at the Red Rocks. A large tree was blazed (the bark cut off) about 4 or 5 inches and I.B. for Indian Boundary cut into it. Many a time we boys were told not to disturb or mar that tree. The Indians would come there and camp, knowing they had a right to be west of that tree." *{Editor's note: George was surely referring to the famous Treaty of 1842 (rather than 1843), which stated that the white man could not move west of this particular 'line' through the Iowa country until midnight on October 11, 1845.}*

[Two of George's uncles, along with his grandfather Matthews, were present at the signing of the Treaty of 1842. Also in attendance was Keokuk, the chieftain of the Sac and Fox Indians at the time. One book on the early history of Des Moines states, "Although the United States had acquired legal ownership of the Iowa country by the Louisiana Purchase, it was necessary to make arrangements for the possession of the land with the Indians, who still regarded it as their home. Sales of their land by the Indians to the whites were known as Indian land cessions. When a cession was to be made, a treaty council was held… after days, sometimes weeks, of bargaining, an agreement would be reached, whereby the government usually promised to pay to the tribe a certain amount of money, and to give them certain goods such as tobacco, cloth, powder, and blankets, in exchange for the desired strip of land."]

Patty's family, the Matthews clan, had put down strong roots in the Red Rock area—one of her brothers built the first sawmill (another original lumber company showing up in our family again!) and one of her brothers also built the first flour mill and opened a general mercantile store in that section of the state. They had all been so helpful in caring for Patty and her children after Enoch left Iowa for California gold. But it was Patty's desire that both of her boys attend the Preparatory Department of the recently founded and Baptist-affiliated school in nearby Pella. [Central College, then called the Central University of Iowa College, did not become affiliated with the Reformed Church in America until 1916.] Homer was 16 and George almost 10 when Patty moved with her sons from Red Rock to Pella in 1857. George wrote of walking barefoot behind a wagon full of their household goods, when a man rode up alongside him on horseback and asked, "Where you moving to, Bud?" George said he proudly answered, "To Pella, to go to school!" He had already loved being a student, but was so excited to love it even more!

My great-great-grandmother, Patty, paid the tuition costs of her sons by boarding other students in a little frame house she rented just across the street from the northwest corner of the school. George recorded that the house they rented had a pump and that it was the first he'd ever seen, having always carried water from a spring to their little home while living in Red Rock. And when first seeing the Central College building, he wrote of his surprise at its size… "It seemed an immense affair... I could easily have been convinced that it was the largest building in the whole world." He also heard a bell ring for the first time in his life, and "finally located from whence came the sound… the top of the College building. I went over and boy-like climbed the stairs and ladder until I was standing by the bell." George began school at Central on his tenth birthday, September 9, 1857. In later years, he wrote, "I have often heard 'Big Ben' in London in the tower of the House of Parliament, claimed to be the loudest bell in the world, but Big Ben never sounded half as loud as did Old Central's bell on the 9th day of September 1857. I have often stood to listen to the beautiful chimes of Bow Church 'Bow Bells' in London, claimed to be the sweetest toned bells in the world, but Bow Bells never sounded half so sweet as did Old Central College bell on the 9th of September 1857."

[Central had been founded in 1853 by the Baptist Church, with a total of 37 students. The first real campus building, known as Old Central, was erected in 1857, the year George and Homer began school there. By then, there were 190 male and female students enrolled in the 'Primary,' 'Academic,' and 'Preparatory' Departments. Annual tuition was $9 for Primary students (like George), and $12 for Academic students (like his older brother, Homer). By the 1859-60 school year, the Preparatory Dept. had expanded to a full four-year 'Collegiate' Dept., and had 227 students—one could now earn a B.S. or an A.B. degree from Central. By then both George and Homer were in the

Collegiate Dept., which cost a whopping $20 annual tuition for each boy.] George just loved that institution and the fact that so many kids from Marion County took advantage of it. He liked being in the same school with his brother and other older students and enjoyed taking part in important activities along with them. In 1860, during the Lincoln-Hamlin Presidential campaign, George helped organize a junior 'Wide Awake Club' so that young students in his grade could take part in debates about the issue of slavery and why it was important to campaign for Abraham Lincoln. He later wrote, "We were in earnest as if the fate of the union depended on these debates."

But then the Civil War broke out in 1861, and all but two (due to physical handicaps) Central College male students enlisted, as did the Dean himself. The school President announced that Central would have to close due to its men leaving for battle, but that didn't actually happen. George's brother, Homer, was so excited about going to war; his little brother badly wanted to enlist along with Homer, but at 13½ was too young. George had been such an excellent and enthusiastic schoolboy but, with no student boarders left to rent her little house, Patty was forced to take him out of Central. Younger students and women had to take the place of their enlisted men in doing the field work and becoming breadwinners for their families, so George followed suit...

He and his mother moved out to the farm of his uncle, George Reynolds, and young George Jewett worked for various farmers. Soon after, two members of the Central faculty [Mrs. Drusilla Allen Stoddard and Professor Rev. Dr. Emanuel H. Scarff] who had grown to love and admire George's educational prowess, drove out to the farm of his relatives to talk with him, suggesting he work in the fields during the day and do school studies during the evenings—they even offered to meet with him on Saturdays to listen to his school recitations. George and his mother found that to be a good plan. In an October 20, 1861 letter to his enlisted brother, George assured Homer that he was still able to be in school after all... "Mrs. Gunn offered me my school free and Ms. Setters offered me my boarding for $1 per week if mother would do my washing and furnish a bed." George recorded that he took "frequent examinations" on the weekends over the next three years, and eventually graduated from the Central institution in 1864. [George wrote that one teacher who listened to his recitations (calling her "Mother Stoddard") was "kind, gentle, and loving but not too lenient; while sympathizing with (me) over hard tasks, she yet commanded that they be mastered. (I) would sit up all night, hard at work on my lessons, rather than see that look of pain cross her face on account of a failure in recitation."]

During the three years living on the farm with his Uncle Reynolds, George got to participate in the famous Underground Railroad, helping slaves escape to freedom like my other great-grandfather, Ambrose Call, had done in a smaller way up in Algona. One historical record states that George Jewett was "driving a wagon of runaway slaves in the silence of night from one home to another, and thus, although but a boy in years, he aided in the work whereby negroes were secretly advanced from one point to another until they reached freedom in Canada." (In a much later 1927 letter to the *Des Moines Register*, my eighty-year-old great-grandfather recounted that amazing chapter of his youth firsthand…

"I am much interested in the articles running in the magazine section of the Sunday Register. I note it spoke about John Brown being at Red Rock in 1857. I remember it well. I was ten years old at the time. I can see him now as he walked about the town with his long white hair and remember the excitement occasioned by his talks about the slaves. In fact, as I heard my elders discuss the matter I too became much enthused and later it bore fruit, as I was working for a farmer and he was a strong abolitionist and he was notified that it was his turn to go with a covered wagon for some slaves. He was not well and could not go and I volunteered to go in his stead. I went to the 'Nine Mile House' midway between Pella and Oskaloosa [near current Leighton, IA] and the next big barn was the station on the underground railway, and here I got them and took them to the big red barn of Allen Tice, just below Monroe… they were to go from there the next day to the barn of J. B. Grinnell, which was the next station." George recorded making two such trips transporting slaves from the station at Nine Mile House.) [And in George's later *Memoirs* (written at age 83), he takes proud responsibility for his *own family's* connection to the Abolitionist events… "John Brown *and my grandfather* Osee Matthews would sit and talk for hours and I stood by and listened." He also wrote that it was *his own uncle*, George Reynolds, who had been too ill to drive the team of horses that night. It is unknown whether or not the personal familial connection had been intentionally omitted from his 1927 letter to the *Register*.]

After graduating from Central in 1864, and having saved up his farming wages of fifty cents per day for three and a half years, George Anson Jewett left for Chicago in January of 1865 to study Bookkeeping and Commercial Law for a semester at a business school there. [Bryant and Stratton's Commercial College had been established in 1854 in Buffalo, New York, and is still in existence in several cities today. Many prominent businessmen have graduated from the Bryant and Stratton programs over the years, most notably Henry Ford and John D. Rockefeller. One of George's letters from school tells of his original meeting with Professor Bryant himself.] George journaled, "While I was there I commenced to pay $5.00 per week for board but soon saw my money would not hold out for me to finish so I and another young man rented a room at 162 Michigan Ave. (old numbering) at $2.50 per week and kept 'batch' and I got through." The next page shows a shot of the seventeen-year-old George Jewett in 1865, after having just graduated from commercial college in June of that year (not looking much like Mark Twain just yet).

George purchased a railway ticket back to Marion County, Iowa, leaving him with $1.00 to his name. After working a short while at the local lumberyard [Snow and Huber's] and helping in the country to harvest fields, he had again saved enough money to leave Pella, this time to find permanent work in 'the big city.' There were no railroads running to Des Moines in those days, so George, while still seventeen-years-old, *walked* the forty miles there in search of a job as a bookkeeper. One history book states, "Colonel Hooker charged ten cents a mile to ride in his coaches, George's purse being short on dimes."

My great-grandfather arrived in Des Moines in early August of 1865. He told me that he remembered standing at the top of the hill where the State Capitol is today and looking to the west where the two rivers joined—that's when he decided Des Moines would be a wonderful place to live. He proudly told me that he paid a one-cent toll to walk across the Court Avenue Bridge. I understand that George then spent time looking for work in the business houses that were clustered around the waterfront, but couldn't find "just the right job." Feeling discouraged, he then walked *yet another* forty miles to visit his aunt and uncle, Eunice (Jewett) Thrift and Josiah M. Thrift, who had by then moved from Des Moines to Boonesboro [now 'Boone']. His uncle Josiah said he could get George a job in a local grocery store in their small town, but that his nephew would be better off to return to Des Moines, take whatever job he could find, and "stick." (Decades later, an elderly George wrote, "I followed his advice and have 'stuck' 65 years!")

The story of my great-great-great uncle, Josiah Thrift, and his importance to our early city and to our country is terribly interesting, in and of itself. I can see why my great-grandfather, George, talked about his uncle and aunt a lot. Mr. Thrift and his wife, Eunice, were considered the very first white settlers of Des Moines and were parents of the first white child to survive birth in Polk County. My great-grandfather said his Aunt Eunice told him about how the friendly local Indians would come to their door to see the little white female papoose. I've often told bits and pieces of their story when talking about the origins of our city since Eunice was the first Jewett to ever live here.

[Josiah Moffit Thrift was born in Virginia in 1815. He became a tailor by trade and eventually applied to use his craft for the government. In May of 1843, he was assigned as the tailor for the soldiers who would be stationed at Fort Des Moines. Thrift was one of the few to come with Captain James Allen on a steamboat up the Des Moines River to the fork of the Raccoon River. The men accompanying Josiah the tailor included a sutler, a blacksmith, two gunsmiths, and the soldiers themselves. The Fort was designed for one purpose—to keep the white man from encroaching upon Indian land west of the river until October 11, 1845 (a date stipulated by the Treaty of 1842). A few months into his assignment, 28-year-old Josiah left for Jefferson County, Iowa to marry and bring back to Fort Des Moines with him 19-year-old Eunice Ann Jewett, the sister of George "Enoch" Jewett. She was the first Jewett to live in Des Moines. Knowing that the tailoring position at the Fort would be only for two years, and that he and the others would be removed from their government positions after October 11, 1845, Josiah made claim to a tract of land just north on the Des Moines River bank, in what is now known as Des Moines' Union Park. The Thrifts built a log home on a knoll there. Their baby, Hannah Jane, was born in the little cabin on March 15, 1845, and was the first white child to survive birth in Polk County. (Two years later, on October 15, 1847, son William Hulbert Thrift was born in the same cabin.)

When expecting their first baby, Eunice Jewett Thrift wanted her parents to be present, so David Lewis Jewett and Marie Bosteeder Jewett came to Des Moines for the birth of their granddaughter and stayed on, later claiming land (old Capitol Park) to farm just east of the Thrift's Union Park cabin. (David and Marie were also the parents of George "Enoch" Jewett, who left for the gold rush four years later; thus, they were the grandparents of George Anson Jewett as well.) David Lewis Jewett had been born in Concord (now called Lisbon), New Hampshire on April 10, 1791, moving with his father Joseph Jewett and wife, Hulda Fenton (of the family of Governor Reuben Fenton of New York), to settle first near Metz, New York in 1805 (where David later married Marie Bosteeder in 1817). David's wife and family (including his parents Joseph and Hulda) then moved to Mentor County, Ohio in 1818, living (and giving birth to their children) on property that eventually became the farm of President Garfield. The Jewett family eventually moved to Jefferson County, Iowa in 1838. Marie Bosteeder had been born in New Jersey; her mother was from Holland, and her father was Henri Louis Bosteeder, who came from France and was an officer in the Revolutionary War under General Lafayette. Marie was the widow of a first husband, David Harris Jewett, who had been killed in the war of 1812 (and with whom she had a son, Caleb Harris Jewett, born in 1811). Documents state that Marie "often said she was not sure" if her husbands, David Harris Jewett and David Lewis Jewett, were related!

By 1846, when Polk County was formed, Josiah Thrift became a member of the first Grand Jury. Eunice Jewett Thrift stayed in Des Moines with their children when Josiah then left for California gold in 1850. By the time he returned two years later and opened his own tailor shop on Second Street, the town of Fort Des Moines had become a thriving place, an important way station on one of the main stage routes to the west. By 1856, Josiah and Eunice Thrift moved forty miles northwest of Des Moines to Boonesboro, where he farmed and became Mayor of the town. Eunice's parents stayed in Des Moines, where her father, David Lewis Jewett, passed away a year later. Eunice's mother, Marie Bosteeder Jewett, ended up moving to Boonesboro, living near her daughter and son-in-law another four years. Marie was buried in a Boone County cemetery in 1872.

Josiah had been mustered into Civil War service in 1862, but was severely wounded in the Battle of Shiloh and taken prisoner for a year—though discharged in 1863, he never really recovered. Ten years later, he and Eunice moved to California in hopes of restoring his health, but Josiah died in Sacramento in August of 1881, just four days shy of his 63rd birthday. Eunice Jewett Thrift remained in San Francisco, losing her home and all possessions to fire caused by the great earthquake of 1906. She then moved in with her son who lived nearby, Sabin D. Thrift, and died at his home on January 5, 1913, at the age of 88. Josiah Thrift's service to our young country was considered of great importance; he and his wife, Eunice, are buried side-by-side in the San Francisco National Cemetery. (Their eldest son, William Hulbert Thrift, went on to serve our country as well and is buried in Arlington National Cemetery. In addition to a long military career in the United States Army and in the Iowa National Guard, William had also served six months in the Northern Iowa Border Brigade, stationed at Spirit Lake to protect settlers against Indian raids—interestingly, that is the same Brigade with which Algona settlers, Captain Ambrose Call and Captain William Ingham, had been affiliated during those years immediately following the Spirit Lake massacre!)]

While George Anson Jewett was putting down roots in Des Moines, his brother (Homer Harris Jewett) was keeping journals of his own life experiences in Civil War service and after its conclusion. According to an excerpt from yet another family history book [Tom Jewett's *Failed Ambition: The Civil War Journals and Letters of Cavalryman Homer Harris Jewett*], there is a letter of record that Homer and George's father, "Enoch" Jewett, had sent money from California to Homer, and perhaps on more than one occasion. But at another time, Homer wrote about feeling 'deserted' and in financial difficulties, so nobody really knows what happened. What we *do* know is that Homer had enlisted on September 17, 1861 ["Co. D, 7th Mo. Cav., at Oquaqa, Illinois, as 6th Corp. Mustered October 3, 1861. Promoted to Reg. Com. Sergt. July 17, 1863. Slightly wounded at Independence, Mo. and taken prisoner; exchanged. Promoted to captain 112th V.S.I.C., January 1865; detailed on special duty; assisted in closing up government business, selling off horses and other supplies at Monroe, La. January 1866."] and had ended up, states one historical source, "working in the secret service… having let his hair grow long, with his dark, handsome face he readily passed for a Southerner." The account continues, "Going through the war with credit, he entered upon the business of buying and shipping cotton. Suddenly letters from him ceased coming, and from that time to this the fate of brave Homer Jewett has been one of the mysteries no one seems able to fathom." Even the records from Central College state, "War Department in Washington say(s) that was the last they knew. He had served as a spy on many occasions, let his hair grow long for that purpose. At Washington, they say he was reported to have been recognized as a one-time spy and shot."

Homer seemed to have inherited his father Enoch's wanderlust, as well as a sense of danger and risk-taking in speculating on new ventures. He may have returned home to visit his mother (Patty) and brother (George) in 1865—I'd like to think that George got to see his older brother one last time before leaving on his walk to Des Moines in search of work. My great-grandfather never talked about his brother around me and, though George was quite a writer, didn't seem to leave much in the way of records about Homer either. But my grandmother, Margaret (George's daughter), said that her father never gave up hope in his lifetime search to find out what happened to his brother. A final letter from Homer had been sent to his mother and brother from Monroe, Louisiana, and was dated March 9,

1866; after that date, the 23-year-old Homer [born May 8, 1842] was never heard from again. The family archives still contain several love letters from admiring women who were patiently awaiting his return home in order to marry them! His mother, Patty, "to the end, longed to know the fate of her never returned home son Homer." Not long after George Anson moved to Des Moines and got settled with a job and a church home, he also brought his mother from Red Rock. Patty lived a full life and was lovingly cared for by George until her passing in 1904, almost 40 years later.

My great-grandfather indeed found work in Des Moines, as detailed earlier in this book. And once he found a job, George's next priority was to find a good church fit. He and his brother Homer had been reared by Patty in the Christian tradition, and both grew to be patriotic men of very deep faith. They had all been members of the Baptist Church in Pella, and George had been baptized in the Des Moines River on February 2, 1860, at age 12. (The first money he ever earned was $1, after gathering blackberries from the woods and selling them in town—he said his mother suggested he give ten cents of that dollar to the church, which he gladly did, and regular tithing became his habit after that… though he paid no attention to stopping at the normal 10 percent). George soon joined [as its 158th member] the new Central Church of Christ (Disciples), where he was quickly elected Church Clerk. The upstart Central Church had just been organized three years earlier, and he was drawn to that group of people by their sincere commitment to helping change Des Moines for the better.

George also became involved right away in other local outreaches and projects. In 1866, at age nineteen, he was appointed a representative of the Smithsonian Institution in Washington, D.C., which was then in charge of the country's weather services. For this position, specific instruments were sent to my great-grandfather here in Des Moines and it is documented that "three times a day he took the state of the weather, which was printed every morning in the *Daily Register* and every week he made his report to Washington… he was the pioneer of the Weather Bureau Service in Des Moines." [No other prior weather records exist in Des Moines other than fragments that had been kept at the Army Post of the original Fort Des Moines from June 1844 to February 1846. Though uncertain where the weather records are archived these days, copies of the few we have show they were at one time, in more recent years, "in possession of State Climatologist, Harry Hillaker, at the Des Moines Airport, 2nd floor."]

George felt that Des Moines should have a religious and social club where its young men could meet in order to address civic concerns; so, by age twenty, he was credited with establishing the first YMCA here! Documents show that George held the inaugural meeting at 8 o'clock in the evening on January 27, 1868 "in the rear of the Business College on Walnut Street, over Coskerry and Tannahill's store." [Once formed, the local 'Y' group met in various locations, including the City Council chamber in 'Sherman Block' at 3rd Street and Court Avenue. Their beginning efforts in Des Moines included morning prayers, doing street preaching, holding cottage prayer meetings, employing a city missionary, and distributing money to the needy. By 1891, an actual 'Y' facility (which included a bowling alley and a large gym) was built at 4th and Grand—the building also housed the first Public Library of Des Moines, which had been chartered in 1866; the Capital City Commercial College occupied the top floor of the same building. By 1893, the city of Des Moines boasted a population of over 50,000, and the sport of basketball was formally introduced to the YMCA. The Young Men's Christian Association continued to thrive, and to become more of a 'physical activity' club in subsequent years.]

Three years after coming to Des Moines, George married Anna ("Annie") Henry, and they enjoyed another 65 years together. I'm not really certain how they met, but it was quite likely at Central Church of Christ, where she was the church's first organist. I'm also not sure what brought Annie's family from Indiana to Des Moines originally, but my great-grandmother and her parents arrived here in April of 1865, when Annie was 17. (George Jewett arrived in Des Moines four months later.)

The Henrys had moved here from the "wealthy locality" of Edinburg, Indiana, where Annie "experienced none of the hardships of pioneer days." She recalled that they came by railroad to the town of Nevada, which was as far as the railroad ran at the time. Their journey south to Des Moines then continued by stage and she told how they often "had to get out and walk around the mudholes!" When they first got to town, the Henrys lived in a house at E. 2nd and Raccoon Streets. It was documented somewhere that Annie was "not college educated due to an illness," but I don't recall ever hearing anything about my great-grandmother's early sickness. I learned that the only time George handed his Smithsonian weather-taking reigns to another person was when he and my great-grandmother were on their two-week honeymoon a couple of years after he had started keeping those records.

[Mr. and Mrs. George Jewett were married on October 28, 1868. George journaled that during their honeymoon trip, he and Annie were guests of Mr. Studebaker, the then-great wagon manufacturer, who gave them a tour of Notre Dame University. Mr. Studebaker also introduced them (on Election Day!) to Schuyler Colfax, who was a Republican Representative from Indiana at the time, and who became the 17th Vice President of the United States the next year, serving under President Ulysses S. Grant. When George was introduced to Mr. Colfax as "a good Republican from Iowa," Colfax asked, "Why is he not home then voting?" Mr. Studebaker spoke up for George, telling Mr. Colfax that George "was on better business, getting married!" There are several stories like this in Tom Jewett's book compilation about George Anson.]

The year after they wed, George and Annie had built that first two-story home at 1219 Locust Street (on the dirt path that was not really a street at all). In 1886, George's half-brother, David, likely moved in with them when he came to Des Moines from California to attend Drake. And at some point, during their 37 years in that Locust Street house, Annie's *parents*, Mary and James Henry, also moved in with George and Annie—records show that Annie's mother and father both passed away (in 1892 and in 1902) while residing at that Jewett address. The Henrys are also buried in the Jewett plot at Woodland Cemetery. [Annie's mother, Mary Oldham Henry, was of English lineage, the daughter of William Oldham and Naomi (Morphew) Oldham. She had been born in Indiana on January 30, 1830, and died in Des Moines on October 26, 1892. The Oldhams originally came from the city of Oldham, Lancashire, England, settling first in Virginia, then in North Carolina and then Tennessee. Annie's father, James Madison Henry, was of Irish lineage, the son of John Henry and Sarah (Massey) Henry. He had been born in Pennsylvania on November 21, 1815, and died in Des Moines on June 23, 1902.]

During the years that the Jewett household was 'growing,' their church was growing as well, thanks in part to the tireless work of members like George Jewett. After his marriage in 1868, George had been appointed a Deacon and was eventually elected church Treasurer by 1879. Church records state that he handled over $1 million for Central Church of Christ in that capacity for fifty-five years, with "never a cent of pay," and "never a cent off balance!" [Not only was he the church 'banker,' but one story written about George states, "Many are the small business men in Des Moines who owe their success in their own enterprises to suggestions and counsels given by this man, who has never been too busy or too exclusive to be approached by others... there is always time for those who seek his advice and help. And not a few people who have known him all through the years have asked him to become their banker—afraid to trust the regular banks but glad to trust their savings to a man whose greatest resource was, and is, business honor and fidelity." The story continues, "Greater than all (his) official positions, he has served his church as soul counselor to hundreds who have been in trouble."]

The same year (1879) that George took over as Treasurer of their rapidly growing church, he was also able to enter business for himself, choosing two good friends as partners and organizing the firm of 'Ewing, Jewett and Chandler, Lumber Merchants.' And last, but certainly not least, George organized the group of four men who met regularly together over the next two years to help found Drake University in 1881... yet another endeavor that will warrant its own chapter in this book!

By 1887, George was appointed an Elder of their church and had also started an outreach Mission Sunday School on the east side of Des Moines (which culminated in the erection of a chapel at East 12th and Des Moines Streets). That very year, he [along with Central Church's pastor, Dr. H. O. Breeden] founded and became editor of (and a regular contributor to) the monthly publication, *The Christian Worker*, devoted for many years to the interests of Christian churches in the city and with a distribution that spanned the country. Central Church of Christ moved into their permanent home on the northeast corner of 9th and Pleasant Streets in 1890. By the turn of the century, that upstart church he had joined, as its 158th member, now had a membership in the thousands (and which later grew to almost 10,000 by the time George died in 1934!). Along with the hats already listed, George also wore those of Bible school teacher and Superintendent, Secretary of the Board, and a member of most church Committees that were formed for one thing or another. One article about him stated, "... his life is a contradiction to the too prevalent opinion that the religious life and the successful business career are antagonistic forces." [Central Church of Christ eventually merged with the University Christian Church in 1971—they jointly took on the name of 'First Christian Church' by 1973. First Christian Church continues to be located across the street from Drake University—two institutions still owing so much to their strong George Anson Jewett heritage.]

I didn't know about all the things he was involved in at church, but just knew that my great-grandfather sure did spend a lot of time there. I remember being chauffeured to Central Christian with George and Annie almost every Sunday (except when I got to go to the Temple with my neighborhood friend or to Plymouth Congregational with Mom). My great-grandfather and I always sat right up in the front row at Central. I don't recall my great-grandmother sitting with us, and now realize it was probably because she was behind the scenes, playing the organ! I was considered a 'chunky' kid, which would one day make my baptism there more difficult. The minister wasn't the one who baptized me—it was another man (who later became a Mayor of Des Moines). All I really remember about that morning was that when he put my body under the water, he had a difficult time lifting me back up out of the tank!

Though Dad had grown up as a member of the Central Christian Church like his mother and her parents, my Mom had grown up as a member of St. Paul's Episcopal Church downtown. Mother later became a member of Plymouth Congregational Church of Christ, probably because it was in our own neighborhood; she usually took Connie there with her (and me too, on occasion). It's likely that my Dad went to one of his offices on Sunday mornings—I just don't remember him regularly sitting in any church pew with us. To be honest, it never even made any difference to me (and still doesn't) why my family members and others chose or belonged to one church over another. I just learned to go along with whatever might be the Sunday morning plan for that week—all that truly mattered to me is that we got together and had dinner as a big extended family afterward. As an interesting side story here, my Grandmother Margaret (George and Annie's daughter) left the Disciples of Christ church tradition in her later years, joining the First Church of Christ, Scientist. It was the building at 38th Street Place and Grand Avenue that had the long spire I used to try to balance on during its construction days when I had the pop stand on the 37th Street corner. Whenever Connie and I spent the weekend with our Jewett grandparents, we'd sometimes ride along when Pops would drop off his wife at the Christian Science Church on Sunday morning. I remember him telling us that it didn't make much sense to him for Grandmother Margaret to be worshipping there because whenever she got sick, she just called for her doctor anyway!

George was a co-founder in 1910 [9/19/10] of the Jewett Family of America, Inc. (JFA), and two years later took over as its President for the last twenty-two years of his life. [The Jewett Family of America was started as a fraternal organization for all descendants of Maximilian and Joseph Jewett (perhaps once known as 'Jowett'). The two brothers had left their home and parents (Edward, 1579-1615, and Mary Taylor Jewett,) in Bradford, England in 1638, setting sail in the summer from the port of Hull in Yorkshire on the ship named 'John of London.' They were the first Jewetts in this country, landing at Boston, Massachusetts on December 1 and calling America their new home. (Also on board the ship was this country's first printing press, later used at Harvard College.) The young Jewett brothers and a band of twenty or so Puritan families spent their first winter in the Salem area, after which they helped settle, with Reverend Ezekiel Rogers, the new town of Rowley, Massachusetts in 1639. Early documents shed interesting light on the reason(s) for the brothers leaving their native England... "Maximilian and Joseph Jewett did not come to this country as adventurers. They were men of respectability, of 'good estate,' and could probably have no hopes of improving their worldly condition by emigration. (But) they were lovers of liberty and men of distinct and well-marked religious views. They were non-

Jewett

conformists. They had too sturdy an independence, as well as too strong a sense of duty to abandon what they held a truth even in the midst of the bitterest persecution. For this reason they left their homes and sought in the wilds of

America a resting place from oppression, a spot where they and their children might enjoy freedom to worship God. They were men of thought and character. The period at which they migrated to America was one of the darkest for the Puritans. Many ministers had been silenced or suspended. Fines and the pillory, mutilation and torture, were remorselessly resorted to by the friends of Archbishop Laud to compel conformity to the ceremonies of the Established Church…"]

Both of George's daughters, along with his half-brother and all three of his grandsons, were also made early members of the Jewett Family of America, according to their Yearbook of 1912-13. As President of the organization of over 300 members at that time, George presented a copy of the Jewett Coat-of-Arms to all existing and incoming members of the Association during his years in office. After Connie and I were born in 1925 and 1930, George made us 'Life Members' of the organization as well. JFA is still in existence today, but with a membership of less than 400. My sister proudly served on its national Board of Directors back in the 1970's, and Jennifer has had a recent discussion with them about getting involved at some point as well, hoping to reignite interest with the younger generations to help strengthen and grow JFA's active membership numbers.

{Editor's note: After requesting current membership information from the organization several months ago, I told the President about this book project and how it has had a way of 'breathing new life' into old family history. He asked for a signed copy of the book once it's published, also requesting a short article about it for publication in their July 2017 issue of JFA's quarterly newsletter. The article was accompanied by a photo of Dad and me, taken a couple of years ago while standing on either side of George's big headstone in the Woodland Cemetery, our city's oldest (established in 1848). That beautiful cemetery of over 80,000 graves has, thankfully, been undergoing a major facelift over the past several months, with hundreds of crooked and lichen-covered stones now being leveled and cleaned. In honor of our ancestors, I was proud to volunteer with a group helping to wash stones last month in Block 10, putting physical action to the spiritual dimension in my very own family's historical plot. Also in honor of our ancestors, and as a surprise to Dad, my sons and grandchildren will soon be made Life Members of the Jewett Family of America.}

George was a member of the Des Moines Chamber of Commerce, and was elected Treasurer of the Des Moines Citizens Association, a "temperance organization that worked for the betterment of civic conditions." He held memberships in the National Retail Lumbermens Association and the Northwestern Lumbermens Association. A charter member of the Advertising Club of Des Moines, George was also a member of the Commercial Club, the University Club, the Grant Club, the Auto Club, the Pioneer Club, and the American Red Cross. Soon after becoming a member of the Iowa Society of the S.A.R. (Sons of the American Revolution), he was elected Secretary of the organization and became the editor of its *Old Continental* publication for the rest of his life. He also served on several Boards, including those of his beloved Drake University in Des Moines and of the other institution so close to his heart, Central College in Pella.

My great-grandfather had been an avid student of American history throughout his life and, in elder years, immersed himself in the field of genealogy. His first book on the subject, *Hunting An Ancestor* (1914), details his ventures into personal ancestral documentation, and his hope that others would do the same. ["(I) thought it might be of interest to study the building of an ordinary American family and to note the many sources from which the blood comes which flows through its veins, and that by relating (my) experience others might be induced to do likewise. By a little calculation you will see that by going back five generations you have sixty-two ancestors or going back ten generations, but 300 years, you have 2,046 ancestors..." That first book details George's trips to the New England Historic Genealogical Society rooms in Boston, then his hiring of an expert to go with him to Concord, New Hampshire after learning of his grandfather's birthplace there. Then he headed back to Boston, and again back to Concord, followed by more time spent in libraries and on the road doing research. He became consumed with detailing his past and with encouraging others to do the same.]

In 1922, George was asked by Central College to write a thesis about his ancestral findings for a Master's degree... "The Beauties of the Study of Genealogy in Connection with the Study of Contemporary History" secured his A.M. degree from that institution. And Drake awarded him the LL.D. (Doctor of Laws in English), an honorary research degree, after which he also became a Phi Beta Kappa. By 1924, George had embarked on an even deeper four-year personal ancestral search, tracing his family tree all the way back to the biblical Adam (neatly compiled in his *138 Generations From Adam*, published in 1929). Through his studies, he confirmed his ethnicity ("3/8 English, 1/4 Scottish, 1/8 Welsh, 1/8 French, and 1/8 Hollander") and discovered that he was related to many royals (i.e., a fortieth cousin of King George of England). He had also traced Annie's ancestry back to Adam through her Griffith line, connecting 135 generations. George firmly believed that most genealogical researchers would find some royal connection when tracing their own histories, due to detailed records kept by royal houses. [George wrote about his researching of tomes like Burke's *Royal Families of England*, Keating's *History of Ireland*, O'Hart's *The Lineal Descent of the Royal Family of England*, O'Clery's *The Annals of the Four Masters*, and numerous other books and documents. He stated that royal families hundreds of years ago "were careful to keep complete genealogical records... the early kings appointed their most learned men to do this." George Jewett wrote in his findings that he was not a descendant of Queen Victoria's line, but "I am of Edward I, king of England; Alfred the Great; Charlemagne; William the Conqueror, and consequently of the old royal house of Norway; of Witekind the Saxon king; Louis I of France; Pepin, king of Italy; Malcom, king of Scotland; Ferdinand, king of Castile (Spain)," etc., etc.]

{Editor's note: I treasure the copy of George's original findings, carefully pasted onto brittle pages of a navy blue leather-bound (and very fragile) 'Composition' book.}

An article that ran in the *Des Moines Register* on February 3, 1929, promoted George Jewett's extensive genealogical research project and his intention to publish the findings in the near future. The article tells of George's printed records that describe his own genealogy, documents that included the name of his ancestor in each generation along with a short history about each of them. [The author of the newspaper article begins with, "Cheer up! No matter how menial you may feel today, you are a descendent of royalty..." George is quoted in the article as saying, "It isn't difficult to trace back to Adam. After you once get started you find the royal lines have kept good records of their ancestry. They had to in order to keep their rank. And in the bible it is very easy to trace lines. The only difficult period is of Irish history." Not long after he published his work, George wrote a series of articles for several editions of *The Christian Worker* publication. In the first article, he addressed some questions that had been asked of him, giving an answer to the most frequent one... "Why do this, you ask. Why trace to the royal lines? Royal blood is no better than common blood. Yes, this is true, but it adds to the interest of history to know of a surety you are a descendent of these historical personages. How did it happen, you ask. Well, during the reigns of the Plantagenet kings and in fact other kings, (the) princes and princesses of the royal family frequently married into families of nobles and knights."]

My great-grandfather was a proud member of the Iowa State Historical Society, the New England Historic Genealogical Society, and the National Historical and National Genealogical Societies. Memberships were also held in the Rowley (Massachusetts) Historical Society, the Piscataqua (New Hampshire) Pioneer Society, and the Governor Dudley Family Association. George had such a keen interest in higher education, and was excited to learn through his genealogical pursuits that one of his ancestors had signed the charter of Harvard College, another had given the ground on which Yale was built, and yet another had donated 33 acres for the site of Dartmouth College.

It probably goes without saying, but George Anson Jewett was listed in an early *Who's Who in America*.

THE JEWETT TYPEWRITER COMPANY

Not only was my great-grandfather quite heavily involved with his family, his lumber business, his church and his community, but George also dove head-over-heels into yet another endeavor. It's pretty important to tell about the Jewett Typewriter Company, because it was quite an operation in those early days of our city.

Prior to establishing this business, George's endeavors had been of a clerical or mercantile nature (bookkeeping, building materials, and real estate), but he really loved gadgets and decided to get further involved in the mechanical industry as well. In his search for such a trade, George became interested in an invention for the application of a new principle in the construction of a typewriting machine known as the 'Duplex,' which had an unusual keyboard and was the latest invention of another Des Moines man [Adolphus S. Dennis, a business college instructor and inventor] who held twelve typewriter patents and claimed that his 'Duplex' was a faster typing machine than the others on the market.

[Homer Jewett later wrote about the uniqueness of it… "In order to understand the Duplex machine we must remember that in those early days of typewriters there was no set way to type. Most people used at most the index fingers of both hands. The Duplex machine had four keyboards—two capitals, side by side and two lower case below the capitals. In typing, if one was to type the word 'the' for example, he would strike the left lower case 't' with his left index finger and the right lower case 'h' with his right index finger at the same time. His next stroke would be to hit the left lower case 'e' with this left index finger and the space bar with his right. The principal was certainly unique and as long as one was only using his index fingers you could actually type much faster." Homer's son, Tom Jewett, recorded in one of his articles for a more recent 2016 JFA *Quarterly*, "In 1886, Remington—up till then the dominant company in the business—gave up their typewriter operations to Standard Typewriter Manufacturing Company. George A. likely sensed an opportunity here, but it would not be easy. Remington had been successful marketing their venerable No. 2 machine since 1878. Over 100,000 of the machines were sold. It was a good machine and held an important advantage over Dennis' machine. The Remington No. 2 had a shift key while Dennis' typewriter used two sets of keys."]

So, nine years after establishing his own lumber firm, my great-grandfather funded the other man's newest idea, and found himself jumping into the typewriter business (in 1888) with only two employees—both were mechanics who were constantly experimenting and perfecting the typewriting machine that was to become the 'JEWETT No. 1,' replacing the 'DUPLEX No. 2.' The plant's headquarters and factory were located in the 600 block of Locust Street, just west of where the current Equitable Building stands. [Ads show the 'Factory and Office' address at 608-610 Locust Street, and the 'City Branch Office' address at 616 Locust Street—both locations had the same telephone number: '868.']

The newly perfected typewriter wasn't ready for marketing until 1892, after which it rapidly came into worldwide prominence, especially after winning the highest awards given (the Medal and the Diploma of Honor) at the World's Fair in Chicago in 1893. Before long, the JEWETT could be found in multitudes of offices around the globe— Europe, India, Russia, Mexico, Canada, etc. In his application for membership in the New England Historic Genealogical Society many years later (1912), George boasted that he had "personally introduced it [his typewriter] into every country in the world." I remember reading that the Bank of England used the JEWETT when that institution's operations were being switched from longhand, which always impressed me. By the turn of the century, my great-grandfather had opened up typewriter company sales offices in France, England, and Germany, and was traveling overseas regularly. (He and his family had often been abroad prior to this time, so he was up to the task. My sister has our great-grandfather's eagle watermarked passport from 1885, on which his age is written as 37, and he is described this way: stature—5'11"; eyes—grayish-blue; mouth—small; hair—black, tinged with gray. George's wife and two daughters are listed as his traveling companions on that particular 1885 trip.)

The JEWETT received the Gold Medallion award at the Paris Exposition in 1900, and by 1901 (the year the Eiffel Tower was completed) it was pegged "The World's Finest Typewriter." By then the machine had also won blue ribbons at the Pan-American Exposition in Buffalo, New York in 1901 and later at the World's Fair in St. Louis in 1904. In excerpts from a 1901 publication devoted to industrial development, the Jewett Typewriter Company of Des Moines, Iowa is highlighted: "… They now have over 200 employees and their weekly payroll distributes some $2500.00 in Des Moines. While they have a good machine to sell, yet much of their success is due to the wise management of the officers and board of directors. They are all of our most highly respected citizens, and men who have been successful in their other business enterprises. No body of men in the state of Iowa stand higher than they do…"

The publication continued, "There is a surprise in store for one going through this factory.

We did not expect to find a shop so well equipped, so systematically arranged into departments as this one is. They have all modern up-to-date machinery. While they are conservative in their management, yet they are progressive. As to the shop equipments, automatic machinery enables one man to do that which under the old system would require five… all parts are made exactly alike, no material is wasted, the shop is clean… the company has adopted the idea of asking their men to think. They offer awards for the best thought for improvement of their typewriters or in the manner of their construction."

And I sure get a kick out of this final section about the company… "We find one of the most complete follow-up systems in use. A corps of stenographers are answering inquiries. If you do not want to buy a JEWETT typewriter, better not answer any of their advertisements, they never let up, you will have to buy to shut off the letters and printed matter they will send you… As soon as a typewriter is started its history begins, a card is made which follows it through the factory with various notations as to dates commenced, finished, inspected, etc. Then to what agency shipped, what date and to whom and when sold. Nor is its history finished then… when it has been out a number of years the Sales Department takes it up again, writing the owner asking him if he is not ready to buy a later improved JEWETT and they do not let up till he does…"

The neatly dressed and outgoing George A. Jewett traveled regularly to his overseas offices, promoting the machine and making a point of meeting interesting people wherever he went. On an early typewriter trip to London in 1897, he was allowed admission to the gallery of the House of Commons and to the House of Lords, with introductions to several members of each. In 1898, he was in the Berlin office when the German War Department placed an order for 1000 JEWETTs, and George had a private meeting with German Foreign Secretary (later Chancellor) Count von Bulow. On June 10, 1899, he sent a postcard home to Des Moines from Berlin with his likeness (wearing a silk top hat) shown next to the typewriter. On the postcard, George wrote, "Dear folks at home. This is the way I looked when I had to part with my last JEWETT. The Kaiser would have it..." Of course, George then headed home and loaded up with more!

On one trip abroad, my great-grandfather became well acquainted with a little girl named Helen and a young boy named Charlie, accompanied by their mother on George's same sailing ship. The girl took interest in the JEWETT that George was selling, and asked him if she could use his demonstrator to type a letter to her Papa. He agreed, only to learn that her Papa was Judge William Howard Taft, then Governor-General of the Philippines, who later became *United States President* Taft! After the ship landed at Le Havre in northern France, George and the Taft family had lunch together, then continued their friendship over the years. George later wrote in his journal (regarding Helen and Charlie) that he "watched with interest the careers of these two young folks."

In 1904, George spent an extended period of time in Paris, running that Jewett Typewriter office himself ("on the Boulevard des Italens, of the Grand Boulevard system") while it was between Managers. George apparently had a private office upstairs, as shown in the picture on the next page, but must have spent most of his time downstairs on the main level while managing the operation that year. He wrote in his *Memoirs* about the lengthier stay in the Paris location… "The front office was filled with young ladies learning to write on the typewriter and they attracted much attention from passersby on the boulevards. One day I noticed quite a group of Africans gazing in at the window. As I had heard that Menelik, the King of Abyssinia [historical Emperor of Ethiopia] was in Paris, I recognized that it was he with his escorts. I went to the door and invited them to come in. One of them acted as interpreter, as he could talk both French and English. They were much interested in the typewriter and bought one for his secretary, as much of their correspondence was done in French… Through the interpreter I asked the King about his country and about his people… On leaving me, I bade him goodbye, he reached into his pocket and took out a silver piece of money the size of a dollar and said as he presented it to me, 'Voila, mon portrait.' And his picture is on the coin."

[George A. Jewett carried the Ethiopian 1 birr (or talari) with him until his death, and the coin remains in the family collection today. In August of 1935, a year or so after George's death, the *Des Moines Register* ran an article detailing that encounter with King Menelik II from thirty years before. It gave some further history about the coin, stating that it "was one of a new unit of currency, which Menelik attempted to establish as its national currency in 1894… (it) bears his likeness on one side and on the other the lion, king of jungle beasts which has long stood as a symbol of Ethiopian prowess. This issue of coinage never reached general use. Most of the natives have continued to use the pre-money system of exchange and barter."]

It's interesting to note that my great-grandfather eventually mastered the French language while studying the literature of that country, and that he read daily from the French translation of the New Testament carried with him at all times. George was running that Paris office in 1904 when he got word that his beloved mother, Patty, had passed away in Des Moines—she had taken ill ten days prior. [Though he made a quick departure from France, George was unable to return in time for his mother's well-attended funeral, held two days later in her own home at 1309 Locust Street, just a few doors west of George and Patty's house. Immediate family members in attendance included her granddaughters, Bonnie and Margaret (and their husbands), and her only brother, Homer Matthews (and his wife), who came from Nebraska. Though not able to be there during her final days, George had certainly been more than present throughout Patty's entire life, and was described in one eulogy as "the mother *he loved so well*." George wrote of Patty that she was "quiet, unassuming, ever ready to lend a helping hand to any in trouble… a devout Christian woman who deeply loved the cause of Christ, and was always faithful in her attendance at the House of the Lord." Patty Maria (Matthews) Jewett had been born on June 29, 1818, near Painesville, Ohio, and died on May 11, 1904, in Des Moines, Iowa, six weeks before her 86th birthday.]

•

George Anson Jewett was just so friendly and outgoing, forever curious and inquisitive when meeting others. And he regularly studied ahead of time to learn about the culture and traditions of the lands he visited. On his many travels, and perhaps being "a bit of a pest" (as my nephew Chan fondly labeled him), George personally met and became quite well acquainted with a number of other prominent individuals and world politicians and leaders, including the Nizam of Hyderabad [historical title of the premier Prince of India, whose secretary owned a Jewett Typewriter] and President Diaz of Mexico [in whose summer home George stayed as a guest]. My great-grandfather considered himself a pioneer in the study of the Mexican Aztec civilization, due to his travels and archeological digs in that country; he lectured often on his explorations using fascinating curios—like old stone idol heads he dug up and brought back with him and that were once on display at the Public Library of Des Moines at 1st and Locust. A fascinating thirty-page handwritten document from George, dated February 23, 1884, was (and hopefully still is) on file at the Cowles Library at Drake University; a biographical piece about him also lists a 1927 book (*Travels and Explorations in Mexico, 1884*) that he published about those trips. [The family has had difficulty locating a copy of this book.]

My great-grandfather also personally met several Presidents of the United States—Grant, Garfield, Cleveland, Harrison, McKinley, Roosevelt, Taft, and Wilson. I guess President Garfield even gave him a personal tour of the White House after George arrived with a letter of introduction from a lifelong Des Moines friend of the President! He never met Abraham Lincoln, but was an ardent supporter of his, and wrote that he had the honor of escorting Lincoln's remains from the Depot in Chicago to the Court House, where the President's body would lie in state for two days and nights. (This was during the 1865 semester that George was living in Chicago to attend business school.)

George's personal journal also speaks of his bold introductions to other individuals such as Mark Twain (pen name of Samuel Clemens), as mentioned earlier. Jewett and Clemens had first met when Clemens was speaking in Des Moines—it was easy to see why they were considered by many as look-a-likes, especially with those full heads of white hair and bushy white mustaches. Grandmother Margaret told me that when they traveled as a family, they would often overhear people mistaking her father for Mark Twain. When reintroduced to Clemens in New York several years after their initial Des Moines encounter, George reminded him that he had several times been mistaken for Clemens, to which Clemens replied, "I do not know whether to be flattered or offended!" My great-grandfather got such a kick out of telling that story. One of Samuel Clemens' Hartford, Connecticut neighbors was Harriet Beecher Stowe (author of *Uncle Tom's Cabin*), and the bold George once decided to call on her when they were visiting there on a family trip. He just loved meeting and getting to know others, like Julia Ward Howe (writer of "The Battle Hymn of the Republic"), poet James Whitcomb Riley (author of "Little Orphan Annie"), Luther Burbank (botanist and horticultural pioneer in Santa Rosa, California), nursing legend Florence Nightingale, and inventor Thomas Edison, among many others... the list just goes on and on.

I have especially enjoyed telling the story of how George Jewett met Florence Nightingale. Here are just a few highlights from the much longer account recorded in his own 1930 *Memoirs*: "One Saturday afternoon in London, I got on top of a bus crossing London Bridge to South London and went to the end of the line. As I looked at the name of the town in my guide book I recalled that this was the home of nurse Florence Nightingale. So, I inquired where she lived and if she ever saw visitors. I rang the bell and a lady came to the door. I told her I was just an American visitor and that I would like to call and pay my respects to Ms. Nightingale. When the lady returned to the door, she took me around the house and there sat the renowned lady. As I approached her, she did not rise from her chair, but held out her hand and welcomed me. I told her that the renown of her splendid heroic conduct in the Russian War was familiar to us in far off America, and that the young ladies in my church had even named a Sunday school class after her. She was exceedingly pleased." I understand that Ms. Nightingale and my great-grandfather had a nice talk before her attendant glanced over at George, indicating that it was time for him to leave. On his way out, he said that Ms. Nightingale "asked me to remember her to the Florence Nightingale class at my church, which I did."

I also like to tell of my great-grandfather's 1885 personal encounter with Thomas Edison, considered yet another look-a-like in his later years. My great-grandfather had been in New Orleans for the World's Fair—also known as The World's Industrial and Cotton Centennial Exposition—likely checking out the newest findings in the field of technology in hopes of coming up with something mechanical that he might get involved in manufacturing (the Jewett Typewriter Company had its beginnings three years later). Also on display at that New Orleans Exposition were elaborate Mexican National Exhibits, which would have been of keen interest to George after the recent publication about his own archeological digs in that country. While talking with someone in New Orleans, my great-grandfather learned that inventor Thomas Edison was hard of hearing, like himself. So, George decided to get on the train and go up to personally call on Mr. Edison in New York, in hopes of getting a suggestion about "the best instrument for the aid of deafness."

[Edison's original laboratories were in Menlo Park, New Jersey, but he had recently also moved to New York City, living near and working out of his labs in both locations. He once held over 2,000 patents!] George said that upon going to the door, Mr. Edison, a man of his same age and with a similar-looking face, "received me very sympathetically" and showed him all through the lab. George reported that he didn't even understand some of the things that the inventor was working on.

My great-grandfather asked Edison why he wasn't trying to invent a better hearing aid since he was also partly deaf; Edison replied that he was, in fact, working on one but that it wasn't yet ready to market. George, who must have still been holding his trumpet-like hearing device to his own ear, then asked where to find the most current and best hearing aid in the country, and was given the name of an outfit in Syracuse, New York. Of course, George got on the next train and went to Syracuse to purchase one! In later years, my great-grandfather owned yet another fancy hearing aid, and I remember it well—there were two large dry cell batteries in a leather case that he carried over his shoulder, with his initials engraved on the case. A strap went over the top of his head, holding a muff-like earphone and two large dual microphones under his necktie. I was told that his was the very first one of its kind in Iowa, which didn't surprise me, knowing George. That hearing aid was huge and looked like it should do the trick, but my family didn't think it worked all that great! I am so thankful that we have family pictures (photos, as well as film loops originally produced with the 1932 8mm Cine-Kodak Eight 20 camera), showing my great-grandfather wearing that 'fancy' hearing device. I wish I had inherited that piece, but don't recall seeing it after he passed away. It would have been fun to experiment and try to get it to work, perhaps even better than the little hearing aids I have worn myself these past few years (generously provided for me by the U.S. Government at no charge, in gratitude for my serving our country around the deafening aircraft noise of WWII).

It's hard to believe just how famous the Jewett Typewriter Company of Des Moines, Iowa became, and the number of traveling opportunities it afforded George during the era of its phenomenal growth. Eventually, however, the JEWETT required some fairly major mechanical overhauling and modifications in order to keep up with other machines that had come on the market. My cousin, Tom, wrote that "the Jewett was not able to match the firepower of the major players who undeniably had more advanced machines. The Underwood No. 5 hit the market in the late 19th century. It would be the most successful typewriter in history. Its two huge advantages over the Jewett were the shift key and the frontstroke design, which meant the typist could now see what had been typed on the sheet. George A. didn't have an answer to these innovations."

George was also getting up in years and not willing to spend time or money to keep up with all that. Family lore sadly states that one of his manager/partners was making back-door arrangements to sell the company while George was away on one of his business trips to Europe. Additionally, George recorded that "Eastern capitalists, deeming it a good thing, began purchasing interest in the stock of the company, so as to remove the plant to their territory," and that he was "resisting their scheme, which has necessitated some litigation in the courts and retarded the growth of the company." After a brave stand, my great-grandfather was saddened to eventually end local production of the machine by 1905; by 1912, he had sold the business to the Underwood Typewriter Company. A 1908 book about Iowa pioneer history recorded that "there is not a civilized country on the face of the globe in which (the JEWETT) is not in use, thus carrying the name of Des Moines to all parts of the world." I'm not certain if this is still accurate, but at one time there was a JEWETT on display in the London Museum of Science and Industry, as well as one in the Smithsonian in Washington, D.C. (along with the previously mentioned two that were donated and exhibited locally).

Though he had sold the typewriter company, George didn't stop pouring his life into his lumber business and many other pursuits. A cute article that ran in the *Des Moines Evening Tribune* back on August 4, 1915, shows my great-grandfather's name under his mustachioed picture on the front page of the paper, with the article headline of, "Celebrates Anniversary By Losing His Mustache." The story begins with, "Above is a likeness of Mr. Jewett as he appeared early yesterday morning. But a picture of him taken a few hours later would show him without his mustache. As he explains it, yesterday morning while shaving he trimmed one side of his mustache too close. He tried to make the other side conform, but couldn't so he did the next best thing—he cut the whole mustache off..."

The article continues, "Today is the fiftieth anniversary of Mr. Jewett's arrival in Des Moines. In celebration of the day, he has planned a picnic supper for all his employees and their families at Union Park [where his aunt and uncle Thrift had built the first log cabin in Des Moines] at 5 o'clock tonight. About eighty-five will be present, he explained." George later said that the gathering was "such a pleasant sight" to him... "like one big family getting together." And I'll bet everyone at the picnic was sure surprised to see their boss without his trademark mustache! I'm not certain if he ever grew it back after that since I don't remember seeing it other than in old photographs.

[George was so beloved by his employees—they seemed to throw parties for him as well, and especially on his birthdays. He oftentimes bragged about their loyalty and commitment, once stating in a national periodical, "You see, our employees are as much interested in helping our customers as I am… Everybody, from the office man who estimates the bill and takes the order, and the yardmen who pick it out and load it, to the teamster who delivers it, can be relied upon." On his eightieth, a *Des Moines Register* article stated that he had been down at Central College for a big celebration of his birthday and, "On returning to Des Moines, Mr. and Mrs. Jewett were to have spent the evening quietly with members of his family at the home of their daughter, but were surprised by the employees of the Jewett Lumber Company who presented Mr. Jewett with a cake with eighty candles." His employees really did regularly recognize his special day, and it often made the papers. On his 83rd, they presented him with a birthday cake "modeled in a caterer's conception of the first office of the Jewett Lumber Company when it was constructed fifty years ago." An article about that birthday celebration described George as "hale and sound in his eighty-third year." It also told of how his travels had taken him to every State Capitol in the nation and to a majority of the country's important cities, and that during another recent trip out east, "He conferred with many leading lumber men and studied agricultural conditions as he traveled… he returned to Iowa convinced that conditions here are better than anywhere in the nation."]

As a little kid, I recall that there were still annual company picnics being held at Union Park every year. Dad and Uncle Homer planned the outings, and they were well attended by the employees and their families. By the time I began running the company, we had some of the annual summer picnics at Ewing Park (named after David R. Ewing, who was once George's partner in the original lumber company), and at Walnut Woods State Park or at the Izaak Walton League lodge on Fleur Drive. We eventually stopped having the summer picnics, but continued to hold our employee Christmas parties at various places around town, such as Ricelli's Steakhouse on Indianola Road, and Johnny & Kay's on Fleur Drive (and at the Top of the Tower in the downtown Holiday Inn after I founded Gilcrest/Jewett Lumber Company in 1985).

As described earlier, George Jewett's love of genealogy as an elderly man often took him to visit extended family members and old cemeteries and libraries around our own country in search of more information about his ancestral line. [George's first cousin, Patty Matthews Wiencke from Grand Island, Nebraska, wrote in a letter to another relative on June 16, 1925, "… A cousin of mine, George Jewett, son of Aunt Patty my father's sister, has rather interested me in looking up family history as he makes that his hobby. He has traced our ancestry back to the immigration of the first Matthews in Puritan times to Massachusetts, and has given me all data entitling me to be a D.A.R…." In another later letter, the daughter of that same cousin recalls that George "used to visit us often in Grand Island… he was so fond of Mother. He had a roadster car. He took us children on rides—we sat in the rumble seat."]

During his travels around the country, George also visited many of his childhood friends from Central College days, keeping in touch with "thirty or more" of them through correspondence or personal visits. And I guess he was regularly being asked to help update for Central their database of former students, providing the school with any new address changes through the years! A 1923 'Alumni Column' details Mr. Jewett's recent travels to visit "several old time Centralites," and his stops to do just that in numerous states and in many California cities. Another newsletter adds, "His schoolmates have been his life-long friends, and such friendships have been to him a constant reminder of his life here, and therefore have added emphasis to its value."

I just love these two photos of my great-grandfather, fully packed down, on a jaunt through Wyoming with his '23 Jewett Touring Sedan. And sure enough, he's still the same old 'Dapper Dan,' even while traveling across mountains and deserts!

DES MOINES KEEPS GROWING

In 1906, about the same time they sold the Jewett Typewriter Company, George and Annie moved out of their big home on Locust and into a three-story brick 'double house'—a duplex or townhouse—in the 1800 block of Grand. A wealthy Des Moines resident and land developer had built the Grand Avenue 'double houses' as an investment, and the first occupants of the new living style were prominent businessmen and city pioneers. ['Double house' developer Lowell Chamberlain was one of the brothers of the Chamberlain Chemical Company family and owned a considerable amount of real estate in the Grand Avenue area. His own large, elegant home at the time, located at 2100 Grand, had been purchased by him in 1900 from jeweler and real estate developer George Marquardt. Mr. Chamberlain also built several apartments in the area, likely including the Argonne Apartments on the northeast corner of 18th and Grand, directly across the street east of the double houses. Additionally, Lowell Chamberlain provided funding for author L. F. Andrews' 1908 publication of a two-volume set of biographies about early Polk County pioneers—George A. Jewett was one of those men listed.]

The photo on right shows the Argonne Apartment building on the northeast corner of 18th and Grand (the building still stands) and also gives a good peek at the double house, which was directly across 18th Street to the west [from lostdesmoinesarchive, "historic buildings," via Jeff Horner, with permission]. From 1906 to 1924, George and Annie Jewett lived in the left (west) half of this first double house, with an address of 1805 Grand Avenue.

Sitting next to the huge columns on the front porch of their grandparents' new double house are my Dad (age 6) and Uncle Warren (age 5). I hadn't even realized that Dad's family originally lived at 1814 Ingersoll Avenue [according to their 1908 Central Church directory], which would have been directly behind these double houses... only a backyard away from their grandparents!

[Almost a century later, a 1999 *Des Moines Register* article about the history of the double houses stated that the George Jewetts housed next door to Mr. Mel born McFarlin, who founded Central Iowa Grain Company. In the next duplex building west were Mr. and Mrs. J. H. Phillip, president of the Des Moines Investment Company. Next was J. A. Fleming, one of four brothers who were general agents of a large life insurance firm in the Fleming Building at 6th and Walnut Streets. The next building to the west—1821 Grand Avenue—housed Mr. and Mrs. Richard Rollins (and Mrs. Rollins, Sr.), who owned the Shops Building at 8th and Locust Streets and who were instrumental in building the Hotel Fort Des Moines. (The younger Mrs. Rollins was a Getchell, whose father had been an original employer of George Jewett in the lumber business.) Toward the end of the block was the Charles Chase family, president of Chase and West Department Store, and his widowed mother.]

Grand Avenue immediately west of downtown was once considered the "grand dame of Des Moines" with its large elegant homes, according to historical memories from a 2005 *Des Moines Register* article. As the downtown grew, many residents like my great-grandparents kept building more houses "out in the country"—further west of their original "out in the country" houses! [The same *Register* article mentions the homes of James C. Savery at 2000 Grand (which was destroyed by fire and rebuilt as the Jefferson S. Polk home), and the homes of the Wests, the Finkbines, and the Hubbells. The big Edwin Clapp brick home at 1800 Grand, on the south side of the street, was built in 1891 and was known for its magnificent round stained-glass window. The home was then purchased by the Harbach family; but by 1916, the entire block on the south side of Grand was sold to the Ford Motor Company— they tore down the Clapp home and built a manufacturing plant for their Model T's (and held the subsequent annual car shows on their lawns).]

The history of Grand Avenue itself is rather interesting. Grand was always one long street running east/west through the middle of Des Moines. It was originally known as 'Sycamore Street' on the east side of town, and 'Greenwood Avenue' west of downtown. Stately elms and other huge trees lined the once dusty path that was converted into a brick paved road in the 1870's, and it didn't become 'Grand Avenue' until 1887. One newsworthy article stated that problems erupted after Grand became a brick street… "Once it was paved, complaints arose about youths racing on horseback, disturbing peaceful afternoons with the clatter of horse hoofs and snagging apples from the trees near the road." Just up the hill and across the street from the Grand Avenue double houses, Benjamin F. Allen (the first millionaire in Iowa) had finished back in 1869 a three-year process of building the 18,000-square-foot Terrace Hill mansion for his family at a cost of $250,000—it must have had an original address of '2300 *Greenwood* Avenue' before it became the now famous '2300 Grand.' [In 1884, F. M. Hubbell purchased the property for $55,000 after Mr. Allen met financial disaster. The home was then given to the state by the Hubbell family in the early 1970's and has served as the Governor's residence since. In 1972, the Terrace Hill property became a part of the National Register of Historic Places.] Today, I enjoy having my own Grand Avenue address here at Wesley, as does my daughter, Stephanie, at her condo just one very long block east of me.

And Steph's friend, who has lived across the street from my retirement community for many years, says he is still convinced that "Life is grand on Grand."

The 'double houses' on Grand Avenue, where my great-grandparents had once lived, were still used as residences here in Des Moines until the early 1980's, and looked much the same as they had seventy-five years earlier… "inside were ornate golden oak banisters winding up the stairway, large fireplaces and deep, plush carpeting," states a 1999 *Des Moines Register* article mentioned in above brackets. The entire block of residences on Grand and Ingersoll, from 18th to 19th Streets, was finally razed to make way for the WHO studios that sit on that block of land today. (Just a few weeks ago, Jennifer and I were in the waiting room of my doctor's office while talking about those original 'double houses.' A gentleman seated next to us overheard the conversation and asked which double houses we were talking about, as he had lived in one on Grand Avenue after first moving to Des Moines as a young college kid. It turns out that he lived on the second floor—by then an apartment unit—of the very double-house of my great-grandparents at 1805 Grand!)

By 1924, George and Annie Jewett moved from that double house, relocating into the new six-story Commodore Hotel in the 3400 block of Grand—it was like a retirement community at that time and was considered one of the nicest places to live in Des Moines.

A 1994 'Meet Me on the Corner' *Des Moines Register* article about the old Commodore recalls that some of the 94 elegant residential apartments were as large as seven rooms. There was also the main dining room and a big ballroom for "festive balls and wedding receptions." The apartments had "bathrooms that you stepped up into, and each had an icebox that could be serviced from a trap door in the hallway, thus avoiding  having the occupants bothered by having the iceman traipse through their apartments."

As a kid, I remember well my great-grandparents living at the Commodore. We sometimes went over to George and Annie's home there for Sunday noon dinner after we got back from their church—they always had an assigned table in the fancy basement dining room. Then my great-grandfather George would take me out to the garage and show me the expensive cars, which he knew I loved—the LaSalles, the Pierce-Arrows, the Lincolns, and the Cadillacs. I thought it was so great that there was a man who stayed with the cars all night long, gassing them and polishing and waxing them, but just couldn't figure out how the guy ever slept if he worked there all night! It's especially meaningful to me that my own current apartment on the far northwest end of the Sargent Building on the Wesley Acres retirement campus looks over at the former Commodore Hotel location (which is now home of Des Moines University, an osteopathic medical and health sciences school). I so often think of my great-grandparents when I look out that window today.

Two years before I was born, George A. Jewett's distant cousin, Harry Jewett (who owned the Jewett Automobile Company manufacturing plant in Detroit, Michigan) had presented my great-grandfather with the new 1923 Jewett four-door sedan as thanks for George's promotion of the Jewett name around the world. My mother, the artist, painted a small family Coat-of-Arms on the back doors of my great-grandfather's Jewett, and George was so proud to be chauffeured around in it during his elder time of life.

[Harry ("Hal") Jewett had made his first money in coal mining. When the automobile invention came onto the scene, Harry felt it would be a lucrative industry, so he (and a few other friends) funded Fred Paige's new prototype vehicle with $100,000. The first Paige didn't do well; within two years, Fred Paige was voted out of the Presidency of The Paige-Detroit Motor Company, and Harry Jewett was installed. While the Paige-Detroit car prices crept upward, Harry saw the need to recapture the lower price market… hence, the 'thrifty' Jewett was born by 1921. It was a huge success, with almost 10,000 units sold in 1922. They built a second plant in Detroit to fill the demand, selling 44,000 units by 1924. In spite of upgrading to a straight eight-cylinder engine, sales started to nose-dive in the next two years, partly due to severe competition from other automobile manufacturers who offered a combined total of 261 new car models in 1926! (Studebaker adopted the lower priced companion-line concept with its Erskine, Hudson did it with the Essex, Chandler with the Cleveland, and later Cadillac with the LaSalle.) Due to the oncoming Great Depression, the car industry was feeling the effects of the economic downturn by the end of 1926. Harry Jewett and his firm had to outsource parts, leaving his company at the mercy of its suppliers who largely controlled the quality and price of their product. Paige-Detroit was purchased by the Graham brothers for $4 million in late 1926. The company was then renamed the Graham-Paige, and their leftover car inventory soon displayed the Paige Six badge (or emblem) by the beginning of 1927. The company existed until 1930, when the brothers went back to producing trucks.]

The Jewett automobile had some unique selling features and was known for its smooth-running six-cylinder engine (advertised as the 'Jewett Six') in a car starting at only $995.

The Jewett was manufactured from 1922-1926, and I enjoy telling people why it was way ahead of its time—it had a 50 hp engine, while the Model A Ford only had a 40 hp one; it also had an electric starter and a locking gearshift and locking ignition. And the final year it was produced, 1926, the Jewett came out with hydraulic brakes—Ford didn't come out with those until 1939!

I picked up a '23 Jewett myself several years ago, after getting word that an antique car collector living in Hudson, Iowa passed away and had one in his estate. I went up to his home where he had a huge garage full of cars, including the Jewett (and even an old Maxwell). So, I purchased his 1923 and sent a lumber truck with a trailer to bring it back to Des

Moines. With that car came another 'junker' to use for replacement parts, which were pretty tough to find. The stripped-down parts car was not much, but it provided an extra engine, transmission, and some wheels, which would eventually come in handy.

My 1923 Jewett convertible was in surprisingly good condition and was originally all black in color. I found out that the company had also manufactured it as a maroon car with black fenders and so forth, so I had mine repainted to reflect that combination. If this book was in color, you could see that it sure turned out sharp, especially with the maroon spokes really helping set off the wheels.

In the summer of 1979, a national insurance company asked if I would display my Jewett auto at their booth in the Varied Industries Building at the Iowa State Fair, which I was happy to do. The month before my car went on display at the Fair, I was supposed to be up in Algona, Iowa, at the big 125th Celebration of its 1854 town founding by my other great-grandfather (Ambrose Call). I had hoped to drive the '23 Jewett up to that gala event, but a huge tornado came through Algona on the night of June 28, just days before the anniversary weekend, destroying a 100-square-block area in two short minutes. Instead of preparing for a gala celebration to mark the city's 125th birthday, the townspeople were dealing with shock and disbelief at the tornado's wrath.

I drove the '23 Jewett around Des Moines quite a bit, but you never knew when something might go wrong with it. One evening Nelle and I were heading to the home of friends in Carlisle when it broke a fan belt or something; we were able to pull into a garage to have it repaired before continuing on our little jaunt. When I built a new lumberyard at 1536 E. Army Post Road in the early 1980's, I kept the Jewett in the showroom of the main offices for several years; then after the merger of Jewett and Gilcrest Lumber Companies, I decided to trailer the car up to Okoboji and drive it around up there for awhile. Eventually, the vehicle was sold to a friend of mine who had a car museum in Spirit Lake, and it remained on display there for three or four years. The new owner really liked to drive it—once when he was in a parade it blew a rod through the block, so he took the engine out of the parts car and replaced it with that. The guy eventually dismantled his automobile exhibition site and got rid of the inventory, including my Jewett, which found a new home somewhere on the east coast.

As mentioned before, my great-grandfather George was very active in so many organizations, and favorite road trips for me were the ones we took to Pella fairly regularly for Central College Board meetings and other functions. His chauffeur, Bill, drove us in the '23 Jewett. (I personally don't ever remember seeing George drive his own car while I was alive, though am certain he was still making several unchauffeured cross-country road trips during those years.) On our outings to Pella, I always got to play with the building caretaker on the huge freight elevator inside the Administration Building, which was not at all like the little passenger-sized elevators in department stores or office buildings. The caretaker and I rode up and down several times in that big thing, which I just loved. My great-grandfather was so proud of everything at Central College, including the trees on campus—he would point and tell me he had helped plant this one and that one.

[When George and his mother and brother first arrived in Pella, the Central campus was "but a vacant prairie, not a shrub or tree around it." One historical record states that George had indeed returned to campus, two years after he graduated, for a big tree-planting endeavor. He wrote of it, "I came back to school especially to assist at the frolic."] Before heading back to Des Moines after our Pella trips, Chauffeur Bill would always stop the car at the watering trough on the northwest corner of the square so that my great-grandfather and I could fill our little cloth bag which was hanging over the front bumper, just in case we needed to put water into our radiator somewhere along the road back to Des Moines— I don't ever recall having to stop to put water into it though.

In the spring of 1929, a very special event took place on the Pella campus, and I made the papers when they reported about it. Seven years before, back in 1922, the Old Central building had burned down, and a famous marble slab in the foyer of Central Hall had been broken. The slab was a revered piece on campus since it listed the names of 23 young men who never returned from the Civil War (out of the 120 from Central who had 'answered the call'). Included on that slab's list was the name of George's brother, Homer Harris Jewett. A new marble memorial plaque to replace the broken one was donated by George and was to be unveiled by him at a dedication exercise in the 'New Central' building during commencement week. Excerpts from a local newspaper article about the unveiling read, "After the singing of the Battle Hymn of the Republic by the audience and a prayer, *happy little three-year-old Jerry Jewett*, great-grandson of Mr. George A. Jewett, proudly pulled the cord which drew aside the curtain, showing the fine white marble slab… Mr. Jewett was the main speaker of the occasion, presenting the memorial to the college. He read the list of names of faculty and students who enlisted in the war and read selections from the diary of his brother Homer." (I do wish I remembered pulling that cord for my great-grandfather's presentation, but can just see myself looking quite proud about it!)

That same evening, the annual Founders Day Banquet was held at the school. For many years George and Annie Jewett hosted that event, which included as invited guests the faculty, the current senior class, the presidents of the other three classes, the presidents of all campus organizations, and the Board of Directors. [According to one Central document, "Mr. Jewett is a man who never forgets a friend, and his love for his teachers of the early days and the men and women who struggled to keep the torch of education lighted at Central during the days when the whole country was plunged into the darkness of civil war inspired him with the happy thought of contributing a generous endowment to the school, the income from which is to be used each year for a banquet known as Founders Day Banquet."]

A newspaper article detailing the afternoon slab unveiling said that several Jewett family members from Des Moines were also in attendance that evening. It's interesting to me that the President of Central was slated to speak immediately following my great-grandfather at a Founder's Day Banquet, perhaps this same one, but that he stood up to say that Mr. Jewett's (historical) remarks had caused him to change the character of his own speech from what he had intended—the college President then spoke instead of the great need in Pella for a Historical Society to preserve those facts "that will soon become only tradition if not recorded and preserved." [George annually attended commencement exercises at Pella too, along with a good Des Moines friend of his (N. C. Towne) who had also been a 13-year-old student at Central when the Civil War broke out in 1861. They were being interviewed together in 1929, and ended up reminiscing about the olden days when they "whispered together when the teacher wasn't looking, stole watermelons out of neat gardens when school was over, and could hit the bull's eye with their sling shots." But their most touching memories had to do with how badly they both had wanted to go to war with the older boys back then, and how disappointed they were when turned away as mere 13-year-olds. George had previously stated, "Our mind reverts to those days of '61, when these boys marched out of Central's halls full of vigor of their young manhood." And Mr. Towne told the crowd that day, "It was a great regret to boys of our age that we weren't old enough to go to war," but added, "We knew one boy named Tommy Cox, 13, who knew how to beat the drum—he went as a drummer boy!"]

On September 9, 1932, George's 85th birthday (and the 75th anniversary of his first day as a student at Central College), my great-grandfather was the honored guest at yet another celebration thrown for him by the school. I was probably with him in Pella for that event too, but don't recall it specifically—they were always having celebrations down there to honor him for one thing or another, and I loved going along. [A local newspaper article from the next day states that 200 people were present for that event, during which George Jewett spoke of his first experiences at the school. His pastor from Central Church in Des Moines also spoke and led in devotionals. A newly retired 40-year faculty member had written a special song for George, and a quartet of four students led everyone in singing the tribute to him.]

In their final few elderly years, George A. and Annie Jewett moved from the Commodore Hotel into that great big home of their daughter, Bonnie, and son-in-law, Dr. Hugh Welpton, at 2413 Grand, across the street from Terrace Hill. It was part of my great-grandfather George's routine to walk every morning from 24th and Grand, west to 28th Street, then down the 28th Street hill to Ingersoll Avenue, and back east a few doors to 'Don's Shoe Shop' on the south side of Ingersoll, for his daily shoe shine. (It's hard to believe that Don did shoe repair work for five generations of Jewetts, even talking to my own daughters about how their great-great-grandfather George Anson Jewett got his shoes shined daily while ready the newspaper there! I remember hearing as a little boy that Don was once held up during a robbery in his store, and that the bandit shot him in the mouth—apparently, the bullet had hit his false teeth and didn't even hurt Don! Whenever I took in a pair of shoes for the guy to repair over the years, even as an adult, I couldn't help thinking of that story… and looking at his teeth!).

Bonne and Hugh Welpton were a quiet couple who also traveled a lot during the early years of Hugh's medical practice, while he did further studies at Harvard, as well as in England, Germany, and Austria. They never had any children, so their house had plenty of room as an eventual co-residence for my aging great-grandparents who lived there until their deaths. I don't really remember a lot about Hugh, other than he had graduated from Drake and had been imprisoned as a missionary in China before somehow escaping because he was able to speak Chinese so well. By the time I was a little kid, Hugh had been partners with Dr. Smouse here in town, but had become pretty sickly from an infection of some sort and was forced to quit practicing medicine. Three years after my great-grandparents passed away, Bonnie and Hugh sold their big house on Grand to the O'Meara Funeral Home people, and I remember them moving into an apartment on 14th Street Place between Woodland Avenue and Pleasant Streets—the big old houses that sat on the west side of the street had been converted into apartments, and they had a nice one upstairs. The couple continued to drive south to a home they rented on Padre Island in Texas in the winter—there was no bridge to the Island yet, so they had to ferry Bonnie's 1937 Plymouth back and forth from the mainland once down there. It was only a couple of years later that Hugh died, and Bonnie then moved into my grandparents' house on High Street. Great-uncle Hugh was such a kind man to everybody, and it was sad that he died so young.

[Hugh Gilmer Welpton was born to attorney James Smith Welpton and Henrietta (Gilmer) Welpton in the town of Salem, Iowa in Henry County on September 5, 1870, and could trace his ancestral lines back to England and Ireland. Both sides of his family came to America prior to the Revolutionary War and all fought for national liberty. His maternal grandfather, Dr. Campbell Gilmer, was one of Iowa's earliest physicians, settling in Fort Madison in 1832. Hugh had graduated from Drake University Medical School in 1897, followed by post-graduate work in Chicago and New York. He then served for two years as a medical missionary in China until captured by insurgents during the Boxer Rebellion of 1899-1901. Apparently, his fluency in Chinese aided his escape. After returning to Des Moines, he went into private practice with Dr. David W. Smouse, a well-known physician and philanthropist, before marrying Bonnie Ella Jewett on November 12, 1903. He never returned to China but stayed interested in that country's affairs. In 1929, Dr. Welpton was forced to retire from medicine after contracting an infection himself following an injury sustained at their home; for the next ten years, he was a partial invalid who was unable to work. He eventually sought medical treatment for heart and kidney complications at Baylor University in Dallas, Texas, where he died on July 3, 1939, at age 68. (Interestingly, his former partner, Dr. Smouse, had retired to California, and had died at his Los Angeles home less than 24 hours prior to Hugh's death!) Hugh Gilmer Welpton had been a member of the American Medical Association, the Iowa State Medical Society, The Polk County Medical Society, and the Des Moines Pathological Society.]

After Hugh's death, Bonnie (also a Drake graduate and member of the Delta Phi Delta art fraternity) continued her art training and travels around the world. Though Hugh never returned to China after being held as a prisoner there, it seems that Bonnie did...

I remember she brought back so many interesting artifacts from her travels. Great-aunt Bonnie was an avid painter, especially of watercolors, and had studied at the Cumming School of Art in Des Moines and at the University of Southern California Art School. And as the eventual 'art custodian' for the Des Moines Women's Club, Bonnie compiled an art catalogue of all the paintings in Hoyt Sherman Place. She also continued to be highly involved in various local public welfare outreaches through the Roadside Settlement House at E. 7th and Scott Streets (that building is still standing).

Bonnie originally drove an electric car for a long time, and I remember just how quiet that thing was! I was a little kid then, but recall that it was steered with a bar rather than a wheel and that it had two flower vases hanging on the inside of the car between the front and rear windows on either side. It was considered more of a lady's car, and I really don't remember anyone else who had one; but the first American electric car had been developed here in Des Moines, so I'm certain that several local people probably owned them. Every day Bonnie drove from her big Grand Avenue house over to the High Street home of her sister Margaret (and Pops Jewett) to fill those car vases with flowers picked from the huge garden that ran along the entire west side of my grandparents' house—the garden I mentioned that my grandfather lovingly tended to every single day. By the time Bonnie and Hugh downsized to their apartment on 14th Street Place, electric cars had dropped in popularity due to gas becoming easily accessible; Great-aunt Bonnie then bought the new 1937 Plymouth, which she owned until 1947. I'll tell more about that Plymouth since she let me take it with me when I was in the service (where it finally saw plenty of action!).

Bonnie had begun showing definite signs of dementia by the time she moved in with Margaret and Pops. When television came onto the scene, and little black-and-white sets became available, my father gave Pops one—it must have been 1950 because WHO-TV, the first local television station in Des Moines, started operating that year. Pops was in the early stages of a several-months-long illness before his spring 1951 death and spent a lot of time up in his bedroom. So, everybody would just gather up there in order to watch the new little television set with the 8-inch screen. Memory-impaired Bonnie always stood right in front of that little TV, blocking it from the view of others, because she thought the man on the screen was talking just to her. Even when Pops and Grandmother Margaret got a bigger console-type television for their den not long afterward, Aunt Bonnie always stood in front of it too. (It's been a longstanding Jewett family joke all these years that if someone is blocking the view of a television set, a family member will surely say, "Get out of the way, Aunt Bonnie!") Though she suffered from dementia, Bonnie outlived all of the

Jewetts, except Warren (and now myself!), passing away in her bed at Margaret's home in March of 1963, just a few months before her 91ˢᵗ birthday. [Bonnie Ella Jewett Welpton was born July 22, 1872, in Des Moines, Iowa, and died on March 11, 1963, also in Des Moines.]

{Editor's note: Whenever visiting the ailing Bonnie up in her room, she was lying in her bed wearing tall lace-up military-style boots. At her funeral, my sister Stephanie and our cousin Chan (both about age 9) got a case of the giggles when one of them whispered to the other, wondering if Bonnie was wearing her boots in the casket. Dad had looked over at me, the eldest great-great-niece at age 11, as if to let me know it was my responsibility to make the other kids stop snickering. It would have been better if I hadn't tried, as their giggles were terribly catching! In mentioning that incident to Dad when working on this book about his life, I was glad that he didn't even recall it. And now, knowing that he has repressed it, maybe I can let it go too!}

Great-aunt Bonnie had been such a wonderful caregiver to her aging parents, George and Annie, and certainly deserves mention for that—it must have been kind of a whirlwind living with the likes of her busy father, George, who was still making the pages of the newspaper even in his later life. And though George received the bulk of press attention during his lifetime of endless activity, his devoted wife was always at his side ("behind every great man is a great woman"), sometimes even getting a little bit of press herself!

This picture apparently ran in *The Des Moines Capital* newspaper in early 1928, when I was still 2 and my great-grandmother, Annie Jewett, was 79.

When she had turned 81, a local newspaper article about Mrs. George A. Jewett stated that she was known around the Des Moines area for her "amazing skill at the piano and (she) never fails to deliver an impromptu number… her fingers, astonishingly nimble for all her four score years, skip over the keys in time that would do credit to a musician one-third her age." Though I don't really remember it so much, my sister Connie said she recalled our great-grandmother's beautiful piano playing when we visited their Commodore Hotel home—I must have been too taken with looking at cars down in the resident garage to remember that! The same newspaper article also tells of Annie's faithful presence at DAR meetings; but then, for some reason, the piece ends with this rather silly piece of information… "She eats two fried eggs (hard!) every morning for breakfast to the despair of dieticians… she doesn't like to cook, she confessed, but does enjoy preparing breakfast every morning—with the help of her husband." I read somewhere that my great-grandparents ate most of their main meals at the 'Des Moines Hotel' downtown, but I don't even know where that was located (if it ever existed)—perhaps the notation just meant that they ate at *some* Des Moines hotel downtown, or may have even been referring to their years living at the Commodore and eating their main meals at that residential Hotel. I do recall they also periodically drove over to the town of Colfax, east of Des Moines, to enjoy the mineral baths, spending a 'spa weekend' and dining out at a big hotel there. I know Annie didn't like to cook, but am glad to learn she and George did at least make breakfast together! *{Editor's note: And Dad used to be pretty good at making breakfast himself, throwing together a mighty tasty fried egg sandwich for his daughters on the mornings after we had spent the night at his place.}*

In another side story about Annie, when the Younker Brothers Department Store (known later simply as 'Younkers') had opened in Des Moines back in 1874, it is recorded that my great-grandmother was their very first customer, arriving by carriage at the 8th Street entrance and purchasing a new hat that day. She must have loved to be out and about, as she even showed up in a gossip column that appeared in the *Iowa State Register* on Saturday morning, October 3, 1874… "Yesterday evening Mrs. George Jewett and another lady were driving down Fourth Street in a top carriage. At the crossing of Locust the fore wheels ran out from under the carriage and that vehicle pitched forward so suddenly that both ladies were thrown out of the carriage, fortunately without injury to either. The horse made off with the shafts and wheels."

I wasn't around when Younkers opened that store, of course, but the next page shows me in their big newspaper advertisement when I was 11 and preparing to enter Callanan Junior High School. Highlighted in the *Des Moines Register*'s August 22, 1937 insert pages were four Des Moines kids who were the newest breed of loyal multi-generational Younkers customers. If only a smart wardrobe would have made a smart student! Younkers was the first store in Iowa to install an escalator ("electric stairs") back in 1939. It was very smart for them to do that since it brought so many more people into the store. At first, we all came just to see the stairs and ride on them, but they were a real nice asset for shoppers— so much faster than taking an elevator and stopping at each floor while the operator announced the goods and exchanged the passengers. I bought a lot of things at Younkers as a kid and through my adult years, especially since Dad was such a good friend of the owners. And most who lived in Des Moines will never forget the Younkers Tea Room with its

famous rarebit burgers—my extended family often went there for our Sunday noon dinner with my great-grandparents after they moved out of The Commodore.

The summer before beginning my high school years at Roosevelt, I also started regularly shopping at the J. C. Penney department store downtown. Much of my fondness of it was due to the guy who headed up the menswear department down there—his name was Sam. Sam was always standing at the ready to greet me, as if I were his only customer. Being just a high school kid, I felt pretty important walking in there, greeted each time with, "Hello, Mr. Jewett. What might I help you find today, Mr. Jewett?" Sam wasn't really that much older than I was, having just graduated from college himself, but I always thought I should be the one calling *him* by *his* last name (if only I'd asked it!). The guy just impressed me as having the charisma it took to make it big someday—I wouldn't have been surprised if he'd ended up managing the whole store! Before my junior year ended, Sam was gone from the Penney's menswear department, and did end up climbing to bigger and better heights… As an adult, I always thought I'd stop into the Wal-Mart headquarters in Bentonville, Arkansas to personally call on Mr. Sam Walton while on one of my travels, and sure do wish I would have done that—Sam ended up dying at a fairly young age, and I regret not having told him in person how much I had admired him all those years before.

My great-grandmother Annie Henry Jewett lived a long and love-filled life, and I was there at Bonnie and Hugh's house when she was very sick and near death. Annie was "an integral part of the social and religious life of the community," according to her DAR eulogy, and was known as "an ardent admirer of art and of nature." She passed away on

New Year's Day when I was just 7 [Annie Henry Jewett was born in Edinburgh, Indiana on March 28, 1848, and died in Des Moines, Iowa on January 1, 1933.] I was also at that house when my 87-year-old great-grandfather, George Anson Jewett, passed away in July of 1934, when he was not quite 87 and I was not quite 9. [George Anson Jewett was born in Red Rock, Iowa on September 9, 1847 and died in Des Moines, Iowa on July 15, 1934.] He had been ill for a couple of months and died from "complications of a few diseases," including pneumonia. Grandmother Margaret always said her father never really got over his beloved Annie's death, an event which unfortunately seemed to take much of the spunk out of him for his last year and a half.

Notice of my great-grandfather's passing was the big bold headline when readers opened their local *Des Moines Register* on Monday morning, July 16, 1934—he had passed at 8:30 P.M. the night before, it stated. On Tuesday, the day of his funeral, the Jewett Lumber Company was closed. And in respect to this man who was bigger than life in our community, all other lumber companies in the city closed early, and Drake University dismissed classes at 3 P.M. More than 500 of us attended George A. Jewett's funeral at the Central Church of Christ, where his pastor [Rev. Floyd Allan Bash] proclaimed, "I never knew a man with a more intense, yet reverent, spirit… he had a great understanding." Dr. D. W. Morehouse, President of Drake University at the time, declared that "the spirit of Mr. Jewett will remain in two indestructible monuments—in the church and in the school," later adding that George Jewett "dreamed great dreams but never let them become his master… he talked with kings but never lost the common touch." My great-grandfather's service was followed by his burial at Woodland Cemetery under the beautiful headstone that proudly displays his well-known signature.

[George's beloved *Christian Worker* periodical featured a long 'Tribute' to him several days after his passing, perhaps the last *CW* edition to be published. These quotes were gleaned from that additional eulogy: "His keen mind adventured in many fields. It was as restless as the wind. He was most happy when exploring some unknown realm of thought… His temple of Brotherhood included not only men of the present generation but its vast arches reach back to include the heroes of a score of generations. Through genealogy Mr. Jewett performed miracles. By it he touched the dead of other centuries into life… As a layman he helped create a new sense of brotherhood in the churches across the world. He occupied pulpits in England and America, contributing good will and fresh courage… He sought Divine guidance." The long eulogy ended with, "To truly know Mr. Jewett one needs to see him not only as a typical American business executive but also see him at the University Club, or at home alike in London, Paris and Berlin; walking with rulers of the earth, and again gathering ragged lads off city streets to organize them into Sunday school classes; see him at the editorial desk or on an ocean liner or in the radiant warmth of his own beloved fireside. Always and everywhere Brother Jewett—the Temple Builder."]

I remember when my great-grandfather's 1923 Jewett was parked in our garage at 213-38th Street Place for several years after his death and I'd go out and just stand and look at it to help remember being with him. I'll forever be thankful to have such terrific memories about that great guy for the first nine years of my life. His unstoppable enthusiasm and endless energy paved the way for me and my other relatives to want to do the same. Since his car occupied the space on the south half of our garage, my folks let me occupy the space on the north half as my own place to hang out. I raked that dirt floor every single day so that it was nice and neat, leaving lines with the rake so that if somebody walked in, I could tell! (And that's also where I eventually worked on cars, as mentioned earlier, including overhauling the Model A Ford engine.)

When he passed in 1934, George Anson Jewett was the oldest living alumnus of Central College. But he also had left quite a legacy with another educational institution…

DRAKE UNIVERSITY GETS ITS START

As a young man, my great-grandfather wanted Des Moines to have a Christian college, and began to meet regularly with three other individuals (George T. Carpenter, Francis M. Drake, and a Mr. Bell [likely Samuel Bell, also a very active Disciples of Christ member at the time], with George serving as the Committee Chairman to get that goal accomplished. Their meetings were held in the upper room of the YMCA, where George Jewett's picture hung in the lobby as the 'founder' of our local Y and its first Secretary. Apparently, the naming rights for the new college were to go to the largest financial contributor. Francis Drake, who had made his money in the railroad industry, outbid everyone when he first pledged $20,000 and then doubled it. George's Committee eventually issued a statement declaring in 1881 (when George was only 34 years old) that the new Drake University "has been designed upon a broad, liberal and modern basis... in its management and influence, it will aim at being Christian, without being Sectarian."

In the early days of the University, all its business was transacted in George Jewett's office and, according to one write-up, "in providing financial resources it is doubtful if any friend aside from General Drake himself, has done so much for it... (Jewett) has had more to do with shaping its policies and directing its course and forming its character than any other man." Even in later years, George insisted on continuing to help Drake financially. But things had gotten tough economically due to the downturn of the economy beginning in 1927, and he had trouble paying property taxes on the big Jewett Building that he had constructed downtown. As mentioned in an earlier chapter of this book, George found a solution when he "sold" the building and its land to Drake University for the total (and apparently secret) sum of $1...

An article in the *Des Moines Register* that ran on November 9, 1927, told of the transaction... "Through the investment of endowment funds and the generosity of George A. Jewett, veteran Des Moines lumberman, Drake University today acquired the Jewett Building and site which extend from Ninth to Tenth streets on the south side of Grand Avenue. The purchase price of the half block of valuable commercial property was not made public. However, it is estimated that the structure and ground are worth between $400,000 and $500,000. It was the largest realty deal ever consummated by Drake University." That same article later read, "The amount of the handsome gift of George A. Jewett which represented a substantial proportion of the purchase price *was not made public* by Mr. Jewett whose past benefactions to the school total more than $100,000." Apparently, there were other transactions handled by George A. Jewett for his beloved Drake University—one account reads, "It was solely through his initiative and largely through his executive work that four land sales were consummated which netted the University many thousands of dollars and saved it from ruin at a crucial moment in its history... the financial responsibility being borne by him when the University had little credit." [When George had been in Portland, Oregon for a Christian Church annual convention back in 1911, one of the social events of the occasion was a banquet held by the alumni of Drake. George was called upon to say a few words since he had been instrumental in its founding and had served as its Secretary and as a member of its Board of Trustees in the years since. After the banquet, George expressed pleasure at meeting so many of the alumni of Drake and said that, "while they told of their beautiful homes in Washington, Oregon, Idaho and California—making them out to be veritable paradises—yet each would say how much he would give to walk across Drake University campus again, or to be in the old college buildings."]

My great-grandfather was so loyal to Drake, pledging money to it every year. And those doggone pledges were made to continue even after his death. I recall how the lumber company sometimes struggled to keep up with those payment promises years later, but my father was also on the Board of the University by then and insisted on continuing the tradition (which we did). After Jewett Hall was built on the Drake campus, they requested a picture of my great-grandfather, which I furnished and placed over the fireplace in the living room of that building at 2707 Carpenter Avenue, which had been designated as the 'Student Residence and Union.' Not so long ago, I was back in Jewett Hall at Drake, having been invited by student residents to come and talk about my great-grandfather and those founding days of their school.

George A. Jewett had assumed the position of Secretary of Drake University in 1883, two years after its inception, and served in that capacity until his death in 1934. He also served on their Board of Directors for almost three decades. During his 50+ years as Secretary, my great-grandfather signed every single one of the diplomas for every single student that graduated from Drake. I enjoyed telling the current students that I often played as a little kid in the school stairwells while my great-grandfather signed some of those 10,000 diplomas and other important papers as Secretary of the Board. I also enjoyed telling them that, for some reason, George had missed signing the diploma of the very first Drake graduate ("J. E. Denton"), and ended up making a special 1923 road trip to Oakland, California in order to do so.

Perhaps George Jewett used that diploma-signing 'excuse' to hop in the car and head west, as he just loved seeing the country and the world. In addition to the Mexican relics he dug up in his many archeological explorations down there over the years, he also collected unique items from other places too, especially things having to do with American history. I'm thrilled to have been given a globe of the world that is supposed to be the first ever in Iowa—I think he had it shipped overseas from some other country, but don't recall the details on that. It would be nice to know where a couple other items ended up... he had a worn shingle from the roof of George Washington's barn and a piece of the first shell fired at Fort Sumter, igniting the Civil War. I also remember him bringing a real fancy pair of binoculars from somewhere—those just fascinated me as a kid, and I have no idea what might have happened to them after he died. I'm hoping the items are all in some of the boxes in Connie's basement, so her kids and grandkids can know what they were and can truly treasure them.

I've already mentioned George's own personal *Memoirs*, written just a few years before he died. In that journal, he had typed this entry about himself: "Loves to travel. Crossed the Atlantic 20 times. Crossed from Des Moines to Atlantic Coast and from Des Moines to Pacific Coast several times by automobile. Have just returned from a 7000-mile trip to N.E. corner of Maine, south to Columbia, S.C., crossed the Blue Mountains from North Carolina to Tenn., north to KY., on into Ind., and home." George had also crossed the English Channel 242 times, from London to the mainland over a period of twenty or so years, most often to promote and sell his beloved typewriters for the latter part of that. The man had certainly come a long way from the 17-year-old youth who went from Pella to Des Moines, then on to Boonesboro and back to Des Moines looking for work, walking all the way because of his "purse being short on dimes."

It's terrific to have these stories about the vision and determination of my ancestors, at first brand-new to a country, then brand-new to a territory and brand-new to a town—men and women unafraid to work hard to make a difference for future generations. They have influenced me, and I hope to have done my part in carrying on their legacies. My sister, Connie, when writing of the connections to our ancestry, once put it so well: "Whether we recognize it or not, we are all—always—holding hands with history."

THE SURPRISE 'JEWETT JEWETT' HERITAGE!

This is probably a good place to talk a little bit more about my grandparents, David L. Jewett and Margaret Jewett Jewett, as they both were born with the Jewett surname for a rather fascinating reason. The intrigue of their love story has always been regarded as kind of a family mystery, but has come into better light more recently. *{Editor's note: After having a rather unusual 'personal encounter' in the Petaluma, California area a few years ago, I began digging into the family archives to help put together the pieces of this particular family puzzle that connects Iowa with California. It is quite a unique story when fully revealed, even according to a certified genealogist who assisted with my research.}*

As already detailed, my great-great-grandfather, George "Enoch" Jewett, rushed off for California gold in 1849, and never returned to Iowa. But Enoch's little 1½-year-old son, George Anson, apparently grew up with the hope of someday reuniting with his father. When George A. became an adolescent, he may have tried to make written contact with Enoch, as his brother had done from the battlefield, but we have no record of that. [Older brother Homer had communicated with their father by letter during the war, and other extended family members and neighbors had been to California and back during that time, so it would make sense that George A. knew, generally, where Enoch was living.] But by the time George A. was in his late 30's, married and with children, he definitely went to California in search of his father. (One account tells that he had gotten hold of a copy of Enoch's 1849-1850 cross-country gold rush travel journal, then followed the same route to the Sacramento area to eventually find him.)

George Anson Jewett indeed found his father, George "Enoch" Jewett, by then a widely known and well-respected gentleman who was considered a 'pioneer' of Sonoma County. Enoch was prominently identified with farming interests and with fruit-growing, a noble pursuit in the wine country area known as Forestville, and was also known for his regularly published articles (especially having to do with politics) that ran in the local Santa Rosa *Press Democrat* newspaper under the signature of "Enoch." George Anson Jewett, the young man who showed up from Iowa, must have been pleased to again meet and better appreciate the father who left his midwest family for the lure of gold all those years before. My great-grandfather never talked to me about the whole situation, of course, but I just wonder what it must have been like for him to find and to reconnect with his father, Enoch. And I also can't help but wonder what his mother, Patty, thought about the news that the husband she had divorced for desertion more than thirty years earlier was still alive and doing so well (with his new wife and ten more children!).

[George "Enoch" Jewett had been born in Mentor, Ohio on February 15, 1820. He left his wife and three children in Iowa when heading west for gold in April of 1849. Enoch died in Forestville, California on March 20, 1908, at age 88. Enoch's California wife, Mary Dahlman/Dahlmann (married 12/22/1862) had been born in Saxony, Germany on March 25, 1838. Mary died at her home in Forestville, California on September 1, 1913, at age 75, after suffering internal injuries resulting from a fall. She was eulogized as "a most loving mother and a noble Christian woman."]

George A. was such a loving man and took a keen liking to all the members of his 'new' California family, keeping in close touch with them from then on. Additionally, he invited his eldest half-brother, David, to come to Des Moines in order to attend Drake University (which George had recently been instrumental in founding) and to live with George and his family while going to school. He's the 'David' I mentioned earlier in this book when telling of his likely moving in with George and Annie on Locust Street after coming to Iowa to attend Drake in 1886. And here's why David is so important to my own story…

Twenty-two-year-old David Lewis Jewett had been born in Petaluma, California to "Enoch" Jewett and Enoch's California wife, Mary. David accepted the invitation extended by his half-brother George, and moved to Iowa. He graduated from Drake's School of Commerce in 1887 and right away got involved in George's lumber business, as manager of Ewing & Jewett's east location. David got married a couple of years later and, as also mentioned in an earlier chapter, sadly lost his wife and their newborn son during (or shortly after) childbirth only two years after they were wed.

Widower David Jewett then remained single for another seven years while waiting to again marry—and believe it or not, the bride he'd been waiting for was none other than George Anson's daughter, Margaret, his own half-niece! Yes, David (or 'D. L'.) became my Pops! (Not many people can join me in saying that their grandfather and great-grandfather had the same father.) David was 35 by the time they married; Margaret was just 21 and a recent Drake graduate [having received her Ph.B. in 1898]. I had understood that my great-grandparents, George and Annie, were not at all pleased with the love affair between their daughter and George's half-brother, fearing that any child born to such a union might have defects. They consulted with doctors in this country and elsewhere during their travels, eventually feeling assured that the blood connection between Margaret and David was not close enough to cause harm. My sister told me that, at one time, our Grandmother Margaret still had a little piece of paper on which George and Annie had figured out and diagrammed mathematically how related Margaret and David were by blood, and that her parents then gave their blessing to the young couple's marriage… but not in *this* country.

So, my grandparents wed in London, England in the summer of 1899 [on July 19]. My great-grandfather George stood up with them and signed the marriage license as their witness. I had always been told that my grandparents, David and Margaret, were overseas visiting George's typewriter sales offices when they decided to get married while in London, but I guess that wasn't the whole story! I had also understood that my grandmother, Margaret, loved Paris so much that she told her new husband, "Let's just stay over here and have a baby in Paris." I guess that's partly true too, but it also wasn't the whole picture…

My father, Gerald Anson Jewett, Sr., was born seven months later, on February 22, 1900, in Paris, France. Dad shared his February 22 birthday with our first U.S. President, George Washington, and we used to kid my father about how he couldn't become President himself one day since he wasn't born in the states. My grandparents did love Europe, and likely stayed overseas with their new baby for a time before returning to America; their second son, David Warren Jewett, was born in Des Moines less than a year after my father had come onto the scene in Paris. (When I was in France as an adult, I traveled to Dad's birthplace—an apartment at '58 Rue Pierre Demours,'—which was very interesting and quite meaningful to me. And my sister, Connie, also had visited it when traveling to Europe with a college tour back in 1950.)

MY TERRIFIC PARENTS,
GERALD A. JEWETT, SR. AND BERTHA SHORE JEWETT

I don't recall that my grandfather (D. L., or "Pops") was overly involved in a lot of civic activities, being so consumed with his work during the day and overseeing his properties at night and on weekends. But his eldest son (my father, Gerald Anson Jewett, Sr.) was involved in numerous civic organizations, much like his own grandfather (George Anson Jewett) had been. Dad was the third generation to be involved with leading the Jewett Lumber Company, working his way up from Assistant Treasurer, to Vice President and General Manager, then to President, and finally to C.E.O. Additionally, he was a Vice President of the Jewett Realty Co. (which had been started by his grandfather), and a partner in D. L. Jewett and Sons (started by his father). As mentioned in an earlier chapter, Dad had also become the Assistant Treasurer and Director, as well as Vice President and General Manager, of Wood Brothers Thresher Company for several years. On top of all that, he was named to the National Production Authority and Office of Price Stabilization in Washington, D.C., and had been appointed by President Hoover in 1931 as United States Collector of Internal Revenue for Iowa. Vocationally, Dad was a member of the Iowa Lumbermens Association, the Iowa Employer's Association, and Hoo-Hoo International; he was a Director of the Northwestern Lumbermens Association, and served on the Retail Lumber Industry Advisory Commission.

My father was President of the Greater Des Moines Chamber of Commerce, had been one of the founders and President of the Des Moines *Junior* Chamber of Commerce (Jaycees), and was an honorary Life Member of the Greater Des Moines Committee. He was a trustee of the Dole Heating and Fuel Company, and a receiver for Lion Finance Corporation and others. Additionally, he served as President of the Des Moines Housing Commission, which operated the Fort Des Moines residential project after World War II by providing quarters for more than 900 families of former servicemen at a time when housing was scarce for them. Dad was also Vice President of the Des Moines Industries, Inc., which financed a factory building and brought the Armstrong Furnace Co. to Des Moines. As President of yet another endeavor, Des Moines Enterprises, Inc., Dad actively supported ongoing organized baseball in Des Moines and played an important part in helping get Pioneer Memorial Stadium built in 1947. That facility later became known as 'Sec Taylor Stadium' (and is now called 'Principal Park'). As an adult, I remember very well going over to Sec Taylor's home with my Dad to tell Mr. Taylor that the stadium was going to be renamed after him, and just how pleased he was about that.

My father was known as "the wheel horse" by his cohorts in community activities, and was the 1950 winner of the Des Moines Tribune's Community Service Award for his "unselfish service in organizations concerned with industrial, civil, charitable and religious progress of Des Moines." Dad headed up fundraising drives for so many outreaches, and served as Chairman of the Des Moines Community Chest and of the United Way of Central Iowa. He was a founder of the Reciprocity Club of Des Moines, and was also a member of the Des Moines Pioneer Club and on the Advisory Board of Mercy Hospital. Dad was on the Board of Directors of the Bankers Trust Company and of the Polk County Federal Savings and Loan Association, and served as a life trustee of Drake University. *{Editor's note: Grandad handed me the diploma when I walked across the Fieldhouse stage at my Drake University graduation ceremony in 1973.}*

At the time of his passing, my father was the longest continuous member of the Des Moines YMCA (63 of his 76 years). He had served as its 1949-1952 President and for several years was on its Board of Directors. Dad took an active part in raising money to build both the YMCA headquarters building at 1st Street between Locust and Grand, and the YMCA Boys Home in Johnston. My father received the YMCA's Distinguished Service Award in 1965—all especially meaningful since his own grandfather, George A. Jewett, was the man responsible for bringing the 'Y' to Des Moines all those decades before. Dad had first participated in the YMCA as a member of a Sunday School class that went over to the 'Y' to go swimming as kids. The building was housed at 4th and Keo at the time, but Dad recalled, "The street was then called Chestnut. The YMCA had the only swimming pool in the city, inside or out, except the old tank at West High School." He said that high school boys of that era could be excused from P.E. classes to take physical training at the 'Y,' for which the schools allowed full credit… "but we had to take all the gym classes and use all the apparatus—the horses, the parallel bars, the ropes; and we played basketball, softball, took swimming course and track, running around the track encircling the top level of the gym." He said the class of boys always swam without suits. Over the years, my father kept up his membership in the local Des Moines 'Y' (even during the time he was away at college). He was an assistant gym instructor, as well as a leader at the YMCA's summer Camp Foster on East Lake Okoboji. As an adult, Dad kept up his 'Y' Athletic Club membership, working out in handball, volleyball, and swimming.

My father was a member of the Central Church of Christ and later the First Christian Church, and of the Wakonda Club and the Hermit Club. He also served as past President of the Reciprocity Club and of the Des Moines Club (the Hermit Club had merged with the Des Moines Club by then, after which they remodeled one of their meeting rooms, naming it 'The Hermit Room'). He was a member of the Jewett Family of America, Inc. and had served as its Vice President in 1934. Dad was an active Republican, like his grandfather, and had been a member of the Polk County Republican Central Committee. He also served as a delegate to many GOP county, district and state conventions. When asked about his hobbies for the Iowa Press Association's 1940 publication of *Who's Who in Iowa*, he listed 'Republican politics.' My father so enjoyed handling the Senate campaigns of Lester Jesse ("L. J.") Dickinson, who had been a U.S. Representative [1919-31] before becoming Senator [1931-37]. Interestingly, L. J. was married to Myrtle Call, the baby sister my grandmother had given to the Indians that day back in the early Algona settlement. In the end, Dickinson was not re-elected to the U.S. Senate, losing by a very few votes to his Democratic opponent, Governor Clyde Herring—the next-door neighbor of my Shore grandparents!

Dad gave of himself in so many ways, but really found greatest enjoyment during his weekends spent at Okoboji, also contributing his time and talents by serving on the Iowa Great Lakes Anti-Pollution League and as one the Commodores of the Okoboji Yacht Club (which included building their first clubhouse and helping to judge sailboat races on the weekends). Perhaps his favorite activities at the lake were the lazy Sunday morning boat rides, when he piloted his wooden Chris Craft full of six adoring grandchildren across to Gull Point State Park for some ice cream and a little cruise!

{Editor's note: Our Grandad always seemed so serious and busy at a task in Des Moines, and I wasn't aware at the time of how overly involved he was in all the activities listed above. No wonder he smiled and laughed so much more on weekends at the lake—it must have been great relaxation for him to be away from that pressure. When not wearing his Commodore hat in the boat, I can still see the wind blowing his thin white hair as we sped across the water to Gull Point for our fudgesicles from the cooler in the main lodge. Grandad was always curious, endlessly asking questions of his grandchildren to engage us in lighthearted conversation. I'll bet he delighted in getting our perspectives and in vicariously enjoying, along with us, our carefree childish pursuits. As the eldest grandchild, I took our conversations quite seriously, doing my best to give appropriate and thoughtful answers to endless questions. But when youngest grandchild, C. J., came around, our Grandad would instantly stop talking—his eyes lit up and he pointed at C. J.

while nodding to everyone else in the room to stop talking and to just watch the little guy. Grandad was full of laughs at absolutely anything that kid said or did, and his laughs were contagious. Those must have been endearing experiences for C. J. too, because in his sweet 91ˢᵗ birthday note to Dad, he expressed thanks for some specific family memories and told of being "grateful for the embrace of the Jewett cottage," which really says it all.}

Laughing and relaxing at Okoboji was pretty commonplace in our extended family. It was a good getaway spot and a time of just being together as one large group. My niece, Darcy, wrote in her own 91ˢᵗ birthday note to me, "Among my strongest and most enjoyable memories of the years in the Jewett cottage are when you and some family friends and a neighbor or two would sit in the wicker chairs in the living room and tell stories. The laughter would grow as the story got further along, first bubbling up and then building and building, until you were all howling. Many times, you in particular ended up taking off your glasses to wipe tears from laughing so hard. We kids were charmed by you grownups having that much fun. And it probably had health benefits—all that laughter has probably kept you young all these years!"

Along with all that comfortable old wicker furniture throughout the house, we also had a big 9-foot long, highly varnished but rough-hewn yellow pine table with two benches that my Dad ordered custom-made from northern Minnesota way back in the early era of the cottage. All those decades, until the mid-1980's, we ate our meals at that table, put together puzzles at that table, wrote letters on that table, talked long hours at that table, and what have you. It was the center of our gatherings, and held buckets of fried chicken we ordered and picked up from The Gingham Inn in Spirit Lake every Sunday night—memories made around that one piece of furniture were priceless. And I get to sit at it yet today, enjoying time with my daughters and grandsons and great-grandchildren around the big pine table.

{*Editor's note*: *Aunt Connie inherited the furnishings from the Okoboji cottage after Nana passed away in 1985. I requested becoming the eventual recipient of the big pine table someday if she had no other plans for it, and Connie graciously gifted it to me. My husband and I designed a living area around the piece when building our own lake house in 1989. What a joy to watch the fifth generation of Jewetts sit around that family heirloom, eating or coloring or working together on jigsaw puzzles. And to serve Dad meals on it is especially meaningful fun. I am delighted to report that additional slight groove marks are still being embossed into the soft pine even today (the piece was already 'distressed' long before distressed furniture was in vogue!)*}

My father and I stumbled into an Okoboji aeronautics tradition for our family back in 1970, when I was able to obtain a two-way aircraft radio from the airport at Waterloo, Iowa. Since we flew to and from Okoboji on a regular basis, Dad and I always thought it would be a great idea to have the title of a 'fixed base operator' at the lake to better communicate from ground-to-air and air-to-ground. But in order to license the radio for use, we had to be the owner or the operator of an airport. Of course, we didn't own any such thing, so my father said, "Let's just call the lake our airport, and get licensed as the Lake Okoboji Seaplane Base." Each time we sent in our application for the license, however, we were turned down by the State—one time we didn't have the latitude and longitude listed, another time we didn't have the height of the antenna listed, and so on. We even used the Iowa Aeronautics Commission as a reference on a letter signed by a friend who was on that Commission; but again, the license came back 'denied' because the Iowa Aeronautics Commission did not own Lake Okoboji or something like that—it was just one excuse after another. Finally, after satisfactorily answering all their questions over a period of several months, we obtained our operating license (dated October 29, 1970) for the 'Lake Okoboji Seaplane Base' and installed a Unicom in a special closet of our living room to communicate with airplanes, on land or sea!

We sure had a lot of fun with that Unicom, especially appreciating the ability to radio ahead when taking off from Des Moines to find out how the weather was at Okoboji. One of my frat brothers from the University of Iowa became a district judge and had a home on another lake in northern Iowa—he obtained a two-way radio too, so when we flew over his home on our way back and forth between Okoboji and Des Moines we could catch up on

the latest with each other. And the childhood friend who grew up living in the Bolton Apartments and racing push cars with me as a kid eventually became a Captain with TWA Airlines—it was a real highlight when he radioed me one weekend while flying over Okoboji on his way from Portland to Chicago. Not only did I enjoy talking with people I knew but, on two different occasions, was also able to direct lost pilots to safe landings from our Base. *{Editor's note: Check out the two small black Dymo labels, with their hand-trimmed curved edges.}*

The nearby little Okoboji airport was unmanned, so our 'Seaplane Base' unit was the point of contact for pilots flying into and out of the area. Dad and I enjoyed the fact that Mom and my sister and all of our kids also learned how to operate the Unicom radio, assisting pilots landing at Okoboji with wind speed and direction by reading that information from the gauges we had hooked up at the living room station. In her 91st birthday note to me, niece Kyle even mentioned the Base unit and her memories of it: "How exciting it was to hear (your) voice on Okoboji Unicom, announcing your imminent arrival, and how we loved to race over to the airport to greet you." And how fortunate for us that the local airstrip had been built only 600 feet away from our cottage—we were able to walk to and from it regularly. [The original Okoboji Airport was further north and east, on the west side of Highway 71, where the Okoboji Summer Theatre is now located; the Spirit Lake Airport had been on the east side of Highway 71, where the current hospital is now located. Two local individuals bought The Inn Hotel on Dixon Beach, and one of them helped build the new 3000-foot runway at the current location, not far from the Hotel (and only 600 feet from the Jewett Cottage). 'Dillon Field' was later renamed 'Okoboji Airport.' The Okoboji Airport was eventually given to the town of Spirit Lake for maintenance purposes, and was renamed 'Spirit Lake Municipal Airport.']

Before we received that operating license, there was a guy on the lake who had a few site-seeing boats working out of Arnolds Park. After we got official designation as the Lake Okoboji Seaplane Base, a twin-engine seaplane also started hopping passengers to do sight-seeing, which was in competition with the guy's existing Arnolds Park boat business. The boat guy was working to get the commercial seaplane off the lake, when one of his boats was 'accidentally on purpose' booted in the rear-end by the seaplane one day. The boat sank, and the crash poked a hole in the right-side float of the seaplane, dropping its right wing into the water. They were able to pull the seaplane out of the lake on the south shore where Boy's Town is, and to take the wings off and load it onto a flatbed truck. The Highway Patrol was called to escort the truck to the airport in the middle of the night when there would be less traffic—believe it or not, a drunk came down the road during that transfer and hit the trailer, demolishing the airplane! (The site-seeing boat was eventually retrieved from the lake bottom—it now sits in the Maritime Museum in Arnolds Park.)

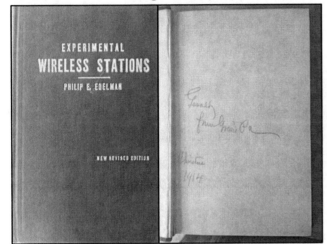

That Unicom being based in our home was a real natural for Dad, who had already possessed a love of electronics from an early age. During his teen years, from 14 to 18, Dad had rigged up (in his folks' third floor attic on High Street) the first wireless radio station in Iowa, with station key letters '9QR'. A 1912 hardbound copy of *Experimental Wireless Stations* by Philip E. Edelman was inscribed by his grandfather, George A. Jewett, when he gifted it to my Dad ("Gerald, from Grandpa, Christmas 1914"). It's hard to believe, but my young father actually understood the technical details described in that 224-page book!

The station must have been quite the set up for my father. Notes typed by his younger brother, Homer, about the components of the wireless station, are very detailed. Uncle Homer kept track of the 'operation' after Dad left home for WWI service training and for college. According to Homer, the pieces of that radio station included the receiving set and the sending set (i.e., a big loose coupler, a glass-enclosed variable capacitor, a small fixed capacitor, the oscillation transformer, the rotary spark gap, and the sending key). I have a few of those pieces on display in my apartment today. The station had a 1 KW power transformer for transmitting with a potential output of 10,000 volts. Apparently, Dad was able to converse in code with other spark station operators all over the globe. On the next page, a young Homer is sitting with headphones at Dad's station desk in 1922, when Homer was 13 (my Dad was by then 22, likely still away finishing his senior year of college). Homer noted, "I am probably listening to Des Moines' *first radio station* play old '78 rpm records." And Homer would be correct about Dad's station being the first in our city—local WHO-Radio didn't begin broadcasting here until 1924!

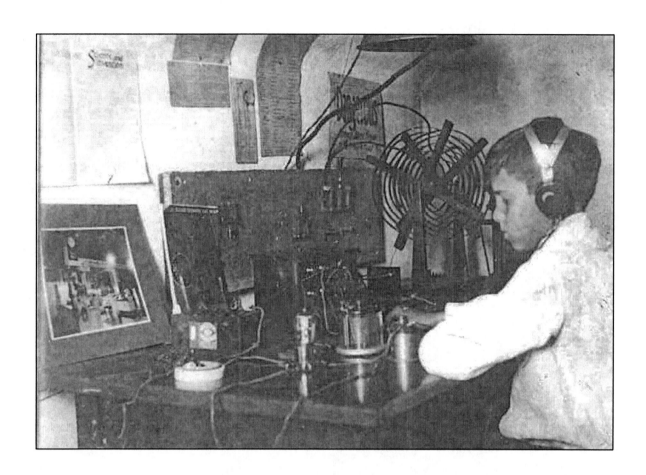

In February of 1918, my father had turned 18 and was of age to enter the service—World War I had been underway almost four years. After graduating from old West High School in Des Moines, Dad officially went into the United States Army at Camp Dodge, where he was issued his clothing and gun. I don't recall hearing much about his short time in that aspect of the service, but understand he was part of a sixty-day training camp that summer.

Though prepared for combat, my father never saw it—in the fall, he left for Pennsylvania to attend Wharton, where he was a voluntary member of the newly formed Student Army Training Corps (S.A.T.C.), which was an organization like R.O.T.C., established that very summer so that young men could train for the military while also receiving a college education. By virtue of being a part of that program, rather than enlisting to go overseas, a young man attained the Army rank of 'Private.' It must have been a terrific opportunity for so many, allowing an education while also standing-at-the-ready if called to defend our country. And I was interested to learn that Dad was a charter member of the American Legion, which was formed nationally in 1918 during his first semester of college! The war reached a conclusion by November of that year, so Dad and the rest of the S.A.T.C. boys never had to serve elsewhere.

One time, while driving his folks' Cadillac Touring Sedan back to Pennsylvania after a school break, my father had riding along with him a Des Moines buddy, a Sigma Nu fraternity brother who also attended Wharton. As usual, they stopped in Chicago where they planned to spend the night. After dinner, Dad and his friend got back into the car and, while they were driving along, a man came up from the back seat with a gun and said, "Keep driving." My father's buddy said, "Gerald, he's not kidding," so my Dad just kept driving. After traveling a number of blocks, they stopped at a light and the man jumped out and ran. [The Sigma Nu college kid who was on this and other trips back and forth to school is the guy who eventually built a big home a block away from the Jewett residence on 38th Street Place—his is the house previously mentioned that former President Coolidge had been invited to use one summer.] I'm not sure it had anything to do with that particular scare, but my Dad's father—Pops Jewett—told me my Dad was always so nervous when driving, that Pops was afraid his son was going to wear the ratchets off their Model T (the throttle had ratchets under the steering wheel to keep it in place). Pops had such a great sense of humor and liked ribbing his three sons, hoping to make them stronger men. He once told me that, after my father graduated with a "fancy degree in Economics" from the Wharton School of Finance, Dad "got such a big head that all he can talk about now are things in the millions and no longer in the thousands!"

Dad not only understood business and finance, but he was a conscientious and hard worker. Pops was correct in noting that his son was usually pretty restless, though, and it was a good thing that Dad's keen mind came up with plenty of opportunities to keep busy. He just always had a good nose for sniffing out an investment opportunity or another project, for himself and for others. Back when Charles Lindbergh flew into town in 1927, I understand my father rented a bunch of tents and had them put up at our former Municipal Airport (which had just been established the year before and was actually located out in Altoona, east of Des Moines). Dad got his friends to manage the tents and sell pop all day when Lindbergh landed there, making a nice $200 profit. It was that kind of creative stuff that kept my father busy and happy.

Even when not at work or going about the business of helping others, Dad rarely seemed fully relaxed. He smoked like the dickens, probably to help settle him down a little. In later years, he supposedly stopped smoking, but we'd often find him sneaking a cigarette when he thought nobody was looking. In an attempt to unwind, he did regularly go to our local YMCA for a swim, a steam bath, and a massage (usually called a "rubdown" back then). And he just loved listening to music, especially jazz. Dad had worked his way through college at the University of Pennsylvania, not only as an arithmetic and business teacher [and apparently football team manager] at St. Elizabeth's High School in Philadelphia, but also as a drummer with his own band. I remember whenever he was listening to music on the radio or television, he was always moving his feet and legs and often his hands to the rhythm—he just loved the beat, and I know it was relaxing to him. In later life, Dad even had a full set of drums in his home that was down the hill from mine. He often could be heard playing jazz patterns on those, while Mom painted in her art room just across the hall in their entry loft area.

I don't actually remember how my father and mother originally met, but it was likely at the old West High, which was located on the southeast corner of 15th and Center Streets. Dad had attended Bird Elementary on 21st Street (now Martin Luther King Blvd.), immediately across the street east of his 2105 High Street home, and Mom had attended Greenwood Elementary a few hundred yards from her house on 37th Street. After graduating from high school, my mother left for Wellesley College in Massachusetts before later transferring to the University of Iowa, where she became a loyal Kappa Kappa Gamma. I'm really not sure why Mom first went to Wellesley, unless perhaps she wanted to go east to be closer to my Dad in Pennsylvania. I do remember some talk about the concern my Jewett grandparents had about Dad getting married before he graduated, and how they didn't want the two of them going to the same school—I wish I'd listened better to that full story.

After graduating from their respective Universities, my parents were married on September 18, 1922, Mom's 22nd birthday. Dad had turned 22 that February. My mother was a terrific artist and could draw or paint on just about anything. She seemed to specialize in oils and pastels on canvas, and we still have many of her Okoboji water scenes (and others) hanging in our family homes today. Mom's mother and aunts were artists as well, so she came by it quite naturally—I understand that Grandma Shore had taken some art training in Des Moines, and also in Paris (probably while her husband, Dr. F. E. V., was doing his own specialized EENT training overseas), but had to set aside many artistic endeavors when their children came along. And you'll recall that my grandmother Shore's eldest sister, Florence Call (Cowles), started her higher education at the Institute of Art in Chicago before transferring to Northwestern University there.

Mom had trained, and even taught design, at the Cumming School of Art in Des Moines. As mentioned earlier, Charles Cumming and his wife Nell were good friends of my Shore grandparents; when my mother was born in 1900, Charles Cumming agreed to be Mom's godfather! Mr. Cumming first ran the Art Department at Cornell College in Mt. Vernon,

Iowa, after which he became the director of the Des Moines Academy of Art. That Academy was so successful that it was renamed 'The Cumming School of Art' just five years later. Mr. Cumming was quite the artist himself, painting a huge mural, entitled "The Departure of the Indians from Fort Des Moines," on the wall above the second-floor balcony of the Polk County Courthouse. He also painted many of the portraits that once hung (and likely still do) in the Iowa Historical Building. Mr. Cumming was considered a pioneer in the early art endeavors of our state, and was soon invited to serve as superintendent of the Iowa State Fair's Department of Art and to also start an Art Department at the (State) University of Iowa. He then formed the Iowa Art Guild, to which my mother was a contributing member throughout her life.

The Cumming School of Art was first housed on the third floor of the newly constructed library building downtown on the river, at 100 Locust Street [constructed in 1903, it was the city's central library until 2006; it has since been remodeled as a museum for the World Food Prize Hall of Laureates]. I understand that Mr. Cumming himself designed all the furnishings for making his studio one with an old Parisian atmosphere. I just love the story about my mother and her younger brother, Dick, who used to ride downtown with Pop Shore to his medical office on Saturday mornings. From there the two kids roller-skated to the main library building on the river, where Mom studied art from Charles Cumming and Dick studied violin from Nell Cumming. Then the two of them would roller skate all the way home to 210-37th Street from 100 Locust Street—Mom talked about how hard it was to skate up the Grand Avenue hill, and I sure can believe it!

Not only was my mother involved with the Iowa Art Guild, but she was also a member of the National Society of the Colonial Dames of America, the Daughters of the American Revolution, and the Junior League of Des Moines. In addition to her involvement in the Plymouth Congregational United Church of Christ, she also kept memberships at the Wakonda Club, the Des Moines Club and the Embassy Club. Mom did some commercial artwork and some commissioned pieces over the years, but Dad really didn't want my mother to earn money outside the home. She was pleased to display her art annually at the Iowa State Fair, however, and at the Des Moines Women's Club shows held at Hoyt Sherman Place where she won many blue ribbons for her works. I remember that Mom wrote a children's book once, and it was full of her own artistic illustrations—I am hopeful Connie still has it safely stored somewhere.

After they got married in 1922, my folks first lived in an apartment at 511-29th Street, on the east side of the road between Grand and Ingersoll Avenues. (That brick building still stands and is currently being completely refurbished.) Across the hall from them was another newly married couple whose pioneer family business, Wood Brothers, Inc., was in the manufacturing of threshing and harvesting machines. The couples soon became best of friends, even traveling together the rest of their lives. I remember a lot of things about that family, but what seems to most stick in my mind for some reason is a hair-growing machine that took up much of their living room in the large family home they had built by the time I was a little kid. The machine had a great big hood that the guy sat under after turning it on. I recall that it was terribly expensive, but I'm not so sure it really worked for him—I don't ever remember the man as anything but balding! Dad was working full-time at the Jewett Lumber Company right out of college, but also soon started working for that guy from the apartment across the hall, first as Wood Brothers' General Manager, and later also becoming its Vice President (as listed earlier). Though they had locations throughout the U.S. and Canada, their main operation was located at E. 18th and Aurora Avenue here in Des Moines. My father was so creative, as I've said already, and once came up with a side opportunity idea for that company, one that involved Sears and Roebuck. Mom and Dad took me into Chicago, where we stayed at the big home of the President of Sears while he and Dad talked business—after that stay, Sears started carrying cast iron skillets manufactured by Wood Brothers' foundry out of Des Moines. And during the WWII years, I recall that my father went to Washington, D.C. every two weeks, negotiating government contracts for various war items that this guy's firm also built (i.e., depth bomb tracks, ammo boxes, etc.) to help keep their company open during those tougher times.

After making it through the rough war years, Dad said to his friend who owned that company, "You've got these sales offices all over the country, but you are undercapitalized. If you would sell out, your family could be fixed financially for life." The man agreed and asked Dad to find a buyer for their business. The hottest prospect was Dearborn Motors, made up of executives of the Ford Motor Company. My father enjoyed so much going to the Detroit area and having lunch from time to time with the likes of Henry Ford, Sr., Henry Ford, Jr., and Edsel Ford. Though he tried to get them interested, I understand they just kept dragging their feet on purchasing the business. So, Dad eventually found another buyer, a guy from right here in Des Moines. And believe it or not, that local man ended up purchasing the company, then later sold it to none other than Dearborn Motors... and for half-a-million-dollar profit!

Dad had taken over the actual presidential helm of the Jewett Lumber company at an early age, due to his own father branching out into the complementary businesses of 'D. L. Jewett and Sons' and the 'Jewett Realty Company' (D. L. then became Honorary President of the Lumber Company). Dad's third occupation as Collector of Internal Revenue made my father a busy guy during those days. As listed previously, he was also appointed by the Courts a number of times as a 'Receiver' to help liquidate businesses that were in trouble financially; Dad did so much court mediation and negotiation that a group of local attorneys even presented him with a 'grandfather' certificate to practice law without a license!

My parents were just such wonderful people. They were true examples of love to me and to Connie. We never heard them fight, and we never heard them curse. We never knew either of them to raise their voices, no matter what happened. I just couldn't have been luckier than to have parents like those two, especially as such an active kid and a busy adult. Dad died far too young, at age 76. He was a decades-long smoker and the habit had caused the disease of emphysema in his later years. He'd survived colon cancer surgery, after which he wore a colostomy bag for a short time, but he couldn't get over the emphysema. Mom faithfully did regular tapping on his back to help loosen phlegm, and would oversee his breathing exercises several times a day with the hand-held blowing device he kept next to his chair. (Whenever I've been hospitalized following some surgery, I've thought of my father while blowing into the same type of hand-held machine, moving that little ball to help prevent pneumonia.)

Dad was a very slight man, only about 5'8" tall and 160 pounds, and seemed to get smaller with each year after about age 70. But he never stopped working. When most folks were retiring by age 65 or 70, my father continued to go to his office at the lumber company every single day, until the day he went into the hospital for one last time. In February of

1976, he and Mom had taken commercial flights out to California, planning to reconnect with personal friends who were key people in the Weyerhauser Lumber Corporation. Nelle and I flew out a few days later to join up with them in San Francisco. Dad wasn't feeling well and was complaining of shortness of breath due to being starved for oxygen during the high-altitude time on the commercial flights out there. He was a good sport, however, and we all four boarded a Weyerhauser-owned twin DC-3 that came down to pick us up and take us to tour their big distribution center in Takoma, Washington.

Unfortunately, Dad never seemed to have full use of his lungs after that trip, and passed away three months later at Iowa Methodist Medical Center from complications of pneumonia. [Gerald Anson Jewett, Sr. had been born in Paris, France on February 22, 1900, and died in Des Moines, Iowa on May 13, 1976.] The pallbearers at my father's funeral were the men who owned the other major lumber companies here in Des Moines—that's how respected he was. [D. L. Jewett's pallbearers in 1951 had also been men from the other lumber companies.] When I turned 76, I just figured that would be the last year of my life too. But here I am, still feeling pretty darn good at 92—it's really hard to believe!

My folks were married 54 years, before Dad's death. For their 50th anniversary, in September of 1972, they threw themselves a very large party with about 250 in attendance at the old Des Moines Club downtown. Many came from out of town and out of state, including my mother's cousin who owned the *Minneapolis Star*—their corporate pilots flew him (and his wife) down for the affair. Mom and Dad, both 72-years-young, looked so terrific that night.

The week before my father passed away in 1976, I had finalized the purchase of my own summer home on Echo Bay at Lake Okoboji and had begun doing some remodeling of it (replacing the roof, adding a breezeway to connect the house with the garage, etc.). Imagine my surprise when arriving at the new cottage one weekend and looking forward to seeing the construction progress, only to be distracted by a big old white toilet perched on top of my chimney! Along with a few junky little bric-a-brac things placed elsewhere around the chimney top, a large plastic duck was sitting in the toilet bowl, with a tall pinwheel sticking out of the rear tank. It had all been put there by some of my so-called 'friends' who had come up with

the hair-brained scheme after a night of too much lake fun—the temptation of using the existing worksite scaffolding to get something up onto my roof was apparently just too inviting to pass up! I had to hire a boom truck to finally get that big old toilet down a few days later, but we ended up with plenty of pics proving it was there. (One of my Okoboji friends thought that the story and this photo should be included, so here it is.)

Since Nelle and I had just moved into our own Okoboji place within a week or two of Dad's passing, I was worried about my mother being alone at their Dixon Beach cottage for the upcoming summer months. Hers was the same lake home that her father-in-law, my Pops Jewett, had purchased back in 1941, and I had always taken care of most of the yard and other items of upkeep at the place all those decades. After Dad was gone, Mom decided to stay up at Okoboji for the entire summer and we talked every day, either by phone or in person, about how she was getting along. She would tell me she was doing well, though on a few occasions she'd say, "I had a little stroke last night but I feel fine today." As always, she never complained about things, and just seemed to learn to live with occasional TIA's [transient ischemic attacks—little strokes]. I may have had a couple of those myself over the past few years—my doctors are not sure, but that (along with drops in blood pressure) might help explain an occasional fall.

As it turned out, Mom got along beautifully and enjoyed having a number of house parties up at the cottage with her girlfriends. Sis Connie, who had her own home further up the lake, was able to keep watch on Mom during the weekdays while I held down the office in Des Moines. And on weekends when back up there, Mom would stop over at my new cottage to visit, which was just terrific. She regularly drove larger cars and, with Dad being mostly a Ford and Lincoln guy, she especially grew fond of driving Continentals. Then in 1982, Cadillac came out with a smaller car called a Cimarron... Mom was ready for a vehicle that was easier to maneuver, so I handled the purchase of a new little navy blue one for her. She looked so happy driving it out of the showroom that day... It certainly came as a surprise when my friend who owned the local dealership called me a couple days later, embarrassed to tell me that Mom's check to them had bounced! I called her right away, and she was so surprised too—surprised there wasn't money in the checking account! She told me, "But there's always been money whenever I have written a check." Obviously, she'd not written a check quite that large since Dad died, and didn't realize that she would need to transfer from savings to checking in order to make that trick work! Though she no longer traveled around the world like she and Dad had done (especially loving their trips to Havana, Cuba during that country's heyday in the 1930's and 40's), Mom found so many ways to keep busy, and enjoyed a wonderful nine years of life after Dad passed. [Bertha Shore Jewett was born in Des Moines, Iowa on September 18, 1900, and died in Okoboji, Iowa on July 9, 1985.]

While she was still living, my mother also had her old beloved 1956 Ford Parklane station wagon ('Nassau Blue' on 'Harbor Blue' in color), which was parked year-round in their lake garage. That vehicle has enjoyed a long history with our family… Dad had made it a habit to buy Mom a new car every other year, but when purchasing her a new Ford in 1958, he wasn't able to get much on the trade for the '56 Parklane (Ford had suddenly stopped production of the model after only 15,000+ were sold in that one year); so, I suggested keeping it in the family as a lake car, which they did. Being an artist, Mom loved filling the back end with canvas pieces and paints and brushes, then piling her grandchildren into it for a drive to a cozy spot where the kids could swim while she painted. I very much wanted to own that station wagon someday, and regularly cleaned it up and kept it running smoothly for my mother. It drove me crazy that Mom also let everyone else drive it, including my sister's babysitters who regularly hauled the kids around in it up at the Lakes—everyone else looked at the '56 Ford as transportation, but I saw it as an original family classic car that could one day be restored!

I didn't drive to the Lakes much myself, preferring to fly up almost every weekend, which meant needing wheels to get around once there. One of my lumber suppliers knew that I was looking for a used car to leave sitting outside up at the Okoboji Airport during the week, and told me about an old Studebaker that had been stored for years in his uncle's garage in Des Moines. He offered it to me for nothing if I could just get it running; so, he and I went over there and put a battery in it, along with some fresh gas, and the doggone thing started—we couldn't believe it! I took it up to the Lakes and drove the Studebaker around for awhile; then after that old thing finally gave out, I picked up various other cars to serve the airport purpose, including a fun white Jeep Bronco and a nice old black Cadillac four-door sedan.

Eventually, I ended up with Mom's 1956 Ford Parklane wagon and kept it as my own Okoboji car (though not regularly leaving it outside at the airport!), and fully restored it to stock quality. It was all repainted by a guy with a small out-of-the-way body shop across the road from a little cabin I built on the river out in Commerce, just south of West Des

Moines. It took the guy a year to finish the paint job—I sure regretted ever telling him to just take his time! After a couple decades of owning that vehicle, I finally got tired of keeping it up and one day surprised my son-in-law by handing over the keys to him. John loves cars and is as fussy as I am about how he keeps them. I know it's in good hands, and am glad that he and Jennifer have such good memories of dating in that car back in the late '60's. It's still in showroom condition, with about 86,000 miles, and they have even entered the wagon in a couple of classic shows—it has been fun to hear about the prizes.

{Editor's note: Though not yet five when Nana got the blue Ford, I remember the subsequent years of 'piling' (as Dad calls it) into that car with my sister and cousins and all of Nana's art materials, sitting in the back end of the wagon to keep her many palettes and easels from shifting everywhere when she 'hauled' us (as Dad also calls it) around. Sixty years later, a smile crosses my face each day when entering my garage and seeing the pristine and vibrant blue-on-blue beauty. And I could almost swear that it smiles back at me, as in this picture, so proud of its history and of its more current license plate— NANAS56—which pays tribute to my wonderful Nana (and to this current Nana too!).}

SERVING OUR COUNTRY

After having graduated from Roosevelt in May of 1943, I volunteered in the College Training Detachment (CTD) of the U.S. Army Air Corps and got deferred to take one semester of college at Drake University. That was especially meaningful since Drake had been founded in part by the efforts of my great-grandfather, and I had such good memories of being over there with him as a kid. But while going to Drake for school myself, I didn't learn very much because it seemed more important to skip classes with a beautiful girl and go to Walnut Woods to spend the day talking and necking.

In February of 1944, I entered the Army Air Corps and started training to be a pilot, which I wanted very much. Most of my friends were smoking, which was the thing to do back then, but my choice to not smoke was because I'd heard that one cigarette could take away ten percent of your night vision. And I've still never smoked (other than as a three- or four-year-old when I regularly lit up one of the two cigars that Mr. Herring had intended for my Pop Shore, and as a five-year-old when Uncle Phil gave me the corn cob pipe! Oh, and there is one other time as an adult that you'll learn about later in this book.) It's interesting that I personally chose not to smoke, then ended up marrying two women who were both quite good at it! That second-hand smoke couldn't have been at all good for me, but I *am* living to tell about it. By the way, my eyesight is still pretty decent, 20/30 and 20/40, which I recently learned is enough to pass the Iowa DOT test to keep a driver's license!

Before leaving for the service, I sold my 1936 Ford convertible to the deaf cement ball buddy, finalizing the sale in the Greenwood Tavern on Ingersoll Avenue. He, of course, was unable to enlist due to his handicap, and I was glad that my car would stay in Des Moines in good hands. I was immediately off to Camp Dodge, and one of the first things we had to endure was a 'peter parade,' where we were inspected for crabs! While in line, a few of my friends were in a group on the side of the lineup, and I asked them what they were standing over there for… they replied, "We have the crabs." Then when *I* got in front of the doctor, he pointed and told me to go over there with that same group. I said, "But Doctor, *they* have the crabs!" And he replied, "Go over and get with that group… you have the crab *eggs!*" Our bunch was then led into another part of the building where we were told to pair up and shave each other's bodies, getting rid of all the hair from the tops of our ears down to our toes. We were then given G.I. soap and told to scrub ourselves thoroughly in the shower. From there, we had to stand up in a straight line, nude, while a soldier with an old-fashioned fly spray gun filled with a disinfectant sprayed our bodies. Then they had us all turn around and bend over while the same soldier came down the line spraying our rear ends, which really burned. After that, we were each given a package with our old clothes stamped, 'CONTAMINATED—DO NOT OPEN—MUST TAKE TO THE CLEANERS,' and were told to address the packages to our homes. Supposedly there were lots of crabs on toilets and wherever else in those days, so it was pretty common... my girlfriend even got infected. (I guess it's important to add that I've never since had a crab!)

A few days later, we were all hauled by bus from Camp Dodge to the Rock Island Depot in downtown Des Moines where we boarded a troop train, not knowing where we were going.

While on the train, a Second Lieutenant asked me if I could cut hair; I said, "Sure," and proceeded to give him a fairly decent cut—lucky for me, he was pretty well satisfied with the results. After a couple of days on the troop train, we ended up in Biloxi, Mississippi, living in tent city barracks for our basic training at Keesler Field—my first day there was February 11, 1944. By March, I had earned a sharpshooter badge, which was ever-so-proudly displayed above my left pocket.

Once officially in training, every guy had an interview with military 'higher-ups' who asked various questions about our lives. One of the things they asked me was, "Have you ever had a broken bone?," followed by several other questions to see if I was a guy prone to bad luck. They made a record of each response, then repeated back all answers to have me verify their correctness. I had never had a broken bone and told them so. At the time, I hadn't realized that answering in the affirmative to any of those types of questions would have actually disqualified me from training as a pilot—they steered away from accepting guys who might have accidents that could be blamed on the military, I guess. (Just for the record, I still can't recall ever having a broken bone to this day, other than that of my right middle finger, which shattered many years later when shaking hands one time with a very enthusiastic fellow!)

One day we were all standing in formation at Keesler Field, and my Uncle Warren, who was a Captain in the Army Air Corps by then, flew in from San Antonio to Biloxi to surprise me. He showed up in his summer dress uniform and was all decorated out with lots of medals—he really looked like an important General. Warren walked up and asked the Sergeant in charge of our large group if 'Private Jewett' was in the ranks. The Sergeant called me out of formation and I enthusiastically walked toward Warren (nobody knew he was my uncle). Two or three other guys in the group urgently whispered to me, "Salute him, salute!" But I just smiled while walking forward to excitedly shake my Uncle's hand.

I was in Biloxi for two months, and during that time we had a seventeen-mile bivouac hike, living in pup tents along the way. My girlfriend in Des Moines had continued to write a letter to me every single day, which meant so much. And her nice soft stationery sure came in handy for toilet paper when needed on that bivouac. The roads down in Biloxi were made out of sea shells and rolled with a roller—when the sun shined they smelled just terrible! We tried to get over that smell by singing songs as we marched, such as "LEFT… LEFT… I LEFT my wife with twenty-eight kids and no gingerbread LEFT… LEFT… I shoulda gone home but I LEFT… LEFT." And, of course, we never grew tired of marching to "99 Bottles of Beer on the Wall." The bivouac finally ended and, after eventually returning to Base, it was discovered that I'd somehow contracted scabies and had to be put into the hospital and quarantined for a number of days—back to being isolated from my friends!

After the two months in Biloxi, we hauled out on a troop train to Kelly Field in San Antonio for a week or so, then loaded onto another troop train taking us clear across the state of Texas to Pampa, which is up in the panhandle fifty miles east of Amarillo. We were on that dang train for two days—one of the reasons it took so long is that our train often had to pull off onto side tracks to let faster trains, or even a two-man handcar, go past us! In Pampa, we had not started our pilot training yet, and I decided to take a nap in the baggage compartment behind the three-place backseat of one of the many UC-78 twin-engine Cessnas called 'Bamboo Bombers,' which were used to train pilots for the multi-engine ratings. While taking my nap, I was suddenly awakened (and in total surprise) when the plane took off with a pilot and instructor in front! I didn't know what to do, and didn't know where I would end up, but hoped like heck it would be back at the same Air Base… thankfully, it was!

{Editor's note: After relating that story, Dad made mention that the Bamboo Bomber sleeping experience was his last nap in airplanes... but we soon came upon this scrapbook photo, aptly labeled 'A LOCKHEED HUDSON USED FOR A NAP.' He then recalled that there were, after all, a few more opportunities for some aircraft shut-eye on later Bases too!}

When we arrived in Pampa in April of 1944, and while standing in formation, we were told that the wind there could blow so strong, and the place would get so dusty, that you could measure the wind speed in this way: if you could not see the mess hall down at the end of the block, the wind was blowing at such and such miles per hour; if you could not see the water tower, the wind was blowing at such and such miles per hour; and if you could not see the church across the street, be sure the ropes on your barracks roof are snugged down good and tight to keep the roof from blowing off the building! While lined up in formation a couple days later, I found out that it was necessary to stand at about a 45-degree angle into the wind to keep a guy from blowing over!

After being stationed in Pampa a few weeks, we shipped to Cincinnati, Ohio for College

Training Detachment, where I finally learned to fly. In addition to our regular studies, we spent actual training time at Lunken Field (fondly referred to by all of us as "Sunken Lunken"). We flew in Aeronca L3Cs, and some of the guys got airsick and threw up... we all learned right then and there that "he who dirties plane cleans plane." On the tenth hour of flying, one of our instructors, when passing close to the field, would regularly throw the stick controlling the airplane out of the plane's window to give us confidence on landing the craft—as you can imagine, that certainly got our attention! (What we didn't know at the time was that the instructor also had a backup stick!) I had accumulated ten hours of flight time when they told me, "You're OK to solo." That was music to my ears.

The U.S. Government had taken over St. Xavier University in Cincinnati. We had terrific food and wonderfully equipped buildings, including two-man dorm rooms with a lavatory in each. (I'm the Elet Hall dormmate on the upper right in this May 7, 1944 photo.)

The only really bad part about being at St. Xavier was that we had to run two miles each day, up and down Victory Parkway. I guess the brighter side of that exercise drill, however, was that the people in Cincinnati didn't see very many soldiers and they were especially kind, even catching up with us along the way in order to talk, to offer us theater tickets, to invite us to their homes for meals, and so on—we felt pretty special.

Though without a car while in Cincinnati, I didn't seem to have much trouble getting around using city transportation. There was a hotel downtown that we service guys frequented regularly if we could get a date. In the middle of the big fancy dining room was an ice skating rink, which made for great ongoing entertainment during a meal! The Ohio River divided the State of Ohio from the State of Kentucky, and Kentucky was off-limits to enlisted guys. 'Coney Island' was just off the shore not terribly far from Cincinnati, though, so we liked to take the 30-to-45-minute riverboat ride up to it. And on the weekends, many women flocked to the boat to meet up with us for dancing.

One time during the five months I was stationed there, my folks brought my girlfriend from Des Moines up to Cincinnati to visit me. She was just a beautiful lady, but never really healthy after that long bout with mononucleosis. In those days, women couldn't get silk hose because of the war, so they started wearing leg makeup to make it look like they were wearing hose, even adding the dark line up the back like the seam. Being summertime, I was wearing what was known as the 'suntan uniform'—and after being with my girlfriend, I ended up with leg makeup all over it. (If I remember correctly, the Des Moines Hosiery Mill [later renamed the Rollins Hosiery Mill after the owner, who also built the big Rollins Mansion still located on Fleur Drive south of Bell Avenue] was the country's first major manufacturer of nylon hose after converting from a silk hose operation. They had a huge plant located on the east side of town, a block from the Fairgrounds, but were also located all around the country. Then I believe they drastically scaled back their business because of not being able to obtain materials during and even after the war.)

We later shipped from Cincinnati back down to Kelly Field in San Antonio, where I also trained out of nearby Randolph Field. Kelly had every kind of airplane you can imagine, including B-29's. You have to look closely to even see me peeking out of the pilot's window of the huge craft (in reality, I never flew one of these, but was just showing off for the camera!).

After only a week or two in San Antonio, I arrived on June 30, 1944, at the Army Air Base at Waco, Texas for another 1½ years of further training. They had every kind of aircraft you can imagine there too. We started with Fairchild Primary Trainers (PT-19s) and then flew Basic Trainers (BT-13s). From there, we progressed to AT-6s, which were Advance Trainers. Fortunately, there was a country club near the Waco Base, with a clubhouse, swimming pool, and golf course; the government had taken over this club, as they had taken over St. Xavier back in Cincinnati, so we had a wonderful place to go and party… WACs, WAVEs and all. My scrapbook seems to have a lot of pictures of our wild celebrations out there! *{Editor's note: For the reader of this book who might also be an airplane enthusiast, Dad's school and military service scrapbook has various additional photos of an AT-7 twin-engine Beechcraft, a UC-78 Cessna, a BT-13, and an AT-11 (which he described as an AT-7 with a glass nose for navigator training). Though completely falling apart all these years later, the 11" x 14" scrapbook is about 6 inches thick and has black construction paper-like pages. Jerry's printing is all in white ink… very stunning!}*

The first few Waco months were 'unassigned' for trainees… basically, that meant they didn't know what to do with us. And that gave us various employment opportunities. Upon arriving there, I drove an ambulance, escorting war-injured men who were just a couple days off the front lines in Europe. The poor guys had been lifted directly from the battlefield and flown over to Miami in evacuation aircraft, where they were then dispersed to Waco and other Bases around the states, according to whatever wounds they had. For those coming to Waco, it was my job to drive them to the McCloskey General Hospital in Temple, which was 37 miles southwest of our Base. Many of these men were "litter cases" who were in pretty bad shape. When I drove them onto the hospital grounds, our wounded guys saw German prisoners of war working in the hospital yards with no fences around them—and after just coming off the battlefields two days before, it made them almost crazy to see the enemy working freely in this capacity. I truly did enjoy being on the road and helping these wounded guys, but it was terribly tough emotionally.

After my stint in ambulance duty I was promoted to driving staff cars, chauffeuring all kinds of military personnel... including some Generals. Being nothing more than an Air Corps Cadet, that was quite an exciting job for this kid. Here I am as the personal driver for a one-star General (note the one star on his windshield!).

Eventually, I had a car down there myself—Great-aunt Bonnie's old 1937 Plymouth sedan, which was just like new. It was the vehicle she bought after getting rid of her electric car and was on loan to me, along with a letter to that effect. In order to pick up her Plymouth and take it down to Waco, I waited for my two-week furlough in November of '44 and got a ride up to Des Moines in the belly of a B-25 bomber. I was issued a parachute before boarding the plane but had never used one and never thought I'd need one. So, I just folded it up beside me and proceeded to take a nap on it. Once airborne, I was sleeping soundly when the bomber hit a huge downdraft—I was so scared after being startled awake, thinking I had fallen out of the airplane without my chute. The plane came out of the downdraft when the quick-thinking pilot shoved the wheel ahead so that it dropped further in order to go with the draft. Boy, was I relieved to be alive!

Over the years, people have often asked if I've ever jumped from an airplane... the answer is NO—I'd be scared to death to do that! Some have wondered if I've ever gone hot-air ballooning, and that whole idea scares me too (as does the thought of zip-lining, like my cousin in Colorado just did on his recent 69th birthday). I've also been asked if a guy like me, who has spent much of his life in the skies for so many years, has ever seen a UFO—to be honest, I sometimes looked around for those, especially whenever there was an article in the paper or talk of others seeing one, but I personally just never did notice any.

Keeping Bonnie's Plymouth at Waco was terrific. I was so pleased to have my own vehicle to tinker with again, even if it meant having to eventually install (with my close pal, in front of our barracks) a new gas tank in it by February of 1945. Back in those days, something always went wrong with vehicles but, as you know, I felt right at home doing that kind of repair work.

While 'unassigned' at Waco, and having a car, I took three of my buddies on all kinds of trips, including one to Mexico. I remember driving us down to San Antonio one night, then one of the other guys offered to drive the rest of the way from San Antonio to Mexico so I could crawl into the back seat for a nap; when waking up a few hours later, I saw a sign that said, "WACO TEXAS." In other words, my buddy drove us from San Antonio back up to Waco by mistake! So, we filled up with gas again at the very same station in Waco, turned around and headed back south to a nightclub in Matamoros, Mexico. (It was eye-opening for us that the women prostitutes in the place handed out business cards with phone numbers to later reach them.) And that's where I learned to drink tequila for the first time— I recall sitting at the bar when my brain sent a signal to my

feet to get up and go to the bathroom, but I couldn't move! Eventually, I was able to stand up, at least enough to play a mean guitar in this picture, dated December 8, 1944 [which was the third anniversary of the U.S. declaring war on Japan, following their December 7, 1941 attack on Pearl Harbor].

Just outside our Waco Air Base was a large sign telling the highway mileage to different towns, such as Dallas. Somebody had hand-written at the bottom of the sign, "BABE'S— 875 MILES." Babe's was the very popular Des Moines nightclub, and that sign always made me a little bit homesick. It helped that we received copies of a smaller *Des Moines Register*—called the *Servicemen's Edition*—to keep up on news from home, but sometimes it only made me want to jump into the car and head north. I had a gate pass that said, "Good Within Three-Mile Radius" of the Air Base, but that wasn't much of a radius for a guy like me. I'll never forget the one time I decided to head to Des Moines (further than the legal three miles) for a long weekend, in order to see my girlfriend and spend time with Mom and Dad. Since 'unassigned,' I thought I'd get by with it. I first stopped by the PX to purchase for my folks eight fifths of whiskey and eight cartons of cigarettes, which were hard to come by back in the day. Then I loaded up the car with those boxes and with extra winter clothes for the Iowa weather, in addition to some extra summer clothes to wear before and after being up north.

I started driving and got as far as Tulsa, Oklahoma when I was stopped at a roadblock checking for stolen cars. After proving with Bonnie's letter that I had permission to be driving her vehicle, they decided I must be deserting the Air Corps due to having all these year-round clothes filling up the backseat. Being the middle of the night on a Friday, they told me I'd have to see the Provost Marshall in the morning; I was taken on over to the Tulsa jail to spend the night. There was about a half inch of 'play' in the jail cell doors, and some drunken locals also in jail were shaking those doors and yelling all night. Finally becoming tired enough, I had to lie down on my woven steel bed and was thankfully able to fall asleep. After a few hours, I heard a rattle under my cell door, and watched them slide a pie tin with white beans and a slice of bread under the door; it almost made me throw up just looking at it. Later in the morning, somebody came to my cell and said, "Mr. Jewett, let's get you out of here." And I said, "I'm ready." They took me to the Provost Marshall, who called my Commanding Officer at Waco and told him they had apprehended somebody they thought was deserting. My C.O. said, "It sounds like he's a little bit out of bounds… Give him special orders to report back to me," which I did the following morning. After walking into his office, my Commanding Officer said, "Mr. Jewett, I'm going to give you the 104th Article of War (which is a written citation) as your punishment, and it will remain here in my right-hand bottom drawer and will never be taken out." So, I got lucky that time! But not lucky enough to have returned with the whiskey and cigarettes—those had all been confiscated back in the 'dry town' of Tulsa, which made me very unhappy. (I want to make certain to add here that this incident was the first and last time in my life to ever be behind bars as a detainee.)

In order to build up flying time in Waco, I volunteered to work at the private Newland Airfield doing a little of everything. (And when later receiving my pilot's license in February of 1945, it was the owner of that field who handed it to me.) I flew regular 100-mile flights into Love Field at Dallas for aircraft parts, and even instructed female flight students from nearby Baylor University. The chief pilot at the Newland Field was also my trainer, a 300-pound guy with a heart as big as his body. The training plane only had a 65 hp engine and whenever I dropped him off and soloed, I was afraid the plane would never come down— it just floated and floated without his weight! After learning in that 65 hp plane, I then got to use mostly PT-19s (with 175 hp) while there. So much time was spent at Newland Field that I borrowed a bed from the United States Government and put it in the back room of their airport office; that way, if there was a student to train in the morning, I could get up and get ready quickly with no driving time across town!

My instructor and his wife liked me very much, doing me several favors and serving me many fine meals. I hoped to repay them somehow and asked if there was anything I could do for them. My trainer's wife said she would sure enjoy having some sugar for baking since it was tough to get that due to sugar-rationing going on during the war. The government kept all their raw cooking ingredients in garbage cans in the kitchen—where I napped on the floor under the tables during my KP duty—so it really wasn't difficult to get some sugar for my trainer's wife; the next day, without looking twice, I filled a great big aluminum pitcher, dipping it into the garbage can of what I thought was sugar. The three of us laughed many times over the following years about how I proudly presented them with a big pitcher of salt that day! I also later presented them with a pitcher of sugar, however, and she even baked me a pie. (Long after that trainer passed away, I continued to keep in touch with his dear wife by phone and in letters even through her elderly time of life, and thoroughly enjoyed having her stay as a guest in my Okoboji home one summer—we even had a date lined up for her, which was a lot of fun.)

Back over at the Waco Army Air Base, I started my actual flight training by piloting Primary Trainer 19 (PT-19) Fairchild airplanes too, as already mentioned—they were two-place tandem open cockpits with 175 hp Ranger engines and were so fun to fly and to do acrobatics in. But I learned first-hand to always fasten my seatbelt because one of my buddies fell out of a PT-19 when doing a loop... luckily, he pulled his parachute, though pooping his pants at the same  time, and landed safely. (Decades later, I was given a propeller from a PT-19, and had it hanging on the wall in my lake home as a talking piece for many years—more recently it was passed on to one of my grandsons, who had requested eventually owning it.)

We also had Basic Training 13 (BT-13) aircraft with 450 hp Pratt & Whitney engines on our Base, then later got Advanced Training 6 (AT-6) airplanes with 550 hp engines. The Waco Army Air Base not only had a good mixture of different kinds of airplanes, but it also had quite a mixture of personnel—we had both WACs [Women's Army Corps] and WAVEs [Women Accepted for Volunteer Emergency Services (in the Navy)] stationed at our field, which kept it interesting. To my knowledge, they didn't train any WACs to be pilots, but the WAVEs were trained. We guys always had fun when the WAVEs got out of an airplane we were getting into… we'd ask them how the relief tube works, to which we got a number of different answers! For some reason, there were a few incidents when WAVEs took off in BT-13s with the trim tab in the landing position… after take-off, the airplanes stalled and soon crashed—that always seemed so strange. We also had Brazilian pilots in training at our field, and when they started flying the AT-6s with retractable gear, they oftentimes came in for a landing with the wheels up. They did not understand English when the tower yelled at them to lower their gear! Soon after that, the government came out with leather straps to hold the landing gear in place. Much time was spent with our training program, including a lot of meetings with special concentration on A.I. (Aircraft Identification)—learning how to identify our own friendly planes, as well as enemy craft. During my time on the Base, half of our class was given a short leave, which I took to go home to see my folks and girlfriend. After that leave, I went back down to Waco, only to learn that while the rest of us were on leave, the other half of our class had shipped overseas! A lot of my good flying buddies never came home, which was tough to face.

Later, at Lackland Air Force Base in Waco, we got to start training in P-51 fighter planes. At first, a lot of the time was spent learning the systems and just sitting in the airplanes going nowhere. I couldn't wait to be flying a P-51 because it always reminded me of being on a fast racehorse and trying to stay one step ahead of it. At night, it was also fun because the exhaust fire from the single engine in front of you came past your eyes on both sides of the airplane. Originally, the P-51 contained three .30 caliber guns in each wing. Then the government changed those to .50 calibers and added two more guns, so there were four in each wing. But the most interesting part was that the .50 calibers they added were closer to the fuselage and were actually timed to shoot between the blades—you changed the pitch and the speed on those planes, and still, these bullets went between the blades! The P-51 was one of the finest fighter planes in existence, but it was quite a maintenance hog. We used to say P-51s took two hours of labor for every hour they flew. And we figured that, for normal flying, they also burned 100 gallons of gasoline an hour. Originally equipped with Allison engines, they later came out with Rolls Royce engines that had more power—they could do about 1530 hp, and also performed much better above 30,000 feet. Immediately after the war, you could have picked up a bunch of P-51s for around $5,000 each… today you'd have to pay about $2.2 million to own one!

During my 16 months in Waco, Uncle Warren (who was still a pilot in the Air Corps and stationed at Kelly Field in San Antonio) called me from time to time—he would inform me that he was coming to pick me up and to fly me in military aircraft to various places, which he did. Uncle Warren would arrive alone each time, offering me rides in a number of different planes, too many for me to even remember… one time he showed up in a Douglas Dauntless A-24 dive bomber, another time in a Canadian Norseman, and once in a Beaver (which was later used in Canada for flying in supplies to the different resorts)—they all provided pretty exciting flying experiences for me.

I'll never forget the time Warren arrived all alone in a B-25 twin-engine medium bomber, like the one in this picture. I had never ridden up front in one of those, and they always carried a pilot *and* a copilot. Boy, was I ever thrilled to be the copilot and to help fly a B-25 for a number of hours. That model of bomber was so much fun and, even while taxiing on the ground, those engines would pop and crackle. I just really loved that sound—it was like a lot of motor boats that do the

same thing. While flying together one day, Uncle Warren said to me, "Don't you think we're patriotic by exercising these airplanes for the government like this?" We actually flew up to Des Moines on one occasion, and were having such a good time there, seeing family and socializing with friends… Warren turned to me and said, "Jerry, don't you think that right engine was running a little bit rough getting here? Maybe we should spend an extra day and have them check over that engine." So that's just what we did!

We have in the family files a July 23, 1945 business letter that my Dad typed to his two brothers, in which he added a few personal updates about what I was doing down in Waco… "Jerry has been acting as dispatcher of the car pool and I think enjoys it very much, although he says it is quite a lot of responsibility. He was just called into a meeting in which they were told they were going to open up cadet training again for bombardiers, navigators, radar officers and flight officers. He was qualified for flight officer and has put in his request to take that training. Warren, you will be interested to know he flew a Stearman Hammond Pusher the other day. Each time he comes up it has been in (the belly of) a Billy Mitchell B-25." I sure enjoyed seeing that letter and knowing that Dad was bragging about me to his brothers. Incidentally, the Stearman Hammond Pusher was a very unusual airplane at that time, and we were lucky enough to have a brand-new model prototype of it at Newland Field.

I enjoyed getting up to Des Moines to see my folks and girlfriend whenever possible. If I could get a ride in the belly of a bomber or whatever else, I'd be there. There were things going on down in Waco, of course, but there was just so much more going on with all my Des Moines friends—and I hated to be so far away from *that* action! These WWII years were certainly lively for many of us who got into the service late—we spent plenty of time trying to do our patriotic part by entertaining the WACs. When in Des Moines for a weekend, those were the nights that we usually ended up after hours at my deaf cement ball buddy's house when his mother was out of town. At these late-night parties, everything seemed to happen. And I was then dating the girl who lived next door to my buddy, which presented some problems… Probably the funniest incident I can remember is when we guys were having a party (with some WACs) at my deaf buddy's house, while my girlfriend was having a slumber party with the rest of our steady girlfriends over at her house next door. Late in the night, the girlfriend group decided to come over to my buddy's house to see what was going on over there. My buddy's WAC date for the night had passed out cold on the davenport, but the rest of the gals were being entertained by us in the living room. As our steady girlfriends came in the back door unannounced, the WAC girls tried to run out the front door. The escape of the WACs was not quick enough, and all the guys got in trouble for having other dates… all, that is, except my deaf buddy with the WAC who had passed out on the couch—he had quickly pulled it out from the wall, then picked up his date and dropped her behind the davenport, pushing it back up to the wall before our girlfriends made it into the living room. Nobody ever found out that she was behind there! (I'm still laughing when recalling that story, as is Jen while typing it.)

In the same July 1945 letter from my Dad to brothers Warren and Homer, he added, "Jerry was up again last weekend. He got a hop with a Captain of Waco. He seems to get one about every two weeks this way. He has applied for a furlough and expects to get up here for his two weeks about the first of August." What none of us knew was that it would only be a matter of weeks before the war would come to an end, and I would have a permanent furlough to Des Moines!

When the war was over, they stopped our training—we shipped, in October of 1945, to San Antonio for discharge. I received my Honorable Discharge at Kelly Field on October 31, 1945, just 10 days after my 20th birthday. (This B-29 bomber picture was taken at Randolph Field outside of San Antonio on October 29, 1945, two days before my discharge at nearby Kelly Field.)

I will always be grateful to have been given such wonderful training during WWII and to have had the opportunity to fly so many different airplanes. I am also grateful that, though my pilot training started out in CTD, I never saw combat—it was tough enough that too many of my buddies never came home.

Prior to leaving Waco for discharge in San Antonio, I had traded cars with my Newland Field instructor. He and his wife drove a 1939 Plymouth which was in terrible shape, and I had Bonnie's 1937 Plymouth which, as I said, was in brand-new condition. The government had put a blue book ceiling on cars, though, so they were selling more on year of manufacture than on conditions... making my trainer's clunky car worth more money than her pristine one, simply due to being two years newer. So, I traded my great-aunt Bonnie's '37 Plymouth (even-up) for their '39 Plymouth, which is the car that took me back to Des Moines upon my discharge. When arriving home, Aunt Bonnie told me she thought she might like to drive again (but fortunately, she never did, so that was that!).

WILD AND CRAZY UNIVERSITY DAYS

After two months in Des Moines following the service days, I enrolled in January of 1946 as a Business major at the State University of Iowa (now known simply as the 'University of Iowa'). Right out of the service, I had been lucky enough to be driving around in a beautiful green 1942 Ford Club Coupe that had been owned by my Dad since new—and that's the car that originally took me on down to school.

My father had been a Sigma Nu at the University of Pennsylvania, and several of my Des Moines friends were already in that fraternity down at Iowa City too (in what was known as the Beta Mu Chapter), so I'd visited and stayed in the house whenever on campus. As an incoming freshman, they all knew I'd be pledging it, so I got to move right in and never did have to live in a dorm. A regular event for Sigma Nu actives was to paddle a pledge's fanny with barrel staves, but I'd already been boarded a few times well before pledging. During the official initiation days, the older brothers did all sorts of stuff to us, and I seemed to get by with less hazing than the others by just staying a step ahead of the game. I'd been visiting once for their 'lilac party,' an annual tradition when the house is decorated everywhere with real lilacs, and knew that the pledges were in charge of cleaning up the house the morning after that big event. So, by the time I was to clean up after one, I just did what I'd seen previously—hauled the garden hose into the living room and began washing down the walls and the terrazzo floors! One time the guys built a fire in the fireplace and proceeded to have a drill—we pledges were supposed to run up to the third floor and get a mouth full of water, then run back down and put out the fire. When the other pledges took off for upstairs, I just turned around and urinated on the dang thing; by the time the rest of the guys came down with mouths full of water, the fire was already out!

It was always hard to believe how messy things could get, not only after a big dance but also after 'boys being boys' while living in a house together. And a lot of my brothers were veterans of WWII, so we were already pretty professional at having wild parties (the service can teach a guy a lot of stuff, and most of us were good learners). I can remember

evenings coming back from the local tavern with the boys… some were football players on the Iowa team and loved to throw together a game in the house living room, even swinging from the ceiling chandelier. I once snapped proof that things could get rather out of control pretty darn fast!

My first roommates in the house were two childhood buddies, and our Dads were also good friends. One was a couple of years older than I—he was the guy who had the head-on collision with the masonry fence at Des Moines Golf and Country Club; the other was a friend who had gone to the local Catholic 'Dowling High School' (we had run around together since he lived fairly close to my home, and we used to listen to records down in his basement). By the end of my sophomore year, the first guy graduated and the other ended up getting married and moving to an apartment—I was in his wedding in Eldora, Iowa and the rehearsal night went just fine. But the day of the wedding, they had put a great big potted plant where I was supposed to be standing. I ended up being allergic to the plant growing in that floor pot, due to my severe hay fever, and spent the entire wedding (and well afterward) sneezing and blowing my nose and wiping my eyes. I was so glad that roommate stayed in Iowa City and finished school. He and his bride moved to a little nearby apartment that was so neat and tidy. I remember when they bought a new cabinet with a countertop and had me come put it all together for them, which was fun. That guy stayed a close friend all my life, and was a groomsman in my first wedding too. He died some time ago, but his family's generous endowments to a local hospital have allowed for multiple renovations and additions over the years, including a most recent $8.5 million project just completed!

My second automobile at Iowa had been a maroon 1946 Ford convertible, purchased new that following February of 1947. (The reason a 1946 vehicle was sold as new in 1947 was due to the shortage of cars after WWII and having to get your name on a list to wait for delivery of one.) My then-girlfriend, whom I'd met in college, was from a nearby town, and I spent some of that second summer of 1947 living at her home while taking summer school classes in Iowa City. She and her widowed mother were happy to have me there to help around the home, and her Mom let me build a workshop in their basement—I was glad to be able to consolidate their various tools from all over the place so I knew where things were and could help take care of fixing up odds and ends around the property. Her mother lived in a bedroom downstairs, and my girlfriend and I stayed upstairs. Every

morning her Mom would come upstairs and check on us, sitting on the side of the bed while the three of us had long conversations. It was a little awkward, as you can imagine, but it worked for the summer. And my girlfriend put up with me leaving for regular weekend jaunts to Des Moines and to Okoboji too—it was nice to have that freedom. She and my '46 Ford both look so sweet in this picture.

But the car no longer looked sweet after my deaf buddy and I ended up in a ditch while coming home from Okoboji after the 4th of July weekend. We had been on our way to Des Moines in the middle of the night, and another friend of ours was driving behind us in my deaf buddy's new Buick convertible. Suddenly, headlights were coming at me on the wrong side of the road near an intersection north of the town of Palmer, so I quickly veered right and took off for the ditch. Seeing my headlights leave the road, the oncoming driver thought I must be turning onto a darkened road going west, so he turned too, following me into the same ditch! We were hit broadside on the driver's side by that oncoming car; my deaf buddy and I rolled over and over, landing upside down in the car in a big cornfield.

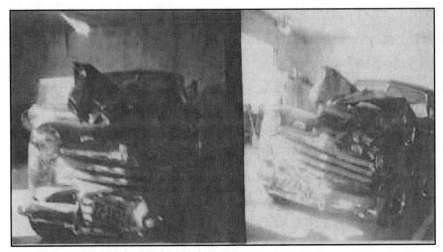

Everything was pitch dark, and we were lying in a heap amidst the fairly well-demolished wreckage of my automobile. The first words I remember were from my buddy, who had lost his hearing aid and kept repeating, "Jerry…Jerry…say something … I THINK I AM DEAD!"

243

Of course, there were no such things as seatbelts back then (Ford eventually introduced those as optional equipment in 1955), so we were pretty darn fortunate to be alive. My poor buddy ended up with several broken ribs, while I sustained only scalp wounds. The once-gorgeous car was hauled to a shop in Pocahontas, Iowa. The wreck made the local papers too. I took the insurance money and ordered a new car; but automobiles were still being rationed so I was placed on a waiting list for delivery of another new 1946, identical to the one that was damaged. I hated that whole idea of waiting, and thought the owner of the Ford dealership in Des Moines where we had bought our cars and trucks all those years (Jensen-Dunn) surely should have made my order a priority, of course. But I was stuck practicing the fine art of patience (and truthfully, admired the owner for being so honest).

During summer break from the University of Iowa that year (and the summer before), my deaf buddy and I had partied a lot up in Okoboji—this included nights at the Okoboji Club, Muriel's Peacock Club, and of course some wild home celebrations. I'll never forget the time that a bunch of us started to dock one of our boats for a big get-together at the home of a friend… when our deaf buddy stepped off, we threw the boat into reverse so that he lost his balance and fell into the lake. The water short-circuited his hearing aid, so all it did was whistle. He took the thing completely apart and laid it on the dock to dry out. We loved whistling at him to get his attention regularly after that, and he laughed every time we did it—his sense of humor was just so terrific. This was in the days of the full quart, no fifths, and that buddy had no trouble consuming a full quart of scotch all by himself in an evening. I couldn't keep up with him, and didn't even try… there were always plenty of other things to do. I can remember leaving him at Muriel's Peacock Club one night while another friend and I went over to Arnolds Park looking for some action. We found a different kind of action when walking into an already-occurring fight with some boys from Spencer. I received a badly cut hand and went back to Muriel's to pick up my deaf buddy, who insisted we go directly to his cottage to bandage me up—he was so upset, and was just sure that I must have gotten into a fight with our own friend with whom I'd gone over to the Park! He kept asking me all weekend if the friend and I had patched things up yet.

I just remembered a cute story about one late summer night several years before that, when my deaf buddy's own *mother* had been involved in an unusual incident after *she* was also leaving Muriel's Peacock Club (obviously, the place had been a popular watering hole for quite some time). A very wealthy gentleman and his wife, who were from Des Moines but who had a weekend home at Okoboji, had also been at Muriel's that night and had offered to drive my buddy's mother home (in her own boat). Turns out, he got too close to Fort Dodge Point, beaching the craft. The three of them decided that the man would go for help, leaving the two women sitting safely in the boat, which was high and dry. The guy took off his shoes and socks and pants, then waded to shore and found the first house with a light on. He knocked on the window, but lost his balance and fell into the window well that was just below it. The owner of the house came out and heard a man groaning, down in the window well. When they finally pulled him out, the homeowners were shocked to see that the groaning guy with no pants was the very wealthy and well-known gentleman from Des Moines. (And the next day, my deaf buddy's mother received a brand-new fancy boat to replace the one that the rich guy had beached!)

Thinking about Muriel's Peacock Club at the Lakes also reminds me that Frenchie Graffaleer played piano up there on certain weekends (I have already mentioned him playing at Babe's Jungle Club in downtown Des Moines too—that's where he met the WAC he ended up marrying). In later years, I flew Frenchie and his wife up to Okoboji a number of times to play at Muriel's place. He was a terrific showman while on the piano, and regularly did other things to keep the audience engaged. like putting a lampshade on his head and so on. Muriel was quite an entertainer herself and, in addition to driving an ambulance in WWI, she had been a Ziegfeld Folly Girl. She would get on stage and give a loud whistle, before singing bawdy songs to a very enthusiastic audience. Muriel's home was right behind the Club; in addition, she had a little motel right there with four or five rooms, and also owned the nearby Roof Garden dancehall in the Park. Muriel lived on the lake herself, and had a small guest house on the water where her son lived—I would stay there with him on occasion so we could party late. One night, while walking to her home in the dark, Muriel told me she had tripped over a couple who were making love in the backyard of the Club—imagine her surprise when she heard the man say, "Thank you!"

After Muriel finally sold her home and businesses at the Lakes, she happened to be in Des Moines and asked me if I would take her back up one more time to say goodbye to her friends and her loyal clientele at Okoboji. I had an extra seat in the plane that weekend, so flew her up and then drove her all around the area as kind of a farewell tour. When we passed by the decades-popular O'Farrell Sisters restaurant, known for their delicious homemade pies, Muriel gave her famous whistle and Edna Mae O'Farrell came to the window and waved. (All three of the original O'Farrell sisters are now deceased, but their restaurant lives on, under new ownership. But that's all another chapter for another book!)

My deaf cement ball buddy and his older brother spent a lot of time up at their Okoboji cottage in the summer, but their business was located in Des Moines—they owned an investment company that was quick to repossess automobiles and airplanes when payments were not made in a timely fashion. Right after the war, cars were selling at quite a premium, so the older brother repossessed a bunch of old worn-out taxicabs from Kansas City and thought he could sell them for a fast buck. One weekend, he asked his younger brother (and me) to go to Minneapolis and repossess the car of some guy who was $170 delinquent in payments to the company. I remember driving one of the old cabs all the way to Minnesota, while my deaf buddy and another friend of ours played gin rummy in the back seat. Everyone thought the two guys in the back had chartered this cab from Kansas City, which served to our advantage since I could park in the yellow zones at the hotels. We checked into The Minnesotan and phoned an old friend who lived in a girl's dormitory there, hoping we could find us some company.

As the evening progressed, a wild party ended up in our room. Everything went well until somebody sat on the wash basin, which fell off the wall and drowned out our party, after which we were kicked out of that hotel. So, we checked into the Radisson, leaving our cab parked out in front in the yellow zone, and continued our party there in two rooms that were connected by an adjoining bathroom. My deaf buddy decided he would clean up, so he turned on the tub and closed the door. But he forgot about having left the water running while he came back out and continued to party in the hotel room. Soon there was a knock on the hall door and the police let us know that there was water leaking into the rooms below. After lots of fast-talk we were not kicked out of the hotel, but we ended the party and went to bed until later that afternoon…

Now it was finally time to locate the car we had come to repossess, so we drove to a very nice neighborhood where the man lived, and proceeded to carry out our mission. I went to the door with my deaf friend, who banged, banged, banged on the guy's door. When he answered, my cement ball buddy said, "Are you Mr. So-and-So?" and the guy said, "Yes." My buddy said, "I am from the company who you owe money to on your car. I must have money or repo car." The man angrily answered, "I'm not paying you anything and you are not taking my car!" At this point, my buddy ran into the big double attached garage and jumped into the man's car, locking the doors behind him. The man picked up a great big rock and told my buddy to get out of the car. My buddy, not finding the key, reached under the dashboard and grabbed a big handful of wires before jumping out of the passenger door—he ran through the guy's front yard and toward the street, right past the old taxi that our other friend was still sitting in. He continued running across the street and ran *right inside* the big home of the strangers who lived over there, locking their door behind him! *{Editor's note: You can't make this stuff up!}*

In the meantime, the man whose automobile we were trying to repossess jumped into that car and drove off. I returned to the cab and waited with our other friend until our buddy hiding in the house across the street decided it was safe enough to come out. We all drove to a nearby telephone to call the older brother in Des Moines who had sent us on this mission. The brother yelled at us, "Forget the whole damn thing and come home!" So, I started driving my card-playing passengers back to Des Moines. We had almost reached the Minnesota-Iowa border when a connecting rod went clear through the side of the engine. We were fairly near a country filling station, so we walked to that and phoned the brother again. He yelled at us, "Just leave that g** d*** old taxi on the side of the road... it's no good anyway!" By now it was the middle of the night and the filling station operator said there was still one more bus that should come through, heading for Des Moines; he told us if he turned on a certain light out by the road he could get the bus to stop, and it did. By the time we were on the bus my cement ball buddy, who had caught a very bad cold during the wild party the night before, kept coughing and loudly clearing his throat, (which sounded like an explosion to anyone with decent hearing, including the sleeping passengers on their way to Des Moines). Then he began complaining aloud about the hum of the bus tires, which he could somehow hear, and the passengers were slowly becoming irate. Fortunately, we didn't get into a fight, though it looked as if we might.

After my maroon 1946 convertible was wrecked and I was unable to get the replacement anytime soon, my grandfather Jewett suggested I take down to school his pristine tan 1939 Plymouth Deluxe—the one that I had driven to and from California for the San Francisco World's Fair in 1939. This shot was taken in the driveway of my folks' Des Moines house before I headed back to Iowa City in it. Pops always had a new car, of course, so he was more than willing to part with the old '39 Plymouth. Come to think of it, Pops had a lot of automobiles, often at any given time. If one of his cars would break down (which they regularly did), he just drove a different one. His 1926 Apperson Six Sport Sedan stayed in storage in his garage for a long time—I don't ever remember him driving it at all! He also had a Graham-Paige that sure impressed me because if it had a low tire, which it did all the time, you just opened the hood, started the engine, and took a little hose out—the compressor connected to that hose blew the tire right back up! One time, Pops got an extra good deal on a rather new Cadillac that he bought from a guy who ran the Polk County Jail garage. A short time later, that guy spent time in jail himself for repainting and reselling stolen fancy cars! My grandfather told me he never said anything to anybody, but it explained why he had gotten such a good deal. Pops didn't ever own a Duesenberg automobile, which is especially surprising since they were being manufactured here in Des Moines right across the street from the Jewett Building when I was just a little boy. And years before that, Fred and Augie Duesenberg had both been repairmen for my great-grandfather's Jewett Typewriter Company! (Recently, in January of 2017, there was a 1930 'Duesie' for sale online, which made me think of that manufacturing company again. This model was listed for $900,000—I know they are going for even more than that, but the ad got my attention!)

Pops loved automobiles like I do, and always drove too fast because he couldn't believe the car was really doing what the speedometer showed. In fact, he once rolled a car at 9th and Grand, speeding around the corner where the Jewett Lumber Company had previously been located. One time I remember Pops driving up to Okoboji, with me and one of my friends as his only two passengers. My grandfather kept passing other cars, which made my friend terribly nervous; whenever Pops would start accelerating to get enough speed to pass, my friend would yell from the backseat, "No, Mr. Jewett, you can't make it this time!" (That childhood friend is the guy who eventually became one of my first Sigma Nu roommates… the one who had made head-on contact with the masonry wall at DM Golf. I can't recall if this jaunt with my Pops to Okoboji was before or after that accident but if after, it would explain a lot about his jumpiness now that I think about it.)

Anyway, I got to have Pops' 1939 Plymouth down at Iowa for a few months, until my sister Connie took it over when she came to the University as a freshman in the fall of '47. I remember when she came to school, and especially about how my father had given me some money to spend on helping her to get settled and feel comfortable. But a day or so later, one of my fraternity brothers got thrown in jail for some darn reason, and I spent that money bailing him out—I guess it was a few days before I was paid back and able to help my little sister get settled! I should mention what happened to that 1939 Plymouth after Connie had been driving it down there for awhile… One very windy day, she was returning to the car from a class. Only half a block away from reaching the '39 Plymouth, the big 42-foot radio tower for the school's WSUI station suddenly blew off the top of one of the school buildings and cut that parked car right in half—"the side of the car was caved in and the frame sprung," reported the *Des Moines Tribune* that evening. Connie wasn't hurt, but the close call did shake her up. Pops then gave her his 1940 Plymouth to replace the wrecked '39, which of course helped soften the blow. (Throughout her life, my sister has seemed to accumulate stories about strange things like that happening to her, always recounting them with such a flair for the drama of each situation—Connie could have a room in stitches so fast with her incredible tales!)

It was a good thing I always had a car down at school, because there were so many things that needed to be done. Like for the annual lilac parties, a group of us typically drove down to Missouri where the flowers had already bloomed, loading up our cars with lilacs to decorate for the dance. It was also important to have a vehicle in order to outdo other fraternities in impressing the sorority ladies. One time a bunch of us removed the bathtub from our downstairs guest bathroom in the Sigma Nu house—I'm not really sure why, but guess we just decided it wasn't needed there. So, after tying that bathtub onto the back of my '39 Plymouth, we towed it over to the Theta house and dug a hole, then planted it in the front yard in wet cement with a sign attached to the tub that said, "Dirty Thetas!" Pranks were common in all frats, of course, and ours was certainly no exception—the list of stuff we did just goes on and on, but you get the idea.

While still waiting for delivery on the second 1946 Ford after wrecking my first one, and having turned over Pops' 1939 Plymouth to my sister, I regularly got to take Uncle Homer's or Dad's company cars down to Iowa for a week or two. I also remember buying a white Mercury convertible from a Sioux City gal I knew in the Delta Gamma house who got a new car every year—I kept that vehicle so nice, and ended up selling it for a good profit after *finally* getting my 1946 Ford replacement. Going through school on the G. I. Bill after just coming out of WWII was great; but a guy can always use spending money, and those months of waiting around for my Ford gave me a new idea to make a little cash on the side… When I'd hear of somebody in a fraternity or sorority who wanted to sell a car, I'd oftentimes buy it and clean it up, drive it around, and then resell it. Before long, cars just came and went for me. I was certainly never short on transportation at Iowa, and even had a boat down there—a kayak just big enough for two people and a case of beer! (And there were airplanes too, but they also will get their own chapter coming up next.)

My next roommate in the frat house was a peach of a guy, and we just loved to pick on him all the time. He was from Des Moines and lived not too far from me, but we hadn't known each other very well while growing up since he was a few years younger. His father, also a friend of my Dad's, was General Manager of a large discount department store chain (the man eventually even moved to Chicago, and then finally to Michigan to take over for the founder of the company!). Our sleeping dormitory was in the back end of the upper two stories of the fraternity house, and we always left those windows open year-round to keep it nice and cool—it would even snow in on us! So, we would do things like turn off my new roommate's heated blanket when he was sleeping, and he'd wake up not knowing why he was shivering so badly. The front of the house was where we had the two- or three-man study/party rooms—he and I had a telephone in ours too, which came in handy for calling the different sorority houses to keep up with any action around campus. One time I drove over to the home of another good friend and frat brother who was by then married and who had a phone in his house. Together we dialed up my new roommate and told him we were calling from the power and light company and that we were going to turn off the lights in the whole town—he didn't believe us, of course. So, I roared over to the fraternity house and ran in the back door… after pulling the main switch for all the lights and blinking them three times, I raced back over to my fraternity brother's home and we called my roommate again—this time he believed us! We did that to the poor guy on several occasions until he finally got wise to it. That type of prank sure would have been lots easier with cell phones!

This roommate and I got along great most of the time, but living in such close quarters could also get annoying. He had a new (but very used) chair, which was a great big overstuffed thing that took up too much space in our little study room. One night we all came in from partying and I stumbled over the chair. I'd had enough of it, and told him that the chair took up too much room; then I opened our huge window and actually pushed it out! He said, "Oh, you want to play *that* way?" So, he picked up *my* chair and threw it out the window too! I guess the thing I remember most about that night is that  my roommate's chair was so big and heavy that it hit the balcony below our window on the way down and shattered into many pieces, while *my* chair landed in a pile of snow and all I had to do was shake the snow off and put it back into our room. We laughed about that incident for years. (And we also laughed about the fact that he had a pair of binoculars to spy out of the window on a newlywed couple living next door to the house— we had finally just moved his desk and chair into the hall to be closer to that window!)

The third year in the house, I was Commander of the Beta Mu chapter of Sigma Nu, and became quite popular because of my theme for a big "Hotel Party," where we guys could take our dates up to our rooms to see where we hung out (which was unheard of in those days). That year I wanted to throw the biggest party of all the Dubuque Street fraternities, and knew I could do it. So, after renting the Czechoslovakian Hall in town, with its tall arched windows and vaulted ceiling, I had carpenters come in to reinforce the second floor so it wouldn't collapse. Then I went around to all the other houses and invited everybody to the gala event sponsored by Sigma Nu. The party was a huge success, with everybody having lots of drinks and lots of fun. Right at the height of the party, somebody switched the women's and men's bathroom signs, so a lot of us just went outside to relieve ourselves. Imagine my surprise (and hers) when I came upon one of my professors squatted next to a tree—I'm pretty sure that's how I got through that class without a failing grade!

After the party at the Czechoslovakian Hall I had been called to go before the Interfraternity Council, and feared I was going to be kicked out of school for putting the big festivity together. As it turned out, my explanation was that I threw such an extravagant affair so that everyone would have a good time and that it would bring the fraternities closer together… they actually thought that was a pretty noble excuse, so I didn't get kicked out of school after all. As a matter of fact, not only did I end up on the Council myself, but was put in charge of planning *all* fraternity parties and rushing programs! After stepping into that position of event planning, we ended up going to a number of locations around Iowa City for regular celebrations—such as The Piccadilly Room of the Roosevelt Hotel in Cedar Rapids, and to a little tavern in West Branch near the house where President Herbert Hoover was born. And we loved partying at the stone quarries near Iowa City where we could easily wash our cars on the edge of the water, and swim and drink beer.

The President of the University of Iowa was a Sigma Nu and a good friend of my Dad's; periodically, we would have him over to the frat house for dinner. I can remember one time when he was there, sitting at the table right next to me and our house mother (we called her "Ma Mu" since we were the Beta Mu Chapter). Suddenly, 'Ma' got hit in the side of her head with a sweet potato that one of our crazy brothers was meaning to throw at another kid—that kind of stuff went on all the time but, naturally, I was very embarrassed to be sitting next to the University President during such a prank. 'Ma Mu' liked me, but I think we all kind of wore her out… she just didn't seem to come out of her room very often. I guess 'Ma' had previously reared several boys, including the father of one of my frat brothers, in a foster-like setting. She really was a wonderful lady, but it seemed to take a little extra effort to make her smile. (I always gave it the 'old college try' though, and especially when sitting next to her for this annual photo!)

While in charge of rush and all parties during my tenure on the Interfraternity Council, I was always thinking up even better ways for us to have fun. By January of 1949, I

figured out how to solve the ongoing lack of transportation dilemma that we faced with most of our big events—I purchased a 1938 Ford police paddy wagon, a Black Mariah, from the Chicago Police Department! After hearing they were buying new Mariah trucks for their guys over there, I went to Chicago and tracked an old one down. It cost me $165 in cash and the help of a friendly policeman, but the deal was closed pretty quickly. After getting it back to school, I couldn't get license plates for the thing, so Dad had me call a personal friend of his, an attorney in Iowa City, to help me out. I picked up the gentleman and we drove together to the Courthouse. He told me to stay in the car and he'd be right back, and a few minutes later came out with my plates.

All of my friends were hauled over to school in the Black Mariah... I was very popular! 'Paddy' was featured in school newsletter pictures and articles a few times that semester. Other than being a real gas hog (one newspaper quoted me saying that it "had a faucet for a carburetor, but it runs like a top"), the paddy wagon seemed like a good investment and sure was a heck of a lot of fun. Right after purchasing the Mariah, I immediately came up with a 'Police Paddy Party' theme for our upcoming Valentine's Day bash—a costume dance complete with underworld characters. Our dates were picked up by 'uniformed policeman' during prescheduled 'raids' and hauled over to the frat house in the back of Paddy. As Sigma Nu President, I pulled off a lot of fun stuff, but using that paddy wagon for our partying endeavors had to top the list for awhile. One time we filled the truck with a bunch of kids and drove over to a tavern in the little town of Solon, backing Paddy up to the front door of the place. Then we just opened the back door of the wagon so everybody could pile into the tavern. As it turned out, any strangers that came along saw the paddy wagon backed up to the front door of the bar. And with 'POLICE DEPARTMENT' on the side, people thought the place was being raided, so we had the tavern all to ourselves!

We've enlarged this photo from the front page of a 1949 Sigma Nu publication so you can see Paddy and a few of our fraternity brothers a little better. That's me stepping up into the front passenger door, wearing the dark leather jacket and dark leather flying cap from my days in the service.

I had a million dollars of insurance on that 1938 Ford truck, and when the Associated Press and the UP learned about me having it, the news went coast to coast. My scrapbook has several clippings all about it from various newspapers. Reporters loved that the truck still had the screened windows, as well as a buzzer system from the prisoner's compartment to the front seat. Plenty of graffiti covered the inside walls, and

Beta Mu News

University of Iowa Chapter of Sigma Nu

Vol. I   IOWA CITY, IOWA, MAY, 1949   No. 3

Big Committee Ready To Tackle Summer Rushing

Time, thoughts, and efforts of an 11-man rushing committee are combining to bring a large but exceptional fall pledge class to Beta Mu next September.

there were still blood stains on the floor! It had steps with handrails going up to the back door, and with a signal bell next to it—the bell was once used for the rear guard to signal the wagon's driver to push a button in his cab and unlock the back door. It was a fully loaded vehicle. (And I kept a mattress back there too, for our guys' own emergency use.)

After only a few days, the local Iowa City Police Department decided they didn't really need our help, and asked me to paint out the word 'POLICE' on the sides of the Mariah. I didn't want to do that, of course, but also didn't want to get in trouble with the local officers. They seemed alright with my suggestion to use black tape to get rid of only the 'P' and the 'O'… then I just kept my fingers crossed that driving a 'LICE DEPARTMENT' truck wouldn't get me in trouble with the local health department next. All that press from around the country was terrific, but it didn't help me in the end… my $1 million insurance policy on that wagon was abruptly canceled when the insurance company found out I was regularly hauling fifteen or so students around! But I kept the Mariah and somehow got new insurance placed on it as a "1938 Ford truck" through another agency; then I went back to hauling my friends until eventually selling Paddy to two fraternity brothers from Spencer shortly before graduating.

AND YES, THERE WERE AIRPLANES

After getting out of the service, and before enrolling at Iowa, I thought I had money to spend. So, my plan was to buy a race car and take on just a few races myself before hiring a driver. When my father found out about that, he immediately said, "Jerry, if you'll forget that race car idea completely, I'll go into partnership with you on an airplane and I'll pay

2/3 of it." So, in 1946, during that first semester of college, Dad and I bought my first airplane, a used 1941 Piper J-5A Tri-pacer Cub Cruiser that was for sale at the old Okoboji airport. That model of plane had kind of a unique fuselage design, with the pilot sitting in the front seat and room for two (if very small) passengers in the rear. It didn't have a starter—you had to 'hand prop' it.

I sure had a lot of fun with the J-5, especially because a Sigma Nu brother from Jefferson, Iowa was in law school by then and had a cruiser identical to mine. Over the years he became such a close friend, and it all started back in our aircraft days at the U of Iowa. That guy had flown B-17 bombers during WWII, and he and his family were well-versed in all things aeronautical—his father donated the land for the very first airport in Jefferson and had also flown his own airplane during WWII on submarine surveillance! (In addition to that, his uncle ran their local airport, later also running the new one they built on the southeast corner of town.)

In the fall of 1947, I won a couple of events at Iowa's largest 'Flight Breakfast' held out at Dodge Field north of Des Moines. Over 170 planes flew in from around the state to enjoy a morning of aircraft fun. Prizes were awarded for various things, and I won a bunch of them. My favorite was a 'Bombing Contest' where we dropped sacks of flour as close to a target as possible. When I won first place for the 'Spot Landing Contest,' it was for flying by at a certain altitude and then landing as near as possible to a designated spot on the grass runway. For my first-place prize in the 'Hurdle Landing Event,' I think we had to buzz some track hurdles as low as possible without knocking them over. Anyway, I won so many things that I couldn't fit all the prizes into that little plane with me and my female passenger (a gal who had asked if she could ride with me to the event, to which I had reluctantly agreed). That woman was really a pain in the neck, to tell you the truth, and I would have liked to have just left her there… which would have made room for the rest of my winnings that day, like the full case of oil!.

Part of the very wise agreement Dad had made when going into partnership with his college-age son was that I would stay away from drinking any alcohol at least eight hours before flying. He said, "And if you haven't had anything to drink yourself, don't even walk into a tavern within that time frame… not even if it's just to pick up a friend." I stuck by that wise agreement all my life and found that it didn't prevent me from still being able to have lots of fun, and logging plenty of hours flying myself and friends to various parties and other events through the years. That first little Piper was such fun—it was just terrific to be able to go here, there, and everywhere. One time I volunteered to take a guy for a parachute jump over Swea City—when we finally climbed to 5,000 feet, out he went! (I actually regret that foolish and dangerous maneuver on my part.) Another time I flew two brothers up to Pocahontas, Iowa, where there was no airport. I had to land the Tri-pacer on a golf course, which was their temporary airstrip—it seemed so strange to watch the golfers move off the fairway when I started to land, but I guess they were used to it.

By July of 1948, I was halfway through college. Dad and I decided to upgrade to a plane that was much faster and had more equipment; so, on July 9, we bought a brand-new 1948 Stinson Voyager and paid to house it in a large hangar once used by United Airlines at the Des Moines Municipal Airport. My little Piper J-5A had sat outside in the weather, and when the owner of the flying service where we bought the new Stinson hit the wing of the Piper with his fist, his hand went right through the fabric! Other than that, my Piper Cub with its many extras was still in fine shape, but it proved the point of paying extra to house my new Stinson indoors. We got a great price for the Piper after listing it in the newspaper, and it was a little tough to see my first airplane sold. But it was so nice to now have a starter and a generator, as well as 'blind' instrument flying capability with the new plane. (Just as a side note here, I learned that my Cub Cruiser later crashed while the two guys in it were hunting antelope from the airplane—sadly, pilot and passenger were both killed.)

When home from college that summer of 1948, I was working out in the yard area at the family lumber company, still climbing the professional 'ladder' from the bottom up. Labor unions were in full swing in many industries in town, and ours was no exception—we had union picketers every hour that we were open. Yard guys from other lumber companies in Des Moines would picket at our office, and our union employees would picket at theirs. The non-union employees (including myself) had to fill in for the picketing guys, of course—we had customers who wanted and needed materials. If we didn't have income, we couldn't pay the salaries of employees, whether they were on strike or not, so it was a real catch-22 for the employer. And the pressure on non-union guys to join a union was real. I remember one time when a customer crossed the picket line to purchase a load of lumber in his own truck. As he started to drive out of the yard, a picketer stood in the way. Our customer got out of his truck and said, "I'm driving outta here. I've been overseas fighting for you guys, and I'm home to build a house for my family now. I have a .38 pistol in the truck if anybody gets in the way and tries to stop me." Then he got into his vehicle and started to drive out, while the picketer continued to stand right in front of the man's truck. Believe it or not, the customer drove right up over the top of the picketer, and the picketer came out the back of the truck unharmed but feisty mad. The customer went on his way. I had seen the guy standing in front of our customer's vehicle after having helped load it, but didn't personally see the actual incident play out. It sure got some attention.

One Saturday I was involved in a memorable incident while working in the yard. Our company closed at noon on Saturdays, so that's when the picketers left. We thought that the afternoon would be a good time to deliver to a new house job at 22nd and Ashworth Road out in West Des Moines. The homeowner came down to the yard to ride with me and show me where to go with his materials. As we both climbed into our loaded lumber truck, I noticed an inside dual tire very low. So, I drove a block or so to the Trax Oil filling station, on E. 6th, just south of Court Avenue, to put air into the tire. While I was down under the truck attaching the air hose to the inside dual, my customer in the passenger seat was approached and grabbed by union workers! I quickly rolled out from under that truck, grabbed a tire iron, and started swinging it around to keep them away from me. They put our customer into the driver's seat of our lumber truck and told him to drive it back to the yard. Being only a block away, I ran back and yelled to my Dad on the intercom to call the police. By that time, our customer drove my truck into the lumberyard, with a picketer on the running board hitting him in the face through the window. The picketers disappeared as soon as the truck was in the yard. The police showed up but just parked at the top of Walnut in an alley and never even got out of their car. My father immediately sat down in his office and wrote what he hoped would be a good union law for our state to implement. Dad was credited with writing an 'open shop' law, which his attorney friend presented to the Statehouse and which was passed. The law is still in effect today and allows employees to join or not join a union, and to not be penalized for either choice.

My father was so often called upon for labor negotiations, not only with the local lumber companies, but also for other corporations like Katz Drug Company, which had its headquarters in Kansas City (their big local store was on the southeast corner of 7th and Locust, and was open 24 hours a day). Dad's keen business mind and ability to come up with solutions that were fair to both sides were the keys to his success in these negotiation endeavors. And he was such a terrific example to me on how to deal with such things in the future. Years later, long after Dad was gone, I started to again have some problems with workers, both union and non-union, at our new yard at 1536 E. Army Post Road on the south side of town. When I fired a teamster, he complained, so the union workers came to my office to defend him. I said, "Wait a minute, you mean you condone stealing?" I proceeded to tell them that we had several yard employees, union and non-, stealing from the company. To obtain proof before firing anybody, I'd hired an undercover person from the Lewis System to be in the yard, posing as a customer trying to work off his lumber bill. Every night after work, this undercover guy typed up a list of the things that were disappearing, and by whom—he got the names of the workers from their shirt pockets. The confessions came rapidly, and we ended up with so much evidence that we actually fired all the boys in the yard, starting over with brand-new employees as truck drivers and yardmen. A very fine law firm from Omaha, specialists in labor relations, was hired to advise us on how to proceed in perhaps becoming a non-union house. The new employees ended up voting against forming a union, and we were finally out of it after all those decades. When we merged with Gilcrest in 1985, the union again approached me and said that we would have to become a union business since Gilcrest had a contract with them. I told them that this was a brand-new company, formed by combining some of the assets of both, and that we were no longer going to be a union operation. And though there was one particular yard guy who tried to organize, the other employees just weren't interested.

While working at the lumber company during the daytime that summer of 1948, I was also earning extra spending money overnight by ferrying new Luscombe airplanes, from their Dallas/Fort Worth factory in Texas to Dodge Field in Des Moines. My close childhood friend owned Central Airways located at that local Field, across the road south of Camp Dodge, and hired me to get the planes up here for him to sell. I got $100 for each airplane I flew, but had to buy the gas for it, and also had to buy my railroad ticket on the Katy Line from Des Moines' Rock Island Depot down to the Luscombe factory. It wasn't a big money-maker but was sure an exciting time of regular travel for me. After a day of work at the lumber company, I'd have dinner with my folks at our house in Des Moines, then they would drop me off at the Depot downtown. I sat up all night in the club car, grabbing a little shut-eye whenever possible, before getting off the train at the factory in Texas and flying a plane back to Des Moines in the morning.

One day I called my folks in Des Moines to tell them there was a terrible storm over Iowa and that I wouldn't be able to fly back home that morning. They said they already knew all about it… As it turned out, the roof blew off the hangar in Des Moines during that July 27, 1948 storm and demolished all the airplanes in the hangar (including my brand-new, three-week-old Stinson, with only 21 hours logged on it!). The owner of the local flying service where we had purchased and stored the plane, generously paid my expenses to the Stinson factory in Wayne, Michigan (which was actually an old Ford Motor factory where they had manufactured the big B-24 bombers during the war years, turning out one every 24 hours). That flying service owner took my insurance check and my old plane and bought me a brand-new Stinson, so I came out OK.

Artistic Mom painted my initials on the front pilot-side window ledge (as she had done on my Model A Cabriolet), but the special piece of art to the right was drawn by a man who came to the Sigma Nu house to do caricatures of the all the guys. Naturally, most of us in the house were given nicknames—if you didn't have one when you came in, you'd have one by the time you went out. (My grandsons have laughed in recent years when I've told stories about "Mo" doing this or "Bit" doing that. "Ding, "Boob," and "Proddy Jones" were good ones too, as was my own, shown here.)

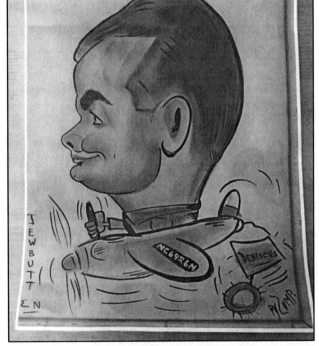

The new Stinson had a registration number of NC6926M—and since 'M' stands for 'Mike' in the radio alphabet, everybody just called my new toy 'Mike.' That plane was such fun—the 165 hp was a nice jump in performance after the little Piper Cub, and it also carried four people, which was really terrific! During the last two years of college, my frat brothers flew with me all over the country. 'Mike' took us quickly and safely to all the Iowa football 'away' games; as a matter of fact, almost every weekend we flew someplace or another—Minneapolis, Chicago, and so on. And many times, when heading to Des Moines for a weekend, I loaded the plane with sorority gals wanting a ride home. I dated a lot of girls at Iowa, from each and every house, but mostly Kappa's, Delta Gamma's, and Theta's—and all were beautiful, of course! One time a local newspaper columnist had just landed at the Des Moines Municipal Airport about the same time I was taking off to head back to school. We were surprised to learn of his little gossip quip about me in the *Register* a few days later (Wednesday, February 23, 1949) ... "When we landed at the chilly airport, I was filled with envy as Jerry Jewett and his three passengers, one of 'em a fearfully pretty coed, took off for Iowa City..." That same reporter made a date to catch up with me for a personal ride when I came home a couple of weekends later—Dad and I took him (and his son) on a short tour over Des Moines, with the reporter seated up front in the copilot spot... his second little gossip article talked about that ride, along with this cute cartoon about the 'campus express.'

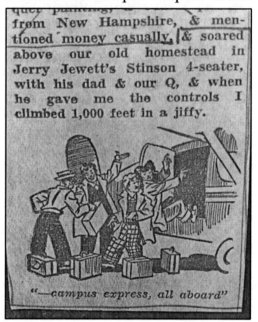

from New Hampshire, & mentioned money casually, & soared above our old homestead in Jerry Jewett's Stinson 4-seater, with his dad & our Q, & when he gave me the controls I climbed 1,000 feet in a jiffy.

"—*campus express, all aboard*"

The night after the reporter's first gossip quip had made the papers, a bunch of guys were hanging around in my frat house 'study room' when a few of us hatched a plan to fly down to New Orleans for the Mardi Gras. My friends suggested also calling my deaf cement ball buddy from Des Moines since he had partied with us before and was always so much fun. So, I called him and yelled, "How would you like to go to Mardi Gras?" He said, "When?" And I yelled, "Tomorrow." He said, "I can't... I have hot date tomorrow night." I yelled, "What about next day?" He said, "Fine... your plane?" I yelled, "No, my plane is full—

meet us down there." He said, "Where?" I yelled, "Roosevelt Hotel lobby." He confusingly said, "Where?" I yelled again, "ROOSEVELT." He said, "Spell it." So, I yelled each letter as he repeated back each one after me. When I got to the 'T' he said, "Oh, ROOSEVELT... why didn't you say so? OK, what time?" I yelled back, "6 P.M." When we got to the Roosevelt Hotel, my buddy was nowhere in the lobby, but we eventually found him at the hotel bar. (And before long, we found *all* of us at a bar, putting away Hurricanes with Schlitz chasers at Pat O'Brien's in the French Quarter!)

I'd completely forgotten that we had a four-hour delay on that trip, with an unplanned stop in St. Louis due to a little magneto problem with the plane. Thanks to keeping a scrapbook, Jen and I came across a Western Union telegram wired to my folks on Saturday, February 26, 1949, informing them that my buddies and I had finally arrived safely in Louisiana.

One of my friends who had flown to New Orleans with us was a Beta at Iowa; since there was no Sigma Nu house on the Tulane University campus, we all became Betas so we could stay in their house and ride on their float in the Mardi Gras parade, which was terrific fun. And we topped off the memorable weekend with some quality time at the horse races before 'Mike' got us safely back to Iowa City.

By the summer of 1949, I was again working at the lumberyard but also had another very interesting 'employment' opportunity present itself while home from college. I had gotten to know the older (and even wilder!) brother of my deaf cement ball buddy, and had been trusted enough to do 'gofer' jobs for him and their investment company. For example, I used to drive their company boat on the Des Moines River while that older brother and a friend played cards and drank cocktails in the back of the vessel. Soon the older brother started to invest in airplanes, rather than in used taxicabs. By now he had learned to trust my flying capability, and made a verbal deal with me to pilot his company airplanes—he had repossessed five by this time and had nobody to fly them. In return, I could use the planes myself whenever I wished (a pretty sweet deal!) … the only catch was that I had to be ready by phone to take him and his friends on any of their planes to any place, and with little advance notice. One very hot weekend day (and with no air-conditioning), Dad and I were painting the kitchen ceiling up at our Okoboji cottage when the phone rang, with the request that I come to Des Moines right then to pick up my summer 'employer' and fly him to another state. I was so very hot and terribly tired, but ran over to the nearby airport [the one under construction just 600 feet from the cottage] and got into their company plane that I'd flown up to the Lakes for the weekend. After landing in Des Moines, I took my deaf buddy's older brother and his girlfriend to a western state where he could gamble, then flew on back to Iowa alone while they stayed out west. After I left, the guy had hired a chauffeured limousine to take him to the dog track and back to a supper club for dinner.

My 'employer' was counting his race winnings on a table at the supper club before he again left in the limo for their hotel. Lo and behold, he and his limo got pulled over by a thief, and when the limo driver recognized the thief (who happened to be the chef at that supper club), the thief killed the limo driver and escaped, while my deaf buddy's brother and girlfriend hid in the ditch in an attempt to save their own lives... which worked! The robber ended up flushing the stolen money down the toilet in order to escape being caught with the evidence. It was a big deal that made the papers, and I was sure glad I'd gotten out of there before all that!

As it turned out, I didn't get to fly that older brother all that many places, really, but got to pilot my deaf buddy (and with our dates, of course) to several states, some islands, and to Acapulco and other places in Mexico, including to the Baja Peninsula... and all in their investment company airplanes! When crossing the border, we always landed at Brownsville, Texas to clear Customs. (Jen asked if we had to show passports during these crossings, but I don't recall ever doing that, not even back during the service days). We had some great trips in those planes of my buddy and his brother, but the aircraft weren't perfect and I had to put up with starter problems and what have you. Eventually, both brothers became licensed pilots themselves, but I was still the one who flew them in their planes all over the place. My deaf buddy was actually a very good pilot with fine coordination but had trouble using the radio, naturally. Once I rode with him on a short hop over to Sioux City, Iowa and was anxious to see how he handled the microphone. He called the tower and told them he wanted to land. The tower answered back in their normal fast lingo, saying, "Twin-engine Piper, land runway such-and-such, wind is (whatever) degrees at (whatever) miles per hour, altimeter setting (whatever)." My buddy answered back loudly, "TALK SLOWER... I DO NOT UNDERSTAND!" The tower repeated details in the same quick manner and my frustrated friend finally radioed back, "JUST SKIP IT!" We then landed in the way he wanted to land. (Needless to say, in this day and age a pilot wouldn't get by with that type of aircraft operation!)

Having my own transportation while in college was just terrific. But admittedly, the cars and planes were a bit of a distraction from the real reason for being in Iowa City—actually getting a degree! My roommate used to keep telling me, "Jerry, you'd better settle down and study, or you'll never graduate." When graduation time came, his mother and father drove in from Chicago, where they were then living, and met up with my folks, who had come in from Des Moines. They all excitedly took pictures of the two of us in our caps and gowns before we headed over to the Fieldhouse for the ceremony. During the graduation, my roommate's name was never called, which was very embarrassing for everybody... turns out *his* grade point wasn't high enough to graduate! He ended up having to take a correspondence course from Chicago and got his degree the following spring. (Though he ended up moving out of state, that guy and I remained such close friends all through the decades, until his death just a couple of years ago. And we never stopped with the stories.)

I became a pretty good student by the time of my graduation in January of 1950 with a degree in Business Administration from the (State) University of Iowa's College of Commerce. And obviously, my folks were pretty happy about it! My grade point average was in the upper 3's, mostly due to the fact that I was engaged by then and could no longer date. Jackie had finished with her teaching certificate the spring before and I really wanted to make certain to graduate, so I finally buckled down knowing the end was in sight.

It was tough not having my girlfriend around for many reasons, of course, and I certainly missed her. Jackie had been such a terrific help in washing the cars and airplanes while in school—as a perfectionist, that was pretty important to me! We loved cleaning cars together over in the driveway of my married friend's house. And here she is after washing 'Mike' at the local field (looking understandably happy to  be done—keeping automobiles clean is one thing; handwashing an airplane is another!).

MARRIAGE AND FAMILY YEARS

Two months after graduating, I married that final college sweetheart, Jacqueline ("Jackie") Berguin, on Saturday, March 11, 1950, at the First Presbyterian Church in Sioux Falls.

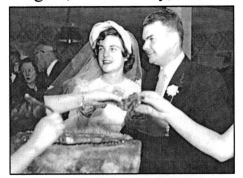

That was her hometown, so my father and mother rented a railroad car and invited many friends to join them for a trip to South Dakota for the wedding. Jackie and I met the train full of guests when they arrived. It was quite a gala affair and everyone had such a terrific time, but there was such a huge snowstorm that I was worried about safely getting out of town to start on our honeymoon trip.

During the wedding reception, one of Dad's friends had asked where we were going for the getaway, and I said, "We are heading south and, with a little luck we hope to get to Florida." He said, "Well, I have a home right on the water in Mississippi, with a deep freezer full of shrimp and a liquor cabinet full of booze, and nobody to use it." Having very little money, I said, "Well, that would be wonderful!" So, he said, "OK, when you get to town, call the Chief of Police and tell him I sent you down there. He'll come and unlock the house for you." That invitation was all the more incentive to start heading south as soon as we could. Before the ceremony, I had parked our car at the nearby fire station, where the firemen assured me it would certainly be safe from my high-spirited groomsmen and their tin cans and soap. I wasn't so worried about my best man pulling pranks because my best man was my Dad! But those other childhood buddies of mine were quite capable of mayhem. After the wedding reception, Jackie and I raced to the station to get the car, only to learn that the firemen *themselves* had filled the vehicle and our suitcases with rice. And we hadn't driven far when there was a thunderous explosion—the firemen had also planted just one "bomb" under the hood to start us on our honeymoon getaway. (That story ended up in the gossip section of the same Des Moines newspaper columnist who had written about my mother serving canned spaghetti to my Italian co-worker all those years ago!)

Jackie and I headed down to Omaha, where we spent the first night. After continuing south and going through New Orleans, we finally got to Mississippi, where we found the lovely home of my Dad's friend—it was more of a southern mansion to us, actually—and spent a week there enjoying his shrimp and booze while overlooking the Gulf of Mexico (and while still trying to get the rice out of our car and suitcases!) The home movies we took with that Kodak 8mm camera next show the Jewett newlyweds visiting Bellingrath Gardens near Mobile, Alabama, then enjoying the Cypress Gardens in Florida. We went to Daytona Beach (and drove around the race track), Marineland, and the old Fort at St. Augustine while down there. The car I was driving then was about a 1947 Buick convertible, which was a gorgeous vehicle I had recently purchased from my deaf buddy (you'll recall that I sold him my 1936 Ford convertible while sitting in the Greenwood Tap back in February of 1944, before I left for the service. He repaid the favor by then selling me for a very good price his nice Buick, a cream-colored beauty with a black top, before we got married). That Buick was a terrific car, but every single time we pulled into a station to get gas, I'd have to say, "Oh, and add one quart of oil to the engine please."

After our honeymoon, Jackie and I drove back to Des Moines, where I began my new career as a salesman and General Manager of the Jewett Lumber Company in April of 1950. I was so proud to be a part of the family firm started almost seventy years earlier by my great-grandfather, George. And I especially enjoyed working with my Dad, but always felt I had to be the first one there in the morning and the last one to leave at night so that I wasn't shown any favoritism. The previous experience that I'd had (by virtue of growing up with the company, let alone working in the various departments and in the yard itself), was all necessary and good for me as I stepped into my new white-collar position. Performing jobs out in the yard was a prerequisite for management positions with our  firm, family or not, and that was a good policy. By 1952, I was also elected Treasurer of our company (and my first task in that capacity was to learn to correctly spell "Treasurer!")

On August 1, 1953, Dad bought a property at S. W. 9th Street and Army Post Road in Des Moines for a new south-side lumberyard location, and sent me to be the manager there for a few years. At the same time, he bought a north-side property on the southeast corner of 6th and Douglas Avenues. This gave the company better coverage of our city, made it easier for the public to shop at Jewett's, and promised more security to its employees as a growing business. Both new locations had been Melvin Lumber Companies, and both were in rather rough shape physically—the S.W. 9th Street place had once been an old stable, and you could see where the horses had rubbed against the wood poles out in the yard. There was a veterinarian next door north, and a filling station owned by a friend of my

Dad's was north of the vet. To the south of the lumberyard there was a Standard Oil filling station; between it and our business was the Parker Drug Store and a little restaurant called Vi's Café. One of the first customers to come into the lumberyard told me he wanted "two six-inch pancakes." I almost replied to him in a cocky manner with something like, "You'd better go next door to Vi's for that." Instead, I stopped myself and radioed out to the yard foreman, "Whitey, do we have any six-inch pancakes?" Whitey said, "Yes," and told me how much they were and where to find them. I wrote up the cash ticket and offered to go out to the yard with the customer to make sure he got the right item (but really to find out what the heck a six-inch pancake was—I learned that it's a round piece of clay that fits into a bell tile to plug the hole in the drain tile; perforated ones are used as floor drains).

The years managing that south yard were so educational—it was certainly the best way for me to learn about the whole operation and to get to know some very interesting customers. One time I had furnished a new home for a guy (who was a bookie) and his wife (who was the madam of a red-light hotel operation downtown). He had me stop over at their house one afternoon to look at and discuss some final details of their construction job. The two of us were sitting at a coffee table in their living room, where all of his records were evidently just a telephone. For some reason, he was telling me that his wife had money stashed in banks all over the country and that he never knew where any of the banks were located. It was a house call that I'll never forget because not long after that, our Assistant County Attorney (Clyde Edsel Herring, who had been rescued from our chimney as a little boy) led a big raid on the wife's red-light operation in her downtown hotel. Among the scores of city, county and state law enforcement personnel who participated in that raid, the Polk County Sheriff told me that they found no prostitutes inside the establishment after several hours of searching.... that is, until someone discovered a hidden button that activated a sliding wall, behind which stood a row of naked ladies!

Another customer of mine was a woman who owned a trendy lounge downtown. She was an overly buxom lady who had been married several times and who was well known all around the city (and around the country due to newspaper articles) for the way she perfectly balanced two glasses on her buxomness while pouring beer into them for her patrons. You had to see it to believe it, of course! Not long after she had opened for business, the woman came into the lumber company to place an order of materials for a new canopy she was going to have constructed over her bar. When she was headed out into the yard to pick up the items, word traveled quickly, and the yardmen all hid behind various forklifts and piles of lumber to sneak a peek when she walked by! I stopped in to see her place with its new project a week or two later and she cussed me out because the canopy was all crooked (which was her carpenter's fault, not ours!). It made me so mad that I never went back after that. She did run a popular establishment, though, and was around town for another twenty years, moving her business from one location to another.

The local distributorship for vending machines and the like (including the slots I used for the lumber dealer outing mentioned earlier) was near the original location of that woman's bar. The owner of the rental place was a nice guy, but a tough cookie who was rumored to have been involved with organized crime since he was a young man. The day I went in to order the slot machines, I asked him about the buxom woman's nearby bar having been recently closed down for awhile. He boldly told me that she didn't rent her jukeboxes and other equipment from him and that the city vice squad "just happened" to find an open bottle of whiskey on a shelf in the men's room at her establishment, so they shut her down! (As a side note, when I placed the order to rent the slot machines, he'd also asked me if I'd like to rent any movies because he had those too. I said no and told him that I thought the police were really hot on those movies being shown. He replied, "Gerald, do you know where I store them? In a locker, over at the police station... they'd look pretty stupid raiding their own place!")

Our south-side lumber location did quite well under my management, as did the new north-side location which was managed by a terrific guy who had begun working out in the yard with me when we were both teenagers. (That man passed away just a few months ago, and we had remained friends all these years.) The south location was about seven miles from my house, and it was a slow commute. As newlyweds, back in March of 1950, Jackie and I

had made our first home at 3602 Crocker Street in Des Moines, loving our little white bungalow with a basement garage that you entered from the back of the house. The entire basement was L-shaped, so both of our cars and my very first workshop fit nicely down under the home. I soon drove a 1950 Ford Coach, owned by the Jewett Lumber Company, and Jackie drove a nice looking and fuel-efficient little yellow Crosley station wagon with a stamped-out steel engine (which I didn't like, so I found another Crosley with one made of cast iron, and then switched out the engines!). The Crocker house was in a very nice neighborhood filled with neat and clean little homes, and I bought it through the Jewett Realty Company for

$5000—my uncles, Homer and Warren, handled the transaction. Then I built the nice efficient workshop in that basement garage… and got along really well with all my neighbors, who came over regularly to have me repair stuff for them!. There were so many other newlyweds in the area, many with whom I had grown up. One childhood friend and original college roommate lived a couple blocks north—he and his wife had me come over and cut out the entire south wall of their garage to make an archway into a big outdoor picnic table room for them, which I loved doing. Another childhood buddy (the son of one of our Governors) and his wife lived just up the street at 38th and Crocker, and across the street from us were the parents of yet another friend. It was a growing neighborhood with lots of activity. One time the sewer line to our house was plugged up with tree roots and I called a guy who had a shop on the south side of Ashworth Road out in West Des Moines to come fix it, which he did. I watched while he sat on a box near the end of the sewer line and jammed this big specially-made snake in there to bust up the roots and unclog the whole thing. The man was involved with a little mom-and-pop drain and sewer cleaning company known for their terrific customer service—who knew the nationwide Roto-Rooter company would have its start in our little neck of the woods?

Jackie and I had some terrific friends in the neighborhood, but also enjoyed being out and about with so many other couples our age. One of them had a big home south of Grand and regularly held impromptu dances in their third-floor ballroom, so we'd head over there quite often. On a November evening in 1951, Jackie and I hopped into the car to go somewhere on a whim like we'd always done—about halfway down the street we both looked at each other in wide-eyed surprise after remembering that we were now parents, and that our brand-new baby was back at our house sleeping quietly in her crib! We quickly turned around and raced back up the street! (It's a little embarrassing to retell the story to Jen, who was that baby.)

The Crocker house was a great starter home and a wonderful place to begin our family. Jennifer had been born in November of 1951 and Stephanie came along in March of 1954… that was also the year we started felling trees on a heavily wooded lot my folks helped us purchase on the west side of 35th Street between St. John's Road and John Lynde Road. The lot was just a couple of blocks from my Pop and Grandma Shore's former home on 37th Street. There were then only two other houses (and they both were sure huge!) on our newly developed street.

The price for my lot was $35 per front foot, which made my one-hundred-foot lot $3500. The guy I bought the property from was a family friend of ours, but he would not sell me just one lot—I had to buy all the property remaining on 35th Street, which included the big lot north of me. So, I went ahead and bought it too, at the same price per front foot (and soon sold that north portion to another childhood friend for the same amount I had paid for it, also giving him an easement to run drainage tile through my backyard.) Originally, there was a building restriction on my land, stating that any houses built on it had to face west because there was a little unnamed city street down the hill to the west, and the city proposed making a big cul-de-sac starting down at that little street, curving up the hill to my property and back down to meet up again with the same unnamed street. But I wanted to have a walk-out lower level off the back (west) side, and also had future ideas for that property down the hill, so really appreciated it when my new neighbor (who lived with her husband in the huge home immediately to the south of my lot) offered to go with me to the City Council meeting to propose having that ordinance changed so that I could build our house facing east like theirs. And we were granted that change.

At the same time that I was starting to construct our house, the City of Des Moines was building the new Veterans Memorial Auditorium on the east side of 5th Avenue, and I purchased from their contractor 40,000 of the paving bricks that he had plowed up out of the street. The nice thing about these particular paving bricks was that they had been laid in sand with no asphalt, so they were nice clean units ready to lay up. Every night after work,

I changed into old clothes and loaded those bricks myself by hand, hauling them in a lumber truck with a dump bed... night after night after night. I was so excited when the first portion of that pile of bricks actually became a foundation, and eventually a full three-story paving brick home. During my semesters at the University of Iowa, I had been constantly drawing and polishing up a floor plan for the house I one day wanted to build, and it was finally becoming a reality. It must have been much like the excitement felt by my great-grandfather, Ambrose Call, with those crude drawings of his own original log cabin built exactly one hundred years before mine.

Our new house was started in 1954 and finished in 1955, the same year my contractor also completed the Lucas Building on the Capitol grounds. The guy had gone bankrupt three decades earlier while building Theodore Roosevelt High School, my alma mater, but had recovered nicely, and I was pleased overall with the job he did on my new place. Jen asked me why I hired a guy who had previously gone belly-up as a builder. That really didn't worry me at all since it happened fairly regularly in that business. A lot of the general contractors I've known throughout my life have been bankrupt at one time or another… they just misplace a decimal point and go kerplunk!

Jackie and I sold our starter home on Crocker to move to 35th Street, which couldn't have been better timing—not long afterward, our little bungalow had to be moved when the new Interstate 235 was built through the heart of Des Moines. Though not huge, our new paving brick house on 35th was everything I wanted and that I could afford to build—a three-story, four-bedroom home with 3½ baths and a full walk-out basement with two exit doors onto a brick patio that spanned the entire backside of the home.

We got to choose our own address, which needed to be an even number between 30 and 120—so, our home became '100' (not only was it easy to remember, but it was also the house number of my great-aunt and great-uncle Cowles immediately west of us on 37th Street). When the City of Des Moines was adding street lights to that new little section of the development, I asked them to install a light directly in front of my place, which they did, so our front yard was well lit all through the nighttime hours. The backyard was full of timber and was totally dark, but adding landscaping lights under the trees gave an attractive view from the upper story at night. Our narrow street was to have no sidewalks, which was (and still is) nice for the homeowner, liability-wise. The two-car attached and fully paneled garage had its overhead door made of special hand-carved wood panels too. The garage itself was oversized at 625 square feet, with built-in cupboards and a walk-in closet providing plenty of room for lawn and garden machines; it also had built-in shelving and a pegboard wall for storing in an organized fashion miscellaneous tools for gardening, barbequing, and what have you. I ran water lines to indoor frost-proof garage faucets, like the ones outside too—that way, along with the floor drain, I could easily wash my cars in all weather! The garage was also heated and later air-conditioned; eventually, an epoxy coating on the floor made it an even nicer area. Jackie and I were part of a square dance group that regularly met in our garage too—it was just a terrific location for so many of our friends to gather, not to mention an awfully nice place to house cars! *{Editor's note: Steph and I have pictures of most of our early birthday parties being held out there as well.}*

I'm proud to tell more about the construction of 100-35th Street since it had some building features not found in other area residences. As a result of using a commercial contractor who typically built large structures, the house had 48" footings below ground, rather than the common 42"; additionally, the footings were two-feet wide all the way up to where the wood started. I used termite-proof (treated) lumber anywhere close to the ground. We put a built-up 'roof' on the basement walls on the ground side, using tarred felt because asphalt deteriorated underground, then tiled the outside foundation to drain down the hill. I also used cast iron for my waste pipe out of the house and down the hill; many people use Orangeburg pipe, which is a composition product nowhere near as strong and which allows tree roots to eventually get in and plug up a sewer. (My friend who built on the portion of land I sold him to the north, and who had an easement through my backyard, ended up using Orangeburg pipe for his home, which later gave way—sure enough, he had to dig up my backyard several years afterward to put in the cast iron I'd tried to get him to use!)

Inside the foundation, I laid ¼-inch thick Meadows pre-molded membrane sheets before the basement floor was poured, turning them up at the walls so that we had a dish-like surface into which we poured the basement floor concrete. All the cement for the basement and driveway was limestone aggregate. Not once, in the almost sixty years I owned that home, did we have any moisture in the basement—never even needed a sump pump. During the construction, I was there myself every single day and added other things too, like fire stops in the walls to prevent any air from fanning a fire. It's said that over 80 percent of heat loss in a house is through the ceiling and not through the side walls, but I went ahead and put in full-thickness blanket insulation in the side walls, as well as a foot of insulation in the ceiling of the upstairs and garage. At the time of construction, I didn't have the money to air-condition the place, but did put in two-inch service pipe all the way from the water main into the structure, so we had terrific water pressure which helped with the cooling system when we finally installed it. I also had put in over 50 runs out of the furnace plenum area to move the air easier, since colder air would be harder to move, so was well prepared when that time came. When the plumber did his installation, I had him use all copper plumbing pipe and put the vents on the back roof so they weren't noticeable from the street side. Before getting ready to apply the heavy hand-split shakes for the roof, I told the carpenters just how I wanted them to be installed—unfortunately, the roofing crew ignored that instruction, and when I came over after work that day and saw what they had done, I got up on the roof myself and tore all of them off... the next day, they were reinstalled correctly. In completing the roof structure, I had put a one-inch ventilation slot all along the soffits, with screen backing to protect it from bugs and to circulate air up into the attic. I also put extra large special-made louvers at both ends of the house for the same purpose. Up in that 312-square-foot attic I built cupboards across the entire length of the house, with a big walk-in cedar-lined closet at one end for the storage of off-season clothes. The attic was accessed through a door in the closet of the guest bedroom, where there was a full set of enclosed and finished stairs that got you up there.

As a good lumberman, the floors were all done in Bruce prefinished select oak, and the walls of each room were paneled with different species of wood—master was walnut, the guest bedroom birch, Jennifer's was pecky cypress, and Stephanie's oak. In each bedroom, large closets contained stacks of built-in dresser drawers. *{Editor's note: And Dymo labels designated the contents of each drawer.}* The living and dining rooms were paneled with an elegant clear pine, and the den was mahogany. The entry hall floor was a smooth

Georgian stone, which we also used for the rough-edged stacked-stone living room fireplace. The basement fireplace was done in the same exterior paving brick, and the paneling and doors down there were crafted of fancy Weyerhauser driftwood. Though we had hired a general contractor, I helped build a lot of the house myself, eventually finishing off the basement by working nights and weekends with a carpenter friend (and with two-year-old Stephanie, who was such a big help with the John Mansville flooring).

When the basement finishing was finally done, I added an upright player piano with plenty of paper rolls full of songs—I'm not even sure where I came up with the big old thing, but it doubled as a nice entertainment piece and as a place for the girls to begin taking piano lessons. *{Editor's note: That 'big old thing' was fun to have, especially for their parties, but had a lousy and tinny rinky-tink sound, not at all desirable for serious pianists! We girls ended up doing all of our practicing and lesson-taking on a nice little studio piano down the hill at our Nana and Grandad's house.}* I also came to possess a real slot machine, another fun item that we kept in the big basement rec room. It sat on one end of the bar, and was robbed once when someone entered the unlocked back door down there—the nickels were all they took! And just to make things more interesting, I put a fully-dressed female mannequin into the furnace closet attached to the basement bathroom, leaving the door ajar just enough so that a person sitting down on the toilet would see the mannequin's outstretched arm as if it were stepping into the room. Boy, did it ever make a party lively when you heard shrieks coming out of the lavatory!

My beautiful and very large two-room workshop was down in the newly finished basement too, and that was where I spent many hours. It was directly under the oversized double garage, which consisted of pre-cast cement floor joists and a concrete floor. One huge workshop room held dimension lumber of various sizes stored on shelving that I built across the length of the wall. An exterior basement door opened from that lumber storage room onto the paving brick patio that ran along the entire back side of our home. A handy drinking fountain was installed on the brick wall, a nice feature when you were working outdoors. I built a picnic table where we had so many memorable meals together during the nice weather months; then every winter, I would box off the patio with 2 x 4's and flood it with water to make a skating rink for all of us (and for the neighbors) to enjoy.

The inner room of my workshop area under the garage was where larger tools were all hung on a pegboard wall, and the smaller hand tools (screwdrivers and the like) were organized underneath that—I had built a wooden rack with slots, and inserted each item according to size and type of tool. It was especially meaningful to me that some of my shop pieces came from the old Jewett Typewriter Company, and a few of the tweezers and other small utensils came from the office of my grandfather, Pop Shore, M.D.

I purchased cases of tall glass olive jars that could be labeled according to size and type of whatever small items needed to be stored in each—the jars were individually organized according to contents, and displayed on custom-designed shelving. After having spent so much time in the hardware department of the lumber company all those years ago, and seeing the picture of my great-grandfather's product shelves in the original store, I was motivated to find a good method of organizing the smaller shop pieces for easy and quick access.

Here's another shot of that workroom from a different angle. This one shows some of the freestanding machines and power tools, as well as the terrific cupboards that I built under the working counter area to hide gallons of paint, bottles of solvents, and other bulkier or less-used items. Everything was so handy.

Once the Dymo Label Maker was invented, I admit to using it for labeling everything in sight, from the glass hardware jars to the containers of various chemicals and other large materials kept behind the cupboards. And I didn't stop with the workroom area but went around the entire house, labeling whatever might need description—like hidden light switches

to reveal what they controlled, and furnace ducts so we'd know where each one went!

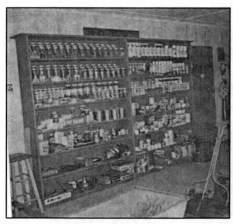

Though putting a nice little workroom into my folks' cottage garage several years earlier, I eventually built a larger one similar to the Des Moines shop in my own lake home garage in order to have "a place for everything and everything in its place" up there too. Nephew Chan mentioned the "impressively organized work rooms" in his note for my 91st birthday. And son-in-law, John (already with his own fully equipped workshop, and now with a few additional pieces from mine) wrote, "Whenever I go into my workroom and pick up one of your tools, I am forever 'cursed' by the expectation that this task must be done perfectly, thanks to you. Your example has helped me to redo something any number of times to get it just right, no matter how long it takes. It's an honor to be using many of those tools to craft things for your great-grandchildren."

After completing the Des Moines house with the huge workrooms, I installed an intercom that went to the kitchen above it, so Jackie could let me know when lunch was ready! *{Editor's note: I used to spend so much time with Dad in his workshop, learning how to fix this and that—what a wonderful lifetime gift from that handyman to this daughter. And I fondly remember our time lunching together up at the kitchen counter after Mom called downstairs on the intercom—our sandwich was always accompanied by a glass of cold milk and an Oreo cookie (still Dad's prerequisites to rounding out any healthy meal). This seems a good time to further address the Dymo Label Maker love affair that my father just admitted to having—his obsession with it extended far beyond the workshops, and well into every facet of our highly organized lives! Those handy little machines could be found wherever one looked—in Dad's office and cars, and even in the boat and the airplane. Over the years this Dymo thing became quite the family joke, hence my husband's idea to somehow incorporate Dad's Dymo-labeled name onto this book cover, as the author (and more importantly, owner) of a memoir about his very own life!}*

In the interior room of my Des Moines basement workshop, I made certain to build an additional storage closet area with shelving, to stock food and other supplies in the event of an atomic bombing by Russia. 'Fallout shelters' gained quickly in popularity around that time, as the Cold War was a real possibility. In reality, my interior workshop and storage area wouldn't have served as much protection for my family from radioactive particles, as it wasn't fully underground. But, for some reason, we all felt reassured by it.

*{**Editor's note:** We had monthly bomb drills during the years I attended Greenwood grade school, and had to employ the 'duck and cover' technique by crawling under our desks and clasping hands over the back of our necks—truly a scary exercise for children. I recall feeling rather uneasy when reading author Bill Bryson's childhood recollections of those same days in* The Life and Times of the Thunderbolt Kid, *accompanied by a photograph that looked just like my own memories of the drills. Bill and I had attended Greenwood together, and I wrote to him in 2007 with congratulations on the success of* Thunderbolt. *It meant a lot to receive a lovely hand-typed and personally signed letter back from England, in which Bill also sent greetings to my Dad and reminded us that he had been our neighborhood* Des Moines Tribune *paperboy (as if I would have forgotten all those cute little freckles!). I then promptly purchased the audio version of* Thunderbolt, *gifting it to Dad on Father's Day along with a copy of Bill's kind letter as a surprise bonus.}*

My next-door neighbor (and close lifetime friend) built a fancy fallout shelter in his basement, with nice beds and a kitchen. When he asked me why I didn't build a big one like his, I told him if he survived a bombing attack and was the only one around, I didn't want to be the last guy left surviving with him! (He was the little boy who got the new wagon that my Pop Shore matched for me back in kindergarten. And he was the kid chasing the car full of friends that rolled over at 63rd and Hickman when we were in high school. He was also the guy to whom I sold the next-door lot for the same price as I paid, and who then had to dig up my yard years later to replace the Orangeburg line that I had advised him not to use.) I was forever ribbing this friend about one thing or another, and could always get a good laugh out of him. He was such an active and fun-loving person, keeping fit bicycling and snow skiing and playing terrific tennis even as an elderly guy. When I last visited him in the hospital a few short years ago, however, he looked at me without a smile and told me he knew he was dying—it was pretty sobering. I seem to have stood at an awful lot of those bedsides and subsequent funerals recently.

Our 35th Street house had taken me two years to finish up the way I really wanted it. In telling about all its nice features, I'm reminded of some of the construction details that were attended to when my great-grandparents built their Algona mansion described earlier in this book, and also of the specifics about my Shore grandparents' building project for 210-37th Street. My own residence had so many hidden extras, apparently not appreciated by its future buyers. When I finally sold the 35th Street house after moving to Wesley, it practically killed me to learn that the new owners had painted the lovely clear pine paneling in the living and dining rooms and the paving brick fireplace in the basement. They removed the custom-made wrought iron handrails from the first to the second floor, and did other cosmetic 'upgrades' before flipping the house to make a few bucks—it's hard to believe that the original quality of construction didn't even seem to matter. It needed a decorating facelift to update it after sixty years, of course, but I certainly expected to get a better price due to the original construction of the place. The market brought what it brought, however, and it was time for me to clean my plate of properties and move on.

Back when we were first living in that house in 1955, I remember that we kept a horse in a lean-to barn down the hill, next to the little dead-end street that was once slated to become a cul-de-sac, as mentioned earlier. It wasn't my own horse, but actually belonged to one of our neighbors down and across the street, and his daughter was typically the one out there with it. I don't even recall the exact arrangement, but am thinking that the guy had told me I could use their horse if I would board it down there for them—I'm not sure I ever even rode the thing, but do remember lugging water down the big hill to that doggone animal, and how it drank so much! Though I always wanted to have a horse, it just never seemed to work out well for me (kind of like when I had 'Pete' as a kid—caring for one was more than I wanted to do). But I'm so glad that my girls learned to love the animals, and that both took riding lessons from an early age. Stephanie especially became quite good at the sport—she spent many years down at a big stable not too far south of our house, greatly excelling in dressage and jumping in various shows.

Then in 1958, as a gesture of love to my folks for all they'd done for me, I offered to give them the west part of my 35th Street property if they would build themselves a retirement house on it, which they did. My neighbor's horse and lean-to barn finally found a home elsewhere, and Mom and Dad's new residence took over the lower back part of our lot, accessed by the short dead-end city street that had no name (for all practical purposes, it had been nothing but a glorified back driveway entrance used by my next-door neighbors to the south). Once my folks built down there, the little city street would now service the utilities going to their home—that meant the street had to be given a name since you can't have a house without a street address. My mother said, "Let's call it Jewett Lane," and the City of Des Moines agreed with that idea. With Mom and Dad living in the backyard, the girls were down there all the time, enjoying being with their Nana and Grandad. We really cherished our time together as an extended family living in such close proximity to one another. (And their white painted-brick retirement house still sits on the property sixty years later, having had three or four additional owners since it was built, but still looking just like it did way back when my folks lived in it. I always laughingly admitted that smart lumbermen build homes out of brick, not out of lumber that deteriorates over time!)

After my parents moved out of the first house they had built at 213-38th Street Place and into the retirement house they built at 3517 Jewett Lane, my sister Connie and her husband purchased and moved their young family into that 38th Street Place home where Connie and I had grown up. The house where Connie and her husband had first started out was on Rollins Avenue, just east of 63rd Street, which was *also* in the eventual path of the new freeway—like our house on Crocker Street had been! I had worked so hard helping Connie's husband finish off the attic in their Rollins home, putting in new wiring and everything, and was so sorry to see it have to be removed to make way for a freeway. But it was also great to see the 38th Street Place house busy again, filled with the next generation of family members. Connie's first husband is a wonderful guy and was a very close friend. His mother was a lovely lady also. He had taken over his father's business as a manufacturer's representative after his Dad passed away. During that time, he and I were good friends, having lunch together on several occasions. And, of course, we spent most weekends together up at the Lakes, with both of our families staying in my folks' cottage for many years. Back in the late 40's, we had such fun together when I took him in the J-5 and out to a less congested area southwest of Okoboji to do some acrobatics—we did a number of them, but he sure loved the full loop (and I hear he still talks about that). I'm sorry to say that we pretty much lost touch after his divorce from my sister, but I enjoyed a recent long phone conversation with the guy several months ago, just before Christmas. I couldn't believe that he recognized my voice as soon as he answered the phone! He now lives out of state, but I'm hoping we will continue to stay in touch—it was so great to chat, almost like old times, and to know that he's still doing so well.

Our new neighborhood on 35th Street started to grow as our young families grew, and Jackie and I certainly enjoyed living there. Back in the days at Roosevelt High School, I had been on the swim team for a short time. Having grown up at Okoboji in the summers, I was a very good swimmer, but never as fast in the water as so many of my friends who actually raced on the school team. And now I was married to a lady who'd not only been an award-winning swimmer in high school in South Dakota, holding the record in breaststroke (and with the nickname of "the female seal"), but who had also been lured to the University of Iowa by a coach there who wanted to help train her for the Olympics!

Jackie was a true competitive athlete and enjoyed trying almost any sport. As a Physical Education (and Sociology) major, she knew a thing or two about it. After we were married, she helped run a girls' camp just east of Camp Dodge, where she was Sports Director, training the girls in various activities. Outside of sports, Jackie also took on several volunteer projects that stemmed more from her interest in social work and other outreaches, such as becoming a caseworker for the Des Moines Juvenile Court system, a district chairman for the United Way campaign, and the area chairman for the March of Dimes drive. She was a member of the Junior League of Des Moines, a rush adviser for the Theta sorority at Drake, and even a Brownie troop leader for the South-Side Community House—I was proud that she was such a busy wife and a good mother.

Not only did Jackie and I enjoy swimming and sailing in the summer months, but we really liked snow skiing and ice skating together in the winter too—we were both pretty darn graceful and good on the ice, making patterns and skating backward as easily as forward. In the winter of 1959, we decided to go with a few other couples to Sun Valley, Idaho to ski. Several of our friends were going, and I also presented the idea to my deaf childhood cement ball buddy and his wife. He was hesitant to join us since he didn't know how to ski, but after I told him how economical the trip would be, he and his wife agreed to come along—he always jumped on a good deal! My buddy immediately advised me, "I will not ski, but I have lots of new stories everybody will love, so I will go." Well, we all had a terrific time while there, and he even took ski lessons (but to no avail). I didn't end up getting my buddy and his wife out there in one of their planes, because the wife didn't like to fly, so they took the train west to meet us.

Jackie and I flew with another couple in our single-engine Bonanza. Flying alongside us was a friend and his wife in their single-engine Bonanza too. We enjoyed talking to each other from plane to plane all the way west, until we unexpectedly had to land in Cheyenne, Wyoming after my tachometer stopped working. We all quickly got to know the fixed base operator (FBO) running the airport there, who was a heck of a nice person—his father owned a dirt-moving equipment company and was the largest customer of Standard Oil, so the man had pulled some strings and got a gas pump close to the Cheyenne control tower so that this son could run the FBO service office and shop out of a small building there. Since Jackie and I had to wait overnight with the other couple for my tachometer to be fixed, I asked the young guy if he knew anywhere some stranded poor people from Iowa could get drunk and go naked overnight, and he said he knew just the place! He picked up the phone and made a call. Afterward, I learned he was calling his wife—she joined up with us and we all had a lot of fun that evening. And the next morning, we even got in some unplanned Wyoming skiing.

Before leaving Cheyenne for Sun Valley, the FBO guy invited the other pilot and me (along with our wives) to go for a ride in a rather new *twin* Bonanza that he had for sale. I was more than impressed with the way it operated, especially at high altitude because of its geared props. It seemed that a twin-engine craft would be a wise next investment for the lumber company, especially since we were wanting to do more direct business with western mills. The single-engine Bonanza I was flying that day ended up being our last one… not long after that trip, I purchased our company's first twin-engine plane, a Cessna. (We later bought a twin Bonanza from the Cheyenne guy, however, who by then also had a small flight service in Indiana. While over in Indiana making that airplane trade of the twin Cessna for the twin Bonanza years later, I noticed that my Cheyenne friend was working on a big DC-3 and had a bunch of the davenports from of it lying out on the ground. The name on the side of the DC-3 was 'MILE HIGH LINER'… the 'Mile High Club' refers to pilots who have made love in an airplane while on autopilot at 5,280 feet or above.)

I kept in touch with that Cheyenne friend for several years—one time he and his wife even flew into Okoboji and stayed with me at my folks' cottage. He was one of those people who was fun to be around because he was kind of a crazy guy and did things on a whim. One time he purchased a P-51 fighter plane in California, though he'd never even flown one. He took his pregnant wife along with him to pick it up, but first spent two days sitting in the cockpit learning the various systems in the plane before flying it back to Cheyenne. The couple eventually moved to Denver and I landed there one day to see him. By that time, he was selling helicopters at Stapleton Airport and was commuting back and forth to work from his home on the top of a mountain west of Denver. One day while playing in his helicopter, the engine quit; he made a forced landing in his yard, but not before the prop hit the roof on his house and did lots of damage—he was lucky to have not been killed.

When our Iowa group finally arrived in Sun Valley after leaving Cheyenne, most of us took ski lessons—it was a good idea to brush up on our skills and was also a great way to meet people from all over the country. One afternoon during a lesson, some lady asked me, "Where are you from?" I answered, "Des Moines, Iowa." She said, "Oh, I met somebody this morning from Iowa, and he told me he was a pig farmer." I had to laugh—what he hadn't told her was that he was also a very prominent banker, part of a family that had a number of private banks around the country, and that he'd formerly served as the national

President of the Bankers Association. Here are a bunch of us together after a class—I'm taking the picture, and Jackie is the fifth one from the right (in the light-colored jacket). And what a spectacular backdrop!

One of the funniest things that happened on that ski trip was after we all had a few drinks one night and got my deaf cement ball buddy up on stage to entertain the big crowd with his stories. In the audience were Lucille Ball and Vivian Vance (Ethel Mertz), who were in town making a movie. At another table were the Gary Coopers with the Ernest Hemingways, just to name a few. (I was walking one morning when Mr. Hemingway was going to get a paper, and we had a nice talk. He said he was being joined by his friend, Jimmy Stewart, the next day. Neither of them were there to ski, but were heading up into the mountains for a hunting trip.) Anyway, my deaf buddy had everyone rolling on the floor with laughter at his stories. The way he could tell a tale, with his eyes twinkling all the while, just kept you on the edge of your seat. And the way he talked, due to his disability, really made it necessary to listen intently. He didn't skip a beat. The climax of that particular evening was when we talked my buddy into going to the table next to ours to ask Lucille Ball to dance. We could hear both sides of the conversation and, although Ms. Ball was very polite to him, she said she did not dance. One of the things I remember about that trip was that Jackie had her picture taken with Lucille Ball—they were both in ski clothes, and it seemed so strange that my wife's were fancier than what the lovely Ms. Ball was wearing!

Jackie and I both enjoyed traveling, and took several nice trips during our first few years together. When we started dating, we had often flown from Iowa City over to Sioux Falls, stopping first for an overnight at my folks' Okoboji house when nobody was there, then heading on to South Dakota. The world-famous Joe Foss was the fixed base operator on the field in Sioux Falls... he would come out and gas my airplane, which I thought was a big deal. (And it was, since Joe Foss was known as WWII's 'Ace of Aces,' and had received a Medal of Honor presented to him by President Franklin Roosevelt. And a few years after our encounters at the Sioux Falls Airport, he became the youngest Governor of South Dakota.) Whenever we flew into Sioux Falls during hunting season, there were always one or two big twin-engine airplanes from the east coast in South Dakota for the season, filling their planes with pheasants to take back to the coast. Jackie's folks had a cottage on Lake Madison north of Sioux Falls, where we'd go spend the weekend, always getting our bird quota. Sometimes her eldest brother would come up from Sioux Falls to join us. I can remember in those days we would sit on the front fenders of her father's automobile while he drove and we scouted out pheasants, since road hunting by car was

legal. She and I also enjoyed inviting a small group of men and women up to Okoboji every fall for a weekend of hunting. The wives didn't carry guns, but they helped walk the fields with us and helped us clean the birds out in the garage at the end of the day. (Jackie is in the plaid hunting shirt here, second from left.) Back then we had a very dilapidated two-car garage with a dirt floor. It was simple to cover the floor area with newspapers before cleaning the birds. And every year or two, a number of fathers of some of our group were also up there hunting, and stopped over to visit and have a refreshment while we were ending the day.

Our lake cottage had a brick and cement manhole in the backyard, which was used to access a water turn-off faucet for the pipes buried well below the frost line. We would always turn off our water when leaving the cottage for any period of time, and especially in the non-summer months when the pipes could freeze. When we arrived back at the cottage the next weekend, we would turn on the furnace until the house had warmed up enough, then go out and turn on the water down in the manhole. I was usually the one to drop the ladder and climb down into the manhole to turn the faucet on and off, but it was approximately 8 feet deep and I got tired of climbing down there every time. So, I rigged up a 2 x 4 with two nails on one end and stuck it down into the handle spokes to turn the water on and off from above ground. Each time I got to the lake for the weekend, all I had to do was open the cover and turn the 2 x 4. When I gave my folks a brand-new garage several years later, we poured the cement floor right over the manhole, leaving room for the cover. We installed a light bulb directly over the hole, which helped us see without a flashlight when we turned the water on and off before and after the car was parked over it. I also built that first nice little lake workshop for myself in the front end of the new garage.

One of the men who came with us on the hunting weekends was another of those lifelong friends of mine. As an adult, he kept busy with several activities, like owning a farm southwest of Winterset, Iowa, where he started a hunt club. It had lots of bedrooms and a beer tap coming out of the wall. A few of us guys regularly went out there for a weekend of hunting—when we got through at the end of the first day, we'd have a beer and barbeque our food, then stay overnight in the club before another day of hunting. The wives would come down to meet up with us after that second day in the fields and we'd all go out to a very fine restaurant in the small town of Lorimor, where they had marvelous food and the waitresses were all in uniform. Jackie had given me a beautiful 12-gauge Winchester Model 12 rifle for a wedding present, which I loved hunting with all those decades. (I recently gave that gun to the one grandson of mine who actually likes to hunt.)

While we had some great times together early on and became the parents of two wonderful daughters, Jackie and I just couldn't come to terms with our differences, and we separated in 1959 after nine years of marriage. Then I spent six more after that just trying to get a divorce, going through District Court and through Supreme Court, then finally getting the job done on the second try through District Court. The big reason we had trouble getting the divorce was that we had both filed for custody of our girls; as it turned out, we jointly shared custody. (Additionally, I would not agree to all the things Jackie wanted, such as the house, the cars, the life insurance policies and everything else, for a total of 72 items!)

It was sad to move out of the lovely paving brick house I'd built for my little family on 35th Street, and especially so soon after my folks had built just down the hill on my property. Jackie and the girls remained in our home, while I found temporary housing arrangements at an apartment in Sherman Hills and then in my folks' house on Jewett Lane for awhile. I finally built a rustic but very neat little cabin just south of West Des Moines, in an area known as Commerce—for all practical purposes, my cute place was just a party house sitting on the Raccoon River where you could literally fish right off the outside deck. The cabin had only one bedroom, but also an open upper sleeping loft where the girls stayed when they were with me. It also became quite the hangout for lots of friends during my 'single-again' period of life. I remember one time, a good-looking gal was at a party there and asked me if I would take her picture in her bathing suit while she was sitting on the lap of a rather well-known gentleman. She went inside to change, and I figured she was doing that in the bathroom. But when I went into my bedroom to grab the camera, she was in it changing clothes—she just stood there stark naked, looking at me wide-eyed, then calmly put on her bathing suit without saying a word!

MY SINGLE-AGAIN ERA

Prior to the divorce, I had become a close friend of the local Sheriff of Polk County and was made an Honorary Deputy Sheriff by 1959. Right away, as part of the secret service detail with my boss, I was assigned to work security during the visit of Soviet Premier Nikita Khrushchev to Iowa, meeting him and shaking his hand when he arrived at the Des Moines Municipal Airport. He had an interpreter with him all the time. I was not in uniform, but carried a gun and wore a certain colored ribbon on my lapel. The Premier spent the night in Des Moines—I was stationed outside the door to his Fort Des Moines Hotel suite and got a kick out of him sending somebody out to get more vodka. The Sheriff and I led the procession the next day from Des Moines to Coon Rapids, and we noticed national guard soldiers on every bridge en route. Security was especially tight since relations between the United States and the Soviet Union [then known as the Union of Soviet Socialist Republics] were extremely tense. Khrushchev was to visit a huge family seed corn farming operation that day. The owner of the operation had been selling hybrid seed to the Soviet Union for many years and had worked hard to help improve relations between our two countries. The Iowa gentleman had traveled to Russia the year before, where he had met and extended to Khrushchev a personal invitation to visit our state. What I recall most about that visit to Coon Rapids was that the owner of the seed corn operation got mad at a reporter and threw a corn cob at him, which made the papers and television news clips.

During that same Coon Rapids trip, there was a big buffet luncheon being held in a large tent, probably 50 feet from the swimming pool. I was stationed at the pool as a Secret Service representative. While on duty, Adlai Stevenson (the former Illinois Governor who was a guest at the luncheon and who many will remember as the Democratic Presidential politician with the hole in his shoes) wandered out of the tent and came over to the pool area. He and I chatted with each other for probably ten minutes—I recall that he was divorced and that he seemed very lonely to me. On another occasion as a Deputy, I sat with our Sheriff and former President Harry Truman in Truman's private railroad car when it was stopped at the Rock Island Depot in Des Moines. (When the former President came back to Des Moines for a visit on another occasion, the Sheriff was looking for me to fly Truman back to Independence, Missouri after some function, which I would certainly have done but wasn't available.) There were so many other encounters with famous people during those law enforcement years, like the November night in 1964 when Count Basie stayed at the Savery Hotel and a bunch of us went to the home of a local Des Moines couple to listen to him play. Those spontaneous happenings went on all the time.

Between the duties I was given as an Honorary Deputy Sheriff, and my own personal involvement with Republican politics over the decades, I have rubbed shoulders with several local politicians and have gotten to know fairly well the Republican Governors of Iowa, especially the times that I served on the very first Committees to help raise money to get them elected. (One of them is now living here at Wesley, and I enjoy speaking to him and to his lovely wife when passing in the halls or in one of the dining areas.) And the Sheriff and I had many drinks with Iowa's *Democratic* Governor Harold Hughes before Hughes reformed. This might be a good place to tell about Iowa's liquor laws since Governor Hughes campaigned for legalization of liquor-by-the-drink. Until he ran in 1962, only beer was allowed to be consumed at a bar in Iowa. Liquor and wine were purchased in state-owned liquor stores and in "private clubs" only. This had been Iowa law since the end of Prohibition in late 1933. One document about it states, "The original idea behind Iowa's liquor stores was to limit consumption. The stores were dark and drab, and liquor was kept out of sight behind a counter." I sure do remember those days…

Each of us who bought liquor had to carry a little book to record our purchases. We'd put our refreshment choices onto a small slip of paper at a big side counter inside a state liquor store, then a clerk would retrieve the bottles and write the purchase down in a ledger that was public record. (I got laughing when telling Jen about the public monitoring of booze consumption, because Pops Jewett seemed to monitor my folks and their entertaining by going through the garbage when he came over, making certain there weren't too many bottles!) The liquor stores accepted only cash, with the idea that Iowans wouldn't go into debt to buy booze. As the liquor monopoly became a source of income for state government, the stores gradually evolved into more modern, self-service cash-only outlets with limited hours, clear up until 1987. Iowa still retains a monopoly on the wholesale distribution of liquor, and imposes a 50 percent markup on wholesale liquor prices, generating tens of millions of dollars for our state budget.

Back in the day, a lot of the bars in Des Moines had liquor available if you knew the owners. And naturally, the private (and not-so-private) clubs and Veteran's Clubs got by with serving liquor-by-the-drink. You could rent a locker box in the back of some establishments, and keep your own refreshments there, to be consumed on-site if the place had a license. I remember that Johnny and Kay's, which was a very stylish south-side dinner place with a private clubroom in the back, had liquor licenses. The owner once told me he got over $50,000 a year in rent from the lockers in the back room of his restaurant. The Des Moines Club had liquor boxes for their members too, and if one of your guests ordered a drink that you didn't have in your booze box, they would just take it out of another box and tell you that you owed a certain amount for it. Illegal alcohol and gambling places were a dime a dozen too. One restaurateur not only had good food, but also had a pretty big gambling operation going on in the back of his place. He made so much money that he kept his bills in garbage cans—$1's in one can, $5's in another, $10's in another, and so on. His big problem was how to get his money to the bank! He was a heck of a nice guy, but lived on the edge with the law. One time I was in there for a sandwich with a friend and noticed he had a hunting boat tied to the roof of his car. I asked him if he was going to another state for the weekend and he said yes. I replied that I didn't know the season was open there yet. He said, "It isn't, but when I get there I'll open it, and when I leave I'll close it!" Some people just get away with that kind of a lifestyle (though I recall he eventually did do some time in jail for one thing or another).

There was a lot of bootlegging out of a number of the drug stores and a number of nightclubs back then too. I remember at the Blue Moon you could buy a pint of whiskey for a dollar—it was called 'Mr. Boston's Spot'. The slogan was that "every drop hits the spot" and the label was open around a little raised glass spot on the bottle. I used to drink scotch, however, and always bought Johnny Walker Red Label because it was in the square bottle and didn't roll out from under the seat. My friend drank Canadian Club and always bought miniature bottles of it and then threw them out the window—that way he never had to have an open bottle of whiskey in his car while driving from one place to another. I know it's hard to believe nowadays that people would ever drink and drive like that, but it was pretty commonplace back then! As an ending to this story about liquor laws, Governor (and later Senator) Harold Hughes got a lot done for our state and for our country as a recovering alcoholic, and established very effective treatment programs for addictions. (On a side note, the only other Democratic Governor of Iowa I got to know pretty well was former Ford dealer and neighbor Clyde L. Herring—not many people can say they sat on a future Governor's lap while he was being served dinner!)

I met and got acquainted over drinks with Minnesota Senator Hubert Humphrey one night at the Kirkwood Hotel with the Sheriff. Then in 1964 when Humphrey was running for Vice President with Lyndon Johnson, I met him again with my girlfriend, Nelle, when we flew from a lumber meeting in Ft. Dodge to Okoboji. Humphrey had been in the Lakes area for an event and was at the airport with his pilot, getting ready to take off for Minneapolis. I reintroduced myself to him and told him to have his pilot check the weather carefully, as the radar had looked pretty colorful between Okoboji and the Twin Cities. In November of 1969, I met Vice President Spiro Agnew at our Governor's mansion, which was then located on Grand Avenue at 29th Street in Des Moines. Texas Governor John Connolly was also here for that function. By then, Nelle was my wife and had the same first name as Connolly's wife (who was actually Idanell, but called "Nellie"). And the guy who tuned-up his air horns at the mansion in my childhood neighborhood and who ended up racing boats as an adult, was at the same Agnew reception that night with his wife, also a "Nellie!" Needless to say, our three wives quickly got to know one another at the reception and enjoyed their own little name-related cocktail party! When I met Senators Lamar Alexander and Howard Baker, Baker had been the Senate majority leader for several years. He became President Reagan's Chief of Staff in 1987 but was also throwing his own hat into the Presidential race once again. A friend of mine was handling the Baker campaign during that time, and told me that Howard Baker had called him one night with the news that he was going to have to drop his own Presidential pursuits because President Reagan was very ill and Baker was going to have to take over many duties for him—apparently Reagan was suffering from signs of Alzheimer's disease by that time.

My time spent in law enforcement was terribly rewarding, and for reasons other than just meeting prominent people. After founding the Polk County Reserve Deputy Sheriff's Association, and drawing up its bylaws with another friend, I conducted meetings as its Chairman. (And by also Chairing the Polk County Peace Officers Association, there was some overlap in my own services to the community.) The Reserve group met monthly at Connie's Skyliner across from the airport and had over 100 people in attendance each time. Our Sheriff was instrumental in getting the various agencies throughout the state together for the meetings, which was terrific—we would have representatives from local Police Departments, Deputy Sheriffs, Reserve Deputy Sheriffs, Iowa Highway Patrol, and the like. Every year we had a representative from a local lock company put on a demonstration, showing how robbers would pour nitroglycerin into a safe in order to blow it open… Believe it or not, after those annual educational meetings there were always some safe-cracking jobs pulled off in Des Moines; we regularly reviewed the list of people attending our meeting but never could pinpoint who, if anyone, from that group might be connected to the attempted thefts!

There were a lot of incidents I got to be a part of during those years as an Honorary Deputy. I've always enjoyed being at the scene of action, and helping out in whatever way I can, so this period was truly exciting. The Sheriff and his wife were lovely people. He was so kind to me, like a brother really, and we enjoyed spending time together. I even took to wearing a big 'official' hat just like the Sheriff wore. My son-in-law wrote, in his 91st birthday note to me, "Fifty years ago this month, when I first met you, I was scared to death of you! I was 15-years-old and your daughter, Jennifer, was the first girl I'd ever dated. We'd been to a homecoming dance at Lincoln, followed by dinner at Bambino's on Ingersoll. You picked us up afterward to go to your house and hang out with our other friends over there for awhile. You were driving a silver-grey Lincoln Continental, sporting a sheriff-style hat, and there was no telling if you were packing heat somewhere. I said 'Yes, Sir' and 'No, Sir' while sweat rolled down the middle of my back…"

After founding the Reserve Association, I installed as my own Reserve Deputies many friends who were Chairmen of the Boards of various large companies (like Tone Brothers, Continental Western, Iowa Power and Light, Willis and Moore, C. B. Florsheim, and others.) With that group of business leaders, we had about seven airplanes to regularly offer for search and rescue emergencies; we also had a number of skin divers and were proud to have retrieved practically every drowning victim in Polk County. All of our services cost Polk County not a single cent—we furnished our own uniforms, our own guns, our own automobiles, our own airplanes—all with no reimbursement. Of course, as Deputies and Reserve Deputies we also attended many functions at no charge (like the State Fair and events held in the Veterans Auditorium, etc.), which was a nice perk for our families. One of my former Reserve Deputy friends recently reminded me of a time that Nelle and I were having drinks and dinner with him and his wife back in the mid-60's, during which I got a call that somebody had broken into our downtown lumber company. My friend recalls that he and I raced downtown and pulled up in front of the office, and that I grabbed my revolver out of the glove compartment and told him to come with me. He said, "No way," and stayed in the car while I went on in. (That's the only problem with the group of Reserve Deputy guys—we were just business owners who hoped to help our community, but nobody truly wanted to be involved in the heat of some battle!)

One time the Sheriff and I were riding around when he got a police call to the east side of town, where a gangster wanted to turn himself in. We went out and secured the location until the officers came and arrested the man. Another time while riding with the Sheriff, there was a call about the police pulling over a pickup truck filled with a load of guns. I said, "Sheriff, I've never seen a truckload of guns… let's drive out there," so we did. On yet another occasion we were tipped off that there was going to be a safe job at a well-known restaurant, so we had a Deputy Sheriff who was an excellent marksman hide in the establishment waiting for the break-in, which did occur. After the burglar got the safe opened and was on his way out of the building with the cash, the Deputy shot the guy in the leg and he was arrested—the Sheriff and I were parked nearby for that whole thing.

And I'll never forget the evening our Sheriff was to speak in Alleman, Iowa and asked if I would go with him. Of course, I said yes, and when we got there he asked permission for me to sit at the head table with him. They had requested the Sheriff talk about the juvenile delinquency problems that law enforcement was encountering in Des Moines. After he got up to speak, that stinker (the Sheriff) said, "The person who really knows more about the juvenile delinquency problems is the founder and President of the Polk County Reserve Deputy Sheriff's Association," and called on me to speak without any prior notice! So, I

got up and just ad-libbed, talking about juvenile delinquency and kids scooping the loop and how, in this day and age, liquor (and especially vodka) led to a lot of the problems. I ended my speech by saying, "And all of that leads to problems with sex, of course; but nobody knows more about that than our fine Sheriff of Polk County, and at this time I'd like to turn the program back to him." It brought the house down. After the meeting, I got into the Sheriff's car to ride back to town and not one word was mentioned about the meeting all the way home—not a thank you, or an apology, or a chuckle, or a scolding, or anything! The Sheriff was ornery as the dickens and was always full of the devil, so you constantly had to be one step ahead. It broke my heart when he passed away several years later, but I was honored to be asked to be a pallbearer—hundreds of people attended the funeral, paying respects to a great guy.

Remaining good friends with members of the City of Des Moines Police Department and of the Polk County Sheriff's office all started back in those days of the Polk County Reserve. And I also stayed good friends with the Iowa Highway Patrol personnel and the Okoboji area police—we even used our airplane a number of times for search and rescue at the Lakes, taking the local City Manager of Okoboji with us. My lake cottage sat at a T-intersection of two roads that ran around the lake, so people knew when I was there. If they saw me out working in my yard or garage, many times the local police would stop and chat or have a coke. I would shine up their badges on my polishing machine in the garage workshop, then clean them off with lacquer thinner and coat them with fresh lacquer so that the badge wouldn't tarnish so badly (much like my great-grandfather's employees did when Jewett Lumber Company had the Santa Workshop to repair broken toys and coat them with Jap-a-Lac!). I bought so much lacquer thinner over the years that Nelle swore I must be drinking it. The stuff has always been terrific for removing spots on carpeting and clothing, or old grease on tools and what have you, because it never leaves any residue. The product isn't sold for cleaning purposes, though, because it's so flammable. *{Editor's note: Lacquer thinner ranks right up there, fairly close to Dymo labels in our ongoing family jokes about Dad. Though he admits to the liquid being terribly flammable, that didn't stop him from keeping a gallon can of it (along with an accompanying stinky rag) in the trunks of his cars and in the storage areas of the airplanes and boats.}*

My early tenure as a Deputy Sheriff kept me a pretty busy guy since those were also the years that my divorce stories were regularly splashed all over the paper. Women I had never met would call or come to the office to ask me on dates. One lovely Italian gal brought homemade cookies to me regularly, then eventually invited me to her home for dinner. On that first invitation, I asked if I could bring a few of my friends, to which she agreed. So, I took along with me three good buddies—the County Sheriff, the City Chief of Police, and the State 'Raiding Constable.' (One of her family members had been involved in a little brush with the law, so I'm sure she was a little surprised with my guest list.) As it turned out, we all had a wonderful authentic Italian dinner together that night, and it was the start of many more over the years. Though that particular connection didn't end up involving any hanky-panky with me, some others certainly did. I had more experiences than I want to relate in this book but, suffice it to say, grass didn't grow under my feet.

I guess it'd be alright to mention a couple of close calls with ladies that were kind of funny. One time a woman came to my office and introduced herself, telling me how sorry she felt about my divorce and wanting to know if I'd like to come over to her house and swim in her pool. So, I went over and she talked me into skinny dipping—it was night and the underwater pool lights were on, which was a lot of fun. After swimming we went back inside, only to be suddenly interrupted when we heard the front door to the house open. She said it must be her husband! What husband? I quickly gathered my clothes and jumped out the first-floor window, running around the side of her house and hopping into my car, never to return. To this day, I can't remember that woman's name and can't even find the exact house (which I went looking for the other day after relating the story to include here). Another 'skeleton' that I brought out of my closet for this book happened with a different gal. She and I were in her home office when her steady gentleman showed up and came walking down the hall. I crawled under the kneehole of her desk and pulled the chair tightly behind me. The guy was sitting out in the living room for about an hour, while I was really sweating and even biting my tongue for fear I'd sneeze! (I do remember that woman's name, but that's all I'm going to say about it.) In my prayers over the years, I've always given thanks for saving my life through several illnesses and surgeries and near emergencies, but also with saving me from so many close calls during my single-again era!

After having to move out of 100-35th Street, I was able to see my daughters whenever I wished, for the most part—which wasn't all that often since I was so busy with work and the many other involvements. We did have a regular time when all four of us were together at the 35th Street house on Sunday nights. I would go over in the early evening to play with the girls, while Jackie made us all popcorn and chocolate malts. The divorce was an ugly one, but she and I did everything we could to remain civil with each other for the sake of our kids. The most enjoyable time for my daughters, as they talk about it yet today, was playing 'rumble car' on the living room floor. They took turns riding on their old man's back while I made sharp turns and fast starts and stops until the 'rumble car' would break down and have to be restarted and ridden on by the other daughter. It was quite a workout for me, as you can imagine, and every Monday morning my knees and back were pretty darn sore. (Eventually, Jackie moved out of the 35th Street house and married another guy, so I got to take back the home I loved. My freezer had once been full of wild game and my liquor cabinet stocked to the brim; but when I got the house back, all that was gone. The girls moved with Jackie to the south side of town, where Jennifer ended up attending and graduating from Lincoln High School. Steph decided she couldn't stand being away from the west side and friends, so moved back over with me to attend Callanan and Roosevelt.)

But before getting the 35th Street home back from Jackie, there was another stop along the way for me...a wild couple of years living with my deaf cement ball buddy, who had become single about the same time I had. My buddy had bought himself a nice large bachelor pad on Lincoln Place Drive, where we each had plenty of room. Grateful that he let me live in one of the master suites at the other end of the house, I worked really hard to be the perfect housemate. *{Editor's note: Think "The Odd Couple" show from the 1970's, with Felix (Tony Randall) and Oscar (Jack Klugman).}* If not on the phone or sleeping, my buddy would be in the living room, with a magazine in hand and two television sets showing different channels at the same time—he would have the volume on one TV turned way up in order to hear it (somewhat) and would be reading the lips of the people on the silent set. And he did all this while absorbing and telling me about the contents of different magazine articles he'd just read! I still don't know how the guy could do that—he was just so smart. He also had a heart of gold, and was always funny and clowning around, especially about his disability—in the morning, after putting on his hearing aid(s), he would say something like, "Good morning everyone… AMC is now on the air… won't you please say something?" I went to work every single day, but my housemate didn't have to do that. After I'd get home from the office at 6:00 P.M., he might say, "Jerry, let's fly to St. Louis for dinner." We'd get ourselves to the airport, flying one of his company planes to St. Louis for a night of fun before returning to Des Moines by 5:00 or 6:00 the next morning. I'd shower, shave, change my clothes and head to the office, while my housemate headed to bed. Then I'd get home that same night and he'd say something like, "Jerry, I just talked to so-and-so in Minneapolis and there is a big party up there tonight… let's go!" I'd answer, "I AM DEAD TIRED!" and he'd ask, "What's wrong with you?" So, we'd end up in Minneapolis that night. And it went on like that for a couple of years.

One time I was flying us home from Illinois in one of his planes during a snowstorm and was fully on instruments. My buddy said, "Where is Des Moines?" and I pointed behind us. He said, "Ho, ho, ho—you miss Des Moines?" I yelled that we were simply making an instrument let-down. He then lit a big cigar and turned on the dome light to read a magazine (flying at night with him was frustrating, as he was always flipping on cabin lights, lighting matches, and even turning on the landing lights to see how the rain, fog, or snow appeared outside the window). After landing in this particular snowstorm, we were unloading the plane and he said, "Jerry, how did you ever find Des Moines?" I yelled, "IT IS VERY SIMPLE ON INSTRUMENTS. WERE YOU WORRIED?" He laughed and said, "No, not a bit… I love to live dangerously!" And he did.

After housing together for awhile it became easier to communicate. There were still occasions, however, when I didn't understand him very well. One of these times was when I was flying to Okoboji through a dense fog while my buddy and my girlfriend at the time (who eventually became second wife, Nelle) were sitting in the back of his airplane drinking screwdrivers from a portable bar. We descended from out of the fog, and I asked him if he knew what town we were over. He said, "Sure," then tried naming the town. I couldn't understand him, so he finally said, "Quack, Quack." He was correct after all—we were over Mallard, Iowa. Another time we were in California and he said, "Let's fly over to SCRAM-E-TOE." After asking him a couple of times to repeat himself, he got put out with me and said, "Jerry, you dumbbell… don't you even know the capital of California?" So, we headed to Sacramento! Even when he was out of town *without* me, which was quite often, he would call while I was living at his house because he just loved talking on the phone. It might be 3:00 or 4:00 in the morning, but he was up and wanting to know what I was doing. I'd remind him that I was sleeping, but he didn't particularly care since he was on his own unpredictable schedule. Oftentimes he'd be wanting me to come pick him up wherever he was, after having taken a commercial flight somewhere on a whim. Naturally, I wanted the opportunity to fly whenever I could, so I'd get up and get into one of his planes and head to Palm Desert (or wherever he was) just to fly him home. On some occasions I'd also try to fill up his plane with other Des Moines people who wanted to fly along in order to vacation somewhere for the day. (And on occasion, when I got to wherever I was to pick him up, my buddy might have decided to stay a little longer—then I'd have to threaten to head back to Des Moines since I had to be at work, which meant leaving him there until I could return later… that always seemed to get his attention.)

The early 1960's were probably our banner ones as buddies. Normally I logged 200-250 hours annually, but I recall chalking up more than double during that time—over 600 miles a year. Most of it was done at night with him in one of his planes—we were on trips all over the country and into Mexico in those few years alone. I recall stops in Chicago, Dubuque, Milwaukee, St. Louis, Kansas City, Colorado Springs, Las Vegas, Santa Fe, Palm Desert, not to mention the frequent trips up to Duluth to see his girlfriend (who later became his second wife). One time we headed together to the wedding of one of our childhood friends from Des Moines, flying to Beverly Hills by way of Phoenix. But on that occasion, I got to fly the corporate plane owned by the family of the guy getting married (he happened to be the one whose tonsils I'd looked at as a little kid while living in his house after I'd eloped with his sister back in kindergarten). People were often asking me to fly their airplanes to one location or another, probably since I was instrument-rated with a commercial license, and authorized for land and sea (single-engine) and land (twin-engine). And, of course, I just loved making myself available to fly whenever possible.

While in southern California for that guy's wedding, we stayed at the Beverly Hills Hotel in a cottage next door to one that housed Elizabeth Taylor and Eddie Fisher—theirs was only about 25 or 30 feet from ours, and we went swimming every day with Eddie Fisher in our hotel pool. Since we were in California, my deaf buddy decided to call another of our friends who had moved to San Francisco, hoping to talk him into coming down for the wedding and to see us. (The San Francisco guy, incidentally, was the kid from our neighborhood who had lived with his family in the big mansion and whose party I attended when the parrot talked to me. His older brother was the one who regularly tuned the air horns on his Cadillac out in their courtyard.) So, when my deaf buddy called our mansion friend on the phone, we were all sitting around a big table down in Beverly Hills with the groom-to-be, his soon-to-be wife, wedding party participants, etc. My buddy was holding his hearing aid so that it would serve as a loudspeaker and we could all hear both sides of the conversation. Our San Francisco friend ended by loudly remarking, "Well, I'm not going to be able to make it to *this* wedding, but tell him I'll try to make his *next* one." I remember how that comment didn't go over very well with the cute little bride-to-be.

The night before that wedding we were in the Grand Ballroom, where an orchestra was playing and the wedding group was dining and dancing with other hotel guests. When the orchestra took a break, our groom-to-be friend went up to the microphone and announced, "We have a very famous entertainer here tonight. I would first like to introduce his manager to present him to us." We quickly figured out that I was to be that manager and my deaf buddy was to be the entertainer. So, I slowly mouthed to my buddy that he needed to tell a story to the crowd. He read my lips and asked me what story he should tell. I mouthed, "Tell about Eskimo Man," then walked up to the microphone and introduced my deaf buddy, who proceeded to tell a slightly off-color joke about the Alaska native who needed to take a leak—the punch line ended up having to do with ice cubes, and the audience roared. The crazy part of this story is that Lucille Ball happened to be in the audience again! (The reader may remember that my buddy had been entertaining a bunch of us on our Sun Valley ski trip a couple of years before, and had asked Ms. Ball to dance back then. By this time, she was not well and was in a wheelchair, but she still seemed to be enjoying a good party.)

The winter of 1961 was colder than Billy-be-damned in Des Moines, and my housemate and I talked about spending New Year's Eve someplace south where it would be warmer. After flying his visiting relatives back to their home following the Christmas holiday, we encountered airplane starter problems as were due to depart Parsons, Kansas. It was getting late so I yelled to him, "MAYBE WE SHOULD JUST STAY HERE OVERNIGHT." And he said, "Hell no, these mechanics are dumbbells!... when we get the engines started, let's head south." I had to hand prop the left engine myself several times to get the thing going. Shortly thereafter, we were airborne and, in two hours and fifty minutes, landed in Houston, Texas. As we touched down, our landing lights went off because the battery went dead. (As already mentioned, my buddy and his older brother did practically nothing to keep up their twin-engine planes—it always seemed to be my responsibility to do that for them!) While in Houston, I called a girl now living there who I used to date in Iowa City and asked her if she'd like to have dinner. She brought along a friend for my buddy and we had a bang-up night on the town. They were experiencing a cold spell in Houston too, so the two ladies agreed to go even further south with us. We headed to Mexico, landing first at Brownsville to go through Customs. Then, about 600 feet out of Brownsville, we lost an engine—after radioing in with the emergency, Brownsville tower said we were cleared to land anywhere; thankfully, I was able to bring us back around for a safe landing at the airport. From there I called the man who was in charge of the service department at the flying service in Des Moines where this buddy and his brother kept their airplanes; he told me the issue with my friend's engine sounded like bad spark plugs. So, we purchased and installed new ones—24 of them (six cylinders, two per cylinder per engine). And sure enough, we had no more problems that I can remember with that particular aircraft. Incidentally, while going through Customs in Brownsville, we were asked if we would also take a Mexican Customs agent with us to Mexico City. We agreed, as I thought it would be very handy to have this guy along as an interpreter for a night on the town. Once in the air, we offered him Oreo cookies and skim milk (I always tried to travel with those staples) and formally asked if he would be our interpreter in Mexico City—it turned out he didn't speak a word of English! Anyway, we all ended up in Mexico City for New Year's Eve, after which the four of us flew on to Acapulco to 'bring in' 1962.

Traveling in Mexico with my deaf buddy was something else, as you can imagine. I had taken two years of Spanish in school and he had taken none, yet he actually got along better than I did in talking with the locals. We had next-door rooms with big balconies right on the water, on about the seventh or eighth floor at the Hotel El Presidente in Acapulco. The first night we came back to the hotel in the wee hours and said good night, going to our rooms. A short time later there was a loud pounding on my door. I opened it to find my blurry-eyed friend holding his "blankety-blank" doorknob, with the key in the lock. He commanded, "Jerry, do something!" and handed me the broken unit. I went to the phone, only to find no night shift hotel employees who spoke English. But before long, the bell captain arrived at my room with two men who were then sent to work on my buddy's door. The repair guys were in his room for quite some time while he was waiting in mine. I kept falling asleep, then woke abruptly when I noticed that my buddy was gone but that his shoes and pants were still in my room. I ran over to his room, which was locked—the workmen had already fixed the door problem and left. I called down to the front desk, learning that the workmen didn't see my buddy come in while they were there. I had them come back and open his door, and we found him sound asleep in his room! When waking him up and checking further, my buddy told me he had gotten tired of sitting in my room and wanted to go to bed, so he had crawled over my balcony railing and across a 4-inch ledge to his own balcony and into his room. After giving him hell for doing such a dumb thing, he said, "Jerry, you forget I like to live dangerously." That was putting it mildly!

Eventually, we were ready to leave Mexico. I first had to hand-pump gasoline into the airplane from a 55-gallon drum on wheels at the airport, then strain the gas through a chamois to fill the tanks. Before departing Acapulco, I asked a guy at the airport if he knew what the flying weather was to Brownsville, Texas and he said, "Oh, it's good." I questioned how he knew it was good, and he answered, "If it's good here, it's good there." I asked if they had a weather bureau at the airport and he quickly answered, "Yes," while pointing to a table with an umbrella top on it. I said, "That's your weather bureau?" He answered, "Yes" again, so I went over to the 'weather bureau' guy and requested information about Brownsville. The 'weather bureau' guy said, "Oh, Brownsville is just beautiful... if it's good here, it's good there!" We never did get an accurate report, but were able to fly safely into Brownsville to clear Customs and get back home.

My housemate just couldn't stop coming up with some travel plan for us. A memorable one was hatched on a Saturday morning in the fall of 1962, when he woke me up to say, "Jerry, I just talked to a girl I met last month in Japan and she lives in Santa Fe and wants us to come right out... she says she has a hot date for you tonight too." So, of course, we headed to the airport and flew nonstop—five hours and ten minutes—to New Mexico in one of his planes. While crossing Kansas, we radioed Garden City and had them use his telephone credit card to call his lady friend and inform her of our arrival time. As we taxied up to the terminal in Santa Fe, she drove up with the other gal—and, as promised, my date was indeed a hot one. That night we painted every picket fence in the area, while also attending a big gathering they threw in our honor. Sometime during the evening, we got a call from Des Moines friends who were vacationing in Colorado and happened to be at a party with the family who owned a famous aircraft corporation—our friends knew that I'd love to get myself to Estes Park that night to meet these aircraft people, and it definitely was tempting to hop into the plane and go meet up with them. But my buddy and I had already been out partying, so had to tell them we couldn't come until the next day...

That next day was September 2, 1962, and at 12:00 noon all non-military airplanes in the U.S. and Canada, including the airlines, were to be grounded [this was the third of three annual Operation Skyshield large-scale military exercises to test NORAD's defenses against potential Soviet attacks]. I'd missed the chance to meet the aircraft people, of course, but we still hoped to join up with our Des Moines friends staying in Boulder, so I had told them we'd leave New Mexico early enough in the morning to make it to Boulder before that noon flight curfew. My buddy and I flew out of Santa Fe by 10:00 A.M. and, due to strong north winds, got into Boulder about ten minutes later than we'd hoped (but still three minutes before the noon mandatory grounding!). We sure had a great time in Colorado, and even drove down to Golden to visit the Coors brewery. Then the next day we flew over to Aspen for a day of play. Believe it or not, my buddy had filled every empty space in the plane with cases of Coors beer (then unavailable in Iowa) that he'd picked up in Golden. It was so crowded in the plane that he had to put his legs up on one of his cases of beer on the passenger side floor—there was just nowhere to put that last box, and he wasn't willing to leave it behind!

We had such a terrific time in Aspen, lunching at the lovely mountain estate of another former Des Moines friend, a gal who had married the guy responsible for bringing the sport of skiing to Aspen (Buttermilk Mountain) just a few years before. He was an amazing skier and did aerial somersaults while coming down the slope. Back when we were little kids going to Greenwood, I especially remember that this girl was taken to school and picked up after school every day by her private nursemaid—the Lindbergh kidnapping case had really frightened parents across the country, and her family was no exception. (And now that I think about it, another classmate, the daughter of a wealthy family on Tonawanda Drive, had installed bars put on her bedroom windows because of it too.) Anyway, after a wonderful time in Aspen with this first neighborhood girl who was now grown up and married, my buddy and I headed back east over the Rockies in strong thunderstorms, with his legs bouncing up and down on that case of beer with each bump.

On a side note, I want to tell something about the Des Moines couple who had been at the cocktail party in Estes Park with the aircraft family. One year I flew them to Palm Desert on one of those day-trips to pick up my deaf roommate—they both ended up falling in love with the place and decided to move out there. So, my friends returned to Des Moines, sold their business and house, bought a great big ranch in a beautiful district of Palm Desert, and opened a furniture and gift store (quickly becoming very successful). One of their customers was Red Skelton, who visited the store regularly and paid cash for all of his purchases—they said Mr. Skelton was a heck of a nice guy who told them he had grown up with no money and just loved buying stuff! (Speaking of Red Skelton, he once came to Spencer, Iowa to perform at the Clay County Fair. During the time he was there, the local Senator had a house party and also invited Mr. Skelton. I certainly enjoyed being at that affair and watching him entertain the Senator's grandchildren—it was just so funny the way he screwed up his face!)

By flying the airplanes that belonged to my buddy and his brother, I learned what kinds of planes I might want to own myself. So, Dad and I had begun purchasing some newer and even faster airplanes for our own use, starting with single-engine Bonanzas. I certainly had some interesting dating experiences, especially with my first single-engine Bonanza that was mainly for personal use. As a divorcee, it was a lot of fun flying different ladies around the country for our dates. I guess we won't put those stories in here, but I had some autopilot fun in the skies back in the day. In her note of memories presented to me for my 91st birthday gift, I was surprised that niece Kyle, when talking about the Okoboji Unicom mentioned earlier in this book, also talked about the different ladies I flew in with for the weekends! She wrote, "Pre-Nelle, we wanted to see what new date would emerge from the passenger side... as there always seemed to be some new "gal" ... always with a big hairdo. Then came the Friday evening that Nelle emerged from the plane, and we all knew, instantly, that she was The One." Kyle was right—once I met Nelle, she was the one.

SETTLING DOWN (SOME)

Before long, we started using little Bonanzas for business more than pleasure. It was so handy to be able to fly contractors, customers, and even employees to various job sites and mills and manufacturing plants. Uncle Homer had suggested that we put the airplane in the lumber company name, with all the business use it was now getting. My Dad replied, "Not unless *you* learn to fly and can benefit from it too." So, our last single-engine Bonanza was purchased by the company, and Uncle Homer learned to fly in it. He really enjoyed piloting but didn't go anywhere much outside of the Des Moines area that I recall, other than maybe to one meeting in Hot Springs, Arkansas. Here's a shot of that last single-engine plane we had, taken in Minnesota at the Wilderness Airport at Sugar Lake. Uncle Homer and I are standing next to it (along with another lumber dealer getting in) as we prepare to leave that conference site.

Since we were in and out of the skies even more than ever before, it became obvious that the Des Moines Municipal Airport would benefit from having some T-Hangars for private aircraft owners like ourselves. So, I headed down to the City Manager's office, taking along an attorney friend of mine who was also a pilot (in case they threw questions at me that I couldn't answer). I'm proud to have gotten the City of Des Moines to build T-Hangars on the southeast part of our airport, which was a real plus for independent pilots. Those hangars were very satisfactory, and I had a winch put into the back of ours so that I could pull the aircraft into it myself. It was terrific to be in control of getting our plane ready to go whenever necessary, and not depending on the flying service to unload their big hangar in order to get ours out at some pre-determined time. It was also nice to know that the craft wouldn't have to sustain any 'hangar rash,' which sometimes occurred when planes were being jockeyed around! Our single-engine Bonanzas were later followed by a twin Cessna 310, which was terribly noisy—like driving in a pickup truck—but it sure was fast. Then the Cessna was followed by a number of twin Beechcraft, the first one purchased in Indiana from that Cheyenne, Wyoming friend, and each one owned by the lumber company. All of our twin-engine airplanes also had automatic pilot controls, and I'd sure learned to depend on that feature. I used to think how funny it was to be able to fly from one place to another, like Des Moines to Florida, and never even need to touch the controls until you landed! Every year a friend and I went over to Chicago to brush up on our instrument flying skills, and I admit that one year I did a terrible job of flying the plane while there because I'd become so dependent on autopilot and had simply gotten lazy.

A few weeks ago, a good friend from whom I used to buy a lot of lumber caught wind of this book that we are writing about my life and suggested getting together to reminisce about a few stories I may have forgotten to include—he knew me very well and didn't want me to come out of this smelling like a rose, I guess! So, he and his wife met up for lunch with me and my daughters to recall and laugh about some of our memories. Among many other things, he reminded me of a convention story that I'd completely forgotten about, but it's cute enough to put here… A bunch of us were up at the Northwestern Lumbermens Annual Convention in Minneapolis, all staying at the very nice downtown Radisson Hotel. Nelle and I had driven up to the event with this same Des Moines couple because there was a massive snowstorm that disrupted our original plan to fly to it. We were all out for dinner with some other lumber dealers from around the midwest. The rest of the story is quoted in my friend's own words: "Everybody was pretty juiced up and now it was midnight or so and we all continued hopping it up, back in one of our rooms. We got a call from the front desk that a couple of guys were raising hell because *we* were raising hell on the floor… they were two over-the-road truckers in shorts and t-shirts, upset about the loud fun we were having. Suddenly the rest of us realized that Jerry was gone from our party room… hey, where'd Jerry go? Next thing we knew, the two truckers showed up in our suite and started partying right along with us. Turns out Jerry had gone to invite them to join us, and they showed up… in their undershorts!"

That friend also reminded me of another time that I flew four of us lumber dealers to Boise, Idaho where my Dad was meeting with the head of Boise Cascade (who had shown some interest in buying our own operation). We first stopped in Cheyenne and all went up to a nightclub I was familiar with just north of there. After our time in Boise, while heading back home over the mountains in the twin Cessna, Dad overheard me on the radio getting in touch with a gal I knew in Saratoga, Wyoming who might show us around that area. Dad said, "What are we doing now?" I replied, "We're landing in Saratoga… it's on the way, and we can visit another mill operation." Dad said, "No, I've got to get back." But we landed, and my gal friend was there waiting for us. (I had met her on an earlier trip while looking for a spot to hold one of our lumbermen outings and had gotten acquainted with her pretty well.) She had a car and took us all over the place, which of course I loved. Everyone else put up with the delay, and we were home the next day.

In being reminded of that trip out to visit Boise Cascade, it also brought back a memory about the time Dad and I met and talked with General Chuck Yeager, the pilot who had broken the sound barrier at 45,000 feet back in 1947. Years later, the owner of a local flying service had brought General Yeager to Des Moines for a big luncheon to celebrate the two of them breaking yet another speed record while flying from Denver to Des Moines. Several other local pilots and business executives were in attendance at the Wakonda Club gathering that day too. Learning that we were in the lumber business, the guest of honor asked Dad if we bought material from Boise Cascade, to which my father answered in the affirmative. General Yeager said, "Well, just keep doing that… I'm on their Board of Directors!"

Because of being instrument-rated and readily making myself available, I was regularly flying somebody else's corporate plane somewhere, as mentioned before… that's how I ended up with thousands of my early logged hours that were purely for pleasure. But business became the main endeavor as I got older. Our company plane landed in such places as Charleston, South Carolina, then Terra Haute, Indiana; those were followed by stops in Anaheim, California, then Osage Beach, Missouri. There were trips to Detroit, Michigan and Tampa, Florida; to Memphis, Tennessee and San Antonio, Texas; to Portland, Oregon and Las Vegas, Nevada; followed by Albuquerque, New Mexico, and Superior, Wisconsin, and Ft. Lauderdale, Florida… the list just goes on and on. Other than Alaska and Hawaii, I've flown to every state in the Union, landing in many of them on multiple occasions. And several of the northern trips to Minnesota and Wisconsin, as well as into Canada, included times spent fishing with our dealers or customers—that was always a great way to get to know one another better. It was on one of those fishing trips, I think after a visit to Edward Hines Lumber Company, that I learned to chew tobacco… if anybody decides to try that trick, I'd suggest you be in a boat because all you do is spit!

I truly believe we were the only lumber dealers in Des Moines who cared much about where their lumber came from, which is so all-important. That's why we flew to many mills to learn about the best lumber and about how to purchase it. We bought our old-growth lumber from the west coast, but from trees that had been grown at a high altitude and on the east side of a mountain. Though the freight can be exorbitant, those timbers have to come from the west coast since they grow larger than the ones in Canada or the eastern empire (east of the Cascade Mountains) or even in the south. When you walk into a building with big exposed beams that have gaps and tears in them—that's due to being built with lumber fast-grown on the west side of a mountain. The prevailing winds from the west will shake a tree and tear the grain at the same time, causing the wood to be inferior (we'd say, "that lumber has shake in it"). The old story about a tree growing up is that every year it acquires a new ring—if a tree grows up fast, the rings are further apart and the wood between the rings is very soft. If it grows up slower and at high altitude, the rings are closer together… that lumber is superior. The strength of the piece of wood is in the ring, and we bought our wood accordingly. And we used to sell a lot of lumber to local smaller yards who did not want to buy a whole boxcar of it. Lumber grown east of the Cascades is obviously closer to Iowa and, as a result, the freight is considerably less (when you buy a piece of lumber at a store in Iowa, the freight alone is reflected in about 25 percent of what you pay). Mills located in the north and south, and ones east of the Cascades, would cut lumber into smaller denominations in size, such as 2 x 4's. And with the littler trees, lots of the lumber was too small for building so it was made into wood pulp for the paper industry. There was always interesting information to learn in this trade.

Back in my day, lumber finally started to be hauled in truckloads—one truckload amounted to about 50 percent of the lumber in a railroad car. Also in my time, they started manufacturing railroad cars that were open and could, therefore, be unloaded with a forklift truck instead of one piece at a time like when it came in boxcars. Obviously, there is so much more to tell about the family industry that I've grown up with and loved all these years. I was fortunate to have seen it through the eyes of people who really cared enough to appreciate high quality. I was also fortunate enough to have been trained so well in flying, which definitely helped take our fourth-generation family business to the next level. The only real downside that I experienced with owning an airplane is that folks regularly asked me to fly them places. People I didn't even know would call and offer to pay gas costs if I could just get them to California or Florida or wherever else they needed to go. I just had to pass up those requests, explaining that ours was an aircraft used for business. (That also gave me a good excuse to not haul politicians, even those who were close friends of mine!)

As already noted, I often succeeded in squeezing in some pleasure while on the business trips. One of the most memorable times was back in August of 1969 when Nelle and I and two other couples had been on a mill trip to Wyoming. After touring Cody Lumber and others, we decided on a whim to take a side excursion before heading home—a raft trip down the river out of Jackson Hole. A bunch of people were all lined up, getting into various rubber rafts with different guides, and ours was a young guy from Minnesota. Everybody was drinking beer and Bloody Marys and whatever else they'd brought along. It was a beautiful day and we were getting pretty relaxed, when our guide pulled out a pipe and a pouch and said, "Do you mind if I smoke a little pot?" None of us really cared. Before long the guide held up his pipe and said, "Does anyone want to share?" while passing the pipe to the rest of us. Then one of the other couples on our raft pulled out two rolled cigarettes of the stuff that they had brought along too. And that's when I tried smoking pot for the first (and last) time in my life, just to say I did!...

When we arrived at our destination, we were all pretty relaxed and our guide was just blasted. His girlfriend was there to meet up with him and get some dinner. We all gave him huge tips and thanked him for such a memorable raft ride. While we three couples dined on hamburgers at a nearby restaurant, our guide and his girlfriend were in the same establishment dining on lobster! We ended up chatting with them for awhile and the gal told us she'd never seen her boyfriend so happy after leading a raft ride.

I am inserting this photo of one of our twin-engine company airplanes, not just because it's the one we were riding in before and after that memorable raft trip, and not just because it was a terrific airplane that served our business so well for many years. But I guess it's proof that I even Dymo-labeled the date on all the pictures hanging on my office wall. (It's easy to forget just how often I printed out and stuck those labels on a lot of things back in the day!)

All aircraft have a private identification number, as mentioned previously when telling about 'Mike,' and I eventually requested our company plane to be '4JL' so that I could radio in by saying, "Beech 4 Jewett Lumber." The next plane had dropping stairs to a side entrance, which was so much easier for passengers to board. We regularly traveled all around the country to visit sawmills, and to attend conventions of the National Lumber and

Building Material Dealers Association, Hoo-Hoo, International, the Northwestern Lumbermens Association, and the Iowa Lumbermens Association. As eventual President of each of those organizations, I ended up with speaking engagements all over the place, and opportunities to also introduce some big-name guest speakers like Larry King, Bob Dole, and George Will when in Washington. D.C. Nelle was such a terrific traveling companion and a gracious hostess to the other passengers, even the times when she was the only female on a trip.

Often getting called on myself to address a group without much advance notice, I was glad to have taken a Dale Carnegie course in my early years, now getting to try out the 'winning friends and influencing people' skills from the podium. I had developed a slick way of remembering opener jokes to loosen up an audience, by always carrying a little slip of paper with punch lines on it—when seeing the punch line, I could quickly recall the joke (of course, that was back in the day when my 'quick recall' worked a lot quicker!)

Other than business, I was also able to fly to annual meetings of the various philanthropic associations with which I was involved. One of the most enjoyable was in November of 1971, when I'd been asked to be in Anaheim, California for the National Convention of the American Heart Association, and got to take Nelle and Stephanie, as well as newlyweds Jennifer and John along as my passengers. The meetings were terrific, and our side trips to Disneyland and to Knotts Berry Farm were great fun for the family. We also got to spend some time with Uncle Ambrose Shore, who lived close by.

During the early 1970's Nelle and I regularly joined two other couples for a few annual trips to Mexico and some winter island hopping in the Caribbean—one of the other guys was a newer pilot but without any instrument rating and, of course, I was always happy to fly wherever he wanted to go. On one occasion, we went down to Cabo San Lucas on the southernmost tip of the Baja peninsula, clearing Customs at La Paz. The year we went to Acapulco, it was fun to first spend some time in Mexico City. Another winter we ended up on Grand Cayman Island, where we all even visited the large turtle farm; while staying there, a couple of us also rented motor scooters and buzzed around all over the island, learning that some parts of the area were pretty wild. In 1975, we flew into Merida on the Yucatan Peninsula and spent a couple of nights in a little old hotel there before heading to a resort further east—I remember that trip the most because several Mexican towns were preparing for a visit from the Queen of England, and we watched workers literally painting up the buildings. We flew out of Merida and circled over the Chichen Itza pyramid on the Yucatan, before heading to Cozumel Island and landing. During our stay, the Queen of England's ship arrived, docking west of Cozumel and east of Cancun, and we got to watch the fanfare. I remember that it was terribly windy, so they couldn't take Her Majesty to the mainland in their helicopter—instead, they dropped a cabin cruiser into the water off the side of the ship and she was delivered ashore in that! As soon as Queen Elizabeth left her big sailing vessel, the flags on it were lowered, indicating that she was no longer on board. After a few days on Cozumel, we had hoped to do a quick jump over to Cuba—I'd always wanted to go there, especially since my folks had loved vacationing in Havana back in its heyday, as mentioned previously. So, I went to the airport to check the weather—they didn't have a weather bureau, just a makeshift tower. I entered that, only to find nobody there and no equipment at all! An airliner had just landed, so I went on board to talk with the flight planner, inquiring about the weather over to Cuba. He reported there was a terrible storm heading that direction, and that we should stay inland—so, on our way back to Brownsville, we stopped and spent time at Veracruz instead. (I'd still like to see Cuba!)

We three couples also tried to take some annual fall leaf-viewing trips to the northeast, regularly flying into Boston, parking the plane at Logan International and renting a van to drive up to Maine to see the colors and to visit stores like L. L. Bean and others. One year, I was flying our own company plane in order to also take care of some business on the east coast, so we landed and parked at the Nantucket Memorial Airport for a short visit. A friend from Des Moines who owned a large car dealership was vacationing on the Island and saw '4JL' parked there—was I ever surprised upon returning to the airstrip that afternoon and finding a personal note from him on the door of the plane! While departing Nantucket, we made it a point to circle over Martha's Vineyard in order to get a glimpse of the Chappaquiddick Bridge made famous by Ted Kennedy's accident. I guess this is a good time to fess up about driving into the Kennedy compound while on the Island too. Against the wishes of most of my passengers, I boldly drove our rental van into the big Kennedy driveway, far enough to see their family houses all around the inner drive of the compound—it was hard to believe we weren't stopped, and that we never even saw anybody after driving in! (Maybe I'm a little like my great-grandfather, George, who didn't seem to shy away from paying a visit to the homes or hangouts of famous people. One year, Nelle and I were driving through Texas for some reason, and I took her to see my former Air Base in Waco. President George W. Bush's plane was parked at the Base, with guards all around it. I thought maybe he might be in town having lunch, which he had been known to do, so we went on over. Though he wasn't there, we had a bite to eat, then I figured we might as well stop by the President's big ranch outside of Crawford since it was only a few miles west. Against Nelle's wishes, I drove on in, but we didn't end up seeing much because of a big hill as you entered the driveway of his 1500-acre place.)

Three years ago, while lying in a hospital bed awaiting a heart cardioversion (and telling my daughters more stories about my life while Jen was videotaping me), I mentioned flying into Nantucket for that trip. Just then, one of my nurses walked in and became involved in the conversation due to having been a pilot herself at one time. She mentioned how scary it was to fly into Boston since you had to come in over water. I told her that was how it used to be in Chicago too, with Meigs Field located just south of the Navy Pier. I was only the fifth person ever to land at Meigs after it was built on Northerly Island back in 1948… After flying my new Stinson over to Chicago and landing at that new airport, their manager wanted to take a picture of the first five pilots to land there. We all lined up in a row standing beside our airplanes for that photo op. Meigs Field only had one north/south runway, which was not very long, so takeoffs and landings had to be precise. I remember years later a Des Moines friend of mine telling me he had once flown over to Chicago in his corporate Learjet, checking into a hotel near the field for a business meeting the next morning. He happened to be watching his company's airplane take off from Meigs when he saw it suddenly lose power and make a forced landing in Lake Michigan after the loss of an engine. Their pilot was saved unharmed, and luckily before the airplane sank!

(Incidentally, I had already been on Northerly Island back in 1933, since that's where the Chicago World's Fair was held when my folks took me there on the train as a seven-year-old kid. The thing I remember most about that particular early trip to Chicago was that a guy who won the Pikes Peak Auto Hill Climb was in a booth at the Fair with his winning car—I'm not sure what that booth was advertising, maybe tires or oil or race cars, but it was fun to see him there since I'd become such a fan of the Peak race. Come to think of it, the other thing remembered from that railroad trip to Chicago as a kid was my father teaching me to always wipe out the stainless-steel lavatory sink on a train after shaving, keeping it nice and neat for the next person!)

With the last Beechcraft we owned, I had some modifications done on it at a field in San Antonio. A manufacturer of jets down there regularly bought twin-engine Bonanzas which were stressed for over 7 g's. He would take the wings off and put them on his new jet planes and sell them around the country. I had the rear window on the left side moved back and then added a new square one in front of it to match the other square ones on the right side, which made the plane look longer. Having windows changed was kind of a big deal, as you can imagine, and they did a real nice job. So, I thought of that same manufacturing company owner several years later when I decided to sell the twin Bonanza, assuming that he might know someone in the market for such a nicely redone unit. I called him up and told him about it, and that I would give him a tip under the table if he heard of a buyer for it who might be sent my way.

Within two days, a guy from San Francisco called and asked questions about the plane. I told him it had all Collins radio equipment, which is the finest available, and that it had de-icing equipment, and could carry a passenger/baggage load of over 2000 pounds. He asked me if it had autopilot, and I assured him it did. The San Francisco man told me he would arrive in Des Moines at 9:31 that night on a United Airlines flight—I'll never forget it. I asked how I would recognize him and he said he would be in western boots and a western hat and a carrying a big black shiny suitcase. I went to the airport to pick him up and was surprised to see *two* men dressed just the same. I took them to Johnny and Kay's restaurant/motel across the street from the airport and they got two rooms side by side. I asked if they'd like to see the plane yet tonight, as it was in a lighted hangar. They said they would, and then they picked up that big black shiny suitcase to bring with them. I said, 'What's *that* about?' They put the case on the bed and opened it, and it was full of cash... all $20 bills in $1000 packets! My knees were knocking. I took them to see the plane, then went to the hotel bar to have a nightcap—they sat on either side of the suitcase and told me, "That plane is even better than reported... if the logbooks are clean, you've got a deal." They asked how wide the cabin door was, and I said I'd never measured it. They asked if it would come off easily, and I said I'd never had it off, but it was just a piano hinge and snubber bar. They asked if the seats would come out easily, and I told them yes, as I had made club seating around a card table for my passengers.

Then *I* started asking the questions. "By the way, what are you planning to use this for?" They quickly answered that it was going to haul parachute jumpers, and I was alright with that explanation. We parted for the night, and the next morning I was to pick them up in front of the hotel to do the financial transaction. One guy ran out and told me the other guy would be out in a minute, but that he was just finishing his Rob Roy! We went to the airport, and they checked out the logbooks. They asked me how much I *really* wanted for the plane... how much did I want under the table? I told them "Nothing," and that I got a certified audit every year. They replied, "Looks like you got a deal." I took them from bank to bank getting checks. I asked to see the bank President each time, telling him that we would need to go into a counting room, as I wanted a cashier's check from these gentlemen. They had money in the suitcase, and in their coats and boots. They had to keep each check under $10,000, so they got several checks in the $9,900 range. Then we went over to one of the flying services and I asked the manager if I could pay him $100 to transfer my airplane to these gentlemen, which he did. The men then handed me the checks and I asked if they would like to see the *inside* of the plane and how to switch the transmitters, and so on, which they did. After doing that, one of the guys said, "Boy, I love that radio gear... I used to do dead-reckoning over water at night outside Italy and I'm not used to that gear." I then asked if they'd like to fly around in a pattern so I could show them how to use the transmitters, and they said no, as they had to be in San Francisco that afternoon. I left the plane and thanked them and wished them well.

A few days later I got a call from a guy who said he was with the FAA Aircraft Registration Department and that he wanted to ask me a few questions about the sale of our plane. I answered all the questions he had, then asked him why he was asking all this stuff. He said, "Well, we know your aircraft is not flying, but we do not know if the pilot turned it to sea and jumped out or whether it crashed in a jungle." It was a disturbing phone call, as you can imagine. A couple days after that, I got a call from a guy who said he was a Special Agent of Drug Enforcement with the FAA in their Tucson office. I recognized the voice and said, "Wait a minute, aren't you the same guy I talked to two days ago from the Aircraft Registration Department?" I asked what the heck was going on with my plane, and he said, "All we know is that it's not flying...the day you sold it, it was traced to San Francisco and rigged for aerial drug drops." I asked him what they did to an airplane to rig it for such drops, and he said they ripped out all the seats and upholstery to lighten a plane and put a trap door in the belly to drop the drugs. That just made me sick, because I had installed all new King Air fire retardant upholstery with blue leather inserts (and an upholstered white leather ceiling)—it was truly first class.

Several weeks later, the Special Agent again called to tell me that my plane had been found... the wings had been cut off to destroy the evidence and it had been buried off the end of a grass landing strip down in Nogales, Mexico, not far from Tucson, Arizona.

*{**Editor's note:** When Dad first learned of this all those years ago, I vividly remember that he had a hard time telling the story without tears in his eyes—that Beech was his baby.}*

After hearing this story, a friend of our family who had ridden in the plane many times with his lumber wholesaler father, decided one day to pull up online my aircraft number, just out of curiosity. He found out that the plane and its logbooks were sold to a man in Minnesota, so he then decided to call that buyer on the telephone! I guess the Minnesota guy was not very friendly—he said he had paid over $30,000 but had never seen the airplane. He told my friend that he learned the airplane was on an aircraft ramp in Mexico City, but that didn't make any sense to me after what I'd been told.

A few weeks later, I again got a call from the Special Agent for the FAA. He told me that the head guy in the operation involving my plane was jailed in Guadalajara, Mexico, but had bought his way out and had been acquitted. They had gotten word that he was in Texas, where he was arrested within weeks. I asked the Special Agent what a guy gets on a delivery of one load of drugs. He answered, "With that size plane, somewhere between $100,000-150,000." I quickly kidded, "I guess I should have done a run or two before selling it," and he said, "You don't fly one or two runs and then end it... you get locked in by them after just one run." The guy went on to tell me that United States Customs had decided to subpoena me to fly to Tucson and identify the suspect, who had testified that he'd never been to Des Moines. By now the Special Agent and I were on a first name basis—I called him by name and said, "I won't do that... these guys play for keeps and I've got mouths at home to feed!" Then I asked, "Why don't you Special Agents just pose as tourists and go to Mexico to get your information?" He said, "Hell no, there's a $10,000 bounty on an Agent's head in Mexico! But we do get good and accurate information, and here's how... we hire criminals and pay them cash. That's how we found out about your plane being at the end of the grass strip in Nogales, Mexico." (This made more sense to me than having the airplane just sitting on the aircraft parking ramp at Mexico City, because they would certainly like to get some money for the plane if they knew that's where it was parked.) The Special Agent told me that the guy in Minnesota kept trying to get delivery on the plane and could not. While all this was going on, my nephew and his wife (who live in Tucson) came to Iowa for a family visit. I told them the story about the plane and about the Tucson agent who kept contacting me, and was so surprised when they told me that they personally knew the Agent's wife! I asked them to please get word to the agent NOT to subpoena me. And I'm assuming they did because that was the end of it!

In April of 1985, I purchased a small used airplane with a childhood friend—the guy who had been one of my first two fraternity roommates in college and a groomsman in my wedding to Jackie (and I a sneezing groomsman in his). He was a pilot who really didn't want to fly anymore, and I was a pilot who really missed flying, so we went fifty-fifty on the purchase of a used single-engine Piper Cherokee with 250 hp. I'd been used to flying two Lycoming 195 engines, so it was pretty underpowered, but it was fun to be piloting regularly again. We just bought the thing purely for pleasure, and basically took ourselves and our wives back and forth between our Des Moines and Okoboji homes in it. Eighteen months later, after two summer seasons of enjoyment, we sold the plane. I don't even remember why we sold it, but guess we just got tired of the expense of it all. After selling, Nelle and I ended up driving to Okoboji on weekends, which was much cheaper and actually kind of fun—we enjoyed seeing the countryside and especially liked finding Maid-Rite locations for lunch along the way. And in order to feel as if we were still flying, I tucked an old airplane altimeter into the left corner of my Cadillac dashboard. (After retiring from flying, I had mentioned to my local flying service that I'd like to get a hold of one of those someday. They called a few weeks later to tell me they had one—it had been removed from an old plane after the altimeter didn't pass inspection because of being too many feet off in its correct elevation. Though kind of a big eyesore, I did enjoy having that altimeter up on my car dash, especially when traveling in the mountains. Today the thing sits on a table in my apartment, where it gets plenty of attention along with a few other items from my past—I seem to have kind of a museum of old artifacts sitting around on display, all of which have fun stories attached to them.)

'NEAR MISSES' AND OTHER TALES

People sometimes ask about any close call incidents with my planes, and I can think of a few times that might be of interest. There were at least two 'near misses' with other aircraft while on instruments… Once, while flying in the service out of Waco, a white airplane tail-light appeared in front of me at night—I just pushed the stick ahead and flew right under it. Another time I was flying east of Des Moines when a single-engine Bonanza almost hit me near Newton. I immediately called Departure Control in Des Moines and asked about the airplane that had just missed hitting me—they were not even aware of the plane. Jen was surprised to learn that an aircraft could avoid radar detection, so I explained that the Bonanza was very streamlined and that when a plane doesn't show enough activity, it won't be picked up on radar. *{Editor's note: …which I find scary and even hard to believe, but Dad seemed very matter-of-fact about it.}*

A few incidents happened back in college with my first plane, that little Piper Cub Tri-pacer… My engine once started to slow up during a flight to Iowa City from Des Moines. I assumed it was carburetor ice, which is common in small planes, but continued to lose rpm even after pulling on carburetor heat. After a forced landing in an open field, and thankfully with no damage to the airplane, it was determined that the problem was caused by a blade of straw in the gas-line to my carburetor—sometimes even the littlest things can become big issues. In another situation, I had to make a forced landing somewhere near Waco, Texas after a carburetor ice problem, only to find out that the heat control had come unwelded and was not throwing any warm air on the carburetor. Then there was the time while flying one night from Iowa City to Des Moines (which I remember was 5½ beacons), that the battery running the lights on my Tri-pacer went dead, and I've already said the little plane didn't have a generator. I was planning to land at Des Moines, but couldn't get the tower's attention without my lights. I kept shining my flashlight down and all of a sudden, the north-south runway lit up and I thought, "Oh good, they saw me." But I wasn't that lucky because, just then, a big twin-engine airplane went zooming by me and landed, and then they shut the runway lights off. So, I went ahead and landed on the dark runway and taxied in, but they never even knew I was there!

Another time, while at the University of Iowa and flying at night, I had a female passenger with me for a ride in the brand-new 1948 Stinson Voyager. This gal had broken up with a guy in our fraternity house; I heard she was pretty wild, so I lined up a date with her…

We got to the airport and I left her sitting in my Plymouth (actually Pops' car) while getting the plane out of the hangar. We hadn't been airborne more than a few minutes when the darn oil cap blew off the engine in flight, and oil completely covered the windshield. With visibility only out of my side window, and needing to land quickly before my engine froze up from lack of oil, I was lucky to bring it down safely at Hunter Airport on the south edge of Cedar Rapids. (Incidentally, the rest of our date went well, but I dropped her like a hot potato after getting back to Iowa City and discovering that she had carved her initials into the sun visor of the Plymouth while I had been getting the plane out of the hangar before our date—that really made me mad.)

I learned the hard way that it was awfully easy to take off in a single-engine Bonanza with the door unlatched—once airborne, you cannot close the door in one of those without landing the plane, so my passenger on that particular flight held fast onto the door the best he could until we could land safely, which we did. And once on takeoff from Des Moines in a different single-engine Bonanza, I hit a flock of birds, which sure scared me—it didn't do any damage to the plane, but I had a lot of feathers to wash off after safely landing. When learning to fly back in WWII, we had been taught to start using oxygen if going above 5,000 feet. One time I was flying out of Colorado Springs to Des Moines in a twin Bonanza, and quickly climbed to 19,000 feet. Suddenly everything looked pretty hazy. I was lucky to have enough brain function to put on my mask—and just that fast, everything cleared up! Oh, and I got hit by lightning once in a twin Beech—it completely melted down the antenna and burned out my radios… of course, I had to land right away.

One time a door window blew out during a flight in that little Piper Cherokee that my friend and I owned later in life for our Des Moines-to-Okoboji hops. He was in the passenger seat and our wives were in the back. It was one heck of an approach into Des Moines, with the wind coming through the cockpit so loud that we couldn't use the radio, but I was still able to land safely. Another time, the four of us were in that same little plane when I started losing rpm about 50 miles southeast of the town of Spencer on our way to the Lakes. Assuming it was the carburetor, I pulled on the carburetor heat but we continued losing rpm and altitude. We made a forced, but safe, landing at the Spencer Municipal Airport [the Northwest Iowa Regional Airport]. I had just picked up the airplane from its 100-hour check the day before and wondered what on earth could have happened. In taking the engine apart at Spencer, they said they found that a compound used to seal the spark plugs had oozed a little and shorted out the plugs.

I seem to have had more than my share of experience in not being able to get a landing gear down for one reason or another. Once in a twin Bonanza with a customer friend and his elderly mother, the gear wouldn't drop. After making a series of dives, I was able to get it down and to land safely at Des Moines. Another time I was testing new radio equipment that had been installed in the twin Cessna, and invited two airport linemen and a very good friend to fly around Des Moines with me for the test flight. Then I couldn't get the darn gear down in order to land. I radioed the Des Moines tower for permission to leave the flight pattern, and they asked, "What are your intentions?" I answered, "To get my wheels down." They granted permission to do a series of dives and maneuvers while cranking, in an attempt to get the wheels to drop. I told my three passengers that we had six hours worth of fuel and that I was prepared to stay up there all six hours if that's what it took in order to not wreck our company plane. After shaking the craft in all different directions for about 45 minutes, I finally got the green light that the wheels were down. The tower told me to fly by at 600 feet off a certain runway and they would do a visual check, after which they said it appeared the gear was indeed down. I landed very, very carefully. It turns out the radio technician had put the new equipment into the nose compartment of the Cessna 310 but forgot to re-hook up the wheel well doors. The craziest part of the whole story is that the tower had tried to find the shop superintendent from the flying service to help me out, learning that the guy was watching a little league ball game at the field downtown. Apparently, they announced his name over the public-address system and said that there was an emergency situation at the airport—an airplane circling with its wheels up—and that this guy needed to come right away to the Des Moines control tower. It seems like half of the population in the ballpark came to the airport to see me crash too! After my safe landing, you could just read their faces as if they were thinking, "Oh darn, no crash!" I was due to be in another town that same night to pick up my new girlfriend, Nelle, but got there late with good reason! (And I guess there was another time when I actually forgot to put down the landing gear during an approach, but I'm not talking about that incident.)

When coming into Okoboji for night landings, I used to find the unlit runway by lining up with a lighted telephone booth that was not far from the darkened airport office. (I also used that telephone booth to regularly heat the engines on my plane by plugging extension cords into the light sockets outside the booth!) One night, Nelle and I were returning to Okoboji with my folks after Dad and I had a business meeting in Minneapolis. I lined up with the lighted phone booth and we landed to the north. There was an electrical wire just across the street from the airport, and I hit the wire while landing. Nobody in the plane knew that I'd hit and broken it—I wasn't even sure of it myself until we taxied back and got out of the plane, and we could see the hot wire smoking all the way down the highway, several hundred feet to the beach road! The FAA thought I would file a lawsuit for having that wire there so close to the strip, so I was never criticized for hitting it. A good friend of my folks lived in a cottage just west of the New Inn, and he happened to be driving by and saw the whole thing—he stopped and told us we'd better come on over to his house for a drink, so we took him up on the kind invitation!

That 'Spirit Lake Municipal Airport' (which was actually in Okoboji, and had been called the 'Okoboji Airport' until given to the town of Spirit Lake for maintenance purposes) seemed to see lots of close call activity over the years. I can think of at least four airplane crashes that I was personally there to witness... One time I was in bed listening to the police scanner at my nearby cottage when I heard them talking about how they thought a plane had just gone down in a field north of the Spirit Lake Airport. I jumped out of bed and got dressed. Nelle asked where I was going and I said, "To a plane crash!" When I got there, I ran to the spot and found the pilot standing on the wing—he wasn't hurt, but the man and wife who had been the passengers didn't look good. The woman was in pain with what turned out to be a broken rib and a broken something else; her husband's face was so bloody that he was unrecognizable. I stayed with them until the ambulance came, and followed as they carried the man from the airplane a couple hundred feet through the cornfield. As he was being loaded into the ambulance, I happened to notice the guy's big fancy buckle on his belt and realized it was one of my Dad's friends who had once been a pilot himself! So, I ran back to the airplane to be with his wife until help arrived for her too. I learned that they had been riding with their pilot, taking the wife to Sioux Falls where she was to catch an airplane to their Arizona residence. Both survived the accident.

On another occasion, there was a big Beechcraft King Air landing at Okoboji when the left engine stopped due to running out of fuel. The pilot was just a block from the airport, where he crashed. Nobody was killed, but practically everybody was cut up. I raced over after hearing it on the police radio and got there before the emergency equipment did. Another time a plane took off from the airport heading south—the pilot thought they had filled him up with gas before the flight, but they had not. He really didn't crash enough to do much damage while putting down in the field just south of the airport. The last crash I got to see was more spectacular, when a twin-engine plane came in 'too hot' from the north and the pilot realized he was going to run out of runway. He pushed the throttles ahead to fly out, but the left engine quit; the other engine pulled the plane around and it crashed into the swimming pool of some nearby apartments, hitting one of the buildings and catching it on fire. By the time I learned about it and got to the scene, a guy living next door to the apartments was standing there shooting a garden hose onto his own house so it wouldn't go up in flames. The apartment building ended up burning to the ground but, amazingly, nobody in the airplane was hurt.

I knew several people who owned airplanes, and also knew better than to fly with a couple of them—it's just not worth taking risks. But one time our plane was in the shop, so Nelle and I caught a winter weekend ride to the lake with another Des Moines guy and his wife. By the time we got up there, the weather was right down on the ground. We came in to land on the surface runway, but he missed it completely and landed parallel to the runway in the grass. I was riding in the copilot seat but never wanted to tell another pilot what to do—knowing we wouldn't crash, I just braced for a rough landing in the snow. There was another close call that same pilot had one Thanksgiving weekend. A bunch of us were all up at my folks' cottage, having dinner at the long pine dining table mentioned earlier. A winter storm blew in and it was snowing like the dickens. By the time it grew dark, we heard an airplane go over our cottage making a lot of noise, and I said, "Sounds like someone missed the approach." Pretty soon we heard it again, and I said, "Something is going on over there… let's go!" So, another guy and I went over to the airport, only to find it was that same pilot friend of ours—he and his wife were trying to land, but couldn't see the lights with the snow piling up. Instead of landing on the runway, he had come in on the east side of it. Thankfully, nobody was hurt, but they were pretty shaken up and came over to our house for a drink. Then there was another incident involving a different Lakes resident who flew in real low over our cottage after we'd been talking to him on the Unicom. This particular pilot was not well-seasoned at all, and had additionally earned the unfortunate reputation of being downright reckless. I asked him where he was and he radioed back that he was lost over Lost Island, which is a little lake about 30 miles south of Okoboji. I talked him in and he landed, skidding right up to the fence at the end of the runway—a bunch of us went over to the airport and helped push him away from the fence.

Though not emergencies, I've had some interesting things happen in flight. One time, back in the mid-50's, Jackie and I flew a building supply wholesaler and his wife out to a San Francisco convention—it was that wife's first airplane ride and she was so excited. But only 30 or so minutes out of Des Moines, she had to go to the bathroom, so we were forced to land in North Platte, Nebraska and take care of that. From there, we also found it necessary to land in Laramie, Wyoming and in Ogden, Utah, and in Reno, Nevada, before finally getting to our destination spot of San Francisco! Another time I was flying a contractor and his wife to Las Vegas, and they wanted to see the Grand Canyon first. While over it, we hit a big downdraft, dropping us so quickly that the thermos cup of coffee being held by the wife lifted right up out of her hands and in front of her startled eyes. On another business trip to Vegas, Nelle and I stayed at the Desert Inn, where billionaire Howard Hughes was supposedly holed up on the top two floors after moving there in 1966. While we were checking in, I asked the Bell Captain what it was like waiting on the guy—he replied that the hotel staff did nothing for the billionaire since his men had blocked off the elevator going to those top two floors. He also told us that the daily rent for Mr. Hughes was $30,000 to stay in that hotel (prior to him just buying the place!). I kept looking around for Hughes to appear elsewhere in the building, hoping to chat a bit about aviation; but of course, that never happened.

That reminds me that, toward the very end of his life, Howard Hughes was living in a hotel in Acapulco. One day in April of 1976, a friend of mine from Ft. Lauderdale, Florida, received a phone call from Howard Hughes' Miami-based doctor, asking my friend to take one of his Learjets down to Acapulco to pick up the very sick Mr. Hughes. (My friend owned a weekend home up at Lake Okoboji, Iowa, which is how I knew him, but he had a jet business in a hangar in the northeast corner of the Municipal Airport in Ft. Lauderdale.) I understood that my friend's son-in-law, who worked with him, indeed copiloted a Learjet to Acapulco to transport a dying Hughes to his hometown of Houston, Texas. Not long after that, Nelle and I were in Acapulco for some function and staying at that same hotel. While taking a tour of the place after checking in, I asked the guide if he had seen Mr. Hughes when he had arrived there, and if he was a jovial man. The tour guide said, "No— he was slumped over in a wheelchair." He also reported that his coworker had seen Mr. Hughes when he moved out and that he was still slumped over in a wheelchair. It got me wondering if Hughes was kept so drugged up that he didn't know what was going on, or if maybe they were covering up the fact that he'd already died and were getting him out of the country that way—I figured we'd never know the real story on that since it seemed like you could say and do about anything you wanted down there with just a $100 bill.

On one of my business trips to a lumber convention in Portland, Oregon, Nelle and I took along a local competitor and his wife—the guy had been in high school with my father, so we really went back a long time. And Dad had just recently passed away, which made it especially nice to have his friend (and pallbearer) joining us. On that same trip, I remember that Nelle and I were able to get some happy mementos for our new cottage, such as a porthole off a Navy ship that was being dismantled there, which we planned to have installed as the window in our new back door. We also were able to get a slightly rough and very large hatch cover from that same ship, which I planned to build into a living room coffee table. Though terribly cumbersome and quite unwieldy, we decided to haul the hatch back with us rather than having it shipped. Once we got that big old thing on board, we were finally able to angle it just right to get it propped up in the aisle. I'll never forget taking off on instruments heading west out of Portland—we flew over the ocean for quite some time and I wondered if Departure Control would ever get us turned around to head back east toward Des Moines. We were finally given the go-ahead to turn and, when we did, the heavy hatch cover also decided to change sides in the aisle… KABOOM! Boy, was it loud, and sure scared me at first—I thought the side of the airplane had fallen off!

As you can imagine, I've flown a lot of people a lot of places, but have also logged many solo hours, and would sing songs out loud to keep from being bored. Here's one that seems to have been quite a hit with my daughters and girlfriends over the years:

> I'm Jerry the yodeling cowboy, from down upon the farm.
> I'm here to bring sweet music, with lots and lots of charm.
> (then I'd start to yodel…
> Oh, little-old-a-lady-hee; oh, little-old-a-lady-hah;
> Oh, little-old-a-lady-ho; lady-a-hee…)

Another tune was not actually my creation, but was my own personal rendition of one that was going around in the early 60's when my girls were young. I twisted it to say whatever I chose it to say (as did most anybody who heard the darn thing). It was about a billboard being blown in half by a windstorm, and how half of a billboard might read, which is why a person could sing it any way they wanted. Here's one of my made-up versions:

> Oh, smoke a Coca-Cola, Heinz catsup cigarettes,
> See Lillian Russell wrestle, with a box of castanets.
> Heinz pork and beans will meet tonight, in a finish fight
> And silent Joe will lecture, on Napoleon tonight.
>
> Oh, feed Bruno to the horses, it is the best in town.
> Castoria kills the measles, just pay five dollars down.
> Ladies fur coats are selling now, a little at a time
> And automobiles taste very good, you only pay a dime.
> (Then I ended the song in good barbershop fashion with: "And buy an arm!")

My girls always thought it was such a fun song, and Jen sang it along with me as we both laughed while writing this section of the book. Another one she and I started singing one day was also mentioned by one of my nephews in his note for my 91st birthday... Chan claims this is one of the memories about his Uncle Jerry that he's "never gotten out of his head." The jingle has actually been around since the turn of the century when my folks were little kids, and also has been changed by me (and everyone else) to whatever I wanted to sing about:

> The horses run around, their feet are on the ground,
> Oh, who will wind the clock when I'm away, away?
> Go get the hammer, there's a fly on baby's head,
> Oh, I hope that grandma's teeth will soon fit Jenny, fit Jenny.
>
> I'm looking through a knothole in father's wooden leg,
> Oh, why'd they build the seashore near the ocean, the ocean?
> Go get the Listerine, sister wants a beau.
> A boy's best friend is his flivver, his flivver.

So, boredom wasn't ever a real problem when I flew, because those songs kept me company. I also found myself singing the old Winnie-the-Pooh tunes from that original crank-up record player, putting in the same warps, skips, and varying speeds that I was always kidded about! Yes, I got tired at times, but worked darn hard to stay alert in the air.

{Editor's note: By now, the reader has concluded that Dad was an exceptional pilot, and it's true. He was always obsessively checking and rechecking weather conditions and the plane's various systems before taking off to go anywhere. Steph and I both told him the other day that we never, ever had a worry when flying with him... he was simply the best!}

I loved airplanes so much that I wanted to start a small local 'fly-in' community back in the 1960's, comprised of a few homes located around an airstrip here in the western part of Des Moines. Several pilot friends were interested in the idea and wanted to buy into it so I really scouted it out, finding a good location just west of 60th Street in West Des Moines (near where the Jordan Creek Mall is now located). It turned out that we couldn't get the project approved because it was located too close to the existing Des Moines Airport. It was a fun idea, but I finally just gave up on it and decided to leave well enough alone. And I guess I didn't want to move from my 35th Street house anyway, which was next door up the hill from Mom and Dad's retirement home.

We've had a bunch of small private airports around the Des Moines area during my lifetime. That's *all* we had until the mid-1920's when our first Municipal one came into being and was located clear out east in Altoona. A few years later, a brand-new city airport was built, and was completed in 1933—it's the one I rode my bike all the way out on S.W. 21st Street to see when I was a kid. For some reason, I'm thinking that my Great-uncle Gardner Cowles bought that land south of town and made the 160 acres available to the city for a new airport, but I'm not recalling the full story on that. (For the record, it wasn't until 1986 that the Des Moines *Municipal* became known as the Des Moines *International* Airport, with an official United States Customs Service office on-site.)

In spite of having a Municipal Airport, several private strips were still around town too. There was once the Herring Field, a grass strip on the northeast corner of Douglas and Merle Hay, but that was before my time. And the Beaver Airfield north of Veteran's Hospital was just a north-south airstrip on Lower Beaver Road—it was owned by two brothers and was the local dealership for Cessna airplanes. One of the brothers was killed in a crash on the way back to Iowa while bringing a new twin Cessna from the factory, and the airport just closed down after that. Dodge Field, south of Camp Dodge, was owned by a childhood friend of mine at one time—he called his flight service 'Central Airways.' He was the guy who hired me to ferry the Luscombe planes from Dallas to Des Moines during that summer back in college. And it's kind of interesting that one of my uncles, Warren Jewett, also used to run the Dodge Field while selling aircraft insurance—that was well before Central Airways was on-site though. There was also North Field, later called Morningstar Field, which was located north of I-80 at Northwest 6th Drive. It was a nice little strip that was home to many private aircraft for over 60 years, and just recently closed back in 2013. Ankeny also had a couple of airports, one northeast of the town and a later one to the south of it. There were several more than these scattered around our area, but it gives a flavor of how popular smaller airstrips were at one time, and why I considered building yet another.

Though I loved to fly airplanes, I also continued to love automobiles. Looking back, I really can't even recall all the cars I've had. There was a period during my adult life that I owned several at any one given time, parking them in our lumberyards around town. After the Edsel came out, I thought I had to have an Edsel, and so on—it was just fun picking up different cars of the era. The one car I always wanted to get, but never did, was a Cord. It was attractive because of its front-wheel drive, but also because of its coffin nose and the exhaust pipes coming out of the hood in chrome—it looked more like a race car.

The owner of the flying service in Iowa City had a couple of them back when I was in college, and one was a beautiful convertible. Then I knew of one for sale more recently, but by then I was no longer a prospect. In 1973, I ended up with a brand-new 1973 blue Eldorado that had a white convertible top—my first Cadillac. I sure liked that car and loved the front-wheel drive, so decided to upgrade to another one. When in San Francisco on a business trip in the winter of 1976, I bought a new deep red Eldorado convertible right off the dealer's showroom floor. I told them I'd be back to pick it up in a week or so. After flying home, I asked Jennifer and John if they would be available to fly out on the airline to pick up my new car and drive it back for me, which they agreed to do. *{Editor's note: ☺}* I remember when the kids called after having pulled off I-80, somewhere in the mountains, with the report of near-blizzard conditions and the legal mandate to drive only with chains on the tires. Other than having to purchase a set of those (and putting the kids up in a motel an extra night along the way), that '76 Caddie seemed to be a pretty good investment.

In 1982, when I was up in Rochester, Minnesota for colon cancer surgery, there was a terrible 16-inch snowstorm and temperatures of 15 degrees below zero. I took some time after the surgery to stop into a local dealership to look at new Cadillacs. On the dealer's showroom floor, there was a maroon convertible with the top down, just looking like it was waiting to be driven to its new home! Even with the extremely cold temperature outside, the convertible was toasty warm driving to Des Moines (but I do remember how every bump hurt my post-surgery body!). Owning all those cars was a pretty expensive hobby, especially back in the days when you had to change the license plates every year, in addition to making certain the batteries were charged and the gasoline was fresh… not to mention the insurance on all of them.

One recent vehicle I had a special fondness for was this white 2007 Pontiac G6 two-door coupe convertible with a large engine and a retractable hardtop. It was fun scooting around town in it for awhile, then even more fun handing the keys to my youngest grandson when done playing!

My most recent collectible as an eighty-year-old guy was a 1923 T-Bucket, which was a very modified Model T hot rod with a 500 hp engine and no top. On our way to Okoboji one weekend, Nelle and I drove through the

nearby town of Milford, where I saw this car with a 'For Sale' sign sitting out in a guy's yard and thought it probably ought to be sitting in my garage instead. It sure looked great, with the gas tank behind the front seat and chrome exhaust pipes going down both sides of the exterior, near the ground. But it wasn't at all easy to get into— the doors didn't open and you had to step over the armrest of them to even work yourself into it, after which you needed to straddle the vertical steering wheel shaft. Once you got settled into the thing, it was a lot of fun to drive; but boy, was it noisy! When bringing it back to Des Moines at the end of that weekend, I wanted to see how much pep it had... the speedometer said '105.' When you stepped on the throttle, it was a bomb—nobody outran me! For years, I sped around Des Moines in it when the weather was nice. My daughters told me on more than one occasion that people asked if it was their old man that had been seen buzzing down Grand or elsewhere in a souped-up Model T!

One day I was having lunch at Skip's, a favorite spot on the south side of town. I was with a group of other retired guys, one of whom was the most recent retired Sheriff of Polk County. After leaving the lunch gathering, I pulled up to a stoplight on Fleur Drive at Park Avenue. The Sheriff pulled up beside me, racing his engine. So, we drag-raced from the stoplight, and I left him in the dust! That Sheriff was a lot of fun and full of great stories, like the Sheriff I had been so close to back in the 60's. My grandsons sure loved that T-Bucket and I let the youngest one, who was about 14-years-old at the time, drive me in it to Okoboji one weekend. When we were almost there, we passed an Iowa Highway Patrol car going the other direction. That's when I decided to take over the steering wheel, thinking it best not to pull the 'former Deputy Sheriff' excuse out of the bag one time too many.

Finally deciding to sell the T-Bucket in 2012, my son-in-law accompanied me to a Mecum Auction at our east-side State Fairgrounds in hopes of finding a buyer. After getting it there, we learned that the engine number didn't match the registration number, so they wouldn't put my car up for sale. The two of us enjoyed spending the day at the auction anyway, walking around looking at some pretty nice vehicles. I drove the T-Bucket home, and soon after had the State of Iowa install the correct number on the high-powered engine block so that I could sell it. *{Editor's note: Hubby and I were watching the news that night when they showed a clip of the auction. John had just been telling me what fun they'd had, and that the place was "mostly a bunch of old men walking around... like those two guys," pointing to the television. All of a sudden, a close-up shot revealed that 'those two old guys' on the film were Dad and John! My husband said his favorite part of the day was just getting to hang out alone with his father-in-law, who was proudly wearing a ball cap embroidered with 'BETTY FORD CLINIC' on the front and 'OUTPATIENT' on the back!}*

I've toyed with purchasing yet another classic, and admit to enjoying looking at what's out there, but really have no business buying. My 2007 Caddie with over 135,000 miles still runs perfectly well—I keep it looking and performing almost like new, and figure it would be silly to replace at this point in my life. (It was fun, however, to recently ride in a friend's brand-new all-electric Tesla sedan. That thing had impressive pick-up and a nice smooth ride, but watching him use his I-phone from several yards away to remotely turn it on and back it out of the parking spot before we even got into it was almost over the top!)

The T-Bucket was a good ending to my classic automobile purchases, and is shown in part of a video of my life that my daughters put together back when I turned eighty. The film ends with an elderly Jerry and his little sister, an elderly Connie, driving out of my Okoboji garage and driveway while waving farewell to the camera as we enter onto the lake road. It reminds me of the video our father took of the two of us on my 8th birthday, when we drove around our Shore grandparents' property, and up and down 37th Street, waving from the little gasoline-driven car Dad had borrowed for me to enjoy on that day back in 1933. Connie and I did that 'elderly drive-off' in the T-Bucket as kind of a Jewett farewell, waving our goodbyes to those we have known and loved—of course, neither of us knew when making that little clip more than a decade ago that we would still be alive today! Jen and Steph have played the life video at a couple of my birthday parties in recent years, and I'm certain it will be showing at my Dunn's visitation as well, so watch for it if you are there. Also at that visitation, you'll see the beloved 1956 Ford Parklane wagon—my son-in-law has offered to drive my four grandsons in it from the funeral home to the cemetery, and I'm sure honored by that. By the way, there won't be a regular service for me—I just don't want one. But I've asked my good friend, a Catholic Monsignor, to lead a little memorial time for my family, to which he kindly agreed. I had gotten to know this priest because he was one of my fellow 'Rotary Bad Boys'—we always sat together at the 'bad boys table' at Club meetings, with some other guys and yet another minister. (I guess those two were supposed to help keep our group in line... as much as possible that is!)

In addition to trikes and bikes and cars and boats and planes, I've picked up a few other 'toys' over the years. Nelle and I liked riding our older classic bicycles around the 35th Street neighborhood, but as we got older I grew tired of taking the hills. After complaining about it enough, she bought me a little Honda 90 motorcycle, which was a lot of fun. A few of our friends also had scooters and motorbikes, and we enjoyed driving down and around the Water Works with three or four other couples, afterward having cocktails and a barbeque in the park. And I kept a side-by-side snowmobile at Okoboji too—it was kind of like a car, with two headlights, two taillights, and a gear for backing up. Best of all, your feet were kept inside where it was warmer.

Due to my lifetime love of vehicles and of law enforcement, I've always had police radios or scanners in my cars and in my houses to listen to the chatter about car accidents or train derailments or robberies... whatever the local police are up to. I understand that the daughter of a good friend of mine was recently talking about the scanner I had in my car back when she and my girls were young. Apparently, she was riding somewhere with us one night and said she remembers well that I drove all of us to the site of a shooting. I don't recall the specific situation, of course, but she told her folks that after the call came over the scanner, I had wanted to go see what was happening. I guess we pulled up in front of the house where the shooting had taken place, and all the police cars were there. She recently told her folks she had really been scared, adding, "Who does that sort of thing with little kids in the car?" *{Editor's note: Our Dad, that's who!}*

Even before police radios and scanners, though, I kept my ear to the ground enough to get in on some exciting events. One time I had gone to a drowning on East Okoboji after hearing about it first-hand. The victim was a houseguest of friends of my folks' and the police used the open boat of another friend of ours to find the body—that got my attention since we had a personal connection with the victim. Another big deal at the Lakes took place in 1944 when the Okoboji Boat Works had a big fire and burned to the ground—I remember hearing about it early and heading over there to see the boat slips all floating around until they filled up with water and just sank!

An accident that surely came over my police radio in Des Moines (though I wasn't home to hear it) was one that involved my own company vehicle. I was driving a brand-new 1959 Chevy two-door Club Coupe, and had parked it downtown on the southeast corner of 9th and Locust, facing east. Immediately in front of me was a parked compact car, and in front of it was a parked four-door Packard driven by a friend of my Dad's—that man and I were both attending the Annual Meeting of the Des Moines Club at 800 Locust when Joe, the doorman in uniform at the Club entrance, came up and into the meeting to get me and the other gentleman, informing us that our parked cars had just been in a wreck. The man and I hurried down to the street level, only to learn that a guy was driving east down Locust when his foot went into the floorboard on the throttle of his car for some unknown reason. His vehicle ran into the rear end of my Chevrolet company car, pushing it so hard that my vehicle jumped up on top of the compact, and both then hit the Packard. It took two wreckers to lift my car off the compact car, and they never knew until after the cars were moved whether anybody was in the compact—thankfully, there wasn't. But in addition to all that, there was a case of whiskey in the trunk of my Chevy, and everybody on the scene smelled booze and thought the driver who caused the wreck must have been drunk. I never revealed the case of whiskey in the trunk. The accident made the papers the next morning. *{Editor's note: It indeed made the papers! I was walking to grade school that morning, stopping first at the home of my neighborhood friend who walked with me every day. Her father held up his copy of the* Des Moines Register *to show a picture of my Dad's wrecked car on the front page! Since Dad didn't live at home with us, I was terribly worried about him and used our friend's telephone to call the lumber company for some reassurance.}*

I was in my Des Moines bed one night when the worst call I could have imagined came over my police scanner. It was the late 1960's, and a local radical revolutionary group had been terrorizing the city and actively burning down several businesses. While listening to the scanner that night of October 10, 1968, I heard about a fire at the Jewett Lumber Company on E. 7th and Walnut! I jumped out of bed, threw on my clothes, and was one of the first people on the scene. I immediately unlocked the door and ran inside to retrieve things, like a large framed certificate in my father's office about his appointment as Collector of Internal Revenue under President Hoover, and the big trophy received when he was elected by the Chamber of Commerce as Man of the Year. The fire had started at the very south end of the lumber company; I was in the north end and it was moving my direction. I thought I had time to save important items, then I stopped short and said to myself, "Jerry, get out of here—you have mouths to feed. All this stuff is insured." I ended up walking out with nothing at all! While the fire was going on, I sat in the front seat of a patrol car driven by the Chief of the Des Moines Police Department, and with the Polk County Sheriff in the back seat—it was reassuring to be sitting with two very close friends of mine. I said to the Chief, "Do you think this was started by the same arsonist group that has been doing this type of stuff around town?" He said, "Jerry, I know that it was… I'll put two detectives on the case and prove it to you." And he did.

The place was a complete loss, but we stayed in business by moving our general offices to a location a few miles west on Ingersoll Avenue and keeping just a distribution yard downtown. All purchases that had been handled at the East 7th and Walnut main yard were then handled through our north and south yard locations in Highland Park and on S.W. 9th. Other lumber companies were so helpful to us during that hectic time—my childhood friend who owned Gilcrest Lumber Company loaned us trucks and  drivers so we could continue deliveries (and when their company burned nine years later, we did the same for them). That reminds me that we also hauled inventory for Dalbey Lumber Co. at 2nd and Grand in West Des Moines when they were flooded and under water on more than one occasion, helping get their goods moved to another location. We lumber company owners were competitors, of course, but continued to be good friends, likely due in part to those annual outings we all went on over the years.

Soon after our fire and during the rebuilding process, my Dad bought out the shares of his two brothers and became the sole owner of the Jewett Lumber Company.

LIFE TRANSITIONS CONTINUE

Just three years before that fire I had married my second wife, Nelle, and had flown with another couple to Colorado Springs to be witnesses at our wedding (that witness friend was now a District Judge, but we had met as fraternity brothers at the U of I back when he was married and in law school, and we both had the J-5 Cub Cruisers). I wanted to be married over Pikes Peak, but Nelle wanted to be married in a church. So, we picked the Broadmoor Community Church and spent our honeymoon in the Broadmoor Hotel a few blocks away. The arrangements were made at the church by a Colorado Springs resident who was the older sister of my good childhood friend—the guy I went to the Temple with as a kid, and who was later a groomsman in my first wedding (and who had then introduced me to Nelle more than a decade later!).

It worked out well for me to find a wiser woman with a good head on her shoulders—Nelle was 7½ years older, and we were happily married for almost forty years. She and I had met in kind of a fun way… Nelle was a well-known beautician in her little town, and a regular stylist for the wife of that same childhood friend just mentioned. The couple had a daughter who was a Playboy bunny in Chicago. One weekend in 1961, they had their daughter bring some of her bunny friends to their home in Iowa for a 'Playboy party.' I was invited to the party since they were always trying to fix me up with somebody after my divorce. So, I drove over to their town to attend the affair. Nelle the beautician was there too— I immediately spotted her and followed her into the kitchen, then into the sunroom, then into the dining room. When the party ended, I got to drive her to her home across town from my friend's house. That night I was a very good boy, and our friendship grew from there. She ended up flying with me to several places, and we continued to fall more in love while dating for the next four years.

That couple used to bring Nelle down to meet up with me at Bob and Frankie's Evergreen Inn, a roadhouse with wonderful steaks in Mitchellville (which was located about halfway between their town and mine). Before long, I just drove all the way to her place in order to see her. Interstate-80 was being built to the east of Des Moines, and when driving late at night, I would get on the unfinished and unopened I-80 for most of my trip. Being a Deputy Sheriff, I thought I could get by with doing that if I ever got caught, but I never got a chance to try out the excuse on those runs! If it got too late while I was at her house, I sometimes ended up spending the night with Nelle before heading back to work in Des

Moines the next day. One early morning I was leaving her house at the same time my childhood friend who had introduced us was taking his children to school. He drove the route by Nelle's house (probably to see if I was over there) and when his kids saw me coming out of Nelle's driveway, they said confusingly, "Hey Dad, there's Uncle Jerry!?"

The wife of that childhood friend of mine passed away tragically and unexpectedly in their kitchen a short while later. After my friend slowly began to be ready to move on, I wanted to help him out with finding him a companion, just like he had for me after my divorce. I asked if he'd like to be fixed up with a widow I'd never met, but about whom I had heard good things through other friends. He agreed, so I called the lady and introduced myself, asking if she'd like to meet my pal on a double date with my wife and myself... I was a little surprised, but so very glad, when she accepted! The night Nelle and I were chauffeuring my friend to pick up his blind date, I still had not met the gal personally. My buddy said, "When we get to the door, *you* do the talking... tell her that you are me and that *I* am Jerry Jewett," which I did as soon as she opened the door. Right away she pointed to me and said, "Well, I know *you're* Jerry Jewett, so this (other guy) must be my date." I guess she must have recognized my voice. *{**Editor's note:** Dad doesn't realize that there is such a recognizable quality to his voice. When calling us on the phone, even to this day, he always begins any voicemail to his daughters with, "Hi Dear, this is your Dad..."}*

So, the four of us drove out to the same steakhouse in Mitchellville where Nelle and I had previously gone on our *own* dates with my friend and his now-deceased wife. We all had a very nice evening on their first date, and from then on things progressed for the two of them. They ended up happily married for decades, until my childhood friend passed away not long ago. Over the years, we've kept in touch and sure have laughed about that first meeting on her doorstep! (I also continued keeping in touch with the older sister of that childhood friend, calling her annually in Colorado Springs on her birthday. When talking with her just a few months ago, she thanked me for calling, but toward the end of the conversation said, "Jerry, this is probably the last time we'll ever talk. I'm really going downhill," which broke my heart. And she passed away this summer at the age of 102.)

For our 30th anniversary in 1995, Nelle and I had flown into Colorado Springs to spend a couple of nights at the same Broadmoor Hotel where we had honeymooned. We also stopped in at the church and found that the same minister was still there. I reminded him who we were and that he had married us right there, thirty years ago, showing him our marriage license and a handwritten note from him since he didn't act like he remembered us. I finally got his attention by telling him I'd come back for a refund—he just stuttered and didn't seem to know what to say!

As we got older, Nelle and I started to spend more time up at our lake cottage year-round. In the winters, we were members of the Snowhawks, a snowmobile club that took winter excursions around the lake. Though we were zipping around in snowmobiles, the lake freezes in most places so completely that people even drive on it with their cars and trucks. One time we

saw a brand-new Chevrolet pickup truck balancing on the ice after the front wheels had dropped through it and into the water. We stopped on our snowmobile to see it, and the two men inside the truck jumped out. *Right then* the truck fell through the ice and went to the bottom of the lake… just that fast! The lake was about 100' deep at that location, and when they pulled the new Chevy truck out, the whole front of the vehicle was smashed in from hitting the bottom. There is a penalty assessed for every day that you leave a car in the lake without getting it pulled out. Under the bridge between East and West Okoboji, the water is fairly shallow and never freezes over very well—that would be the one place *not* to ever drive a vehicle on the ice, not even a snowmobile. It has always been amazing to me how many people have tried to drive on the ice under that bridge, only to have their vehicle drop through to the lake bottom—it seems like at least one car falls through the ice every year up there! One winter day in the late 70's, I was in the Standard filling station not far from that bridge when a man came in and said his car had fallen through the ice under the bridge, and wanting to know what it would cost to have the station operator (the most well-known man in town for the job) remove it. When the filling station operator told the guy that the price started at $2,000, the guy got mad and walked out. I was told he later came back and hired the man to retrieve it after all.

Nelle and I did some ice fishing one year—right in front of our cottage the first time, and later at the southern part of the lake. I took a power-driven auger and drilled the holes several feet down through the ice. Once we even rented a little ice house, which was toasty warm inside, but it was spooky when a car went by and you heard the ice crack all around you. We parked our own lake car, my mother's old '56 Ford, right next to the ice house; it was kinda fun to look down into the water below the ice hole we cut and see the fish swim by the bait… and to sometimes go for it. We caught a few good ones that year, then I cleaned them and Nelle fried them for our dinner. Those are great winter memories.

One time some Des Moines friends who lived straight across the lake from us were also up at Okoboji on a winter night, having a nightcap with another family from their beach. The ice had just gone out for the season, and the cold water was uncharacteristically flat and eerily quiet. After seeing lights on at our cottage, our friends called us up on the phone and told us to go outside to see if we could hear them yell at us across the still lake (maybe a once-in-a-lifetime happening if we were somehow able to hear one another from over a mile away). So, I went outside—it was probably about 10 pm—and my friend yelled, "Jerry, can you hear me?" I answered, "I sure can… now come on over and have a drink." The family they were having cocktails with had an old fourteen-foot aluminum boat. So, the first couple and the guy with the boat loaded up in the tiny vessel, along with the boat owner's son and their big dog. As retold by my friend just recently, "It was such a cold damn night, and here were these five bodies loading down this little boat, with the icy cold water only about six inches from the top of it… and all that, just to cross the lake and go have a drink with Jerry and Nelle!"

The partying really never stops at Okoboji, even during the winter season. The University of Okoboji (a fictitious college that was established in 1981 with the lake as its campus) started a few years ago holding annual 'Winter Games' each January. It's a weekend of great fun that includes lots of happenings on and around the lake… there's a 'polar plunge' at the Arnolds Park pier, a 'swimsuit and snowboot' competition, a 'human dog sled' race, a 'brain freeze trivia and scavenger hunt', a 'guns 'n hoses' boot hockey tournament, 'ice broomball,' and the like. Hundreds of people turn out to take part in or just to watch the annual Winter Games, where a terrific time is had by all! I like to mention my regular participation as a student at the University of Okoboji, especially since I have a framed diploma hanging in my apartment, showing my 'Ph.D. in Lumber Management' awarded by its 'College of Forestry.' That diploma always reminds me that I'm in the company of former President George H. W. Bush and other famous celebrities who also hold U of O honorary doctorates! It has been such fun to be a part of the annual steady growth of a school that isn't even a school.

One December weekend in 2004, Nelle and I drove up to Okoboji for a couple of days, just to get out of Des Moines and see what was going on up there. We went to our usual winter haunts on Friday and Saturday nights, then for Sunday breakfast at a favorite bar and grill before heading back to Des Moines. Nelle was sitting on a bar stool next to me, chatting with the other locals. When finished with breakfast, we both got up to leave and were standing at the bar when she suddenly froze with a big grin on her face. I said,

"Nelle? Nelle? Nelle?" but she didn't respond. The owner of the bar said, "Jerry, I think she's having a stroke," and called 9-1-1. In the meantime, the person sitting next to us helped me lift Nelle back onto the stool and hold her there until the ambulance arrived. The EMT workers first took her to the little Dickinson County Hospital, which wasn't equipped to handle her case. After they gave her a scan, they asked me if she'd ever complained about headaches and I said she never complained about anything. They reported that she had a big tumor on her brain.

After the scan, they took her back to intensive care, where I phoned her two sons from her bedside. While talking with the first one, I said, "Your Mom can't talk, but she can certainly listen." I handed the phone to her, and she suddenly talked up a storm with him! Then when she got through talking to him, the last thing she said to me was, "fresh chicken in the trunk." (That morning we had loaded food, including a chicken, into the car from the cottage so that we could leave the restaurant and head straight back to Des Moines.) So, I drove the car back to the cottage, removed the chicken from the cooler in the trunk and put it back into our refrigerator, knowing she would later ask if that got done. Upon returning to the hospital, the team of doctors told me they had decided to take Nelle to Sioux Falls, but I said I wanted her to go to Des Moines. They told me that Des Moines was too far out of their territory, and that they needed to get her to the closest larger hospital right away. It was too windy to take her in the helicopter, so they took her by ambulance and I followed in my car. After being in intensive care for about three days, they said if Nelle lived she would be paralyzed the rest of her life. With permission from me and her two sons, Roy and Tom, who were then both present, Nelle was moved to a larger hospice room at the Sioux Falls hospital so that her sons and their wives and my daughters could see or even stay with her—she remained there for another three or four days. During the time in hospice care, Nelle never spoke a word. One time, however, I was telling the nurse about how she wore great big dark horn-rimmed glasses, then went out to the car and brought the glasses in—when the nurse put them on Nelle, she suddenly opened her eyes!

Roy and Tom were both there with me when Nelle passed away on December 18, 2004. [Nelle Frances Paulline had been born March 12, 1918, in Albia, Iowa.] Her sons meant all the world to her and, though unable to communicate, I know she was comforted just having them there during those final days. I had met Nelle as a young widow with two boys, and they all immediately became an integral part of our family after we married. My nephew, Chan, wrote this about them in his note to me for my 91st birthday: "It says a lot about Jerry that Nelle loved him—a lot that is good. Nelle knew life and Nelle knew herself, and when

Jerry brought her into our lives, mine was transformed—and by transformed, I don't just mean the higher probability that I'll get emphysema from breathing in all her second-hand smoke—I mean that something funny and smart and naughty and free." Chan's note continued, "Best of all for me, she also brought along two new male step-cousins who became the older brothers I desperately needed right then. Yes, they beat the s**t out of me, and blew cigar smoke into my face when I slept, and taught me awful things, but I loved every single minute of it. I am so deeply grateful to you for marrying that warm-hearted, gutsy woman with her two brawny sons. It was a gift you gave me without intending to. And that gift to me—of Nelle, Tom and Roy—has never stopped giving. So, Uncle Jerry, on your 91st... thank you for all you have done for me, for your generosity, for your sense of humor, for your naughty, devilish side, and for Nelle and her boys."

I guess this is as good a time as any to tell about my nephew Chan's wedding to a sweet gal from Los Angeles (Holmby Hills) several years ago. The wedding took place at her home, which was Lana Turner's old house. President and Mrs. Ronald Reagan were there, as was their Governor and many other well-known celebrities—450 were in attendance. The bride's parents' house sat on about four acres of land. After you drove through the gate and walked into the front of the house, you were greeted by a winding stairway with string orchestra members playing from the different steps up the stairs. Connie told me that the bride's father used to write the musical arrangements for the Tommy Dorsey Orchestra (and for Les Brown and his Band of Renown, who played at the wedding). The ceremony itself took place outdoors in a huge white tent that extended over the two tennis courts with a wood floor covering the court surface, and had a specially-built stairway going down to the tent from the house level on the upper hill—even the tent ropes were wrapped in white material. Nelle and I were seated at the head table in the tent, along with my sister Connie and her second husband. Chan's brother and sisters were there too, of course, and my niece Kyle was seated at a nearby table with President and Mrs. Reagan.

The wedding was such a beautiful event, with the different orchestra and band members playing in various places on the property and by the swimming pool. When people were seated around the grounds during the reception, I suggested to Nelle that we go over and talk with President and Mrs. Reagan," which we did. I said, "Mr. President, my name is Gerald Jewett from Des Moines, Iowa, and I used to hang out at the same Moonlight nightclub that you did when you lived there." Even though he suffered from dementia at the time, Mr. Reagan said, "Oh I understand they've torn that down." I said, "Yes, Sir, they have." Then he said, "Well, they sent me the sign off the front of the building."

(I had already heard that he had it hanging in his ranch out there.) Mrs. Reagan didn't say anything to us, and we moved on to meet other guests. The Reagan's were very, very close friends of the couple whose daughter had just married my nephew. In fact, her father was an honorary pallbearer after President Reagan's death, and the couple rode on Air Force One to accompany the President's body back to California for the service and burial at the Reagan National Library. Nelle and I certainly enjoyed being invited to that wedding, and considered it one of the highlights of our many travels. And though we loved flying to so many wonderful places, and being a part of so many terrific functions, we especially cherished our weekends up at Okoboji, with just the two of us spending time together at our cottage. She was my second wife, and not the mother of my girls, but she surely was my soulmate. Going up to the Lakes after Nelle passed was just never the same again for me. I missed being with her and am so glad that our final time together was spent up there on a quiet winter weekend, after a nice Sunday breakfast at one of our favorite places.

Not long ago, I almost died at Okoboji myself. It was Father's Day of 2012, and I'd had a colonoscopy earlier in the week—a regular routine for the thirty years since my 1982 colon cancer procedure. They'd taken out a whopping 26 or so polyps during this latest colonoscopy, however, which was well over and above a 'normal' removal rate for me. My girlfriend was at the lake with me that weekend when I suddenly began to have some serious rectal bleeding. After being admitted to the little Dickinson County Hospital in Spirit Lake, it was quickly apparent I was losing blood faster than they could replace it—and after seven transfusions, the hospital was actually running out of blood! They said that they would need to transfer me to a larger hospital, the nearest one being in Sioux Falls. I immediately responded, "Doc, my first wife and I were married in Sioux Falls, and my second wife died in Sioux Falls... Sioux Falls has been nothing but bad luck for me!... Get me on an ambulance to Des Moines!" The doctor replied, "You wouldn't live long enough to make it to Des Moines, Mr. Jewett." At my suggestion and persistence, they called Iowa Methodist Hospital in Des Moines, requesting that their Life Flight helicopter immediately come get me. The two young medical workers and the pilot who flew to the Lakes to pick me up couldn't have been nicer, and the helicopter ride was an adventure— I just wished I had been sitting up and participating in the flight. I'd always thought it would be fun to own a helicopter (though they are maintenance hogs) and had only been in one several years ago, with a friend in the skies over the Lakes... that friend was the guy who had a jet hangar in Florida, flying a Learjet back and forth from Ft. Lauderdale to Okoboji on the weekends. Anyway, on this Life Flight ride as a patient from Okoboji to Des Moines, I talked to the pilot all the way so it seemed a quick trip. I was grateful to be met at the Iowa Methodist Hospital rooftop elevator door by my daughters and by the very doctor who was to immediately repair the leaking polyp. I was never so thankful to be back in Des Moines, in the hands of competent folks who were whisking me into a nearby emergency operating area. My girlfriend was stuck driving my car all the way back to Des Moines, joining my daughters at the hospital once she arrived a few hours later.

I always thought the old 1982 cancer surgery was my scariest medical emergency, but that 2012 event really got my attention. In addition to having my own emergency on that Monday, Steph had also almost died earlier in the month… Jen and I sat vigil in her hospital room every day during the twelve days of her medically-induced coma following emergency surgery because of an infection surrounding her heart, and with subsequent infections running wildly unchecked throughout her body. *{Editor's note: Additionally, Dad's first wife and our mother, Jackie, had passed away just a month before Steph's coma, so it was an especially tough time of adjustment for our nuclear family.}* [Jacqueline Frances Berguin was born May 19, 1929, in Sioux Falls, South Dakota and died May 6, 2012, in Tucson, Arizona.]

After those incidents, I wanted to stay closer to my Des Moines doctors, which meant deciding to sell my Okoboji home. It was a difficult decision after having spent more than eighty years of my life up at the Lakes, but I told my daughters, "There comes a time for everything." Neither one of the girls were interested in taking over the cottage that Nelle and I had purchased, and I was thankful they respected my decision to sell and that they helped empty the house of any furnishings and mementos that family members wanted to keep. (Ironically, the eventual buyer of my Okoboji home happened to be a 35th Street Des Moines neighbor who lived just two doors from me!).

I have been back to Okoboji only four or five times since selling my cottage, mainly to visit my sister, Connie, whose Parkinson's and its accompanying dementia has gotten quite bad. Connie and I have remained so close throughout our lives, and it's sure tough to watch that ruthless disease stealing her once-endless vitality. Sometimes she has a fairly good day and perhaps knows who I am, but I don't count on it. A year ago, in July of 2016, her kids were able to get Connie to a Marilyn Maye show, and it was terrific to be sitting around a big table together, once again watching our childhood friend sing and strut her stuff. Cabaret singer Marilyn Maye had grown up playing at our folks' Okoboji cottage and has remained such a good friend of my sister's all through the years. And it's been wonderful watching Marilyn's success… believe it or not, she was on Johnny Carson's 'Tonight Show' more times than anyone else—like 67 appearances or something!

When Nelle passed away in 2012, Marilyn immediately learned of it. As I got into my car in Sioux Falls to drive back to the Lakes to throw out that dang chicken from the cottage refrigerator before heading to Des Moines, Marilyn called me on the phone and talked to me all the way to Okoboji. Then on my 90th birthday in 2015, she called to sing 'Happy Birthday' to me from Carnegie Hall in New York where she was performing—she told me she was going to be back at Okoboji singing again in the summer, so I made plans to be up

there to see her a year ago. And then this summer, after leaving the Algona Founders' Day celebration on July 9, Jen and John and I continued heading north to Okoboji so that we could visit Connie at her home (I think she knew who we were!) and take in yet another of Marilyn's performances at The Inn, where she has sold out shows for 61 seasons. It's really hard to believe that the woman on stage, belting out her tunes while still doing a couple of high leg kicks, is soon going to be 90-years-young!

Incidentally, while at Okoboji this July, we also took some time to visit several friends around the area before heading over on our way out of town to spend a couple of hours at the unbelievable automobile museum—Okoboji Classic Cars—located just south of the Lakes. The kids hadn't seen the place and were almost dumbfounded when entering the unique 48,000-square-foot showroom designed to look like the 1950 downtown main street of Spencer. We all thoroughly enjoyed the guided tour, and highly recommend it to others. (I was able to ride with the tour guide in an electric golf cart, which was also nice!)

Though I miss being a part of what goes on at the Lakes nowadays, it sure felt good to sell my Okoboji place awhile back. So good, in fact, that I soon decided it was time to also sell the 35th Street house that I had built in Des Moines almost 60 years before. I wish one of my girls or my grandsons would have moved into it, but nobody seemed interested in that. *{Editor's note: I had never mentioned it to Dad, but seemed to regularly sense an eerie 'presence' in that house in more recent years, and was personally glad to see it sold, to be honest. This next part of Dad's story helped confirm it for me… }*

In her 91st birthday note to me, niece Darcy talked about staying in the guest room of that house when she came to Des Moines to attend a funeral just a few years ago… "You and I went to dinner, and I attended an event at the lumber company with you. It was just delightful to spend time with you then. You were a wonderful host and I still tell a lot of people about that trip, because I am quite sure I was visited by a ghost that night! No clear sighting, but there was something quite white and translucent in the air, and my bedroom door suddenly closed. I am not sure who it was. After I told Mother about it, she casually asked you if you knew you had a ghost, and you said no, you didn't know that. I still chuckle about how both you and Mother discussed it so calmly, without any drama." I never felt anything like that in my house, but it's probably worth telling for the record.

When I headed south to Marco Island, Florida for the winter months almost five years ago, I asked Jennifer to handle cleaning out and dismantling the three-story house on 35th Street and to get things donated, sold or moved to the homes of my kids and grandkids. The pieces I really wanted to save, along with a few things from Jen's home and office, went to furnish my new 500-square-foot apartment on the Wesley Acres retirement campus—she and her husband took over decorating the place, choosing paint color, carpet color, hanging the pictures, arranging the furniture, and everything. My mother's beautiful oak game table is in the middle of the living room, and I love sitting at it every single day. Mom's old drop-leaf desk holds my computer, another of her little desks serves as my office area, and her marble-top end table with carved drawer handles stores several important odds and ends. The place is kind of a museum, like I said before, with displays of many things that have had special meaning to me over the 92 years of my life.

Even the walls tell a story, with pictures of Jewett automobiles, historical lumber company snapshots, a Federal Duck Stamp album done in metal, and one of my mother's original oil artworks she completed while looking out of the living room window of her house on Jewett Lane. Over the bed is a lovely framed scene from Marco Island's Tigertail Beach, and in the kitchen are two watercolor drawings of Aspen, Colorado (as well as a framed poster of an Oreo cookie with a bite out of it, a gift from a well-known lawyer who also loved those too!). Knowing of my boyhood crush on Shirley Temple, one of my special Wesley friends recently gifted me with a framed picture of that little cutie dancing, so it's on my wall now too. On the stove sits a grey pottery crock showing a blue depiction of my great-grandfather Ambrose Call's log cabin, a meaningful item picked up at the 150th anniversary celebration in Algona back in 2004. And one of my earliest special memory pieces is also in my kitchen—it's the silver napkin ring that I used at every meal as a kid.

Sitting on top of the ring, still in silver, is a little boy with a dog leaning up against him. And now inserted into it is a pretty linen napkin monogrammed with my initials in blue, which looks terrific when next to a setting of my favorite plates [Pfaltzgraff 'Yorktowne' pottery] that Mom had started collecting up at Okoboji in the late 1960's. I'm so glad to have somehow ended up with those!

Along with the little table I crafted for my grandmother in the junior high classroom in 1939, my apartment has an antique hand-carved table holding an intricately designed Parian lamp from the 1860-1880 era—both were in the home of my great-grandparents. On that table are a few components from Dad's first wireless radio station, pictured here.

Also displayed on that very table and the long window sill next to it are a wide variety of keepsakes: a spark coil from a Model T Ford, a kerosene lantern used on miner caps, a wooden printing block from India, an antique knife from a Third World country, an antique wooden planer that my grandfather Jewett had, a couple of wooden decoys from my hunting days, a brass Navy compass gift from one of my Dad's friends, and the handcuffs I carried as a Deputy Sheriff next to the badge with my name and number.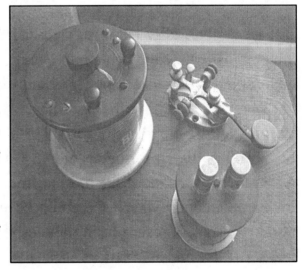

Across the room on my computer desk visitors can see a heavy black metal antique embossing machine, once used to stamp official papers with the Jewett Lumber Company corporate seal. Additionally, there is a pair of antique dual-lensed eyeglasses that Pop Shore apparently used when examining railway men—Connie's note accompanying the glasses says that they were found in the Railroad Workers exam room in Valley Junction.

While getting my new Wesley residence ready for me that winter, Jennifer regularly emailed me in Marco Island pictures of the decorating progress, and I got so excited looking at photos that I came back to Iowa a month early just to begin living in my new home with its nice balcony that overlooks the Chamberlain mansion's front yard where I'd played football as a little kid. (The Chamberlains were in the cosmetics business, as were their Weeks relatives. It's interesting to me that the Weeks' Armand Company with its cosmetics, and the F. W. Fitch Company with its shampoos, and the Chamberlain Medicine Company with its hand lotions, were all famous personal care businesses that originated in right here in Des Moines and had their heyday during my early years when I hung out with kids from each of those families.) After nearly five years owning this apartment here on the Wesley retirement campus, I'm still loving it. Until this summer, I had preferred to spend most nights over at the south-side condo of my girlfriend, and she usually chose to put up with me. Most medical emergencies or scares had happened to me in the wee hours, and I wasn't sleeping as well the nights spent alone in my apartment. Also, I admit to having enjoyed being a bit spoiled by reading the morning paper over a breakfast of fruit and coffee on her porch and keeping my car cleaner in the underground parking garage (and if you don't want to wash or detail your own vehicle, or put air into your tires or recharge your battery, they will have someone do those things at the rate of $7 for 15 minutes—those were nice features for this car lover).

Last December, after being so sick due to a nightly drop in my blood pressure, I told my doctor I just wanted to drive into Dunn's Funeral Home and have myself embalmed! Then I had another of those blood pressure drops that caused me to black out last January. I don't remember falling that morning, which is scary. And I couldn't blame my girlfriend for not wanting me to stay over at her place until it got resolved. After a battery of tests in the hospital ER, my doctor didn't want to admit me, even just for an overnight of observation, because of all the pneumonia illness throughout the hospital. So, I went to Stephanie's condo where she could keep a keen eye on me and monitor food intake and blood pressure. It's sure been nice, especially as I get older, to have a daughter who is a licensed R.N. and is certified in health care quality management. Steph even wrote two books sharing her expertise—one about legal nurse consulting and one about medical transcription services. She then got her M.B.A. while serving as the Administrator of a local ambulatory surgery center a few years back, and today works from home as a national nurse reviewer for auto injury solutions. I'll mention here what Jennifer does as well… After receiving her undergrad degree with Special Ed. certification, Jen taught school four years before leaving town for her husband's graduate school stints in Texas and in California. Upon returning to Iowa in 1978, they opened a private counseling clinic in the western suburbs, with Jennifer serving as Office Administrator to the group of therapists there. She continues to be involved in that and so many other side pursuits, not the least of which is wordsmithing, editing, copyediting, and proofing articles and books like this one! My daughters are both so talented in what they do, and are so different from one another in many ways. But they've told me time and again that the one thing they will always have in common is loving and caring for me… and that's pretty special for a Dad.

So, after the fainting spell and subsequent non-hospitalization last winter, the girls and I visited my regular physician in his office the next day following that ER visit, where he determined the incident had been caused by two of my daily medications working together to lower my blood pressure just too much—I was relieved to at least know there was an explanation for what happened. Doc wanted to see me in a week, rather than in a month, and I appreciated his keeping on top of it—the guy does know his medications, and the two of us get along so well. (He told me a few weeks ago that I remind him of a 'naughty little imp,' which I'm trying to take as a compliment... he'll really be calling me that after reading this book!) Being alone at night isn't bothering me these days, and I do love staying at my own apartment all the time now. But I take blood pressure readings each day just to assure myself everything is fine.

Steph and Jen recently reminded me of one more pretty scary medical emergency that I'd almost forgotten about. It had all started a week or so before a great big 80th birthday party the two of them were throwing for me in October of 2005, twelve years ago. I somehow got cellulitis in my leg after a physician did a perhaps-less-than-sterile procedure on my toe, landing me in the hospital for several days while medical personnel worked to stop the infection from spreading quickly through my body. I was lucky that it got turned it around, and that they were able to finally release me, though it was just an hour or so before my big 80th party. The discharge came with strict instructions to remain seated and with my leg elevated throughout the evening—which wasn't easy, as several hundred dear friends showed up to honor me that night! (And I admit to cheating, standing up to greet each person as they arrived.)

LOOKING BACK

Since retiring several years ago, I have had more time to reflect on many aspects of my life, and especially on my wonderful position(s) in the family lumber business. It was an honor to be a part of it and to give back in whatever way I could, carrying on the tradition of my great-grandfather George by continuing to make the operation a strong one. My cousin, Tom, wrote for my 91st birthday, "A number of years ago my Dad said something about you that has always stayed with me and makes it clear that there is a lot more to you than someone who knows how to have a good time. Dad mentioned that he was really proud of Jerry for his hard work at building up the Jewett Lumber business at a time when it needed such leadership." I so appreciated those kind words from Tom (and originally from his terrific father, Uncle Homer).

Our company was sure something to be proud of, and had many notable 'firsts' (in addition to the tilt-up construction for our main office building discussed earlier in this book). We were also the first lumber company in Iowa to have a power-driven lumber truck (1906). It was called the 'carter car' and was a cab-over design with no top. The cab sat on a two-cycle, two-cylinder engine (right photo).

Jewett Lumber Company was the first in Iowa to use a 'straddle truck' carrier (left photo), which was sometime after 1913. The beauty of the straddle truck was that it was open on the front and the back, allowing for longer lengths of boards to be moved. Once a pallet was loaded with lumber, the straddle driver just pulled right up over it and attached to the pallet, running the lifting mechanism without ever even leaving the truck. Though we had been the first in Iowa to use forklift trucks, the straddle was a neat innovation because it allowed loading and unloading without forklifts or cranes.

We were also the first to have removable truck beds—all designed by Uncle Homer. Our hoist system at the E. 7th Street location would remove the empty bed frame (which was on wheels) from a truck after a delivery, and another pre-loaded bed would then be hoisted up onto the truck for the next delivery. The guys were able to go right to work loading up the empty bed that had just arrived, in order to have it ready to  hoist back up again when the unloaded truck returned to the yard. It was a pretty slick system of rotation and certainly helped in getting the goods to the customer in record time.

Inside the main offices, our firm was the first in the industry to utilize cash registers and the first to employ a mechanical billing computer to post invoices with the use of an old flatbed Elliott-Fischer machine. We were the first to use electronic data processing and the first to have a pension plan for our employees. Jewett's was also the first to have an automobile used for lumber company business—it was assigned to the Credit Manager who, in addition to collecting bills, would drive the company President from home to office and office to home (as well as to and from church on Sundays!). We were one of the first in Iowa to have two-way radios in our trucks and company automobiles, and one of first to have dial telephones in those cars. Ahead of the two-way radios in all the trucks, we had two-way radio communication throughout the yard and offices starting back in 1958. Our main location on East Walnut had one of the first time-lock safes, which opened automatically at the beginning of the workday and couldn't be opened until then. We were the first to have compensatory pricing—loss leaders—and the first to be a stockholder in the lumber mills and in the huge member-owned HWI (Hardware Wholesalers, Inc., doing over $500 million in volume). Our company was one of the first to manufacture pre-hung doors. And of course, were the first to have a company airplane to service accounts outside city and state limits, as well as to assist in the acquisition and purchasing of building materials directly from the mills.

My great-grandfather began our family business back in 1879 based on strong morals and ethical habits, and those were carried on over these decades by my grandfather, my father, and myself. We never hired a person out from under a competitor, nor did we call on a competitor's customer; we ran regular sales meetings, and continued to have a breakfast strategy meeting each Tuesday morning at 7 A.M. to keep lines of communication open with our sales personnel; we personally trained all of our estimators and salespersons, and had a certified audit every single year. But more than anything else, we were honest with our customers, from the minute they walked in the door, through the estimate stages, and after delivery of the goods.

Looking back, I realize that my favorite company gatherings over the years were our Annual Board Meetings, which meant being together as an extended family to make sure the business ran smoothly. Until Pops Jewett died in 1951, we met in the dining room of my grandparents' home on High Street, with most family members present—all Officers were family members, but not all family members were Officers, of course. After the Annual Meetings, we had a big lunch together. I don't recall if my grandfather made the lunches for us, but I'm fairly certain he did. Pops loved to cook and did such a great job at it... I remember his waffles in the mornings and his dumplings at night whenever we stayed with my grandparents as kids. What I *do* know for certain is that my grandmother *did not* prepare our lumber company Annual Meeting meals—as with her own mother, Annie, I never once saw her cook! Even in her elderly time of life, long after Pops had passed away, Margaret had a woman who took care of all that.

This might be a good spot to mention that, unlike the rest of the family, Grandmother Margaret had very dark features. And she was just a little thing... I remember the day as a kid when I surpassed her in height after a growth spurt. *{Editor's note: We great-granddaughters loved the fact that Margaret wore a size 4 shoe. When we were over to visit her as little girls every Sunday afternoon, it was such fun to clomp around in her various fancy high heels!}* Pops Jewett stood a head taller than his wife, but they made a nice-looking couple. And if you think they look somewhat alike, as I still do, it helps to be reminded that

they were descendants of the same guy—Margaret's father (George Anson Jewett) and her husband (David Lewis Jewett) both had the same father (George "Enoch" Jewett)! That's still a little mind-boggling for me, and probably for most readers of this book.

Pops was sick for a few months before his death at age 87. [David Lewis Jewett was born in Petaluma, California on November 14, 1863, and died in Des Moines, Iowa on April 9, 1951.] Jackie and I had just learned that we were expecting a baby shortly before Pops died, but we didn't tell him for fear it might do more harm than good. We were careful not to excite him enough to give him a heart attack or something—he ended up dying of that anyway, and I always wished we'd gone ahead and told him that he was going to be a great-grandfather. His wife, Grandmother Margaret, lived another fourteen years, also passing away at age 87. [Margaret Jewett Jewett was born in Des Moines, Iowa on December 6, 1877, and died in Des Moines, Iowa on March 2, 1965. She was fourteen years younger than her husband, David, and lived fourteen years after he passed.]

It was just wonderful to have so many decades in active management of the Jewett Lumber Company. In 1979, exactly a century after my great-grandfather founded the firm, I purchased a five-acre parcel of land on the far southeast side of our city [at 1536 E. Army Post Road], to become the new main office headquarters and south location for the lumber operation. After additional construction and remodeling, the new site was opened for business on April 1, 1980. Unfortunately, that was also the start of a nationwide economic slump which severely hit a number of industries, with lumber being one of the most devastated. It was tough to compete with the big national chains who were selling building products. This recession continued until 1983, so I closed our north-side location in Highland Park and our longtime distribution yard in downtown Des Moines, and we operated out of the new Army Post Road location only.

The years 1983 and 1984 took a definite turn for the better, and I felt it was a good time to firm up my company's standing in the marketplace. I contacted a competitor (and good childhood friend) of mine to discuss the possibility of merging our two Des Moines family-owned pioneer lumber businesses—we were the main yards that came to one another's rescue after each of our big company fires. My friend and I only wanted to work ten more years; I had no immediate family members who really wanted to take over the presidential helm of the Jewett Lumber Company, though my stepson, Tom, remained involved. After much discussion and many months of meetings, Jewett Lumber Company and Gilcrest Lumber Company became Gilcrest/Jewett in 1985. It was a wise decision on both of our parts. My friend passed away before his ten years was up, but I filled out my ten and 'retired' at age 70. Though no longer actively involved in the company, I continue to have a beautiful large office there the rest of my life and to be affiliated with it as Chairman Emeritus. And I would probably go there more often if it didn't require climbing such steep stairs to get up to my second-floor location! (They used to put my partner into a special box they had built to hoist him in a forklift up to his office at our earlier location, but I'm not one bit interested in doing that.)

My years in the lumber business were terrific. And involvement in local, regional, and national lumber associations, along with the travel opportunities that came with all of those, gave me so much additional satisfaction. We always had a company airplane during my tenure there, and I was the pilot who got to fly to the various job sites, conventions, and wherever the business would take us or wherever customers needed to go. There was also a lot of involvement in those many terrific civic organizations and other outreaches, with opportunities to travel for those as well. I found myself meeting a number of people who

had truly left their marks in this world, and it was humbling. For an active pilot, it doesn't get much better than having one's picture [permission courtesy of the Conrad Foundation] taken at a local event with Capt. Charles "Pete" Conrad, USN Ret., NASA's third man to walk on the moon while Commander of Apollo XII. He also commanded Gemini 11 and the first manned Skylab mission too. (People often ask me if I'd like to have been an astronaut, and the answer is no—that just seemed far too 'iffy' to me.)

Since we are beginning this book with my obituary already prepared for the newspaper, Jen suggested I tell something about the various involvements listed in it if they haven't been mentioned in this memoir already. It seems silly to have such a lengthy obit, but I just can't decide what to eliminate. In the long run, I guess it shouldn't matter so much to me how it ends up looking since I won't be opening the newspaper that morning to read it! The next few paragraphs should touch on most of what's not already been covered…

As a volunteer Committee member of the Employer Support of the Guard and Reserve (ESGR) for Iowa, we worked to help convince local business owners to hire servicemen and then to support those employees by giving them a leave of absence without losing their jobs if they were called to serve. I read recently that our local Principal Insurance Group won an award this year for its participation in such a program. Some of the ESGR

Committee traveled around to a number of different bases, like the Marine headquarters in California, the Jacksonville Navy facility, and several other military spots. When this next picture was taken at the re-commissioning of the USS Iowa in Mississippi in 1984, I noticed they had .50 caliber guns in pairs all around the ship (which reminded me of the .50 calibers on those P-51's back at Lackland, so close to the fuselage that they shot through the propeller). They told us that when they shot one of those .50's from the USS Iowa, the guns would line up and intercept the enemy flak

and just destroy them! On a side note, it was interesting to learn that no drinking of alcohol was ever allowed on board a Navy vessel, not even to be carried onto a ship—somehow that seemed hard to believe! I had been asked to become a member of that ESGR Committee for Iowa by a close friend of mine who was a two-star Major General. When I first got out of WWII, that fine gentleman had tried to get me into the Air National Guard—he told me if I would join, I could do all the flying I wanted and that he would make me a Major (I guess a two-star General could do that). I was honored by his offer and his ongoing persistence but was looking forward to a good job in my family lumber business, and with an airplane to allow all the flying I could want. (And at that early time, I didn't realize just how *much* flying and travel time I would actually be getting over the ongoing years.) Right after he made that final plea to me, the Iowa Air National Guard was activated and sent to Bangor, Maine, so I was pleased to have not accepted the offer!

There were some awfully nice all-expenses-paid trips through the business too, such as one to Spain and Africa when Nelle and I were guests of Weyerhauser. Another memorable one was to London and Ireland as guests of the Georgia Pacific Corporation... we also invited Nelle's son, Tom (and his wife, Gay), as well as my daughter, Jennifer (and her husband, John) to join us on that lovely trip. Nelle and I went on another overseas jaunt that seemed almost like a prize vacation, after getting a call from a guy who taught law at Drake and who was also a travel agent with a charter tour business. He and his wife (she hosted a local radio program) said one of his charters had fallen through, so he was calling various people to see if they'd like to go to Europe and back for $99 each. I immediately said, "Yes, how many seats can I save?" He said he'd save ten if he had the money in hand. I was quickly able to get four other couples. After we boarded the plane that day, we were all just looking at each other—none of us could believe we were flying to Europe and back for $99 each. But it really was true... we landed in Detroit, then flew nonstop to London on a Stretch 6 (DC-6). During that week, we also took a side trip to Paris, which allowed me to see my father's birthplace, before then returning to London for the flight home.

As one of the founders of the Polk County Heart Association and as Chairman of the American Heart Association/Iowa Affiliate, I did a little traveling, such as the 1971 Anaheim trip already mentioned. I also recall treks to Jamaica and to Miami (one of our programs had Jack Benny as Master of Ceremonies, which was certainly memorable). AHA was a great organization, and I was pleased to promote it, especially coming from a long line of ancestors who have had heart conditions (not to mention my own). I always wanted to be a doctor myself, and particularly a surgeon like Pop Shore—it's probably my only real occupational regret. During those days of involvement with the Heart Association, I seriously toyed with enrolling as a fifty-year-old guy at Des Moines University (it was called 'College of Osteopathic Medicine and Surgery' back then), but would never have made it, having to study like that. So, I did the next best thing to becoming a heart surgeon—I convinced one to let me scrub up and be in on watching him do open-heart surgeries a few times! Not only was that doc a fellow pilot and a good friend, but he served as President of the Iowa Affiliate while I was Chairman of the Board. Watching the surgeries was terribly interesting, and I consider those rare opportunities in the operating room (other than as a patient) some of my life highlights.

Serving several years on the Board of the Mercy Foundation involved some local car trips, raising funds for the hospital where my grandfather had been Chief of Staff. And I don't recall ever traveling as Chairman of Mercy Properties and of Mercy Home Supply, other than to all 27 parcels of ground they owned around the Des Moines area. The bylaws of Mercy Properties said you could only serve nine years on that Board, which I did, then they put me on as Chairman of Share Care, Ltd., which oversaw their home supply equipment sales. With Mercy Share Care, Ltd., "travel" meant walking across the street from the hospital to the southwest corner of 6th and University!

One of the gals I had dated in high school stayed a close friend through life, and taught me the fine art of fundraising. Many remember Maddie Levitt Glazer as an extremely generous woman who donated her time and talents to the betterment of so many institutions in our city. That fine lady and I worked on several area projects, especially fundraising together for local hospitals back in the '60's. She was one of the few people who knew

349

I couldn't say my 'r's as a little kid, even when reciting my own name, and continued to call me 'Jee-wee Jewett' throughout my entire life. It was so sad to walk into her funeral at Dunn's… that is, until her daughter, Suzie Glazer Burt, saw me and laughingly greeted me by that very same name! (Suzie said her mother would have badly wanted to be a part of this book about my life, and offered permission to use their names and this picture in it.)

My travel opportunities were numerous for the Des Moines Chamber of Commerce, as the chairman of their Membership Committee and of their Aviation Committee. Every year, the Chamber had a 'Goodwill Tour' that included a three-day trip by private train to different parts of Iowa, helping to spread the message to buy from local merchants, because they buy from the Des Moines wholesalers (Chamber members). The trips were a lot of fun for all the guys. On one occasion, Speck Redd played piano in the club car on our way to Iowa City. The year I was Chairman of that Goodwill Tour, we went to Fort Madison and all through the state penitentiary, which was interesting but kinda spooky.

It must have been 1983 when I chaired the Aviation Committee for the Chamber and was in charge of the big Air Show to celebrate Des Moines International Airport's 50th Anniversary. I picked as my co-chair a female pilot and good friend. We had great plans and a commitment to have the Blue Angels perform for us, but they ended up getting into an argument with our airport manager over various things like where they would park their planes and so forth. They finally told our manager to "just forget our show being there." So, we had to hustle to come up with something to replace such a big act. My co-chair and her husband had their pilot fly us in their corporate plane to Oshkosh, Wisconsin to the Experimental Aircraft Association (EAA) Annual Air Show, where we sat on the flight line and picked the different forms of entertainment to have at our own 50th celebration. That's when I decided that those wing walkers are absolutely crazy, doing their stunts with no parachute and no safety cord. But crazy or not, they were entertainers and we hired them to perform for us—they were such a big hit! I had also telephoned my cousin, Gardner Cowles, Jr., who was on the Board of United Airlines in New York, to see if we could get a United plane at the airport for the visitors to tour—he provided one and it was very popular too. The gala celebration was so well attended by the citizens of Des Moines and by hundreds from around other parts of the state. We also threw a side party for all of the entertainers while they were in town.

Immediately after being discharged from the service, I had accepted an invitation to become a member of the international Aircraft Owners and Pilots Association (AOPA), which was a great way to get to know others with the same interest in this lifelong hobby. Though no longer a member of that particular group, I have really enjoyed my membership in (and serving as a past President of) the Des Moines Hangar of Quiet Birdmen ('QB')—another association of pilots from all walks of life. To be eligible for QB, which is by invitation only, you must have a minimum of 500 flying hours certified by the FAA. At our local monthly meetings, we have cocktails then barbeque our own steaks out at Rube's Steakhouse west of Des Moines. After dinner, we say the Pledge of Allegiance with the flag present and give a toast to any QB's who have 'gone west' since our previous meeting. Then we all go around the room to each attendee, who can quickly talk about anything he wants (or even tell a joke!). QB has been a popular fraternal organization in our country for many years—Eddie Rickenbacker and Charles Lindbergh were both members. Male guests (and occasionally female, if on the program) are sometimes invited to attend too. Mr. Piper of Piper Aircraft was our local guest once, as was Max Conrad who ferried the first single-engine Piper across the ocean for that corporation. (After that flight, Max had delivered a number of their single-engine airplanes around the world. I was able to personally ask him if he always got a radio signal to confirm his navigation and he said, "Oh no, some days I didn't get any signal, but then the next day I would!" That sure seemed strange to me.) When there is a funeral of one of the QB guys, each attendee meets up with the other members before the service so that we can walk in together. To be honest, I haven't gone to a QB meeting since my best friend died last year. We always rode together from Wesley, and he bought me a drink once we arrived—it's just not the same now.

Another fun fraternal organization back in the day was the Shrimp Club, of which I was a past President. The group was basically formed to get a bunch of guys (business owners, doctors, lawyers, educators, etc.) together for some weekend male companionship. Our luncheons consisted of packages of hot shrimp, along with cold beer; after lunch, we told jokes, which made for a fun Saturday afternoon. The group started out meeting years ago at the Des Moines Club, but that facility ended up being closed for Saturday lunch, so we moved our gatherings to the downtown Holiday Inn. Though it's no longer in existence, Shrimp Club was a terrific way of getting to know a wide variety of fine gentlemen from Des Moines and surrounding areas.

With such a strong ancestral heritage in our city and in our state, I'm especially proud to have served as a past President of the Pioneer Club of Des Moines. It has continued to be a very active organization since its inception in 1894. The Club is made up of members who have lived in Iowa for something like 40 years and longer. While I was more active in it, we met annually for a luncheon at the Fort Des Moines Hotel and invited some excellent speakers to address our group (like the President of Drake University, and many others), telling stories about life in Des Moines over the decades. Our most recent meeting in August 2017 was held out at Wakonda, and the dining rooms were full.

One of the most interesting outreaches with which I was involved was the Polk County Society for Crippled Children and Adults, an association designed to take care of meeting special needs of the handicapped. Their office was located on 31st Street south of the Veterans Hospital and was run by a friend of mine who had been injured in WWII and was the recipient of a Purple Heart. He was our full-time Director who worked on raising monies, and we would discuss in our meetings various projects that needed attention with those funds. We had one little girl that reminded me so much of my daughter, Jennifer. But the gal was born with no arms, so we got her equipped with artificial ones; and later, as her body grew, we replaced the arms with even longer ones. When I asked her doctor what would cause such a thing, he said they thought it was due to an injury the mother had in her second month of pregnancy. It was all an eye-opening experience for me, and I was truly honored to have served as its President.

As a Board member for about 15 years on the Executive Committee of the Mid-Iowa Council of Boy Scouts (after which I moved onto the Advisory Council), we had monthly dinner meetings at the Fort Des Moines Hotel with various volunteers, as well as with the Scoutmaster. There were usually 25 or 30 people present to discuss the newest projects that the local Boy Scouts had going. It was basically a fundraising think-tank to come up with ideas to complete big projects, like repairing the swimming pool at the 'Camp Mitigwa' Boy Scout Camp or how to best add another building… things like that. Along with their famous popcorn sales event, we had a drive every year that included a list of people we each agreed to call, in hopes of coming up with monies for the projects the Committee determined to be most important. There was so much more that was accomplished, of course, but that's a good thumbnail sketch of what went on in meetings.

As a good Executive Board Committee member for the Boy Scouts, I even went so far as to take Stephanie's eldest son, Ryland, on a scouting expedition overnight at Camp Mitigwa when he was nine or so years old. I must have been about 70. We took a couple of nice used cots, but his Mom forgot to pack us any pillows! There was a big storm that came up in the night, and our tent leaked water all over us, which fortunately took our attention away from the daddy long-legs that had invaded our tent. And just to top off the night, my borrowed cot broke and I ended up on the floor. Another Committee member friend of mine was in the tent next to ours with his own grandson, and they had a miserable time too—he and I had even taken a couple little airline-size bottles of vodka to enjoy once our grandsons were asleep, but we never got that far! (I just recently saw that Committee member friend of mine, and asked him if he'd slept in a tent lately, to which he loudly answered, "NO!"). After my uncles were in that 1918 neighborhood Boy Scout picture with former President Teddy Roosevelt, I guess the troop membership in our family died a slow death. Ryland was a Scout for a couple of years, with Steph serving as Den Mother, but that was about it (though the kid who lived across the street from them became an Eagle Scout!) Ryland's little brother, Kingsley, was part of a troop himself, but only for about two weeks… King said he had the flu while at a den meeting in some guy's garage, and threw up all over a model home the boys were supposed to be constructing. He tells of running out and never going back!

My niece, Kyle, was a Girl Scout and recalled for me an event that took place when she was young. Her Dad wasn't able to attend a particular Scout function, so I went with Kyle in his place. She wrote to me for my 91st birthday, "On the actual night, I put on my green uniform and the sash with all the badges I'd earned. You picked me up and drove us to Plymouth Church. During the drive, you asked me questions about the troop and who my friends were in the troop. The event was in the church basement. You were asked to sit in one of the little low chairs provided to all the fathers. I remember it was so low to the ground that your knees nearly touched your chin. But you didn't seem to mind. I handed you some sheets of artwork that I'd done. I remember your expression as you studied the artwork, nodding intently as you studied one sheet, then another. And I remember your telling me I had done a good job. I felt proud… The older I get, the more I appreciate what a sweet thing that was for an uncle to do for his niece. It was only a Girl Scout gathering, but Uncle Jerry understood that this was important to me." The Scouts are a terrific organization for kids and I'm pleased to have been a very small part of their outreach.

I was on the Board of the Des Moines Club when they moved from 800 Locust to the top of the Ruan Center. The late Mr. John Ruan had his corporate pilot fly us on their private jet into Chicago's Furniture Mart to pick out all the furnishings for the new Club, which was fun. At our Board meetings, we always heard a report from the Manager, then discussed how the Club was doing and ways to improve it. One time the Manager reported that they had just, the previous Saturday night, had their largest turnout for dinner in the Club, serving 256 dinners. I mentioned to the other Board members and to the Manager that I'd just been out to the very small but very crowded Johnny's Vet's Club for dinner, and had asked the chef how many dinners *they* had served that night—their count was over 500 dinners, and all served out of a teeny-little, nothing-fancy kitchen. I asked our Manager why, with all our Club's square footage and two beautiful large new kitchens located on two floors with an elevator in between, do we only serve 256 dinners? Our Manager replied, "Because of the view! People come and just sit here and drink wine or cocktails and we can't turn our tables."

It seems that there was once a heyday for private Clubs, but they are way down in membership these days. I still retain mine at the Des Moines Club though, lunching there almost every Tuesday with a group of about ten or twelve fellows, and also oftentimes having drinks before a dinner of free hors d'oeuvres at the Club a couple times a month. I don't drink much these days, of course, but once liked martinis made with straight gin and ice (until finding out I wasn't man enough to drink them anymore). If I have a cocktail before dinner now, I usually order gin diluted with plain water, served over ice, which makes me last a little bit longer. I don't eat much in the way of large meals either, but find that the Des Moines Club is definitely still the place to go for the view! And it holds good memories for me—I can still remember as a young boy going there with my mother and father for various activities, back when it was at 800 Locust. And as mentioned earlier, that was the location for my folks' 50th wedding anniversary celebration in 1972. (Incidentally, I recently attended a 100th birthday party for the long-time Des Moines Club hostess. She and I go back a long way—we used to sit and chat over a drink in the basement bar at the old Commodore Hotel. The gal really smoked up a storm back then; I can hardly believe she is still alive and somehow looking even younger than she did several years ago!)

We used to have our big monthly Sigma Nu luncheon meetings down at the Des Moines Club too, with thirty or forty local fraternity brothers attending—any Sigma Nu would be welcome at those, and at our annual Christmas party, which always included the wives or dates. There was a time when we had senior members my father's age at the table, along with young pledges from Iowa State and the University of Iowa as guests at the luncheons. I was once very active in keeping that going, serving as President a number of years, but our group has shrunk to about four or five guys nowadays. Until recently, we were still meeting monthly for lunch, but more intimately at The Ember's on Ingersoll. It finally got down to only two of us regularly attending, so we no longer even have those luncheons at all. I still donate annually to the Sigma Nu Educational Foundation, as a believer in keeping fraternal organizations alive and well at some level. Social media has replaced much of the need for that more personal type of networking nowadays, I guess, but it seems somehow sad after my own lifelong experiences with such wonderful Sigma Nu connections. Only two of my own four grandsons pledged fraternities in college. [Jennifer's youngest, Jake Dilley, was a Sigma Chi at the University of Iowa and Stephanie's youngest, Kingsley Jewett, is a Pi Kappa Alpha at Iowa State.]

For many decades, I have been quite active in the Izaak Walton League, serving as an Honorary President and on various Committees over the seventy years as a member—one summer, even helping mow their lodge yard every Saturday! I sure have donated a lot of lumber to expand both locations that Ikes have had in town—their first one was on the Raccoon River across from the Water Works on Fleur Drive; the second (and current) one is on George Flagg Parkway on the west side of the Water Works, just a mile or so southwest of the original lodge. Their general contractor told me that if I would donate paneling for the new dining room, I'd have to help install it…. so, I did! Among other things, Izaak Walton members are an association of individuals committed to conservation and nature. We promote gun training for children, have fishing parties for kids, and hold an annual sweet corn feed for anybody who wants to come. A short business meeting follows each of our weekly dinners. We used to have 2000 local members and were the largest chapter in the United States—today, we're down to about 500. They had to start taking in women a few years ago, so a lot of the guys just quit going. While we typically once served over 500 dinners at our weekly meetings, we now serve about 125, which includes the five or ten women who attend.

Retaining my membership in the Ad Club of Des Moines was mostly to network with other executives and to learn from one another how to run worthy advertisements, how to keep purchasing locally, and the like. We shared specific ideas to help grow one's own company, and had great speakers who taught various techniques to use in business. While going to those meetings I would think of my great-grandfather who, as already mentioned, was a charter member of the local Ad Club. One of the things I learned from him was to never run an ad without showing your name and phone number, which helps assure the consumer that you aren't hiding something—buyers want to know where you are located, how long you have been in business in the community and what your specialty is, as well as to feel that you have maintained honesty and integrity with your customers.

Being a part of Rotary International was a wonderful experience too. Rotary is a Club devoted to peace and goodwill globally, and to applying high ethical standards in one's business and community. I always felt as if such a large group of citizens committed to a specific goal (like theirs of eliminating polio around the world) could truly change things, a little at a time. And they do. I reluctantly pulled out of Rotary awhile back, after a perfect attendance for 19 of my 30 years as a member. To be honest, I just got tired, and it had become a challenge to find a local chapter with which to meet when I was traveling out of town or out of state. I continue to wish my fellow Rotarians well in their efforts.

My main involvement nowadays is in the Reciprocity Club of Des Moines, which was co-founded by my Dad. The group is comprised of 84 men who each represent a different local profession (one lumber dealer, one office supplies dealer, one jeweler, one attorney, one luxury car dealer, etc.). A couple of us longtime members are considered 'lifers' now and continue to be included even though the firms we represent have supplied a non-retired member to be in the Club. (Gilcrest/Jewett Lumber Company has a newer employee who is a CPA and seems to be a nice asset to the Reciprocity Club now.) The purpose of the organization is to promote and patronize the businesses of the Club members. Each week we gather at the top of the Holiday Inn downtown in their Tower dining room, where breakfast is served and each of us fill out a slip of paper showing our attendance that day, how many businesses we patronized that week, and how many leads we gave for people to do business with others in the Club. The one-hour program that follows consists of a Club member presenting information about his own business or bringing in somebody from outside our membership to talk (i.e. a football coach, or the head of another company). In a recent stroke of good luck, our speaker just happened to be a new attorney member specializing in copyrights and other intellectual property matters—meeting with such an expert was already on our agenda as the final step in finishing up this book, so Jen and I made an appointment!

At each Reciprocity breakfast, we have a drawing for $10; to be eligible you must have registered during the week in the Reciprocity Book kept at the speaking member's place of business. If nobody wins the drawing one week, ten more dollars are added and that new total carries over to the next week. It's just been a wonderful fraternal experience for me, and I look forward to the craft talks and sitting around the assigned tables getting to know that particular month's group of guys (our Club Secretary mixes up the members to seat everyone at different tables with different guys in order to get better acquainted). Every year we also have a big Christmas party with our wives or dates, which is quite a gala affair. And during that holiday season, we also help the Salvation Army by ringing bells— my spot was typically on the skywalks, which wasn't at all bad in the winter weather.

There are other social events that Reciprocity guys throw every now and then, and I try to attend those too. On my 90th birthday in 2015, which just happened to fall on our regular Wednesday meeting day, the guys surprised me with a big birthday cake and champagne, along with singing me the birthday song. I was really taken aback, and their kindness sure meant a lot. (And it still meant a lot when they again did it this year, a few days before my 92nd!) It probably goes without saying that I am the oldest member of the group and the one who holds the longest tenure, about 67 years now. Interestingly, long before I became a member of Reciprocity, I used to go as a guest to some meetings with my father. At that time, they met in the Rendezvous Room at the Randolph Hotel where my deaf buddy and I had hung out as younger guys. When walking in there to have their meetings on Wednesday mornings, the Reciprocity men were always met by the reek of smoke and booze. The Club finally got smart enough to leave that location and meet elsewhere.

My out-of-town memberships still include those having to do with my summer presence in the Lakes region. The Okoboji Yacht Club is basically a tax-deductible school for young sailors to learn how to sail. Dad was one of its earlier Commodores, as mentioned previously, and those guys met every week, promoting and teaching kids sailing skills, as well as judging weekend boat races. They still meet weekly during the season, as far as I know. The Yacht Club is a member of the Inter-Lakes Yachting Association, with sailboat regattas at Iowa's Clear Lake, Minnesota's Lake Minnetonka and White Bear Lake, Kansas City's Lotawana, and so forth. All through the years, so many of our members would regularly haul their sailboats on trailers to these various locations to represent Okoboji in the regatta races, where trophies were awarded—I've already talked some about my active involvement in all that, back in my own sailing days. While active in another group up at the Lakes, the Okoboji Protective Association, I met with the other Board members every week during the summer to help promote things like clean water and lake safety. Regular tests were run through the Iowa Lakeside Laboratory to ensure good water quality and to give temperature readings at various water depths. We had a large Annual Meeting of people interested in supporting the Association and in learning about what was being done to protect our beautiful lake. Certificates were also given to members to place in the windows of homes for security purposes. Though no longer owning a residence up there, I am still a dues-paying member and believe in the good work this Association provides. My final non-local membership is actually an out-of-state one—several years ago I was commissioned as a Kentucky Colonel (never even realizing that the family of my own great-grandmother, Nancy Henderson Call, hailed from that great state!).

Because of a career of being on this Board and that Committee back in the day, my eldest grandson wrote a high school essay about me in 1997, when he was getting ready to graduate from West Des Moines Valley. The assignment was to "Select an individual that you know from your community who has demonstrated the responsibilities of being a citizen of a community, then write a 500-word essay on what this individual has done for his/her community." I was certainly honored when grandson Joe Dilley chose me! At the end of the essay, he wrote, "The Jewett Coat of Arms carries the French motto, 'Toujours Le Meme,' which means 'Always The Same.' I certainly see that motto in the lives of my ancestors in the areas of entrepreneurial and community service, and am both humbled and proud to be following in such big generational footsteps while striving to do the same."

I guess that's what it's all been about, so now I can relax and let the next generations take it from here. Frankly, it's a relief to keep a much less hectic weekly schedule nowadays—in fact, I don't know how I ever found time to do it all! There's something pretty nice about waking up slowly, taking my time listening to the news or reading the paper and emails before whatever is on my calendar for the day—just getting ready takes so much longer now. Every Wednesday morning, I'm still up at 5:00 A.M. to get showered and shaved and headed downtown by 6:30 for breakfast and meeting with the Reciprocity guys; then my daughters come over for our weekly lunch together in The Bistro at Wesley (or sometimes at another haunt in town just to mix things up a bit). Jen and I have been working on this book for a few hours on those afternoons, and I've headed out to her office in Clive a day or two later to again work on it. Tuesdays find me meeting with 'the lunch bunch' down at the Des Moines Club. On the other weekdays, I had met regularly with some retired guys out at Skip's on Fleur Drive—unfortunately, all but one other man from that original group of twelve or so have died. The two of us still get together sometimes, and a third guy has been regularly joining up with us too, enjoying a martini with his lunch. But it's just not what it was. I'm getting the message, now that so many of my meetings have shrunk in size (I notice that my good friend who owns a number of funeral homes seems to watch me pretty darn closely every Wednesday morning at Reciprocity Club too). I had been going to the Izaak Walton League most Tuesday nights, but have backed off on that; and I'd regularly been out to QB the first Thursday of every month for the steak dinner until my best friend passed away a year ago like previously mentioned.

A lot of the guys I know retire in order to play golf in the nice weather months, but it's no longer something I do. I actually didn't pick up that sport until about age 75, which is hard to believe because Jackie was a trophy-winning golfer in the Des Moines and Central Iowa area while our girls were growing up (and throughout the rest of her life). I had been too busy with work and civic activities, and all that, to find any time to golf. But in 2000 or so, I decided to hit the links, using my Dad's old clubs, and especially enjoyed golfing with Jen and John at some easy and not-so-easy courses around the Des Moines area… River Hills, Ponderosa, and Glen Oaks. I wasn't ever planning to be a good golfer but did enjoy the recreation of it. For a few years, I took my clubs with me down to Marco Island, Florida in the winter, where I got in some rounds with a friend in nearby Naples and with my stepson, Roy, when he and Barb came to visit. And I took my clubs up to my cottage at Okoboji during the summer weekends, where I enjoyed playing with three good friends there too. The very last time I golfed was with those three guys in my regular Okoboji foursome—they all passed away within a short time of one another, and I just never picked up my clubs again (finally giving them to my youngest grandson, who may or may not find time to take up the sport). In addition to golfing at Okoboji in my later years, I also looked forward to having coffee every morning with a bunch of guys at a couple of local restaurants up there—some mornings we had as many as 25 show up to chat about this and that, and everything else. We liked to think of our times together as necessary for solving the problems of the world, but my sister used to joke that our gatherings were just a way to twist local gossip until it ended up as completely incorrect information! I liked the camaraderie though. When back at Okoboji this summer to see Connie and visit others, my son-in-law John came with me to meet up with the guys for coffee again. There were about eight or ten of us—it was sure fun to be back solving the problems of the world.

About the same time that I took up golf, at age 75, I also I bought my first personal computer and loved being able to communicate that way. Nelle and I were at a New Year's Eve party at the home of friends on Marco Island, and one of the other guests was a computer nut who talked me into purchasing a used machine from his firm. Then another friend of mine down there spent a good share of the winter of 2000 teaching me to use it. *{Editor's note: I'll never forget the day, sitting at my office computer, when an email came in from 'jerryjewett@yahoo.com.' With no prior knowledge of this potential new endeavor, I was truly shocked (and, of course, a little leery of opening up the piece of mail). Calling Dad right away, he assured me it was indeed true—he said he'd taken the advice of his daughters and had stepped into the computer age, literally overnight! So, I opened his email, only to read in all caps, "HI JEN. IT IS YOUR DAD. THIS IS NOT EASY."}*

Using the computer keyboard (we used to call it typing) was no problem for me, but neither was writing in longhand. I have tried to have legible handwriting throughout my entire life. My writing teacher at Greenwood (who had also been my mother's teacher) once told us, "If you're going to write something, write it so somebody else can read it… or else, why write it?" And that really stuck with me. But everyone in our family also typed, including all the males. I still have some personally-typed weekly letters received from Dad when I was in the service and at college. Dad once said, "We've no great skill, but we all type!" He used the hunt-and-peck system and was fairly fast. Great-grandfather George had learned to type in order to demonstrate his new product all over the world, of course. And I learned the keyboard in a class at Roosevelt—I had signed up for Typing as a 'snap course,' but it turned out to be one of the most valuable things I could have learned. Another snap course I took was at the University of Iowa in how to write a business letter, which was taught by a guy who actually had a doctoral degree in Business Letter Writing—one of the only Ph.D.'s in that, he told us. I have used what I learned in that course more than most other things I ever learned in business. (And for the record, another snap course in college was supposed to be in learning to play the piano, but that didn't last long because the teacher got pregnant—not by me—and had to quit. That was the end of my piano-playing career, though I think Grandmother Margaret secretly hoped the tunes she taught me as a little boy would carry over into some serious playing in my adult years.)

Nowadays, I'm on Facebook and receiving more emails than I even want to open—many times over 100 in a day, which kind of wears me out. And my fingers no longer move as fast on the keyboard, which is frustrating. When I first got the computer and spent so much time on it all those years ago, Nelle called it "The Devil" since it took me away from doing a lot of the other things I typically spent time on—and there may be something to that. (My father sure would have loved this computer day and age. I remember when I got my first cell phone and thought about how excited Dad would have been with one of these wireless phones, after having had the first wireless radio station in Iowa. I remember just how giddy he was in 1958 when we put those two-way radios into the company vehicles.) Though recently toying with getting myself a 'smart' phone, I'm afraid I wouldn't be smart enough to operate it, so am passing for now! I can still flip mine open whenever I receive or make a call, and that's plenty good enough for keeping in touch with others.

One day this past January, while sitting here at my mother's lovely four-place oak game table, there was a beautiful soft snow falling outside. I got thinking that the fun part about dictating this book to my own daughter is that we both get to sit here in my corner apartment with its sliding door looking out to the north at Grand Avenue and down 35th Street to Ingersoll, and with my northeast windows looking out next door to where our ancestors' Commodore Hotel residence once stood. Right here is where it's all happened for me over my lifetime. I'm always thankful to be in my cozy home, but on that snowy January 2017 day also found myself wishing I could return to Marco Island, Florida, where I spent most winters for about forty years. My docs just didn't want me to be quite so far away, and I can appreciate why—that first low blood pressure scare was just the month before. I'd even looked up several of the friends Nelle and I used to run around with down there, hoping to reconnect, but learned that almost everybody I wanted to see is now deceased (other than two or three couples in our South Seas condo complex who are still around). Though it would be nice to go back for a month or so this coming winter, my doc still says 'no' to being away for any length of time. And now that Hurricane Irma made landfall in Marco, it may be quite a mess getting around down there this year anyway.

While mentioning Florida, I'd better tell about the one spring not so long ago that I decided to stop at a nudist colony on my way back to Iowa. I'd always wanted to see one of those, so I checked in (and checked it out!). The place was located 18 miles north of the Tampa Airport and was a very nice facility. There were dining rooms, a number of bars, a huge swimming pool with co-ed locker room, and quite a few permanent homes for residents. And since nobody had anything to hide, most residents and visitors never pulled their shades! Everybody (except employees) was nude, walking down streets or going to dances or into the bars or dining rooms; and everybody carried a towel to put on the chairs. They had a clothing store, massage parlor, barber shop, tattoo booth, and so on, with golf carts parked outside and drivers to take you wherever you wanted to go—it was worth the stop!

As for hanging around Wesley more often these days, I usually enjoy meeting up with other residents for daily afternoon coffee in the shop on the first floor designated as the 'Gather and Gab,' and have made some really good friends here. Every day the shop is run by a different volunteer hostess, and one of them even brings me my own little package of her homemade cookies on her day of serving. She is a lovely widow who met and fell in love with a resident a few years ago while volunteering here—that resident happened to be one of my childhood friends and fraternity brother who had twisted my own arm to consider living at Wesley myself. He's also the guy who I had brought into QB as a member, and was the one who helped write the bylaws for the Reserve Deputy Association way back when. As I already mentioned, that good friend of mine became my best friend in more recent years, since we lived and spent time in the same places. He passed away from a sudden and unexpected virus over a year ago, but his sweet girlfriend still hostesses in the 'Gather and Gab' every Tuesday. And I understand the other residents are jealous of her bringing me the special package of homemade cookies!

Another lady is a resident who I have gotten to know quite well due to being involved in the daily coffee time and learning about our overlapping pasts. She actually graduated from Roosevelt the year before I did, and had worked in the Treasurer's office at the Courthouse for many years. We had lots of friends in common in that same building because I spent so much time at the Sheriff's office there. In talking today, we just can't believe we hadn't ever met prior to moving to Wesley as elder adults... before marrying another man, she dated for a long time a guy who graduated from high school with me; then she and her husband regularly went to so many of the same haunts where Nelle and I hung out (like Johnny's Vet's Club). But our paths just didn't cross for some reason. We sure enjoy finding so much past in common when we chat nowadays—she's become a very close friend, and recently gave me that picture of the little dancing Shirley Temple.

Also living here at Wesley are a couple of guys I went to Greenwood Grade School and to Callanan Junior High with, which makes it fun. (By the way, just a few months ago, I got to take a tour of dear old Greenwood, personally led by one of Steph's friends who is a teacher there... I was surprised to see that the Principal's office had moved from the spot where I'd once spent quite a bit of time!) One couple moved to Wesley not long after I did—high school sweethearts who graduated with me in my class at TRHS. They are great people, and it's nice to see folks my age holding a 72nd wedding anniversary party here. The guy was a B-24 and B-29 pilot during the war, so we are never short of things to talk about when we pass in the halls or see each other in The Bistro or at coffee; he was also quite a cycler after graduating from Roosevelt, riding a bike over 100,000 miles, like from California to Iowa and so on. Neither of us can believe we are living here as guys in our 90's, however, sharing stories of life in Des Moines since the 1920's!

That's how it is with most of the residents at Wesley, where such friendly 'hellos' are exchanged when passing in the halls. It truly is nice to have a community of folks my own age to chat and reminisce with. There are regular programs to take advantage of here too— you could attend something every single day if you wanted to, but I'm out and about enough that I don't make it to some of the wonderful activities that are offered. Every month there is a Veterans Luncheon where residents and others can gather to hear a speaker tell about his or her time in the service, which is always interesting. Last winter, I was that speaker for one meeting, and the topic was "How the Air Force Trained an Iowa

Boy to be a P-51 Fighter Pilot in WWII." In spite of a big ice storm outside, we had a great turnout that day. I sure enjoyed telling some of my service stories—the feedback was terrific and so was the time of questions and answers.

Most of the residents here talk about our aches and pains, of course, because that's what's going on when you've put this many miles on the old car. But some of us do various things to strengthen our bodies. I try to work out for about thirty minutes on the elliptical machine down the hall—sometimes my legs just hurt and I don't want to ride the thing, but do believe the exercise has helped a lot. (I used to get cortisone shots in my knees to alleviate some of that pain too, but the last round didn't do a thing anyway.) On occasion, I've also taken physical therapy to help with strength and with balance, and my doc has given me more conditioning activities too, asking me at each visit how well I'm doing with those… that routine is admittedly kind of hit-and-miss, like his telling me to take a one-hour nap (what's that?) every afternoon in order to sleep better through the night! But visits to his office monthly, and sometimes more, help keep this old guy in check. On occasion, I've even walked into his place without an appointment because of feeling punk (usually a bout with low blood pressure—my body doesn't like it when the lower number goes below 50).

Congestive heart failure has been an item on my medical chart for quite a long time and I wear a stint that was put in a decade or so ago. It was necessary to have a cardioversion procedure due to atrial fibrillation (AFIB) two days before Thanksgiving in 2014… fortunately, that shock procedure worked the very first time. (The cardio team was going to try me on a light blood thinner for a month before deciding whether I needed the procedure, but it quickly became obvious I wouldn't live that long if they waited. My daughters had to stand on either side of me to help walk me into the cardiologist's office that day, and wouldn't leave until the doc agreed to admit me to the hospital right then and there. I just know I'm alive because of the ongoing medical persistence of Steph and Jen in recent years. And that's a good thing, or this very book would never have been written!)

Being more proactive about my health has slowly become a necessary priority, and especially after one hospitalization a couple of years ago that was followed by a short stay downstairs in the Health Center here at Wesley. That's what really got my attention. I was considered a 'fall risk' for a day or two, so was confined to a little bedroom and had to ring for assistance if I even wanted to go to the bathroom. Boy, did I *hate* being down there… they even locked the doors at night, which brought back memories of being in my crib with double pneumonia as a baby or being in that Tulsa jail overnight while in the service.

Maybe if I'd agreed to using a walker back when it was first suggested, I wouldn't have had to 'do time' downstairs! When I finally got released from that place, I sure didn't want to stay alone in my apartment, but my girlfriend didn't want me over at her place either until she could be assured I was not going to fall. Those were a few tough days for me!

Last April, my physician finally prescribed a walker since I'd been feeling a little unsteady, in spite of decent blood pressure. So, I caved! The thing has four wheels and hand brakes and a seat with storage underneath which is supposed to make it fancy, I guess. It's known as my 'blue Cadillac,' and I'm actually getting accustomed to racing around Wesley with it. When I leave the building, though, it's usually parked. But I sure don't want to fall… my doc explained that a broken hip could wreak havoc, telling me an injury like that would likely "paint us into a corner," and I don't have enough lacquer thinner to clean up that sort of a paint job! It must be a real trick for him to help balance my heart issues with my chronic kidney disease—one requires drinking extra water, while the other requires just the opposite… it's confusing! My weight can vary weekly by a few pounds, depending on how much water is being retained, so they are always making adjustments to my water pill. (I've lost about thirty-five pounds these last couple of years though, which is by design.)

{Editor's note: Dad called to report that his blue walker had been 'taken' during a wine and cheese party at Wesley less than a week after we picked it up. Though he had stuck a couple of return address labels on it (where's a Dymo Label Maker when you need one?), another resident inadvertently drove off with the thing. An hour or so after discovering the walker was gone and reporting it to the front desk, the 'blue Cadillac' was returned intact. He has since tied a red ribbon and a green ribbon to the handlebars, for easier 'port and starboard' identification, I guess; more importantly, he also put a bra on the front of it for awhile, proudly calling it "Jerry's hooter-scooter!" (no surprise to the other residents)}

Things have geared down for me quite a bit, especially in recent months, and I like it that way. It's been nice to be more a part of the lives of my family now, spending time with the girls and grandsons and great-grandkids—that's probably the benefit of living this long and slowing down enough to smell the roses. A man asked me this summer what I considered my greatest accomplishment in life; after thinking awhile about all I've been a part of, the answer was, "My daughters." They do make me proud. This is a probably a good place to brag on my grandsons, too, who have turned out to be such well-rounded young gentlemen. I'm known to all four as "Grandad," which is also what the girls called my Dad…

Jennifer's eldest is Dr. Joseph Brandon Dilley, a 39-year-old clinical psychologist (like my son-in-law) in private practice with his wife, Dr. Carrie Dilley, also a clinical psychologist. Joe graduated from the U of I (my alma mater) and received his Ph.D. from Northwestern Medical School in downtown Chicago (*not* my alma mater!). In addition to his patient load, Joe is a published author with regular speaking engagements around the country. Carrie completed her undergraduate work at Ole Miss and received her Ph.D. from Fuller's School of Psychology in Pasadena. Carrie Northrup Dilley is a native of southern California, where she and Joe reside with my great-grandchildren, Ashton Sophia Dilley (age 7 this month) and Jack Cohen Dilley (age 2½).

Jen's youngest son is Jacob Brian Dilley, a 34-year-old artist and musician, and with a Master's degree in Film. Jake was a Sigma Chi at Iowa and moved to Minneapolis out of college to further hone his many artistic skills. Just a couple of years ago, he became a southern California resident too, thoroughly enjoying life in the milder climate of North Hollywood (and just 20 miles due west of his brother). Jake is currently 'batching it' with his dog, Ziggy, and is doing well with many commissioned artworks and local film endeavors. He's always been such a creative kid, and I love learning about and seeing the latest things he has become involved with, including designing the front cover for this book about his Grandad! I do wish the California kids lived closer—I don't get to see them as often as I'd like—but it was terrific to have spent several good hours with them when they were here over Father's Day. I may even try to take a trip to California to visit them over Christmas (if my doc agrees, and if I feel up to such a long day of being in airplanes).

Stephanie's eldest is 30-year-old Ryland Gerald Jewett (with that middle name, he is known as "Jerry" to a lot of his friends!). Ry holds the title of a Plan Reporting Analyst with the Principal Financial Group here in Des Moines, and works with auditors of several big-name institutional clients to file their retirement plans. Prior to this position, his title was that of a Corporate Tax Paralegal Analyst, working with the VP of Corporate Tax and the VP and Assistant General Counsel in the legal department, serving as a liaison between the two groups to ensure compliance with annual new tax regulations. Ryland graduated in Accounting from Iowa State University and originally began working for Wells Fargo, processing HUD loans and leading a team that specialized in individual home loan retention work. He is a wonderful father, and I have especially loved being able to attend the recent t-ball pursuits of his two terrific sons, Anson Trice (soon 6) and Jonah Charles (age 4½). It's terrific to be included in their Saturday morning breakfasts or Sunday noon luncheons on the weekends when Ryland has the boys.

Steph's youngest son, Kingsley Berguin Jewett, is a single 22-year-old who is now into his final year in Construction Engineering at Iowa State University, with an emphasis in Project Management. He also served as President of his Pi Kappa Alpha fraternity up there. King has always been quite the entrepreneur, starting his own Jewett Lawn Care business at the age of eleven, and faithfully keeping it going (and growing) until finally selling it once he became too busy with college. Always interested in the building trade, King's recent summer was spent interning for a commercial construction firm out in Denver, gaining valuable on-site experience (much like he received when taking on a full-term internship leave from ISU to work for the busy Ryan Companies here in Des Moines prior to his junior year). It's almost unbelievable that King already received several job offers for full-time employment starting next spring, and is excited to have just accepted a nice position as a Project Engineer with local Neumann Brothers, Inc., effective May 28, 2018!

Even though I keep coming up with more material each time we write, eventually Jen and I need to bring this book to a close and get the thing to a printer while I'm still alive. Looking at the caricature that Jake drew for my book cover was pretty exciting, and now I'm anxious to see it done. *{Editor's note: We had planned to self-print and distribute this memoir, but got pretty excited about how it was turning out—the manuscript appeared to be of a high enough quality to perhaps be picked up by a publisher. After a lot of research into the top print-on-demand companies with whom we would retain rights, I sent the final copy to a very selective one that rejects the vast majority of submissions coming their way. (Frankly, if they didn't feel it was good enough, then I still had work to do!) After their screening process, we were excited that BookLocker felt the memoir was indeed of superior quality in its subject interest, salability, and technical prowess! Their works are distributed worldwide by Ingram, so Dad's book will be available in all bookstores around the globe, and online through Amazon, Barnes and Noble, etc. The publishing process has definitely slowed us down (especially with their reformatting of the original manuscript pages, which required further editing and changes), but has also taken it to the next level. And now that Dad is a published author, we had to add yet another item to that long obit!}*

A few groups want to have signing party events for me, which is nice; but I'm not real crazy about it, for fear I'll be too tired to talk to folks and to then sign my name after only a few books—writing for long periods is a chore nowadays. Because of that concern, I recently stopped by a local Office Depot and picked up a packet of white address labels, then spent several hours signing my name to a few hundred of those—it seemed like a good backup idea if necessary to use them. (Yes, I admit to thinking about using a Dymo machine to print out some cute name labels!) Even though this project has become kind of a monster, it's been fun too—writing a book about one's life sure does keep the memories and the people alive, and I would recommend it to others. But I really didn't know it would be this much work… for my daughter, that is! *{**Editor's note:** Agreed!}*

Someone asked me just the other day how life has been treating me, and I had to admit that it's been treating me pretty darn good for the most part… I'm 92 and still looking at the right side of the grass! Many thanks to all who have taken the time to read this—you have been my friends and loved ones, and I am grateful. The book title was chosen because of my signature toast given to special people on special occasions. And now I raise my glass yet again, this time to each of *you*:

"Here's to it.
And to it again.
If you don't get to it
to do it,
here's to it to do it
until you get to it
to do it again."

Love, Jerry

APPENDIX

A partial bibliography of related sources and resources that may be of interest to readers. The listed entries have likely been consulted, but not necessarily used, in this final project compilation.

Algona Republican, various articles and dates, 1872-1902. Public domain.

The Algona Upper Des Moines, various articles and dates (including Sesquicentennial edition, July 8, 2004). All articles (including from archived public domain *Algona Republican*) used by permission.

American Families—Genealogies and Biographical Information from Most Authentic Sources Including Much Valuable Material Drawn From Hitherto Unpublished Family Records with Accurate Reproduction—and Descriptions of ancient Emblazonry Compiled by Masters of Genealogic and Heraldic Science, New York: The American Historical Society, Inc. 1921. Public domain.

Anderson, Robert Charles. "The Great Migration Begins: Immigrants to New England." *Great Migration Study Project, Volume III*. Boston: New England Historic Genealogical Society, 1995. Used by permission.

Andreas, A. T. *Historical Atlas of the State of Iowa, 1875*. Des Moines, IA: State Historical Society of Iowa, 1975. Used by permission.

Andrews, L. F. *Pioneers of Polk County, Iowa, Volumes I and II*. Des Moines, IA: Baker-Trisler Company, 1908. Public domain.

Beta Mu News, University of Iowa Chapter of Sigma Nu (front page photo), Vol. 1, No. 3, May 1949 (also group house photo and additional Sigma Nu references throughout work). Used by permission.

Bicknell, Thomas Williams. *The History of the State of Rhode Island and Providence Plantations: Biographical*. Chicago and New York: American Historical Society, Inc., 1920. Public domain.

Biographical Souvenir of the Counties of Delaware and Buchanan, Iowa. Chicago: F. A. Battey & Co., 1890. Public domain.

Blanchard, Charles. *History of Drake University: Building for the Centuries—Volume I*. Des Moines, IA: Drake University, 1931. Reference source listing only.

Bluth, John A. "Harry Mulford Jewett: DAC's Renaissance Man." *A History of DAC Sports*, DAC News magazine, Detroit Athletic Club, October 2001. Used by permission.

Brigham, Johnson. *Des Moines, The Pioneer of Municipal Progress and Reform of the Middle West together with The History of Polk County, Iowa—The Largest and Most Prosperous County in the State of Iowa* (two volumes). Chicago: S. J. Clarke Publishing Co., 1911. Public domain.

"The Brothers Ralph and William Sprague and Some of Their Descendants." *NEHGS Register*, April 1909. Public domain.

Bruckard, Gerry Howe Sprague with Sicks, Esther Bretthauer. "Gerry Remembers: A History of the Howe Family of Port Orchard, Washington." 1997. No excerpt used.

Bryson, Bill. *The Life and Times of the Thunderbolt Kid: A Memoir*. New York: Broadway Books, 2006. Reference made. No excerpt used.

Call, John R. and Vanessa. *The Diaries of Asa Cyrus Call: March 28, 1850-December 26, 1853*. Derby, KS, December 1998. Used by permission.

Call, Simeon T. *Genealogical History of the Call Family in the United States*. Emington, IL: The Joker Press, 1908. Public domain.

The Canada Lancet, Volume 38. University of Michigan: Lancet Publishing Co., 1905. Public domain.

The Canadian Teacher, Vol. 12. Toronto: Educational Publishing Co., 1907. Public domain.

The Central College Catalogues, 1857-1858 and *1859-1860*. Pella, IA. Used by permission, courtesy of Lammers Archives at Central College, Pella, IA.

Central College newsletters and local newspaper articles. Pella, IA, various dates. Used by permission, courtesy of Lammers Archives at Central College, Pella, IA.

Central University Record. Pella, IA, July 3, 1861. Used by permission, courtesy of Lammers Archives at Central College, Pella, IA.

Chamberlain, George Walter, M.S. *The Spragues of Malden Massachusetts*. Boston, 1923. No excerpt used.

The Christian Worker, Volume 47, Number 7, September 1934. Ended publication 1934, likely with this edition highlighting eulogy about founder George Anson Jewett.

Clarkson, Anna Howell. *A Beautiful Life and Its Associations*. Astor Place, NY: J. J. Little & Co., 1899. Public domain.

Cooper, Anderson and Vanderbilt, Gloria. *The Rainbow Comes and Goes: A Mother and Son on Life, Love, and Loss*. New York: HarperCollins Publishers, Inc., 2016. No excerpt used.

Cory, Constance Jewett. 1989 typed letter to Iowa Senator Jack Hatch (with copy to Gerald Jewett, Jr.) regarding history of residential property located at 696-19th Street, Des Moines, Iowa. Original copy reproduced for family use.

Cowles, Florence Call. *Early Algona: The Story of Our Pioneers 1854-1874*. Des Moines, IA: Des Moines Register and Tribune Co., 1929. Used by permission.

Cutter, William Richard, ed. *Genealogical and Family History of Northern New York*. New York: Lewis Historical Publishing Co., 1910. Public domain.

Daily Iowa State Register, various articles and dates, 1871+. Public domain.

Deiber, Camilla and Hirst, K. Kris. *Leading Double Lives: The History of the Double House in Des Moines*. Hiawatha, IA: J & A Printing, 2005. No excerpt used.

Des Moines: The Pioneer of Municipal Progress and Reform of the Middle West, Volume II. Chicago: The S. J. Clarke Publishing Co., 1911. Public domain.

The Des Moines Leader, various articles and dates, 1885-1900. Public domain.

The Des Moines Register, various articles and dates, 1915+. All articles after 1932 used by permission.

The Des Moines Rotary Week newsletter, November 29, 1984. (Material provided by Gerald Jewett, Jr.)

The Des Moines Tribune, various articles and dates, 1908-1982. All articles after 1932 used by permission.

Des Moines Tribune-Capital, July 10, 1929. Used by permission.

The Developer (publication), *Devoted to Commercial, Industrial, Mining, and Railway Interests*, 1901. Public domain.

The *Diaries of Ambrose Adolphus Call*, covering 1862-1875 (and various items of interest from the scrapbook on Nancy Eliza Henderson Call), Des Moines, IA: Hutchison family collection and works, 2003. Reproduced for family use.

Directories, Central Church of Christ, Des Moines, IA, 1891 and 1908. Public domain.

Documents Relative to the Colonial History of the State of New York, Volume I. Albany: Weed, Parsons & Co., 1856. Public domain.

Donnelly, Jim. "Harry Jewett." *Hemmings Classic Cars*, August 2008. Used by permission.

Duncan, Jim. "Who Are These Guys? The People Behind the Famous Des Moines Names." *Cityview*, November 2, 2016. Used by permission.

Elston, Hattie P. *White Men Follow After*. Iowa City, IA: Athens Press, 1946. No excerpt used.

Email correspondences between Tom Jewett, Jennifer Jewett Dilley, and Beth Kuper regarding Iowa history of the George Enoch Jewett/Patty Maria Matthews family, numerous dates 2015+. Used by permission.

Email correspondences between Tom Jewett, Jennifer Jewett Dilley, and Rebecca Jewett regarding California history of George Enoch Jewett and Mary Dahlman/Dahlmann family, numerous dates 2015+. Used by permission.

Email correspondences between Jennifer Jewett Dilley and Channing Gibson, Kyle Gibson, Darcy Gibson Berglund, C. J. Gibson, Tom Jewett, and John Dilley regarding memories contained in 91st birthday remembrances for Gerald A. Jewett, Jr., numerous dates 2016-2017. Used by permission.

Gardner-Sharp, Abbie. *History of the Spirit Lake Massacre and Captivity of Miss Abbie Gardner: The Raid of the Santee Sioux Against the Iowa Frontier Settlements, 1857.* Leonaur, 2011. No excerpt used.

Gordon, Charlotte. *Mistress Bradstreet.* New York: Little Brown and Co., 2005. No excerpt used.

Grant, H. Roger. *The Biographical Dictionary of Iowa.* University of Iowa Press (Digital Editions), 2009. Used by permission.

Gue, Benjamin F. *History of Iowa, Volume* I: *The Pioneer Period.* New York: Century History Co., 1903. Public domain.

Hammer, Ilda M. *The Book of Des Moines.* Des Moines, IA: The Board of Education, 1947. Used by permission.

Hamilton, Carl, ed. *Pure Nostalgia* (signed copy). Ames, IA: The Iowa State University Press, 1979. Interurban photo, p. 164. (Not used—copyright transferred to Wylie & Sons; permission unattainable.)

Heusinkveld, Harriet. *Red Rock, Iowa: Annals of a Frontier Community 1943-1969* (signed copy). Pella: Pella Printing Co., 1993. Used by permission.

History of Kossuth, Hancock and Winnebago Counties. Springfield, IL: Union Publishing Co., 1884. Public domain.

History of Kossuth and Humboldt Counties, Iowa. Springfield, IL: Union Publishing Co., 1884. Public domain.

History of Pella, Iowa, 1847-1987, Vol. II. Dallas, TX: Curtis Media Corp., 1989. (Use of any excerpt(s) unknown. Publisher no longer in business; permission unattainable.)

Hunter, Dan. *Des Moines Confluence of People and Resources.* Des Moines, IA: Public Library of Des Moines, 1982. Used by permission.

Hutchison, Dorothy. Personal handwritten letter to Tom Hutchison detailing descendants of Thomas Call, 1972. Reproduced for family use.

Iowa Citizen, various articles and dates, 1855-1860. Public domain.

"Iowa Formula." *Time*. July 1, 1935. No excerpt used.

The Iowa Heritage Digital Collections. Drake University Cowles Library Special Collections, Des Moines, IA, 2006. Reference source listing only.

Iowa: Its History and Its Foremost Citizens, Volume II. Chicago: The S. J. Clarke Publishing Co., 1915. Public domain.

Iowa Medical Journal, Volume 7, July 1901. Public domain.

The Iowa Star (first newspaper in Des Moines, Iowa), various articles/dates, 1849-1855. Public domain.

The Iowa State Leader, various articles and dates. 1876-1885. Public domain.

The Iowa State Register, various articles and dates, 1860+. Public domain.

Jaques, Sue Cowles Shepard, ed. *Florence Maud Call Cowles Excerpts from Letters, 1879-1884.* Des Moines, IA, 1994. Reproduced for family use.

Jewett, Frederic Clarke, M.D. *History and Genealogy of the Jewetts of America, Volume 1.* New York: The Grafton Press, 1908. Public domain.

Jewett, Frederic Clarke, M.D. *History and Genealogy of the Jewetts of America: A Record of Edward Jewett, of Bradford, West Riding of Yorkshire, England, and of his Two Emigrant Sons, Deacon Maximilian and Joseph Jewett, Settlers of Rowley, Massachusetts, in 1639.* Wentworth Press, 2016. A 'Scholar Select' work designated for public domain.

Jewett, George Anson, *Hunting An Ancestor*, Des Moines, IA, 1914. Public domain.

Jewett, George Anson, *138 Generations From Adam*, Des Moines, IA, 1929. Original copy reproduced for family use.

Jewett, Tom, ed. *Failed Ambition: The Civil War Journals and Letters of Cavalryman Homer Harris Jewett.* 2004 (revised 2015). Used by permission.

Jewett, Tom, ed. *George Anson Jewett: Pioneering Iowa Entrepreneur.* 2006 (revised 2015). Used by permission.

Jewett, Tom, ed. *It is One Grand Rush For Gold: George E. Jewett's 1849-1850 Gold Rush Journal.* 2007 (revised 2015). Used by permission.

Journal of the Iowa State Medical Society. Fulton, MO: Iowa State Medical Society, October 1915. Public domain.

Kerstein, Bob, Jewett Typewriter article on scripophily.net/jewtypcom. Used by permission.

Kent, D.L. "The Sprague Family of Charlestown Massachusetts." *The New England Historical and Genealogical Register.* Boston: New England Historic Genealogical Society, 1978. Used by permission.

Kossuth County Advance, various articles and dates. All articles used by permission.

Kuper, Beth, ed. *The Story of the Matthews Family, 1st Edition*. (Personal documents of Patty Frances Matthews Wiencke and Matthew Immanuel Wiencke). October 2, 2015. Used by permission.

LaFoy, R. Aubrey. *Okoboji Remembered* (signed copy). 2010. No excerpt used.

Letters and file notes, handwritten and/or typed, of Gerald A. Jewett, Jr., Constance Jewett Cory, Tom Jewett, Homer H. Jewett, David Warren Jewett, Gerald A. Jewett, Sr., Bertha Shore Jewett, and George A. Jewett, various dates. Reproduced for family use.

Lewis, Paul W. *Scouting in Iowa—The Values Endure: The Story of the Mid-Iowa Council, Boy Scouts of America*. Des Moines: Mid-Iowa Council, Boy Scouts of America, 1999. Used by permission.

Matthews, Amanda. *A Journal of Traveling: Red Rock, Iowa to California*, April 18, 1852-September 9, 1852. Public domain.

Matthews, L. A. "Amanda" E. *Reminiscences of the Past—1906* (A personal reconstruction of the 1852 'Journal of Traveling: Red Rock, Iowa to California'). Public domain.

The Midwestern, Vol. II, No. 10. Des Moines: Greater Des Moines Publishing Co., 1908. Public domain.

Mills, George S. *The Little Man with the Long Shadow*. Des Moines: The Trustees of the Frederick M. Hubbell Estate, 1955. No excerpt used.

Milne, A. A. *The World of Pooh: The Complete Winnie-the-Pooh* (1926) *and The House at Pooh Corner* (1928). New York: NY, E. P. Dutton & Co., 1957. No excerpt used.

Milne, A. A. *When We Were Very Young*. New York: E. P. Dutton & Co., 1924. No excerpt used.

Mitchell, Nahum. *History of the Early Settlement of Bridgewater, in Plymouth County, Massachusetts*. Bridgewater, MA: Henry T. Pratt, 1897. Public domain.

The Palimpsest. Iowa City, IA: The State Historical Society of Iowa, July 1954. No excerpt used.

Personal 'proof' papers (including birth, marriage, and death certificates and other legal documents of all ancestors) for Jennifer Berguin Jewett Dilley, documented member with dual lineage of Jewett/Jewett and of Sprague/Call, *The National Society of the Colonial Dames of America in the Commonwealth of Massachusetts*, 2005. Reproduced for family use.

Personal 'proof' papers for Bertha Shore Jewett, *The National Society of the Colonial Dames of America in the Commonwealth of Massachusetts*, 1968. Reproduced for family use.

Personal 'proof' papers for various female family members. *Daughters of the American Revolution*, various dates. Reproduced for family use.

The Pioneer and Historical Review, Vol. XIII, No. 7. San Francisco: The Pioneer Publishing Company, July 15, 1898. Public domain.

Polk County Historical Society newsletters, March 1974 and September 1988. Permission requested.

Quarton, Bertha Cowles. Forward to second printing of *Early Algona,* and containing *Eda's Cradle.* Des Moines: IA, 1964. Used by permission.

Quarton, William Barlow III. *Lucky Man.* West Branch, IA: Herbert Hoover Presidential Library Association, 2005. No excerpt used.

Reed, Benjamin F. *History of Kossuth County, Volume II.* Chicago: S. J. Clarke Publishing Co., 1913. Public domain.

The Register and Leader, various articles and dates. Public domain.

Ritchey, Charles J. *Drake University Through Seventy-Five Years: 1881-1956.* Des Moines, IA: Drake University, 1956 (republished 2012, LiteraryLicensing.com). Reference source listing only.

Rock Products and Building Materials. Chicago: The Francis Publishing Co., September 22, 1915. Public domain.

The Roosevelt High School Annual Roundup. Des Moines, IA, 1942 and 1943. Used by permission.

Schiff, Stacy, *The Witches: Salem, 1692.* New York: Little Brown and Co., 2015. No excerpt used.

Spear, Burton W. *Search for the Passengers of the Mary and John, 1630: Updated Ancestries.* Toledo, OH: The Mary & John Clearing House, 1987. No excerpt used.

Sprague, E. G. "Ralph Sprague Genealogy." Montpelier, VT: The Capital City Press, 1913. Public domain.

Torrey, Clarence A. *New England Marriages.* Baltimore, MD: Genealogical Publishing Co., 2004. No excerpt used.

Trigiani, Adriana. *Don't Sing at the Table: Life Lessons from My Grandmothers.* New York: Harper Collins Publishers, Inc., 2010. No excerpt used, though permission (with cost) was granted.

Upper Des Moines-Republican, various articles and dates. All articles used by permission.

The U.S. Biographical Dictionary and Portrait Gallery of Eminent and Self-Made Men, Iowa Volume. Chicago and New York: American Biographical Publishing Co., 1878. Public domain.

U.S. Census Records for states of Massachusetts, Vermont, Rhode Island, New Hampshire, New York, Ohio, North Carolina, Virginia, Tennessee, Kentucky, Indiana, Illinois, Iowa, various years: 1700's-1900's. Reproduced for family use.

Watkins, Joan, correspondent. "The Sprague Family from Dorset, To Massachusetts and Gibraltar." Manning family website, 1992. No excerpt used.

Yearbooks and *Quarterlies*. The Jewett Family of America, Inc., Rowley, MA, numerous articles and dates. All articles used by permission.

Zeller, John. "From the Real to the Ideal: Images of Des Moines in the Progressive Era." *Historic Des Moines 1904-1914*. Des Moines, IA: Drake University, 2005. No excerpt used.

A multitude of topics were researched through various helpful internet sites including, but not limited to: americanancestors.com, ancestry.com; archive.org; artprice.com; desmoineswomensclub.com (used by permission), familysearch.com, findagrave.com; freepages.genealogy.rootsweb.ancestry.com; genealogycenter.org, genealogytrails.com; geni.com/people; iagenweb.org; lib.drake.edu/site/about Cowles/history; Lib.drake.edu/heritage; newspapers.com, myheritage.com, publications.iowa.gov; tenneyfamily.org, theodore-roosevelt.com (used by permission); webjourneymen.net, wikipedia.org

CPSIA information can be obtained
at www.ICGtesting.com
Printed in the USA
FFOW01n1157151217
43870245-42900FF